MADE IN OCEANIA

First published in 2011 by
Sean Kingston Publishing
www.seankingston.co.uk
Wantage

British Library Cataloguing in Publication Data
A catalogue record for this book is available from the British Library.

The moral rights of the authors have been asserted.

Printed by Lightning Source

ISBN 978-1-907774-11-9

Made in Oceania

✳

Social Movements, Cultural Heritage and the State in the Pacific

Edited by Edvard Hviding and Knut M. Rio

SK publishing

Sean Kingston Publishing

www.seankingston.co.uk

Wantage

Contents

Preface

❋

This book is a major outcome of the large collaborative research programme 'Pacific Alternatives: Cultural Heritage and Political Innovation in Oceania', generously funded by the Research Council of Norway for the period 2008–12 (Grant No. 185646). The 'Pacific Alternatives' programme is based at the University of Bergen (Department of Social Anthropology, Bergen Pacific Studies Research Group), and maintains strong collaborative links with the University of Hawai'i at Manoa, the East-West Center, The British Museum, and a number of other universities and national museums in Europe, North America, the Pacific Islands and Australia. For this funding, and for substantial additional contributions from the University of Bergen (Department of Social Anthropology and Bergen Museum), we are very grateful. It is a privilege to be given the opportunity to engage intensively in studies of the great region of Oceania from our base at a Norwegian university, and to be allowed the resources to collaborate with a wide international network of colleagues.

The volume represents two separate scholarly events organized by the editors. During 9–14 October 2006, the symposium 'Cultural Heritage and Political Innovation in the Pacific' was hosted at the University of Bergen by the Bergen Pacific Studies Research Group, drawing together scholars in anthropology, archaeology and political science and two directors of national museums in Melanesia. Funding for this symposium, which in large measure focused on the Solomon Islands and Vanuatu, was provided by the Research Council of Norway (seed funding for international research cooperation, Grant No. 175023) and by the University of Bergen (Department of Social Anthropology and Bergen Museum). The week-long flow of presentations, discussion and diverse exchanges (including the opening of a museum exhibition and exploratory work in the Bergen Museum's ethnographic storerooms) provided fertile ground for the initial development of the 'Pacific Alternatives' programme. Chapters by Bolton, Foana'ota and White, Regenvanu and Geismar, and Lindstrom have their origins in presentations at this symposium. In 2008, during the conference of the European Society for Oceanists at Verona, we organized an invited session on 12 July entitled 'Cultural Heritage and Political Innovation: Relations of the State and Alternative Social Movements in Oceania'. Most participants at this session generously came and joined us at Verona on their own funding, for which we are most grateful to them. Chapters by Pigliasco, M. Scott, Hviding, Dalsgaard and Otto, Alévèque, Hanlon, R. Scott and Henry have their origins in presentations at this session.

The titles of the two events at which the chapters in this book were originally given as papers are a good indication of the present volume's subject matter. From a collective perspective drawn from many years of experience in fieldwork, research and cultural policy work in Melanesia, Polynesia, Micronesia and Australia, the editors and the contributors share the belief that the region of Oceania and its immense cultural diversity provide some intriguing examples of locally driven development of innovative political forms that, more often than not, are steeped in 'tradition' and 'cultural heritage'. This, we argue collectively, requires a fresh comparative examination of both cultural heritage and political innovation, and of the many diverse connections between them. The Pacific region is unique in terms of its diversity of both culture and political forms, and as such the wide-ranging contributions to this volume may collectively provide a significant reorientation of our understanding of how people deal with life-worlds over whose circumstances they have only, at best, partial control.

For teaching us these and so many other lessons we are indebted, and in profound gratitude, to the peoples of the Pacific who are so intensively engaged in forging new connections between the cultural and the political in order to influence the power relations in which their lives are entangled. There are also some specific acknowledgements that we wish to make as editors of this book, and as organizers of the events that resulted in it. First, to participants at the Bergen symposium in 2006 who participated significantly in the discussions, but whose contributions are not in this volume: Cato Berg, Ben Burt, Annelin Eriksen, Tarcisius Kabutaulaka, David Roe, Graeme Were and Terence Wesley-Smith. Second, to the fine and large audience at our conference session in Verona in 2008, whose comments and questions fuelled the creative intensity of an already tight programme. In particular, we are grateful to Marshall Sahlins, who came to attend the session and who took on a prominent role as spontaneous discussant. Finally, we are grateful to Ane Straume for her dedicated editorial efforts on all chapters, to Tom Mountjoy for some particularly strong editorial contributions, and to Sean Kingston and an anonymous reviewer for detailed, constructive and inspiring suggestions concerning the entire book.

Edvard Hviding and Knut M. Rio, Bergen

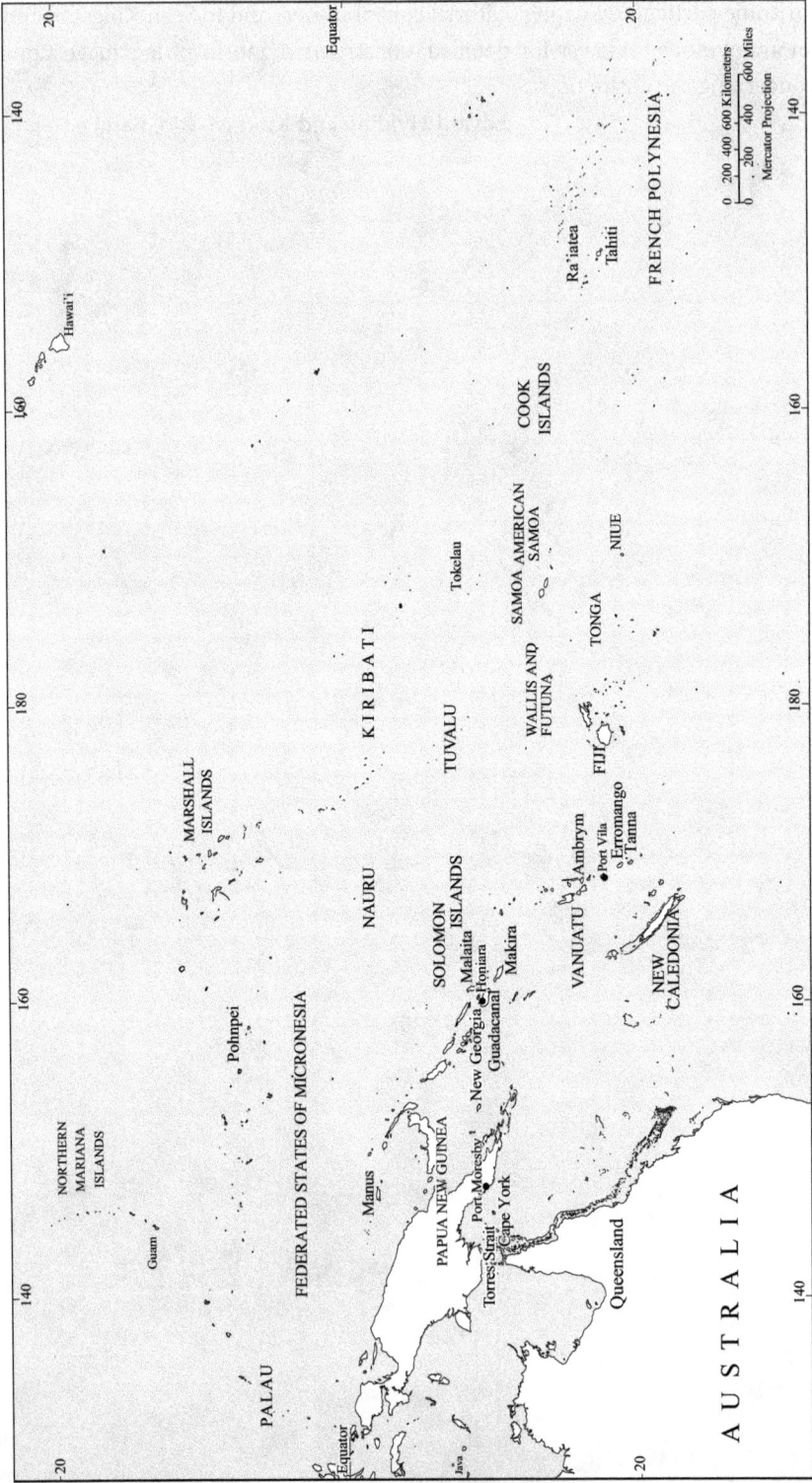

Map 1   *Oceania, showing locations of key relevance to the book's chapters.*
Map by Kjell Helge Sjøstrøm, University of Bergen. Map data source: University of Texas Libraries.

Pacific made

Social movements between cultural heritage and the state[1]

✳

Knut M. Rio and Edvard Hviding

Any national cultural policies must be based on local cultural ideas and practices. A national cultural policy must not be imposed from the top to the bottom, but must come from the bottom to the top. It must take into account matters such as traditional copyright systems, connections between cultural heritage and local identity, and people's authority over their own custom.

Cultural leaders at all levels should be advisors in local and national cultural policy formulations. Policymakers need to consult closely with existing cultural leaders.

National cultural policies must address all levels of community, including the provincial and the village. These policies should coordinate all functions relating to culture that might be performed by various governmental and private bodies and agencies.

All who might be involved in cultural policy formulation and its implementation must have a clear idea of what is meant by the terms custom (kastom) *and* culture (kalja). *National cultural policies must attempt to make clear to the people that culture is a living thing; that it does not refer to archaic matters or objects such as artefacts in museums; and that it covers all aspects of people's lives.*

> Willie Bongmatur, Former President of Malvatumauri
> National Council of Chiefs, Vanuatu
> (Lindstrom and White 1994:85, emphasis as in original)

Social movements, nation and state in Oceania

This book documents two parallel social developments of the contemporary Pacific. One, evident all over this widespread region, is grassroots movements' mobilization of energy from their cultural heritage in a way that may be unique in the globalized world. The other is the closely related current that we might term state-making, which continually runs up against this grassroots political innovation and meets it with legislation and efforts of circumscription.

In the statement by Chief Willie Bongmatur of Vanuatu, quoted above, we see an extraordinarily clear formulation of a perspective on culture and cultural heritage that mediates between the state and the people. In Vanuatu, the particular position of the National Council of Chiefs in the national constitution has indeed been to occupy this significant in-between space in the formation of a modern Pacific nation. For observers of Vanuatu politics, the institution has come to be seen as crucial for the maintenance of the nation's stability (see Bolton 1998).

We think Bongmatur's statement captures some important general insights when it comes to the relationship between nation and state in Oceania, and also with regard to the crucial role that cultural heritage has played in the formation of the nation-state in the region. Through a range of different perspectives, and from detailed, ethnographically grounded examinations of past and recent events in many parts of the Pacific, this book examines how concepts of cultural heritage have served as templates for Pacific peoples through successive forms of political challenges in colonial and post-colonial history. Our argument is that throughout the Pacific local cultural heritage has been a central element in political innovation, in and beyond the local. Across the Pacific region colonial power and resistance, the construction of nations, and ideas of the global have been historically formulated within this very potent cultural space of customary objectification. But, and maybe surprisingly so, in Pacific social environments cultural heritage has also been set free from its Western bearings as a codified concept, and has often become a driving force in local social movements – only to be misunderstood in anthropological analysis of these movements as 'cargo cults' or as examples of the 'invention of tradition'. From this observation, the present volume proposes a focus on social movements and current processes in Melanesia and the wider Oceanic region that defy such simplistic tropes. This ambition is founded in the collective experience of the authors: the chapters convey the insights and perspectives of scholars, many of whom have worked for several decades in the localities and nations of which they write. In addition, we are privileged to have the participation of distinguished practitioners in the cultural and political fields of Melanesian nations: the former director (for more than 35 years) of the Solomon Islands National Museum and the former director of the Vanuatu Cultural Centre and National Museum are both contributors to this volume.

The chapters in this book relate to Bongmatur's arguments in several important ways. In particular, this volume rises to the challenge of rethinking assumptions about how the 'grassroots level' of everyday life and political ambition is configured in Oceanic models of the social world and of the relationship between this level and the state. In Oceania – including the levels of parliament, law and national media – decision-making and the quest for crucial knowledge often focus on local circumstances, at inter-village and inter-personal levels. With regard to configurations of cause and effect in political life and the tendency for locating authority at the localized level, to the scales of persons or objects, there are interesting challenges to much contemporary thinking around centres and peripheries. The chapters of this book explore such alternative ways of configuring authority, wherein the varying distribution and composition of central persons, objects and places of key cultural significance determine decision-making on all levels including the national. The book offers descriptions of social movements and politically charged events that locate and develop elsewhere than in the institutions of government, parliament, law, statehood or foreign intervention. While some of these movements have been ridiculed in the media and downplayed in the anthropological literature as vain cultic movements or as superficial performances of culture, we believe there are reasons to take them seriously as efforts to search for alternative social orders. Social movements throughout the Pacific present new values, new social structures, new aesthetics, new ways of ordering space and a re-location of authority, generally to a much greater degree than scholars, political commentators and journalists have been willing to consider. The on-the-ground perspective of political life examined in this book can serve to exemplify alternative ways of understanding the functioning of the state.

The second of Bongmatur's points that we highlight here relates to the inherent tension in Pacific nations between the concerns of the state and the emergent or performative qualities of cultural heritage. As Bongmatur expresses it, the museum as a state institution is always at odds with people's lives, just as culture (seen as *kalja*) is somewhat at odds with custom (seen as *kastom*). This is specifically examined for Papua New Guinea, Solomon Islands and Vanuatu in chapters by Dalsgaard and Otto, by Foana'ota and White, and by Lindstrom. This tense but elaborate and diverse relationship is further exemplified by movements aspiring to political power and explicit autonomy, as examined in chapters by Hviding and M. Scott, and by the performative aspects of cultural heritage that may amount to 'diplomacy' between the local and the state, as examined in chapters by Henry, Alévêque, R. Scott and Bolton. The friction between cultural heritage and the state finds its most marked expression in the formulations of national cultural policies described in the chapters by Foana'ota and White on Solomon Islands, and by Regenvanu and Geismar on Vanuatu. Moreover, the chapters by Pigliasco, Hanlon and Rio show how cultural heritage represents an agency for change and instability in the eyes of the state in a range of Pacific settings. It follows that this book deviates from a glorifying view of cultural heritage, as it pinpoints both the conflicting values at play in questions of cultural heritage and the subversive power of cultural-heritage movements that may call for responses of state legislation and regulation.

It is important for the collective approach proposed in diverse ways and settings in this volume to maintain that cultural heritage is of interest both as an idiom for state policies and as constitutive of the generative dynamics of social movements – i.e. in terms of the relations it mediates between people and the momentum it adds to social values and claims. Our ambition is to highlight the importance for Pacific peoples of their own vibrant social movements in their efforts to challenge wider social orders, such as the state, legislation and religious orders, as well as in their desires to gain and maintain increased control over the conditions for everyday life. We are made aware that cultural heritage objects, sites and performances hold a particular power that threatens pre-assumed social orders such as those that the state attempts to hold together. Through examining localized, and perhaps chaotic and exotic, values and strategies we learn about social movements that are neither 'traditional' nor 'new' – but that in their own totalizing social motion appear in their own right as agents for the creation of both unity and continuity.

Kastom and cultural heritage

Several chapters in the volume are concerned with contemporary articulations of culture under state governance. It is of interest here to follow the development of codified concepts like *kastom* in Melanesia, as well as the intense discussion around the 'invention of tradition' among scholars and political activists in previous decades, not least in the context of Oceania. In the special issue of *Mankind* entitled 'Reinventing Traditional Culture: The Politics of Kastom in Island Melanesia' that appeared in 1982 (Keesing and Tonkinson 1982; see especially Keesing 1982; Tonkinson 1982; Larcom 1982), and in the special issue of *Anthropological Forum* entitled 'Custom Today' that appeared a decade later (Lindstrom and White 1993; see especially Tonkinson 1993; White 1993), the concept of *kastom* was treated with academic rigor and from a regionally comparative perspective, as an enormously diverse rhetoric of tradition flourished concurrent with independence and nation-building in the Melanesian island nations. Hobsbawn and Ranger's *The Invention of Tradition* (1983) was a key text that informed the theoretical foundations of many of the writers about *kastom*. The time saw heated debate among scholars on the topics at hand, exemplified by the exchange between Marshall Sahlins and Nicholas Thomas in *American Ethnologist* (Sahlins 1993; Thomas 1993) leading on from the publication of James Carrier's collection *History and Tradition in Melanesian Anthropology* (Carrier 1992; especially Thomas 1992). No less heated were the confrontations between scholars and indigenous political activists over Pacific issues, notably the exchange between Roger M. Keesing, Haunani-Kay Trask and Jocelyn Linnekin that ran over several initial issues of *The Contemporary Pacific* (Keesing 1989, 1991; Linnekin 1991; Trask 1991).

Heated scholarly debates and dismissals from indigenous activists notwithstanding, the advantage of the turn towards a historicizing of 'tradition' and 'culture' was that a lot of academic work came to be invested into interweaving understandings of global processes with down-to-earth indigenous perspectives and life-worlds, not least in the Melanesian setting. In terms of the Melanesian part of the Pacific, this body of work made it possible to realize that the concept of *kastom* was undoubtedly of the most importance, coined as it was by indigenous populations themselves so as to accommodate and appropriate colonialist visions of 'culture' and 'tradition'.

In actual fact, the currency and widespread discussion of Melanesian *kastom* revealed the indigenous concept as signalling a deep pre-existing understanding of 'cultural heritage' that, not long after the intense debates about *kastom*, was adopted by UNESCO and by policy-makers throughout the world. When Lindstrom (this volume) comments that *kastom* can translate directly into 'cultural heritage', it indicates how the concept of *kastom* itself grew out of a Melanesian understanding of 'culture' as pressed upon them from the colonizers (see also Rio, this volume). On the other hand, if we look at the genealogy of its usage, cultural heritage really gained its global currency only after taking into account an anthropological concept of culture – specifically a Geertzian notion of culture as knowledge – with a subsequent attention to 'intangible cultural heritage'. In what has been called the 'anthropologizing' of cultural heritage and the move away from the renaissance and enlightenment concepts of heritage (see Butler 2006), Pacific experiments with *kastom* and politics and national cultural policies have played an important role in informing the international audience about a new apprehension of cultural heritage. For example, *Our Creative Diversity*, the report of the World Commision on Culture and Development, opens with a quote from Marshall Sahlins on culture as 'the total and distinctive way of life of a people or society' (UNESCO 1995:21). When proceeding further into the anthropological understanding of intangible heritage, the report's tone echoes Pacific conceptualizations of *kastom*. We note that Thomas Hylland Eriksen

(2001) in a critique of this UNESCO report focuses on the concept of culture that emphasizes difference and the production of local art forms, and which in his view is overly relativist. This could partially have been a description of the Melanesian concept of *kastom*. This is not to say that local conceptualizations of *kastom* are similar to UNESCO's culture concept (see Mosko 2002; Leach 2003), only that Pacific peoples in their concern with culture have perhaps been especially sensitive to the Western preoccupation with heritage. The contributors to this volume address in many different ways how the globalized concept of culture continually engages, nurtures, or borrows from its localized counterparts such as *kastom*. Simultaneously, as several contributors point out, *kastom* itself is also continuously gaining importance in new ways (see Akin 2004; Lindstrom 2008). Indigenous concepts of culture are undergoing historical developments and are adapting to particular political and socio-economic circumstances – more precisely, to the compartmentalization and stratification entailed by modernist or capitalist economies and post- or neo-colonial state-building.

A common definition of *kastom* has been 'exchangeable, relational and partible intellectual property' (see Dalsgaard and Otto, this volume), thereby representing the standing stock of a group's, lineage's, village's, island's or even nation's means for expressing their cultural specialities. Although *kastom* is considered by all Melanesians as something crucial to a local way of life – in the meaning of 'we live inside it' (not unlike the way we think about culture in anthropology) – it can also be handled as a thing; something that can be 'borrowed', 'destroyed' or 'lost'. In the case of exchange between islands, *kastom* can be performed and, even, bought – through the ceremonial purchase of ritual elements such as songs, dances or titles, or even the purchase of another language. As described by Rio (this volume), *kastom* in this sense was indeed a partible entity before it came to stand for the cultural property in a nationalist sense (see also Larcom 1982; Foster 1992; Harrison 2000). However, in parts of Melanesia there are current indications of a move towards the more essentialist concept of *kalja*, with a focus on identity, unity and eternal, inherent and inalienable qualities of distinctiveness. As shown in the chapters by M. Scott, Hviding and Lindstrom, the search for unity in local movements is today about building micro-nations, rather than about elaborating local and fluid variations of *kastom*. A further case in point is the chapter by Dalsgaard and Otto on political developments in Manus, Papua New Guinea. Here we see a shift in both vocabulary and practice towards an essentialist understanding of culture as first and foremost a given identity. As formulated by Simon Harrison (2006:66), we are dealing with important processes of modern nationalism, wherein the nation stands forward as a 'possessive individual' with a claim to autonomously possessing culture as a property of itself.

Nation-making despite the state: the problem of 'invented tradition'
The processes examined in these chapters thus connect directly to the literature of recent years on 'nation-making' in the Pacific (Foster 1995, 2002; White and Lindstrom 1997; Otto and Thomas 1997; Picard and Woods 1997; Babadzan 1988, 2000; Hirsch 2007). Much of this literature has explored national sentiments with regard to the nation-state, or the lack of national sentiments with regard to post-colonial states. For Foster, nation-making is about 'both the production of a collective definition of "peoplehood" and the construction of individual "personhood" in terms of such a definition' (1995:2). As such, nation-making is not only about communal sentiments and the creation of organic social totalities; it is also a thoroughly modern form of movement that attributes a particular status to the individual.

So far, what has been underplayed in these debates is the way in which Pacific peoples have tended to search for alternative ways of nation-making, rather than through nation-state structures (see Kelly and Kaplan 2001). In our experience, there is a current pan-Pacific interest in expressing visions of nationhood that bypass state organization, as exemplified by social movements that operate laterally through making connections, and that work at the level of grassroots infrastructure. One such movement is described in the chapter by Hviding: the Christian Fellowship Church of New Georgia in Solomon Islands has built an organization that suggests its very own way of constructing a strong island-based identity, with an economic infrastructure of logging (in liaison with Asian transnational companies), forest plantations, education and logistics, a way which simultaneously springs from a unitary religious formation with a Christian flavour, grounded in the original work of a local prophet. This is an example of a clearly circumscribed local movement of unity that has ambivalent relationships with a state that it partly replaces and partly assists. There are also more recent developments in the Pacific region in which unity is sought in larger movements of religion or *kastom*, drawing in the nation as a strong counter-movement to the state.[2] We might speculate about the nature of the sentiments and social movements that aspire to establish new identities of a national character by drawing together bits and pieces of existing cultural heritage, both tangible and intangible, and which potentially override existing state boundaries or government regulations. Whereas it has been argued that the newly independent states of the Pacific in the post-colonial era have been 'states without nations' (Dinnen 2007:3) – artificial creations without a sense of shared history or identity; it is suggested that today the actual formations of national sentiments and identities, some small-scale, some large-scale, are oriented around cultural heritage rather than existing state forms – 'nations without states' – and actually explore new, alternative ways of state-making.

A well-known example serves to introduce our view of cultural-heritage movements as a particular form of nation-building in the Pacific. The Polynesian Voyaging Society of Hawai'i, although it may not have any explicit pretension to build a specific nation, has the character of a search for regional – at the very least pan-Polynesian – cultural unity that more small-scale Melanesian movements mostly reveal only on a local scale. As described by Rolf Scott (this volume), since its start in 1973 the movement has managed to re-territorialize the Pacific Ocean, creating an ocean space of linkages that cross-cut the various state boundaries that exist as colonial leftovers. In Hawai'i, the movement has become much more than a community of seafarers, with an educational programme that teaches traditional leadership and navigation skills to thousands of school children every year, and that has lifted the consciousness of native Hawaiians and has influenced the way in which they see their relation to the United States. Some detail on the Polynesian Voyaging Society's 1995 expedition sets the amazing circumstances of this remarkable movement into view.

> The 1995 Voyage to the Marquesas, called Na 'Ohana Holo Moana
> ('The Voyaging Famil[i]es of the Ocean') carried on the work of the 1992
> voyage – training new crew members and navigators, sharing voyaging
> traditions across the Pacific, and re-connecting Polynesian peoples through
> the heritage of the canoe. On the voyage from Tahiti and the Marquesas
> to Hawai'i, Hokule'a was joined by five canoes, Hawai'iloa and Makali'i
> from Hawai'i, the Maori canoe Te Aurere, and two Cook Islands canoes,
> Takitumu and Te Au o Tonga.
>   (Polynesian Voyaging Society website, http://pvs.kcc.hawaii.edu)

The account by anthropologist Ben Finney, a founder of the movement, of this boundary-crossing expedition from Hawai'i to Tahiti and back in 1995 is full of surprising events (Finney 1999). As the Hawaiian canoes joined with the other Polynesians of New Zealand, Cook Islands, Tonga, Tahiti and Marquesas, just off the island of Ra'iatea near Tahiti, they were led ceremonially through 'The Sacred Pass', through the reef, into a lagoon and to the location of the ancient stone temple Taputapuatea. In front of an eager audience, an ancient mystery was unravelled, and a historical tension was finally resolved under ceremonial circumstances:

> As the last of the sailors were taking their places, a spare Tahitian man in his
> early seventies, dressed in wrap-around *pareu*, with a short, feathered cloak
> over his thin shoulders, welcomed the voyagers onto the marae with more
> 'come hither', pronounced three times in Tahitian, then in Tuamotuan, and

finally in Hawaiian. Then he told the assembled crews how 'our mother', by which he meant Taputapuatea, was throbbing with maternal joy because 'you, the children, the descendants' of those who centuries before had set sail from here to find new lands, had this day returned on your canoes from the 'four sides of the dark, dark sea of Hiva', sailing through the Sacred Pass to at least remove the tapu that had isolated Ra´iatea and their own islands for so long.

(Finney 1999:5)

Finney (1999) launches a radical critique – which seems to have been subsequently largely overlooked – of the theoretical idea of the 'invention of tradition'. His critique is important because it demonstrates empirically where the theory fails. In short, the 'invention of tradition' literature presented us with the idea that 'traditions' are always shallow historically and manipulated politically for motivations of power. Traditionalist movements were thus seen as political movements rather than cultural creations, and as such were assumed to flourish in the modern era because 'tradition' is one of the few assets that formerly colonized peoples possess on the globalized political scene. This view undeniably carries some strong assumptions about what culture is, how the constitution of society takes place, and the role of politics in socio-cultural development. Not least, the view implies that the concerns of the people in question are mainly political.

Important critical contributions from Sahlins (1994, 1999) made suggestions about culture that would render many scholars' problems with invented traditions unnecessary. It was never the pretence of culture, Sahlins argued, to be unchanging or un-innovative – nor was it ever the promise of humans or society to merely live according to one correct, unitary history. The long-standing arguments about invented traditions offered us 'explanation by way of elimination' (Sahlins 1999:407) – resulting in analyses that eliminated many aspects of social life and of people's efforts to live their lives – in order for power, desire, greed and conflict to stand out in the analysis. We believe this is an absolutely crucial point. Empirically, Finney's detailed accounts of the many-stranded work of the Polynesian Voyaging Society (e.g. 1994, 1999, 2003) provide an alternative vision of a traditionalist movement, by focusing on the movement's revelation to itself of its own structure and history, and even its own cause, in the form of a mystery. The Society's ambition to revive open-ocean navigation meant that virtually everything had to be 'invented', since all concerning the technology, skill and knowledge of constructing and sailing the large canoes of a distant past was lost in Hawai'i. But immediately after the initial phase of construction and learning, in the course of actual sailing, and through the connections that emerged as the Society's first canoe

Hokule'a visited various islands of Polynesia, the voyaging itself brought back to reality a cultural memory that was very much alive. The technology of sailing turned out to be only a precondition for a technology of cultural remembering. Thus the gathering in 1995 at Taputapuatea commemorated an ancient Polynesian union and pact, constituted in ancient times through marriage between royals from distant islands. It brought back into recollection that this very site had been a ritual and political meeting point between far corners of the vast ocean for many generations, ever since the institution of the alliance. This union had been broken at a point long before the arrival of Europeans. Following a quarrel and the murder of a high priest, the delegates from the western islands had fled the scene, never again to return. A taboo had allegedly been put on inter-island travel and on the temple at Ra'iatea. When the first missionaries visited the islands to the west, the people were still well aware of that murder as 'the sin at Awarua'.

Over a century later, in 1976 when Ben Finney first landed in the *Hokule'a* at Ra'iatea, the island's inhabitants had cleared the ancient temple at Taputapuatea, and the orator Parau Rahi (lit. 'Big Talk') started recalling a prophecy. In his version – uninfluenced by the literature on the subject – he explained that the taboo had been placed on the temple and on the 'sacred passage' and overseas voyages because Ra'iateans had once sent out an expedition eastwards – to Hawai'i – that had never returned. The orator could therefore declare the lifting of the taboo, since the *Hokule'a* had now returned with the descendants of that expedition – if it had not been for one essential mistake: the *Hokule'a* had arrived at Ra'iatea's official port of entry, and not through the 'Sacred Pass'. The details of this event and the historical pieces that fell into place are amazing. The Polynesian Voyaging Society – founded in Hawai'i but reaching out to and creating energies among Maori, Tahitians, Tongans and others – managed to map a completely new seascape between the archipelagos, with the Taputapuatea temple as the new 'vital cultural centre' (Finney 1999:17), with new routes being constituted between the islands, and with an overarching new emergent sense of shared Polynesian identity – sustained and verified in already-existing myths, prophecies and in tangible and intangible cultural heritage.

It is in this sense that this movement can be seen to represent nation-making – while bypassing state boundaries and state legislation, and through establishing and affirming identities across a (re-)unified ocean space. Is this not a presentiment of a pan-Polynesian nation based on a shared vision of geographical and historical location and of shared time-space, on a mythico-religious model that offers a shared understanding of the way these far-flung islands and their peoples are connected by eternal bonds? And is it not a glimpse of the *longue durée* implied in Epeli Hau'ofa's vision (1993) of Oceania as a 'Sea of Islands'? Here, we do not wish to enter into a political discussion about independence, unions or similar future developments in Polynesia, but simply to establish our point that nation-making in the Pacific is continuous in social movements that do not necessarily have a political agenda of either state-making or 'invention of tradition', but which stand out as truly alternative structures. Furthermore, cultural heritage has been central in the articulation of these movements by generating historical truths and shared beliefs about origin, identity and futures in the islands. But do shared identity and history necessarily invoke the nation as a construct?

At this point, we suggest, it does – because nationhood has become a natural and perhaps necessary ingredient in people's contemporary lives. In global discourse, an overall concern persists for people to be able to identify themselves vis-à-vis significant others; and in this particular case the 'others' may themselves be identified as state citizens, submitted to the authority of states. Maori activists can identify with Polynesian nation-making in opposition to being citizens of the New Zealand state, in the same way – although of a different scale – that the people of Makira celebrate their identity through the Makira proto-nation in both opposition and complementarity to the Solomon Islands state (M. Scott, this volume), and the followers of the Christian Fellowship Church envisage themselves as living in their own unitary nation-like existence within a movement that pools the ownership and development of customary land and operates as a viable alternative to, yet within, that same Solomon Islands state (Hviding, this volume). The Polynesian Voyaging Society is unique in terms of the immense pan-Pacific scale and momentum of its activities, but not in its way of incorporating into its own structure, and outlook for the future, the language of nation and national person-making.

Social movements and political innovation

We believe that this specific character of social movements – a potential for political innovation through nation-making in a close relation to state-making – has been underestimated in the documentation of developments in the Pacific. It has been a constant logical problem for processes of state-making that local social movements do not clearly formulate their ambitions in terms intelligible to a 'state-way-of-seeing' (cf. Scott 1998). The Nagriamel movement of Vanuatu can be mentioned as a case in point (cf. Tabani 2008). During the 1960s and 1970s, as this movement grew in Vanuatu, it first appeared to the colonial administration as a harmless traditionalist movement. It was constructed around the ceremonial men's house as a religious unit, and was striving to create an inter-island movement that could unite through its cultural heritage – i.e. a somewhat shared ritual hierarchy, the prevalence of boys' circumcision, of bride-price and of prescribed marriage-rules, pig sacrifice and ceremonial displays of food. But the movement was further geared to economic and infrastructural development by establishing custom ownership of land and community organized plantations on a large scale. It spread quickly across the country as a unitarian movement with an ethos of traditional values and a claim for independence from colonial influence. The Nagriamel movement was not so much imitating the colonial administration or trying to install government or law in the sense of creating a state, as it was up-scaling Melanesian values of authority, leadership and relation-making to a national scale. In this it came to look more like a workers' union in terms of organization (Van Trease 1987:164). It was not until its last days of 1980 that the movement was pressed into taking up a competitive position vis-à-vis the Vanua'aku Pati, as the latter formed government in the newly independent state of Vanuatu. That Nagriamel should form an alternative political movement to the independence movement was first and foremost something pushed onto them from, on the one hand, the capitalist interests of a US corporation that wanted to set up a free-trade paradise, and on the other, the French navy that wanted to counteract British influence on the independence movement (see also Beasant 1984).

What we want to achieve by invoking these examples is to underline that our initial use of 'political innovation' is meant to emphasize the energy with which social movements in the Pacific are experimenting with political forms – something quite different to the idea that there is self-interested innovation in cultural politics. In this type of experimentation with political forms, with nation and with state, cultural heritage provides social movements with their values and orientation and informs the alternatives they constitute. 'Cultural heritage' viewed through a Pacific lens is likely to be seen quite differently to 'cultural heritage' in the generalized, conventionalized sense. Many chapters in this book describe how social movements continually draw on cultural heritage – not merely in the form of objects, practices or knowledge of the past, but as totalizing phenomena that keep appearing and reappearing in people's lives. When a Makiran underground army of ancestral spirits, mythical creatures and past warriors suddenly reappears in people's visions during a time of national turbulence (M. Scott, this volume) it is indicative of an unexpected, alternatively desired or strategic, reappearance of cultural heritage. Cultural heritage is not necessarily used politically in the general sense or for some specific purpose of political gain – in many cases in the contemporary Pacific, it seems rather as if cultural heritage itself determines and dictates politics.

Cultural heritage in, against and beyond the state

In Rosita Henry's chapter an important observation is given that has key relevance to the above argument. Henry describes the performance of cultural heritage by various Australian indigenous groups as diplomacy: '... a form of political engagement where the participants employ various performance tactics of etiquette, to announce whatever claims are at stake and with the intention of avoiding open conflict.' Keeping in mind the above discussion about 'invention of tradition', we acknowledge that the performance of cultural heritage often takes place in the particular circumstances of inherent conflict: with claims to be made and acknowledgments to be given, with indigenous rights, ethnic identities or at least group distinctiveness at stake. Henry's case is concerned with the relation between Australian Aborigines and the Australian nation-state. On the local level, cultural heritage is articulated in dances and performances as a social movement not fundamentally different from the kinds that flourish in the rest of the Pacific, but in the direct encounter with the state-as-institution, at the opening of Australia's parliament in 2008, the movement is able to express itself through the subtleties of the very language of performance.

In these types of contexts we also see the potential for heritage movements to create alternative political spaces. Cultural heritage does not itself carry a language of state-making or state-resistance, but expresses itself on a different level, by evoking emotional responses of belonging. The diplomacy of events such as examined by Henry amounts to a meeting point and a form of communication between two different levels of social organization, one bottom-up, one top-down (see also Alévèque, this volume). This creates a context for the state's responses to cultural-heritage movements, in which there will necessarily be an appropriating attempt to adapt the sphere of cultural heritage to modalities of state control.

In the case of David Hanlon's chapter on the extraordinary archaeological site of Nan Madol in Pohnpei, it is clearly shown how various colonial state configurations have attempted to adapt the site to their own nation-making, but without ever entirely succeeding. This is also what Pigliasco's chapter is about in essence – to try to map Pacific state responses to various kinds of cultural-heritage movements. One case in point is the idiom of 'cultural property rights', through which states and the international community have taken it upon themselves to create legislation to safeguard indigenous claims to ownership (see also Hirsch and Strathern 2004). This process is not unproblematic, and Pigliasco comments: 'Note that if we turn culture into property ... its uses will be defined and directed by law, and culture is going to become the focus of litigation, legislation and other forms of bureaucratic control' (see also Leach 2003). Furthermore, vis-à-vis the state, the social movements that circumscribe cultural heritage as their own always appear as potentially uncontrolled forms of nation-making. Although cultural heritage may seem benevolent and indeed a moral high-ground for state purposes, there is always the pressing need for the state to be part of the mapping and organization of heritage. A fair claim seems to be that cultural heritage becomes codified as such in moments when it appears before the state as an undomesticated or wild force. This, then, becomes a concern for the state institutions of cultural policies and national museums.

Henry's argument about the need for diplomacy in cultural matters may have been less than alien to the cultural institutions that existed in the Pacific before the eras of colonialism and the modern nation-state. For the Maori of Aotearoa New Zealand, the *marae* ceremonial house functioned as a place for storing and teaching knowledge, with its own staff and with an emphasis on taboos on entering storage rooms as in modern museums (see Cochrane 1999). Today it is interesting to note the great curiosity, energy and creativity that Pacific nations and smaller communities across the region invest into building museums or cultural centres (see Eoe and Swadling 1991; Lindstrom and White 1994; Healy and Witcomb 2006; Bolton 2006; Stanley 2007). Local cultural centres have flourished throughout the region, not first and foremost for the purpose of storing historical objects, but as spaces for historical contemplation, for the sharing of memories and for bringing back into life knowledge and practices. What type of state-like or counter-state codification is taking place inside these institutions?

In our own experiences from Solomon Islands and Vanuatu, islands abound in groups of youth, women or elders, or any combination of these social categories of gender and age, that try to institutionalize their desire for cultural assembly houses. The sensation that *kastom* has been dormant or 'dead' is often combined with a desire to reawaken essential parts of it, sometimes for purposes reaching beyond the nostalgic (e.g. Hviding 1993). Tim Curtis (2002) describes how the Na'hai Cultural Centre that opened in 1998 in South Malekula provides villagers with facilities for recording stories and interviews, how it is a venue for holding workshops on issues of *kastom* practices, and how the *filwoka* (fieldworker, see below, and Bolton, this volume) of the centre may take up the role of cultural expert in the community when it comes to disputes over land or resources, or in negotiations with the state. These types of local institutions are outwards looking, seeking funding from NGOs or other agencies, as part of their contemplation of rural development and sustainable resource management. But they also maintain a separate agenda of creating social movement and of generating energy for the community itself – in Curtis's terms: 'the motivation for all this is less nostalgic reminiscence than energetic concern for the future ... appealing to a *kastom* for tomorrow' (2002:52).

On the national level we see the same concern – and here we again touch on the bottom-up perspective of heritage management in Pacific Islands nations (see Foana'ota and White, and Bolton, this volume). We will once more mention Vanuatu as a case in point, since that nation has a cultural institution – the Vanuatu Cultural Centre and National Museum – which since independence in 1980 has been able to carry out its work ideologically unhindered by political turbulence. We consider this to be the most successful example of the tendency to turn a colonialist concept of cultural heritage in the favour of living practice and national development. Inside the institutional framework of 'museum', the Vanuatu Cultural Centre (VCC, locally known also as Vanuatu Kaljoral Senta, VKS) has become an institution not so much built around objects and heritage preservation, as it is an active agent that invests funds and personnel into supporting and recording cultural events (both in rural and urban environments), that transfers knowledge between people and between generations, that carries out research into the lives of young people in contemporary Vanuatu, and that hosts annual workshops for an veritable army of indigenous rural fieldworkers who come together to share the results of their recordings and thoughts about their respective islands' *kastom* (see Bolton 2006, and this volume). An influential leader in these processes, former VCC Director, Ralph Regenvanu, comments:

> Fieldworkers are assisting their own communities to develop their own culturally distinct approaches to the management of their own cultural resources. This is, in effect, diluting the role of the of the Cultural Centre as the custodian of the national cultural heritage and 'dissolving the walls' of the institution, in fact – and refocusing it as both facilitating, training and co-ordination body for local-level cultural heritage initiatives and preservation-oriented national storehouse for the cultural property of indigenous cultural groups.
>
> (Regenvanu 1999, quoted in Curtis 2003:106)

With reference to the state, the Vanuatu Cultural Centre and the Vanuatu Cultural Council have during recent years been developing an alternative political agenda – most visibly through the project of a 'traditional money bank' (Huffman 2005; Regenvanu and Geismar, this volume), and through launching 2007 as the 'Year of *kastom* economy'. These influential initiatives for the nation have taken place against overt resistance, with severe conflicts of interest with the Vanuatu state as a progressive, liberalist tax-haven. Alongside the Vanuatu Council of Chiefs, the Vanuatu Cultural Centre represents an interesting nationalist alternative to state governance. This conflict recently surfaced in an open confrontation between the police and representatives of

these alternative 'cultural' authorities. In December 2008, one of the prisons in
Port Vila was set on fire by inmates as a protest against what was claimed to be
inhumane conditions and violence by correctional staff. Some of the escaped
prisoners fled and sought refuge in the meeting house of the National Council
of Chiefs, and Ralph Regenvanu, former director of the Vanuatu Cultural
Centre and since 2008 an independent Member of Parliament, was arrested
as he advocated their protection inside this realm of chiefs' and *kastom's*
authority. Over the next weeks the situation was largely resolved through
diplomacy in which chiefs, the media and a number of parliament members
challenged the authority of police and government.

Through this conflict we can perhaps envisage a situation where cultural
heritage no longer is a force 'against' the state – something that states have
to control and codify, and that creates friction and embarrassments between
governance and grassroots – but where cultural heritage becomes a driving
force in governance. In this vision, museum becomes parliament, and vice
versa.

Overview of the chapters

The cultural politics that we see played out in situations such as the ones
we have discussed here reflect the unique character of cultural institutions
in the Pacific: there are actual possibilities that in future developments the
'cultural sector' of many Pacific Islands nations can manage to redirect the
paths of state governance. For example, the 'difference that makes a difference'
in Vanuatu has to do with the way an ideological and moral '*kastom*-ist'
movement is now featured with its own bottom-up-model of governance and
authority, as exemplified in the quotes by Bongmatur at the opening of this
chapter and Regenvanu's comments above. Here the unity and well-being of
the nation goes along naturally with the people's projects of moving along the
paths laid out for them by their locally singular and differential *kastom*. But
such processes are not exclusive to the Vanuatu politics of the cultural field. In
all the contributions to this volume, ranging right across the Pacific Ocean, we
can see how people's own fields of cultural practice are in diverse ways at odds
with, yet also often feed into, the equally diverse states and politics concerned.

In Chapter 1, a conversation between Ralph Regenvanu and Haidy Geismar
describes the most recent and most impressive of the Vanuatu Cultural
Centre's projects so far, 'Traditional Money Banks in Vanuatu' (TMBV), whose
ambition it is to attack the influences of global economy through a revival of
local currencies such as pigs, mats and shell-money. Geismar considers the
process that led to 2007 being 'the year of traditional economy' in Vanuatu,
and examines the articulation of state, nation and grassroots. An interesting
feature of the TMBV is the way it articulates the relation between state –

with all the ministries involved with their respective policies, UNESCO backing it financially, Vanuatu Kaljoral Senta formulating its aim, in line with contemporary, mostly Australian, anthropology – and the grassroots, as mediated through the fieldworker programme and the people generally in all their exchanges of marriage, school-fees, banking etc. In one sense the project can be seen as a form of social engineering on behalf of anthropology and *kastom* together, in an effort to let culture overrun economy – what Geismar calls a 'synthetic national economy'. In another sense it reflects the Vanuatu Kaljoral Senta's way of defining cultural heritage, not as something of the past or of the material museum realm, but as something that gives one a tool for operating on the nation and its politics.

In Chapter 2, Edvard Hviding examines a powerful but far from well-known social movement in the Western Province of Solomon Islands. The Christian Fellowship Church has a long history, and a complicated relationship with the state. Founded in New Georgia in the 1950s by a local prophet, it was long seen by Solomon Islanders and outside observers as a cult with strange practices of worship. But operating as a somewhat secretive indigenous movement with control over large areas of customary land and a substantial communal labour force, the church has pursued strong agendas of rural development and self-reliance. As a social movement it bridges the secular and the religious, the 'modern' and the 'traditional', as well as the local, national and global. Over the decades, the Christian Fellowship Church has developed a resilient social organization and has built its own economic and educational infrastructure, with the explicit aims of supporting rural social stability and promoting appropriate economic development. These aims have been not least significant in the more recent situation of government collapse in Solomon Islands. The rise of the Christian Fellowship Church into a substantial economic force, with considerable political power wielded by what was once viewed as a remote rural cult, is noteworthy for the ambition to replace, alternatively assist, the provincial and national government – depending on the political situation at hand – and for the movement's everyday use and spectacular public performances of New Georgian cultural heritage in a search for demonstrations of 'unity'.

Moving to the other end of the Pacific Ocean, in Chapter 3 Rolf Scott describes the history of a very different social movement, the Polynesian Voyaging Society of Hawai'i. He highlights the cosmological and ontological character of the voyaging movement as it has served Hawaiian identity and, perhaps, brought on the launching of a wider Polynesian identity in the last decades. Scott asks the question: if ocean voyaging and wayfinding by non-Western methods is a rite of passage for the seafarers and the indigenous Hawaiian population, and if the ocean is the liminal space to be explored and expanded, who is being transformed in the process, and where do the social changes become visible? Scott hints at the wider aspects of transformation of a national Hawaiian identity. He examines the biographies and viewpoints of the Hawaiian voyagers and their imaginary Polynesian nation and sees a radical transformation of global space though the contemporary performance of navigating canoes across the Pacific.

This is immediately relevant to Chapter 4, where David Hanlon describes the politics of cultural heritage related to the famous megalithic site of Nan Madol on the island of Pohnpei in the Eastern Carolines group of Micronesia. He follows the history of representations and the way the site has served different political interests and colonial endeavours. Most recently it has become an important element in the National Historic Landmark programme of the United States, figuring on the US list of sites that matter most to all Americans. Through this history we see clearly how institutions of cultural heritage (of which Nan Madol is a great example) complicate the relation between state and nation. In this case it is the colonial, outsiders' perspective and narrative that clash with Pohnpei's development of its own narrative of lineage models and questions of authority – as Nan Madol emerges as an agent and driving force for certain directions in Pohnpei popular movements.

In Chapter 5, Steffen Dalsgaard and Ton Otto examine a change in attitude towards culture and tradition in the Manus Province of Papua New Guinea. They report on a development that diverges from a view of exchangeable traditions to be given back and forth, and even sold, between groups as relational entities of language, performance and objects. Tradition or *kastom* as a concept is to a larger degree becoming defined by unifying and totalizing cosmological visions of culture – or *kalsa*. Through a biography of one man, Sounin Kilangit, emphasizing his multiple roles as leader of a dancing group in the capital of Port Moresby and, upon his return to Manus, the organizer of a cultural festival, as well as a candidate in the elections to parliament and local government, this chapter articulates the complexity of politics and conflicts that underlies any definition of culture. The chapter raises a number of questions that are central to this book as a whole, by empirically describing an operational line between concepts of culture and cultural heritage.

In Chapter 6, Guillaume Alévêque gives an account of cultural festivals in northern Tahiti. We can perhaps say that the Tahitians approach their cultural heritage from a completely different angle to that of the Manus people. Their ceremonial spectacle starts out with an ambition to 'bring culture to life', and in this respect they emphasize that the ceremonies are 'more real' than cultural shows. In these cultural ceremonies they actively seek out and use archaeological sites, museum objects and traditional spiritual substances for getting in touch with ancestors and for removing themselves from the modern world. These occasions offer opportunities to get 'inside culture' and represent investigations into the 'feeling of culture'. It presents people with an 'immemorial identity' shared by all Tahitians, across divides of religion and against government agendas.

In Chapter 7, Rosita Henry provides a comparative analysis of a number of dance performances by Aboriginal and Torres Strait Islander Australians, and how this enactment of cultural heritage serves as a form of 'diplomacy'. By drawing attention to dance as 'political protocol' and 'an etiquette of diplomacy' she asks what these performances achieve by only partially revealing what they express. She considers three levels of performance. The first is a birthday celebration in the Torres Strait Islands, in which it is the 'felt vitality' – the vigour, the noise, the smell etc. – that causes the audiences to relate to it. The second is an Aboriginal cultural festival in Cape York, where a dance group somewhat controversially celebrated their mixed Aboriginal and Torres Strait Islander heritage. The third case is the opening of the Australian House of Parliament in 2008 (the day before the historic 'Apology to the Stolen Generation'), which was the first time that the parliament opened with an Aboriginal ceremony – the historic moment when Aboriginal performance became political protocol. Henry addresses the issues raised in previous chapters and calls for a deeper understanding of the way cultural heritage works, especially in relation to post-colonial state formations.

With Chapter 8 we move into a section dealing more explicitly with the way Melanesians articulate their *kastom* in the contemporary situation. Michael W. Scott describes recent events taking place on the island of Makira, in the south-east Solomon Islands. There has been news of a reappearance of an underground army, in league with both the *kakamora* – primordial beings of Makira – and possibly ancestral spirits – that in a time of turbulence and disempowerment has paved the way for a vision of Makira becoming the 'strong island' and even the 'chosen land' of the Bible. This represents a total mobilization of cultural heritage for independence from the state, in the name of indigenous Christianity and riddance of foreign ways. Most potently it emerges as a social movement that attempts to reorganize the Provincial Assembly and the Council of Chiefs, preparing for a turnover of government and finally leading towards independence for Makira. Here, it is not the search for a cultural identity and revival of tradition that is delegated to cultural heritage, but rather it is cultural heritage (ancestors, *kakamora*, warriors, island *kastom*) that presses itself upon the people, and urges them into thinking and acting in specific ways and thus forcing an intense interplay between grassroots and government.

In Chapter 9, Knut Rio describes the mobilization around the concept of *kastom* that took place in the colonial era on the island of Ambrym in the neighbouring nation of Vanuatu. Coined as a commercial movement, a veritable industry developed from the communications between chiefs and colonial personnel circling around the value of cultural heritage. Rio describes a historical process of codification and regulation of *kastom* that culminated in the independence movement of the 1960s and 1970s. He explores how the concept of *kastom* has in many ways served as an ideal appropriation of 'cultural heritage' – a concept that was very much at the core of the colonizers' experience of native life. Rio also argues that whereas cultural heritage and *kastom* were well integrated in the colonial state-apparatus of the New Hebrides through the authority held by chiefly assessors, the Vanuatu state's appearance at independence came about through overtly violating *kastom* and compartmentalizing cultural heritage.

In Chapter 10, Lamont Lindstrom presents a framework for how 'Melanesian culting hopes to bind together and create new unities among … diffuse and variously directed people', and he explains the way in which the famous John Frum cult on Tanna, Vanuatu hopes to create totalized social unity through their 'law'. The concept of law here indicates the true order of things as well as regulations for disciplining people's behaviour with regard to such matters as sex, sorcery and economic transactions. The dream of unity is closely linked to cultural heritage, or *kastom*, defined as the ever-changing tool kit for appropriating new impulses that come ashore as foreign influences: 'islanders continue to invoke the best, unificatory aspects of their *kastom* – their cultural heritage – to pull strange people and strange cargo flows into local circuits'. Lindstrom searches deeply into the phenomenology of that concept of unity.

In Chapter 11 Lawrence Foana'ota and Geoffrey White look back on decades of experience with the sector of cultural development and policy in Solomon Islands. This chapter serves as a review of the history of the Solomon Islands National Museum and Cultural Centre and its varying relation to politics and nation during the colonial and post-colonial periods. The authors analyse and problematize the complexity of joining colonialist and Euro-centric ideas about cultural heritage and tradition with local concerns about culture and development, political fluctuation and turbulence. They pinpoint the role of this cultural institution, however much it may have been founded in a European vision of history, as absolutely crucial in the move towards independence in 1978 as a site of, and for, the cultural politics of a new nation. It is intriguing how this process on the national level also generated a parallel movement of institutionalizing culture on grassroots levels – in terms of local 'cultural centres' that popped up throughout the archipelago.

In Chapter 12, Lissant Bolton takes us to a case of cultural policy that has come a few steps further than the Solomon Islands situation. In Vanuatu, the

Vanuatu Cultural Centre (or, Kaljoral Senta) has proven to be a major drive for political change, and has over the recent decades launched several projects that have taken on the task of submitting national education, economy and politics to the specific character of the country's cultures. Bolton describes the indigenous fieldworker programme of the Cultural Centre as taking a specific perspective on cultural heritage. With reference to the example of one fieldworker and his effort to revitalize the building of traditional yam towers on Erromango island, Bolton contemplates the purpose of revival for the fieldworkers. As she observes, revival becomes both a form of description of, and a form of agency for, the island *kastom*.

In Chapter 13, Guido Pigliasco provides a survey of the field of Intellectual Property Rights (IPR) and the way this has manifested itself in law, legislation and policies across Oceania. He points to the ambiguities, paradoxes and contestations inherent in transporting the concept of cultural heritage into the realm of property and law, in the attempts to label indigenous heritage, and the character of 'soft law' that is in practice too vague and fails to actually protect and uphold the rights to those cultural groups concerned. Even though IPR was initially meant to enhance people's cultural identity and self-esteem, it has inevitably become a new framework for reification, economic bargaining, politics and dispute – in addition to raising 'vexing questions concerning origin and boundaries'. Pigliasco argues that cultural rights and property in the understanding of Pacific islanders often denote complex networks of relationships that regulate people's behaviour with regard to both things and other persons, and suggests a shift in the vocabulary from 'property' to 'custodianship' of heritage.

In different ways, and from different vantage points in time and place, each of the following thirteen chapters shows that the decisive moment for cultural heritage is when it denies its own status as policy-defined cultural heritage, and becomes a creative force that engages people in diverse courses of action towards new political orders.

Notes

1.   We would like to express our gratitude to the many constructive suggestions on this introductory chapter given to us by the book's contributors in the course of successive revisions. Many thanks also to an anonymous reviewer, and to Sean Kingston, for their critical comments and insightful advice.

2.   See A. Eriksen (2010) for the case of Pentecostalism in Vanuatu, or Tabani (2008) for the case of the strongly nationalist movement of Nagriamel in Vanuatu. Ecumenical organizations of national scope in Island Melanesia have also exemplified this potential in forging images of national unity through Christianity

in opposition to what is seen as a state that does not support the well-being of 'ordinary people'; this was certainly the case in Solomon Islands during the armed conflict and collapse of government from 1998 onwards (e.g. Joseph and Beu 2008).

BIBLIOGRAPHY

Akin, D. 2004. 'Ancestral vigilance and the corrective conscience: kastom as culture in a Melanesian society'. *Anthropological Theory* 4(3):299–324.

Babadzan, A. 1988. '*Kastom* and nation-building in the South Pacific'. In *Ethnicities and Nations.* (eds) R. Guidieri, F. Pellizzi and S. Tambiah. Houston, Rothko Chapel, 199–228. Huston, Austin: University of Texas Press.

Babadzan, A. 2000. 'Anthropology, nationalism and "the invention of tradition"'. *Anthropological Forum* 10(2):131–55.

Beasant, J. 1984. *The Santo Rebellion.* Honolulu: University of Hawai'i Press.

Bolton, L.1998. 'Chief Willie Bongmatur Maldo and the role of chiefs in Vanuatu'. *Journal of Pacific History* 33:179–95.

Bolton, L. 2006. 'The museum as cultural agent: the Vanuatu Cultural Centre extension worker program'. In *South Pacific Museums: Experiments in Culture.* (eds) C. Healy, and A. Witcomb, 13.1–13.13. Melbourne: Monash University ePress.

Butler, B. 2006. 'Heritage and the present past'. In *Handbook of Material Culture* (eds) C. Tilley, W. Keane, S. Küchler, M. Rowlands and P. Spyer, 463–80. London: Sage Publications.

Carrier, J. (ed.) 1992. *History and Tradition in Melanesian Anthropology.* Berkeley: University of California Press.

Cochrane, S. 1999. 'Out of the doldrums: museums and cultural centres in Pacific Island countries in the 1990s'. In *Art and Performance in Oceania* (eds) B. Craig, B. Kernot and C. Anderson, 256–66. Honolulu: University of Hawai'i Press.

Curtis, T. 2002. 'Kastom as development: opening the Na'hai Kaljaral Senta'. *Cultural Survival Quarterly* 26:49–52.

Curtis, T. 2003. 'Vanuatu Cultural Centre's fieldworker network: capacity-building from inside out'. In *Linking Universal and Local Values: Managing a Sustainable Future for World Heritage*, 105–8. World Heritage Papers, 13: Paris: UNESCO World Heritage Centre.

Dinnen, S. 2007. The Twin Processes of Nation Building and State Building. Briefing note, 1/2007, State, Society and Governance in Melanesia. Canberra: Research School of Pacific and Asian Studies, Australian National University.

Eoe, S. and P. Swadling (eds) 1991. *Museums and Cultural Centres in the Pacific.* Port Moresby: PNG National Museum and Art Gallery.

Eriksen, A. 2010. 'Healing the nation: in search of unity through the holy spirit in Vanuatu'. In *Religious Movements, Emergent Socialities and the Post Nation State* (eds) B. Kapferer, K. Telle and A. Eriksen, 67–82. Oxford: Berghahn Books.

Eriksen, T.H. 2001. 'Between universalism and relativism: a critique of the UNESCO concept of culture'. In *Culture and Rights: Anthropological Perspectives* (eds) J.K. Cowan, M. Dembour and R.A, Wilson, 127–48. Cambridge: Cambridge University Press.

Finney, B. 1994. *Voyage of Rediscovery: A Cultural Odyssey through Polynesia.* Berkeley: University of California Press.

Finney, B. 1999. 'The sin at Awarua'. *The Contemporary Pacific* 11(1):1–33.

Finney, B. 2003 *Sailing in the Wake of the Ancestors: Reviving Polynesian Voyaging.* Honolulu: Bishop Museum Press.

Foster, R.J. 1992. 'Commoditization and the emergence of kastom as a cultural category: A New Ireland case in comparative perspective'. *Oceania* 64 (4):284–94.

Foster, R.J. (ed.) 1995. *Nation Making: Emergent Identities in Postcolonial Melanesia.* Ann Arbor: University of Michigan Press.

Foster, R.J. 2002. *Materializing the Nation: Commodities, Consumption and Media in Papua New Guinea.* Indianapolis: Indiana University Press.

Harrison, S. 2000. 'From prestige goods to legacies: property and the objectification of culture in Melanesia'. *Comparative Studies in Society and History* 42(3):662–79.

Harrison, S. 2006. *Fracturing Resemblances. Identity and Mimetic Conflict in Melanesia and the West.* Oxford: Berghahn Books.

Hau'ofa, E. 1993. 'Our sea of islands'. In *A New Oceania: Rediscovering Our Sea of Islands* (eds) E. Waddell, V. Naidu and E. Hau'ofa, 2–16. Suva: University of the South Pacific. Reprinted in *The Contemporary Pacific* 6:148–61 (1994).

Healy, C. and A. Witcomb (eds) 2006. *South Pacific Museums: Experiments in Culture.* Melbourne: Monash University ePress.

Hirsch, E. 2007. 'Looking like a culture'. *Anthropological Forum* 17(3):225–38.

Hirsch, E. and M. Strathern 2004. *Transactions and Creations. Property Debates and the Stimulus of Melanesia.* Oxford: Berghahn Books.

Hobsbawn, E. and T. Ranger (eds) 1983. *The Invention of Tradition.* Cambridge: Cambridge University Press.

Huffman, K. 2005. *Traditional Money Banks in Vanuatu. Project Survey Report.* Port Vila: Vanuatu National Cultural Council.

Hviding, E. 1993. 'Indigenous essentialism? "Simplifying" customary land ownership
    in New Georgia, Solomon Islands'. *Bijdragen tot de Taal-, Land- en
    Volkenkunde* 149:802–24.

Joseph, K. and C.B. Beu 2008. 'Church and State in Solomon Islands'. Discussion
    paper 2008/11, State, Society and Governance in Melanesia. Canberra:
    Research School of Pacific and Asian Studies, Australian National
    University.

Keesing, R. 1982. 'Kastom in Melanesia: an overview'. *Mankind* 13:297–301.

Keesing, R. 1989. 'Creating the past: custom and identity in the contemporary Pacific'.
    The Contemporary Pacific 1(1–2):19–42.

Keesing, R. 1991. 'Reply to Trask', *The Contemporary Pacific* 3(1):168–71.

Keesing, R. 1992. *Custom and Confrontation: The Kwaio Struggle for Cultural
    Autonomy*. Berkeley: The University of Chicago Press.

Keesing, R. and R. Tonkinson (eds) 1982. 'Reinventing traditional culture: the politics
    of kastom in Island Melanesia'. *Mankind,* Special Issue 13.

Kelly, J.D. and M. Kaplan 2001. *Represented Communities: Fiji and World
    Decolonization*. Chicago: University of Chicago Press.

Larcom, J. 1982. 'The invention of convention'. *Mankind* 13(4):330–7.

Leach, J. 2003. 'Owning creativity', *Journal of Material Culture* 8(2):123–43.

Lindstrom, L. 2008. 'Melanesian *Kastom* and its Transformations'. *Anthropological
    Forum* 18(2):161–78.

Lindstrom, L. and G.M. White (eds) 1993. *Custom Today*. Special issue of
    Anthropological Forum 6(4).

Lindstrom, L. and G.M. White 1994. *Culture, Kastom, Tradition: Developing Cultural
    Policy in Melanesia*. Suva: Institute of Pacific Studies, University of the
    South Pacific.

Lindstrom, L. and G.M. White 1997. *Chiefs Today: Traditional Pacific Leadership and
    the Postcolonial State*. Stanford: Stanford University Press.

Linnekin, J. 1991. 'Text bites and the r-word: the politics of representing scholarship'.
    The Contemporary Pacific 3:172–7.

Mosko, M. 2002. 'Totem and transaction: the objectification of "tradition" among
    North Mekeo'. *Oceania* 73(2):89–109.

Otto, T. and N. Thomas (eds) 1997. *Narratives of Nation in the South Pacific*.
    Amsterdam: Harwood Academic Publishers.

Picard, M. and R.E. Wood (eds) 1997. *Tourism, Ethnicity, and the State in Asian and
    Pacific Societies*. Honolulu: University of Hawai'i Press.

Regenvanu, R. 1999. 'Afterword: Vanuatu perspectives on research'. *Oceania*
    70:98–101.

Sahlins, M. 1993. 'Cery Cery Fuckabede'. *American Ethnologist* 20:848–67.

Sahlins, M. 1994. 'Goodbye to Tristes Tropes: ethnography and the context of modern world history'. In *Assessing Cultural Anthropology* (ed.) R. Borofsky, 377–94. New York: McGraw-Hill.

Sahlins, M. 1999. 'Two or three things I know about culture'. *Journal of the Royal Anthropological Institute* 5(3):399–421.

Scott, J.C. 1998. *Seeing Like a State: How Certain Schemes to Improve the Human Condition Have Failed.* New Haven: Yale University Press.

Stanley, N. (ed.) 2007. *The Future of Indigenous Museums: Perspectives from the Southwest Pacific.* Oxford: Berghahn Books.

Tabani, M. 2008. 'A political history of Nagriamel on Santo, Vanuatu'. *Oceania* 78:332–57.

Thomas, N. 1992. 'Substantivization and anthropological discourse: the transformation of practices into institutions in neotraditional Pacific societies'. In *History and Tradition in Melanesian Anthropology* (ed.) James Carrier, 65–85. Berkeley: University of California Press.

Thomas, N. 1993. 'Beggars can be choosers'. *American Ethnologist* 20:868–76.

Tonkinson, R. 1982. 'Introduction: *Kastom* in Melanesia'. *Mankind* 13:302–5.

Tonkinson, R. 1993. 'Understanding "tradition" – ten years on'. *Anthropological Forum* 6:597–606.

Trask, H. 1991. 'Natives and anthropologists: the colonial struggle'. *The Contemporary Pacific* 3:159–67.

UNESCO 1995. *Our Creative Diversity.* Report of the World Commision on Culture and Development. Paris: UNESCO.

Van Trease, H. 1987. *The Politics of Land in Vanuatu: From Colony to Independence.* Suva: Institute of Pacific Studies, University of the South Pacific.

White, G. 1993. 'Three discourses of custom'. *Anthropological Forum* (Special Issue) 6:475–95.

White, G. and L. Lindstrom (eds) 1997. *Chiefs Today. Traditional Pacific Leadership and the Postcolonial State.* Stanford: Stanford University Press.

CHAPTER 1

Re-imagining the economy in Vanuatu

An interview with Ralph Regenvanu

✳

RALPH REGENVANU AND HAIDY GEISMAR

The following interview took place at the conference 'Pacific Alternatives: Cultural Heritage and Political Innovation in Oceania' at the University of Hawai'i at Manoa, March 2009. The discussion focused on the implementation of the Year of Traditional Economy in Vanuatu and the ways in which it has provided an avenue for rethinking the role of government in villages and for reconceptualizing the basis of economic sovereignty. The introduction and conclusion contextualize this project both in the context of cultural and economic initiatives in Vanuatu and within the broader theoretical framework of Pacific Alternatives, which have been rearticulated in this volume as 'Made in Oceania'.

Background to the 'Traditional Money Banks Project' and the 'Year of Traditional Economy'[1]

In June 2004 a project emerged that had originated with a ni-Vanuatu fieldworker of the Vanuatu Cultural Centre, James Teslo. James recognized that there were not enough pigs to do traditional ceremonies, which meant these ceremonies were not being done, which again meant that transmission of *kastom*, viewed in the context of the Vanuatu Cultural Centre as a form of intangible cultural heritage, was not occurring. The vitality of his culture was therefore being threatened, and he suggested the establishment of a pig 'bank' which could provide the required pigs. With the assistance of Tim Curtis, an anthropologist doing fieldwork in the area at the time and who later went to work for UNESCO, the project documentation was produced. The name of the resulting project, the 'Traditional Money Banks Project', reflected a wider focus on all traditional wealth items needed for use in ceremonies, such as red-dyed pandanus mats, shell money and yams. The project partners were the Vanuatu Cultural Centre and the Vanuatu Credit Union League, with funding provided by the Japanese government through the 'Japanese Funds-In-Trust for the Safeguarding of the Intangible Cultural Heritage' via UNESCO.

The stated objectives of the project were:

1. to survey and understand the production processes and investment and saving/banking mechanisms for traditional wealth items in Vanuatu;

2. to raise awareness of the significance of traditional monies and the need to preserve and continue to transmit the intangible knowledge relating to skills and techniques for the production of these monies;

3. to develop a strategy for promoting the use of traditional wealth items in Vanuatu;

4. to develop strategies to facilitate the use of traditional wealth items to pay for services currently paid for in cash (e.g. school and medical fees), especially in rural areas;

5. to establish laws and policies at provincial and national levels to support the use of traditional wealth items as part of the formal economy of the country;

6. to strengthen the foundations of the traditional economy within culturally appropriate frameworks with a view to stimulating income generation within local populations;

7. to provide infrastructure and resources needed to establish effective and viable 'traditional money banks'; and

8. to establish the viability for extending this concept to other areas of Melanesia.

At the most basic level, the principal objective of the project was to maintain and revitalize living traditional cultural practices while stimulating the generation of cash income. It was envisaged that this would be achieved by:

1. encouraging people involved in the production of various forms of traditional wealth (tusked pigs, mats, shell money etc) to continue producing such wealth;

2. encouraging people who are primarily involved in the cash economy to access the traditional valuables and to use them for ceremonial activities; and

3. facilitating the exchange of cash and traditional wealth items between the informal and formal economic sectors, both to generate income for people involved in the traditional sphere of economic life and to encourage the revival of traditional practices amongst those primarily involved in the cash economy.

The first activity of the project, a survey of the situation of the production and use of traditional wealth items, was completed at the end of 2004, with the survey report being published in July 2005. The report found that the traditional economy was strong in some areas, while in other areas the know-how still existed but was no longer practised because of growing monetization, specifically as a result of a need for money to pay for state health and education services. Despite the greater focus on cash crops, there was still a strong and widespread interest in revitalizing traditional ceremonial exchanges and traditional cultural expressions.

By this stage, there was a growing realization that this project involved more than just cultural heritage issues; rather, it required a broader focus on macro-development approaches and policies. This was an awareness that had been growing for some time within the Vanuatu Cultural Centre, as its work to assist local communities to maintain and revitalize aspects of their cultural heritage was consistently undermined by government policies, which did not reflect these community values and concerns. The need to address the broader national development agenda led to a key decision to form a partnership with the National Council of Chiefs and to cement a relationship with the Prime Minister. This was to become the key strategic alliance that eventually led to the government's declaration of the Year of Traditional Economy in 2007. This initiative was extended into a second year in 2008.

By the beginning of 2007, the project was providing seed funding to support the establishment of 'pig banks' throughout the country, as well as numerous other projects to promote traditional wealth production in local communities. An awareness team comprising VCC fieldworkers, chiefs and national and provincial government authorities were touring all areas of all islands to explain the meaning and purpose of the Year of Traditional Economy, to some bemusement from local communities, who had been 'doing it' all along. Policy makers in the national capital, ironically, were the least ready to accept what they saw as an 'about face' in national development policy.

The Year of Traditional Economy and its aftermath

HG: So we are going to have a conversation about some of the issues that have come up around culture and economy and development in Vanuatu in the wake of the Year of Traditional Economy and the Vanuatu Cultural Centre (VCC) project to investigate the history and continued resonance of traditional economy (known colloquially as the 'Pig Bank Project').

In 2007 the Year of Traditional Economy was legislated by parliament and came into being. What kinds of policies have already been set into place? What happened between policy and the grassroots? What are the interconnections between policy and practice and do the Cultural Centre and the government mediate them in different ways or in similar ways or increasingly converging ways?

RR: The Year of Traditional Economy started on 17 November 2006, which was a national day of culture. There was a march from the middle of town up to the National Museum and the chiefs' *nakamal*, their meeting-house. It was interesting, because the Prime Minister and the President showed up in their traditional dress, wearing all the marks of their ranks, with their wives, which may have been the first time ever, in the capital, that this happened. This was widely covered in the media and it was perceived as a very strong commitment by the government to this Year of Traditional Economy. It reflected a very strong commitment by the then Prime Minister (Ham Lini), who is himself a high-ranking leader in North Pentecost.

Every person who marched was supposed to come with some item representing the traditional economy. Some people came with bags of taro, coconuts, there were a couple of pigs, sugar cane, kava ... [they] marched with these and then they were exchanged between the different provincial groups represented in the march, and between chiefs, government and the heads of church. They all presented pigs as their contribution. Normally they donate cash or money, but the idea was that this year they give us what we have in our currency. So that was a very good start to the whole Year of Traditional Economy. There was a high level of commitment and practise of actual exchanges going on in the chiefs' *nakamal*, which was showing what it's all about.

However, there was also a lot of confusion about what the Year of Traditional Economy means among policy-makers and right down to grassroots. There were questions about how are we going to use pigs and mats to pay for a Hilux: how many mats does it take to buy a double-carry Hilux from Asco Motors? There was also talk about how is the traditional economy going to provide jobs and where are the jobs going to come from. So it was obvious that the main focus of the year was going to be raising awareness.

✳

So, one of the first things we did was put together a policy matrix of all the different policies that were part of the objectives and activities of the Year of Traditional Economy. The matrix allocated responsibilities to the Cultural Centre, the National Council of Chiefs, the fieldworkers, to communities, to the Department of Agriculture, Department of Heath, Minister of Education, Judicial Service Commission, even the USB Chamber of Commerce and various NGOs. One of our first activities was to provide an awareness of what the *kastom* of Vanuatu is. I pretty much did that with an article I wrote that came out in the newspapers early in the year. I provided a lot of explanations in Bislama that went into brochures, t-shirts – all kinds of promotional activities. I think probably the main thing that happened in the year of *kastom* economy was that we sent a group all around Vanuatu, raising awareness not only in the islands at grassroots level, but also in Vila with policy-makers.

What we found at the community level was that they just thought 'Yeah… well what's new.' In some places they expressed the view, 'All these years the government has been telling us to do other things and now you come after 28 years and tell us, no, you do what you've always been doing.' There was a feeling of frustration there, but basically at the community level, people got into it very quickly. At the policy level, it was a totally different matter. People couldn't understand. It was very hard for them to understand how this is going to be implemented, there was the conception that 'we don't want to go backwards, but into the future.' And obviously for them, the future meant a more Westernized future.

So yes, the policy level was the challenge. However, sometimes it was a case of going back to existing policy. For example, the Education Ministry already has a policy allowing school fees to be paid in kind, and this existed before the year of the *kastom* economy. The ministries of education and health have decreed it acceptable for people to pay for medical consultation fees, for school fees, in kind, in traditional items. The policies are there; it's just a matter of the school committees and health committees facilitating them somehow.

HG: So did that start to happen?

RR: It was already happening and it started to happen a bit more.

HG: Can you describe how this system of payment in kind works? How is it formulated, those kinds of payments?

RR: The best situation is a boarding school or a hospital. In those cases, it has been happening for quite a while: parents can pay a fee in foodstuffs, which then go to feeding the kids at boarding school, or to feeding the patients.

HG: So that's a place that you can avoid money transactions completely?

RR: Yes, and where one can also achieve the other objective of the Year of Traditional Economy, which was eating more traditional food, getting the health benefits of all that. So that's already happening and it happens through the hospitals and boarding schools. They receive food by weight and pay by weight. They have scales.

HG: They know how many days of school are worth how many pounds or kilos of produce?

RR: Yes. The problem is that there is a lot of coordination that needs to go on. For example, in a school, if you were going to have a menu with taro on it, then you would need enough taro for that meal at that time. So if you were receiving, for example, taro enough for 15 kids, what are you going to do with it? You have a cooking infrastructure there that has to deal with this stuff, so it's a matter of coordinating the different parents who want to contribute. It's the same with hospitals.

HG: How does this system potentially change people's traditional practices? Do they suddenly have to intensify their gardening and take time away from cash cropping (and from *kastom*), for example, to grow enough food to pay for their kid's school fees? Is the idea to try to develop a completely alternative economic sphere, or is the idea that you'll borrow or get food from your immediate family and continue to cash crop as well? What sort of knock-on effects are there from trying to get people to pay with produce rather than money?

RR: Well, the Department of Agriculture in collaboration with the Vanuatu Chamber of Commerce, which are the two organizations working particularly on increasing local production of traditional foods, as well as any kind of produce that can make money as well – cash crops, have long had a policy, which was promoted within the year of the *kastom* economy, of encouraging three gardens. Everyone is to make three gardens: one for your own food consumption and household consumption; one for *kastom* ceremonies; and one for market, for cash crops, to sell. This policy has been promoted because of the problem people sometimes face when they start to market food and then do not have enough to feed themselves.

HG: Was it the same with the project to set up 'banks' of pigs by giving fieldworkers fences to use in the setting up of breeding areas. Was the idea that these pigs would be divided into three kinds – *kastom*, commerce and subsistence?

RR: Yes, but with the giving of foodstuffs as hospital fees, hospitals are actually purchasing food items. Because the issue is not so much an individual garden being able to supply all of the food, but of coordinating a number of different food producers. This requires a different infrastructure, which is why one of the other policies of the Year of Traditional Economy was that each hospital or boarding school needed to set up a cooperative, a branch of the Department of Cooperatives to deal with this kind of stuff.

HG: Can you talk about working with the Vanuatu Cooperative Society and the Credit Union League, and trying to connect them to ideas about the traditional economy?

RR: Well, one of the fifteen overall objectives of the *kastom* economy was to assist ni-Vanuatu to save cash money, to assist in setting up savings clubs at village level. The 'savings club' is a concept that comes out of credit unions and cooperatives. People get together and start a savings club and decide to commit a certain amount each week or something, to put in the club and so on.

HG: And each person gets to take out the whole kitty at regular intervals?

RR: Well they can take out as much as they've put in, but not more – at certain points. There are rules set up by the savings club as to how you can do that.

The idea with the Year of Traditional Economy was that we would encourage people to set up savings clubs at the village level. At the sub-area or ward levels credit unions can take together a number of different savings clubs. One of the ideas the Vanuatu Credit Union was already promoting in savings clubs was that you could use traditional wealth items as collateral for a loan. The system that was already set up with some credit unions was that a person could allocate a pig, for example, as collateral for a loan of a certain amount – whatever the value of the pig was, for example 10,000 vatu. What would happen was that the savings-club or credit-union manager and the chief would visit the person who wanted to have the loan, would look at his or her pigs and then identify the pig to be collateral. They'd all look at it and agree: this is how much it's worth, and then he would get the loan and he would continue looking after the pig. If he didn't pay back his loan, then you could take the pig and give it to someone else, and the chief would be there to witness everything, and be the authority saying yes, I agree that you did guarantee this. So that was the idea of using traditional wealth items. Actually, I think two years ago, the government passed an act to make it possible to use personal property as collateral, including pigs and traditional wealth items.

HG: Is the idea of personal property based on individual ownership, rather than the kinds of group ownership or relations of reciprocity and debt through which pigs actually circulate in *kastom?* Does it allow for that kind of fluid ownership of traditional wealth items?

RR: The legislation itself is strictly for a Western sense of collateral. There's a person who borrows against collateral, and when he repays, it gets given back to him. So group ownership wasn't recognized in the legislation, although it is recognized in the savings club. The whole savings club idea is based on a community of people who set rules for each other and help each other to meet their obligations and so on. Another objective that was promoted in the Year of Traditional Economy with regards to the objective of getting ni-Vanuatu to save cash, was that savings clubs should be set up using the clan system. So you set up a savings club based on an extended family, given the realization that the extended family is the traditional unit of production. The extended family is the production unit, the resource-owning unit, in Vanuatu. So if you were to set up a savings club across that unity there'd be a real incentive, because you would be building up your own extended family, your own clan. Using it that way promotes the organization of savings along those lines. Also, the idea was to try and have savings clubs or credit unions that include the 'four legs' of society, the chiefs, women, churches and youth. The year of the *kastom* economy, the traditional economy, is largely about trying to bring governance down to the community level. It's not about state governance, but about strengthening traditional governance – clan units, chiefly systems and, of course, communities as a whole, which is indeed the current reality in Vanuatu. Which is why we talk about the four legs of community, like a table – chiefs, women, youth, churches – and try to make sure they're involved in all management, in all governance decisions.

HG: Did you feel, in your observation of what happened as these projects were being introduced into communities, that there were structures in place to implement them, or was one of the issues that you needed to create new bureaucracy to administer and orchestrate these programmes?

RR: Yes, there was a lot of mistrust of cooperatives because of what has happened in the past, when a lot of the time they have been used by political parties, and managed in other ways that didn't follow traditional lines by individuals, or individual committees made up of individual men who ended up squandering the money. So we were asking people to organize them in a different way as a solution to the issue of ensuring the cash is looked after and managed well. If you go back to the original traditional money bank project, these were two of its objectives: one, to revitalize traditional practices; and two, to generate incomes. We have tried to revitalize the belief in cooperatives and, in a lot of cases, to reorganize how they were run and working. Often we had to reintroduce the idea of savings clubs, because the first things to go in the cooperatives were their savings and loans wings, which had been the first to be decimated by bad management.

HG: One thing that I see in the project is an attempt to bridge a divide between the cash economy and ideas about *kastom* and tradition, and to take advantage of the benefits of what can happen when you bring them together in ways that are informed by *kastom* but which don't exclude the possibilities of making profits in cash. This presumably is really what everybody wants – to maintain their traditional base but also be able to have cash. I think a lot of the preconceptions at a higher level, or maybe at an urban level, are that going back to the traditional economy means leaving cash behind in some way. This is the way that the project seems to be successful, in bringing the two together. Did you feel it did this? That you got people to think about cash from a traditional basis rather than just the capitalist basis, and to realize that cash can be valued in different kinds of ways?

RR: Yes, but what happened was that everyone in the rural areas really knew all this. It wasn't anything new. They live with this reality every day. They live in their traditional economy and they're trying to make cash to pay for government services and things like that; mainly government services. Government services are the biggest burden, which is why we're targeting school fees and medical fees, because that's what people need cash for. It's like the government is forcing people to get into the cash sector because of the fees it imposes, so it's not helping at all. The idea was to see how the state, mainly, can be made to stop charging people money, so that they can manage.

HG: Then more money would actually be freed up for medicine and equipment, rather than for feeding patients and paying for food, for example.

RR: That is an aspect as well. Some political parties in Vanuatu argue that these services should be free. But I think communities are willing to contribute, it's just that they don't have the cash, so other resources need to be mobilized.

HG: Can you talk about what happened in town, where the situation of access to traditional resources is really different?

RR: In town what happened was that there was a lot of focus on developing policies that promote easier and cheaper access to traditional foods, and on trying to put regulations in place to stop the influx of unhealthy, imported foods. So, for example, we spent a lot of time in the Year of Traditional Economy on trying to assist the Codex Committee, which is part of an international system about food safety in trade. It is able to look at foods, for example the colorized rice we import huge quantities of to Vanuatu, and say, look, what's the nutritional value of this food, what are its health benefits? Then, according to the international trade regime, typified best by WTO, though we're not a member, we say on these grounds we don't want to import this food anymore, and you can't penalize us, because nutritionally it's a danger to our health. So, these areas of national policy, which have been neglected, we have been trying to strengthen. There was a draft for food regulation that had been around for years and years, but no one paid any attention to it. In the Year of Traditional Economy, we really took it up and pushed it, and said, who's doing this? We raised it on the priority agenda, saying this is something that needs to happen. And I'm glad to say it was passed, as a result of this pressure. We looked back at the Vanuatu National Food and Nutrition Policy that had been formulated in 1986 and finally approved in 1998, at this government document and its specific objectives to increase the consumption of local foods to improve food self-sufficiency, to reduce dependency on imported food and beverages, to improve security at a national level, to improve disaster preparedness, to improve the quality and safety of local and imported foods. Unfortunately, what had happened was that this stated objective of the department was being sidelined by 'glamour–projects' such as the Chinese-funded oil pump foundation at Santo or the Chinese-funded tuna processing plant in Port Vila; these kinds of big export, revenue-earning projects. Down at the department level they were still talking about food security. They were talking about planning a three garden policy. We started to question the priorities that were already in government. It's the same in education. Policies exist to get a national curriculum that reflects local culture, which reflects local realities. We went back and tried to revitalize it. This was part of the activity matrix of the policy matrix of the year of the *kastom* economy – to improve education.

HG: So what do you see as happening with rice in the future, realistically?

RR: One of the big things we were pushing in the year of the *kastom* economy was the need to process local foods to make them convenient for urban dwellers. So that if an urban dweller comes home at five o'clock in the afternoon – you know, you've worked all day, you haven't got time to sit down and peel a taro or whatever – then you could either open a plastic bag of rice and chuck it in the saucepan, or you could open a plastic bag of processed taro, and it would be the same price. I think that if it was the same price and the same convenience, then people would go for the local one for sure.

So, you need to provide that alternative. It's like when you talk about paying bride price, but not paying cash, but instead paying with traditional items. That's all very well to say, but where do you get the pigs? Where do you get the mats? These things need to be made available. So it came down to issues of markets, of improving trade linkages to the islands and to things coming into Vila.

I still think the solution to the rice problem is processing urban food, made convenient for urban dwellers, who are the people you want to eat this stuff, because on the islands they're eating it anyway.

HG: Do you see this as dependent on foreign business investment – to set up those businesses – or do you see them as being generated by ni-Vanuatu?

RR: Ideally, it's generated by ni-Vanuatu. It's already starting. The biggest local food producer is Lapita Café. They're doing the most processing of local foods, and that's owned by a local person. It's also in government plans in the Department of Agriculture – somewhere in their list of things they want to do, and this is the thing about getting priorities re-ordered on that list – to set up plants on each of the major islands, so that people can bring their produce to one place, get it processed and sent to Vila and the urban areas, so that you start having a situation where you can have the same level of convenience with local foods that you have with rice. Because that's the advantage of it, there's nothing else really. There is the status stuff that's added onto it, but I think it's the convenience that's really the issue.

HG: Changing tack, let's talk about the role of the Vanuatu Cultural Centre in relation to government. It seems to me that this project marks a significant change in role for the Cultural Centre, to having a major impact on policy and government. Do you see people, or government, opening their eyes to the notion that *kastom* is now being influenced by the Cultural Centre, or that the position of the Cultural Centre has changed as a results of these kinds of projects, in terms of policy making and state governance?

RR: I think so. I believe the Cultural Centre now has equal input into other departments when it comes to development issues: which is different from before.

HG: They are coming to the Cultural Centre?

RR: Yes, we're being invited to participate in all the meetings. Now, for example, the stuff about the *kastom* economy awareness has a budget line in the government's overall budget. There is support for an office promoting the Year of Traditional Economy. It won't be the Year of Traditional Economy anymore, but a Traditional Economy Secretariat. There is funding for staff positions and travel around the islands. Of course you have to supplement it with the Cultural Centre Budget, but at least it's now in the budget system.

HG: Do you think an avenue has opened for the chiefs and other customary leaders to feel they have greater participation in governance and other policy-making? You talked about the idea of devolving the state and taking the administration and implementation of these policies down into communities and their structures. But on the other hand it seems that greater access to the state is also being allowed. It's not about forgetting the state, but about making the state much more present, so people feel that they are more connected to the nation.

RR: There is still a problem with the state not coming down to the level of the people. More avenues being opened for the participation of chiefs through legislation. More laws now that state that the chiefs have a role. But one of the big bottlenecks is that we have to identify chiefs. This issue is coming to a head because the more we advocate for traditional leaders and chiefs in state policy-making, the more quickly you get to the point at which you have to legislate *who* the chiefs are. For example, when a law gives power to a minister, there's a process. You know how a minister operates. This is how a minister is put in this position. There is a process that is already in the law. When you give power to a director general of a department, it's all there already, you know what you're talking about. You know it is one person. For a chief it's not like that. So, we're stuck in a dead end – we can keep giving power to chiefs in laws, and yet have a position in which the laws are ineffectual because you don't know who the chiefs are and anyone can step up, and then they're contested. To move forward on the issues of chiefs being involved in governance we're going to need to solve that problem.

HG: There are some compromises there, because once you legislate you lose the fluidity and the ways in which chiefs are embedded in dynamic systems that are negotiated, that are community based.

RR: I think the awareness in the Cultural Centre and in the National Council of Chiefs about the direction we need to move in is good. And that direction is: you have the state chiefs, who are legislated for, and then you have the traditional leaders, chiefs and so on, who aren't legislated for, but who are separate. For the state chiefs, the first bit of legislation is now coming into being. The structure is new, but it clearly says that there are now fourteen councils of chiefs in Vanuatu. One is the Port Vila Council of Chiefs, one is the Luganville Town Council of Chiefs, and then there are twelve island councils of chiefs. Some are big, like the Malakula Council of Chiefs, and then some, the Futuna Council for instance, are small; it depends on the island and how people think about it, but it's fitted to those realities. It's not very contentious. So in some cases, like in Futuna, you just have the island council of chiefs, whereas in Malakula you have the island council of chiefs, and then you have the area council of chiefs and so on. It depends on how big the geographical entity is. For example, the National Council of Chiefs is comprised of the chairpersons of each council of chiefs – fourteen members in all. This was never the case before. Plus you have the Port Vila Town Council of Chiefs, which consists of chiefs chosen by the island council of chiefs. So Jacob Kapere, who is the chief representative of people from Tanna in Port Vila, was chosen by people of Tanna.

In the past there have complaints that the Port Vila Town Council of Chiefs was very discredited and disconnected from the islands; and that people could walk around saying 'I'm the chief from Aneityum in Vila', despite everyone from Aneityum knowing that he is not. No-one would contend that role because of some sort of respect, but there is no authority there. So one of the things about this legislation and also about the approach that the National Council of Chiefs has taken, is that power has been given to councils of chiefs, not chiefs themselves. The council has the authority, not the chiefs. That's really good. There is also a registration system for chiefs, which didn't work in the early eighties because of resistance from chiefs. But the model is very good. There is a forum, and the chief is nominated. The people who have to sign are the leader of the churches, the leader of the women, the leader of the youth, the leader of each clan, and then chiefs of neighbouring villages. If they all sign: this is the chief.

HG: So it has to be really consensual.

RR: The thing about State Chiefs is that they are going to be given power by legislation and so on; they are basically community leaders.

HG: What will they be called?

RR: They'll be called State Chiefs.

HG: So you won't be able to tell, just by somebody's title, what kind of a chief they are, you'll have to know by the context in which they've been created chief.

RR: Yes, but they're community leaders. Then you have the other chiefs, who are the heads of clans. Although 'chief' is not an indigenous concept, the closest you get to one in Vanuatu is the leader of a clan, and that role existed prior to colonization – the person chosen by the clan to be their spokesperson. So that's still there. And then you have all the graded systems as well.

HG: And then you have MPs, elected officials to represent areas...

RR: But I suppose they're not chiefs, right?

HG: Right, but doesn't that then divorce community and state leadership even more?

RR: Yes, and that's why one of the big pushes here, in the Year of Traditional Economy, was to implement Article 30, Sub-article 2 of the constitution, which says the Malvatumauri National Council of Chiefs should be given the power to endorse any legislation to do with land, *kastom* or language. The most recent case is the family protection bill, which gives chiefs power to intervene in a household between a man and his wife – if the man is beating his wife up. The chief has the legal right to come and kick the guy out of his own house. This power is given not only to chiefs but also to teachers, to women's leaders and to church leaders. But chiefs are one of them.

HG: And who oversees the chief? What if the chief is beating up his wife?

RR: Yes, see now, that's the thing. Now you have one of these other leaders step in.

HG: So there's a kind of parallel between different domains of power?

RR: There is equal power, but these people have to be recognized by the state. The state has to decide: these are the main people in the community empowered by this law. So it's going to have to name the chief in the community. Which might conflict with the chief as recognized by some other party. Essentially there has to be some mechanism – if the chiefs are going to be involved in governance at the state level – to have laws formalized in a way that is recognized by written law and state law

HG: Moving from the Cultural Centre into government, you must be aware of obvious contrasts – some people seemingly participating in capitalist markets and government and legislation for their own purposes, others struggling to really create indigenous models and to base policies on ideas about *kastom*. Do you see a split between all these other power structures and government, or do you think that they're coming together now? After all, all this legislation is going to affect the way in which the government negotiates with the World Trade Organization.

RR: Potentially, but these things haven't happened; there are no official structures or ways to do that yet.

HG: Are people frustrated with the framework that's been imposed, or with the structure of government that's been adopted in the country, and which you are trying to adapt and trying to change?

RR: Yes. There is much frustration, but there is also a lack of models; a lack of conceptualizations of how it's going to work.

HG: Are there other countries in Melanesia or other places in the Pacific that you look to for guidance?

RR: There are lots of models, the problem is we don't know about most of them. We know about some, but it would be good to learn about more.

HG: So what kind of models would you say you drew on, in formulations of the traditional economy, apart from the project of understanding community interests and community frameworks, which has been going on for a long time through the Cultural Centre fieldworker programme?

RR: I think it's more a question of models of alternative development from the development field; alternative ways of empowering communities towards development goals. That's where the models have come from. Our culture is the alternative for our communities, because that is what they're doing anyway. That is their knowledge base. So that's the way the alternatives are going to be articulated. Because that is what the experience is. And that is what's working and has proven to work more than anything else. Because it has been doing this, providing these sustainable outcomes, livelihood outcomes, and the spiritual outcomes, as well as economic ones.

HG: Do you feel that those lifestyles are sustainable in town, in Port Vila, given the projections for growth and development there? If we shift the focus back to reliance and traditional products – is there sustainability to the reconnection of people to their traditional base? Furthermore, could you talk a bit about what you spoke of as honouring the traditional landowners in Vila and the region? Obviously land is going to become the huge issue in town if you want to commit to this system...

RR: There are the policies of the Year of Traditional Economy, which were the kind of policies I espoused in my campaign to get into parliament ... which people want. I mean, they voted for them.

For instance, different island communities in Vila or Luganville, the two main towns at this stage, should have their own *nakamal* or meeting house. Everyone must have a *nakamal.* Everyone needs a place where it can be their place to meet, their place to sort out problems. If they want to teach *kastom*, that's their place. Everyone should have land and a building, and communities should be given land to grow gardens, in town. These island communities, they'll be identified in different ways. For example, in Malakula their meeting houses won't just be a Malakula *nakamal*, they'll be Wala, they'll be Rano, they'll be Urapiv; while Futuna might just have Futuna. So it might follow the areas, according to the Malvatumauri, which I think is the best kind of structure we have for governance in the country. It starts at the village level and goes to the national level. There is a clear line. So one of the big things we proposed in the year of the *kastom* economy was that the provincial structures and the national structures have to align, so we have one structure. And I think that the chiefly structure is the best one, so far. So, we should perhaps have the island communities in Port Vila following that corresponding structure. They have their land, they have the *nakamal*, they have their garden areas. For example, when the Tanna/Ambrym conflict occurred in March 2007, the Ambrym community had to reorganize to form an entity that could speak on behalf of that entire community because the existing structure that they had wasn't representative. This shows that there is a need to reconstitute the way the island identities are organized in Vila, so that they can represent a particular area in a sustained way.

So, as an MP, I'm spending a lot of time helping communities that are trying to get these structures. One way to do it is to try and get them to set up bank accounts, so that I can feed state resources to these communities; this also helps them to try and organize themselves, to have a bank account. I also tell them I want a woman to look after this account, no-one else. Or it can be the youth account, or someone else's. But there are key people you have to have, and the chief has to assent to it for the community. These funds, when they come, who are the people who are going to approve what they're used for? So, I am helping them to get these types of organizations. Then the next step, of course, is getting the land, and for that you have to be in government, basically. But there is a whole lot of privately owned land that is vacant. And my policy in the campaign was, in essence, we're going to take all of this land and make it into gardens. The government has the power to repossess land and give compensation. We really need to do this in Vila now. There is all this land that is vacant and that we can't build on. We have to start making provisions for gardens. That is the way this traditional economy is going to incorporate the urban areas.

Concluding comments

It is clear that the Year of Traditional Economy and other projects to reformulate and revivify a national and state recognition of the viability of subsistence and community – as models for economic engagement – is embedded within a critique and commentary on broader structures of power and governance in Vanuatu. In reference to the argument of this book about politics, 'Made in Oceania' (see Introduction, this volume), there is a powerful contribution to the notion of a 'Pacific' alternative – in that the Pig Bank Project uses the infrastructure of government, but to quite different ends. In doing so, it builds an alternative into the mainstream, with a powerful potential for reconfiguring national agendas. The contribution that the Vanuatu Cultural Centre and the Vanuatu state may make to international models of political innovation is in exploring the ways that alterity may be mapped into the heart of governance. Just as the category of *kastom* itself is both an index of indigeneity and a nationalist (and regionalist) movement, so projects like the Year of Traditional Economy reposition alternative visions with the explicit intent of nation-building.

In making Vanuatu Cultural Centre fieldworkers the key agents of the Pig Bank Project, in promoting regional credit union activities alongside cultural centres, biodiversity projects and traditional resource management projects, and in linking traditional wealth items to UNESCO funded projects around intangible cultural heritage, the Pig Bank Project and the Year of Traditional Economy have explicitly re-imagined the national economy in Vanuatu. As Regenvanu notes in our conversation, in the absence of models, the customary economy itself becomes a good platform for envisioning political transformation. If intangible cultural heritage may be criticized by some as a peculiar form of cultural reification, a globalizing concept that homogenizes the idea of culture as performance, whilst at the same time drawing boundary lines between naturalized 'Western' nation-state cultures and indigenous, minority and 'non-Western' cultures, then it is also a remarkably efficacious alternative model for the economy and economic development that allows grassroots definitions to infiltrate internationalist theory and institutional frameworks (see also Pigliasco, this volume). It opens up avenues for international participation and allows ni-Vanuatu to travel and have their voices heard in key international forums. As a global category, intangible cultural heritage may solve some of the perennial problems of property *qua* commodity taken for granted within much economic theorizing, namely providing a space for understanding resources as total social facts, even as it raises problematic issues around the boundaries between the material and the immaterial, especially in terms of the rights and entitlements that such materialities usually entail.

In another talk, Ralph Regenvanu has called the Pig Bank Project a 'Trojan horse' for *kastom* (Regenvanu 2006). The Traditional Money Banks Project was, and is, therefore strategically subversive. It intends, by sneaking *kastom* into a domain that usually excludes it, to provide a set of practical solutions to the persistent questions that underlie contemporary life for many ni-Vanuatu (and indeed many other Melanesians). Some of these questions are: why is our access to money and the fruits of international investment and development still so limited? Why has our government failed to deliver on its promises of self-reliance and development? How can we reconcile the international interests of finance with local desires to develop a strong 'cultural' base? And, how can we make more money without selling out (which is often abbreviated to how can we make more money)? In short, ni-Vanuatu, like many contemporary anthropologists, are interested in exploring the seemingly divisive relationship between the 'economy' and 'culture' and in developing new ways of thinking about their entanglement.

The imaginary synergies between, for instance, pigs and money, which have led to a productive model of economic development, have not only emerged from within Vanuatu or in UNESCO led initiatives. In 2006, the Happy Planet Index, devised by the London-based New Economics Foundation (whose tag line reads 'economics as if people and the planet mattered'), announced that Vanuatu was 'the happiest place on earth'.[2] Their pronouncement was based on a quantitative algorithm that incorporates the indices of life expectancy, the subjectivity of 'life satisfaction' and a measurement of 'ecological footprint', linking the sense of 'happiness' to environmental policy and ecological well-being as much as to national income based on GDP.[3] 'In doing so', NEF writes, the report 'strips our view of the economy back to its absolute basics: what goes in (natural resources) and what comes out (human lives of differing length and happiness)', factoring out political instability, war and other such blips in human experience.

Within the index, islands perform well (with all of the G8 countries scoring particularly lowly on the chart). Vanuatu, along with the neighbouring Solomon Islands, ranks so highly because of the relatively high numbers of people living off the land (70% according to the 1999 census), the relative under-population of the country, and the lack of integration into global consumption of natural resources. These two economic imaginaries, global and local, bring into being a series of straw men that interlock and are encompassed by one another. Firstly the spectre of 'the economy' (which analyses well-being in association with access to and consumption of resources, viewed in terms of Gross Domestic Product and a monetary standard) is encompassed by a view of the economy that uses the language of heritage and resource management, with its emphasis on the 'right to culture' (Eriksen 2001:127–48), as a model for a new form of economic regimentation. The New Economics Foundation connects itself to the growing movement within economics that theorizes happiness. This concept of happiness is increasingly used to justify economic policy-making with emphasis on, say, environmental protection rather than corporate profit in terms of resource management.

Like many grassroots projects that intend to resist and reformulate global economic practices, a 'social' theory of economics is built into the implementation of the practical solutions proposed through the Year of Traditional Economy. At this early stage of the project more has been modelled than enacted. However, it is apparent that a utopian movement is emergent in Vanuatu in which the basic structures of governance are being provocatively re-imagined. The challenge is to see whether these imagined economies can be made into concrete national models or if they work best at a grassroots level within smaller rather than larger spheres of exchange.

NOTES

1. This section has been taken from Ralph Regenvanu (n.d.) 'Making policy to support living cultures: a case study in "mainstreaming culture" from Vanuatu', paper presented at the 'Islands as crossroads: Cultural diversities in Small Island Developing States' expert meeting, Seychelles, 11–13 April 2007.

2. In the second iteration of the index, published in 2009, Vanuatu was not included due to inadequate data. So we need to take the conclusion that Vanuatu is the happiest place on earth with a pinch of salt. What is important is the creation of an alternative index, which positions countries like Vanuatu in surprising relationships to countries like Australia and the USA.

3. 'Like previous indices, it is multi-dimensional, composed of distinct variables, each reflecting different aspects of the human condition. However unlike, previous indices it ... makes no explicit use of income or income-adjusted measures ...

utilizes both objective and subjective data ... combines fundamental inputs and ultimate ends... The HPI reflects the average years of happy life produced by a given society, nation or group of nations, per unit of planetary resources consumed. Put another way, it represents the efficiency with which countries convert the earth's finite resources into well-being experienced by their citizens.' (http://www.happyplanetindex.org/calculated.htm, last accessed September 18, 2006). Even Vanuatu, with a HPI of 68.2 failed to reach the target index set by NEF of 83.5. Another interesting point is that the remoteness from international markets in Vanuatu is cited as a possible cause of increased happiness in its population!

BIBLIOGRAPHY

Eriksen, T.H. 2001. 'Between universalism and relativism: a critique of the UNESCO
    concept of culture'. In *Culture and Rights: Anthropological Perspectives*
    (eds) J.K. Cowan, M. Dembour and R.A. Wilson, 127–148. Cambridge:
    Cambridge University Press.
Regenvanu, R. 2006. 'The "pig bank": a Trojan horse for custom'. Paper presented
    at the panel, 'Vanuatu Taem: 1606–1906–2006', the Association for Social
    Anthropology in Oceania, February 6, 2006.

CHAPTER 2

Re-placing the state in the
Western Solomon Islands

The political rise of the Christian Fellowship Church

✳

EDVARD HVIDING

Rural resilience in a 'failed state'

During 1998–2003, Solomon Islands experienced civil unrest, armed skirmishes on the island of Guadalcanal between militia groups (the Isatabu Freedom Movement and the Malaita Eagle Force), corruption and extortion at gunpoint of government ministries, a spiralling decline of government services, and a collapse of the national economy (see Dinnen 2002; Fraenkel 2004; Moore 2004; Dinnen and Firth 2008). Following armed conflict in rural Guadalcanal, a coup in June 2000 unseated the government of Prime Minister Ulufa'alu, and violence escalated in and around the capital Honiara and in parts of rural Guadalcanal, which saw large-scale displacement of Malaitan settlers. Although a peace agreement was reached later in 2000, a number of militia leaders from both sides refocused on extortion and small-scale strongman tactics both in Honiara and in Guadalcanal's rural hinterlands. Rarely has a Pacific Islands nation been regarded with such aversion by regional observers, particularly in Australia, where the 'failed state' of Solomon Islands was at one point regarded as a 'petri dish in which transnational and non-state security threats can develop and breed' (ASPI 2003:13).

This conflict-ridden recent past, and images and stereotypes of the Solomon Islands situation conveyed by international media and political commentators (again, particularly in Australia), gave a widespread impression that the Australian-led RAMSI[1] intervention in 2003 – which by any standards was quite successful and relatively peaceful in its opening stage of disarming militants and establishing 'law and order' (see Kabutaulaka 2005; Moore 2005) – was one of reinstalling peace in a country in which every corner was war-torn and any economic activity was on its knees. In international media coverage of the armed intervention, and in the continuing Australian-led RAMSI involvement in policing and in filling the national public sector with expatriate advisers under the banner of 'development partnership' (AusAid 2006), a notable dimension has, however, been ignored. Even during the most intense conflict at the height of the 'tension',[2] everyday village life went along relatively undramatically in many parts of the Solomons outside of Guadalcanal and Malaita. Unwanted visitors (especially from the Malaita Eagle Force, given the high number of Malaitans who reside in other parts of the Solomons) would at times pass by, and in the Western Solomons there was some presence of armed ex-militiamen from nearby Bougainville in Papua New Guinea. But, by and large, the villagers of the western and eastern parts of Solomon Islands lived their lives as usual. Which is not to say that the effects of the 'tension' were not felt. Throughout Solomon Islands, the years from 1998 into the twenty-first century saw little government capacity at national and provincial levels, and rural people experienced a virtual disappearance of government-operated services of infrastructure, health and education.

The majority of the Solomon Islands population of about 560,000 (2011 estimate) still lives in villages, and continues to engage in a subsistence economy based on shifting agriculture, lagoon fishing and food gathering in rainforests and mangroves and on reefs. Most land, reefs and inshore seas are held by kin groups as ancestral estates under constitutionally sanctioned customary law. During the years of the 'tension', this robust subsistence sector provided a strong buffer against the decline and disappearance of government services and the disruption of supply systems for the modest import goods desired at village level. Indeed, an intensification of rural subsistence, made possible in most places by ample land and sea resources under local control, developed in response to the collapse of the rural cash economy as tourist visits disappeared, copra marketing ceased and trade stores lost their supply of imported consumables. Meanwhile, churches of different denominations, some already with significant infrastructural involvement, took over even more of the operation of rural schools and health clinics.

Thus, while national government and economy in the nine provinces of Solomon Islands slid into impoverished standstill, village-level activities in a number of provinces not directly affected by the conflict on an everyday basis developed in interesting ways, demonstrating the capacity of rural Solomon Islanders for improvising by falling back on their own natural and social environment. In this chapter I shall examine what is perhaps the most extraordinary of these rural initiatives. In the country's resource-rich Western Province, the Christian Fellowship Church – a somewhat secretive indigenous movement founded in the 1950s as a breakaway movement from the Methodist Mission (Harwood 1971, 1978; Tuza 1977; Hviding 2005) –

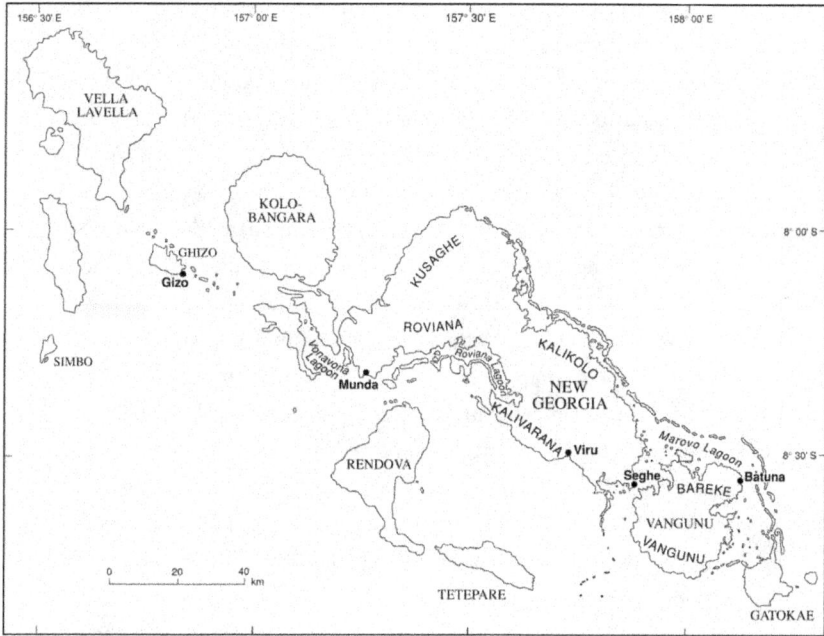

Figure 1   *Map of New Georgia and the main islands of Western Province, showing major districts of CFC influence (Kalikolo, Kusaghe, Vonavona Lagoon and Roviana Lagoon).*

efficiently supported and stabilized large rural areas in the New Georgia group of islands (Figure 1) in the face of state collapse.

The Christian Fellowship Church, conventionally referred to in the Solomons as the CFC, had its beginnings in the prophetic visions of a charismatic leader, and was viewed by European observers (especially missionaries), as well as by Solomon Islanders of other denominations, mainly as a cult with 'deviant' worship. But from a broader view of its more recent engagements, the CFC appears as a powerful social movement that bridges the secular and the religious, the 'modern' and the 'traditional', the 'local' and the 'global'. In the twenty-first century this indigenous and entirely independent church has emerged as the major actor in the reorganization of pathways of power and the rebuilding of economic infrastructure in the Western Solomons, fusing old-style Methodist doctrines with ancestor worship, traditional chiefly hierarchy, modern corporate business ventures and agendas of rural development that aim for independence from both government and NGOs.

In May 2005, the Prime Minister of Solomon Islands, Sir Allan Kemakeza, toured the Western Solomons. Towards the end of the tour he called at the

Christian Fellowship Church headquarters at the boarding-school village of
Duvaha, a rather remote location in Kalikolo, an area in the northern reaches
of the Marovo Lagoon of New Georgia. The visit, although billed as a simple
courtesy call, was duly reported in the national newspaper *Solomon Star*:

> PRIME Minister Sir Allan [Kemakeza] and his 20 member delegation on
> Saturday visited the development projects of the Christian Fellowship
> Church (CFC) during a courtesy call to the area. Led by the spiritual leader
> Reverend Egan [Ikan] Rove, Sir Allan and his delegation were shown the
> various project undertakings by the CFC community. The projects include
> forest, oil palm, cocoa, poultry, rice and copra. Commenting after the field
> trip to the area Sir Allan congratulated Rev Rove for undertaking such
> developments adding 'it was a true manpower work'. He said if all Solomon
> Islanders do exactly what Rev Rove did to his community the country could
> improve for the better. He cited that the system of development undertaken
> by Rev Rove reflected the principles of discipline, obedience and community
> participation. 'These are the true pillars that brought Christianity and
> because of that it shows what to do in the bush', he said. Sir Allan stated
> that Rev Rove's leadership should be the model for all Solomon Islanders to
> follow. He called on the citizens of Solomon Islands to visit the development
> and learn from there. 'You are now sitting on millions of dollars where it is
> important for the country'.
>
> (Wate 2005a)

The ability of the CFC to display such an impressive range of 'project
undertakings' in a national situation of urgent rebuilding, after years of
economic standstill and government incapacity, is without parallel in the
Solomon Islands. This situation has deep structural and historical foundations.
Unlike any other church in the Solomons, the CFC exercises traditionally
derived, centralized authority over huge areas of customary land with lowland
rainforest and abundant timber resources coveted by global extraction
economies. Since the 1980s, royalty income from continued logging on
CFC-controlled lands has been a mainstay of the movement's stable financial
system. From a secure base of accumulated capital, the CFC pursued agendas
of rural social stability and appropriate economic development during the
'tension' years, pouring in funds to encourage rural well-being in a situation
of government absence. Considerable welfare discrepancies developed in the
Western Solomons between villages of the CFC and those of other church
denominations, as the latter lacked the organizational and financial means to
operate schools and health clinics. However, the tendency of the CFC to also
extend assistance, in cash and in kind, to neighbouring non-CFC communities

Figure 2 *His Grace, Reverend Ikan Rove KBE, the Spiritual Authority of the CFC, relaxing in his hideaway house at Tita, northern Marovo Lagoon, September 2007. Photo: Edvard Hviding.*

made these discrepancies less grave than those still apparent today between the Western Solomons and the rest of the nation.

I shall focus on this rapid rise into a powerful political and economic agent by a movement long dismissed as a remote rural cult with strange religious practices. Certain aspects of the CFC's political practice that rely on the everyday usage and intermittent spectacular public displays of pre-Christian, pre-colonial elements of characteristically New Georgian cultural heritage are also of interest.[3]

Logging economy, rural development and social movements

The scattered archipelago of the Western Province – since 2000 a self-declared State of Western Solomons with its own flag (Scales 2007) – has recently been the scene of extraordinary paths of locally driven development, not so far described in ethnographic detail (see McDougall 2008 for an exception). In contrast to the strong strategy formulated and pursued by the Western Provincial Government in the 1980s – an era of economic optimism and environmental concern (see Western Province 1985) – major inputs for recent processes have been village-based, not emanating from the provincial capital of Gizo. Notably, the foundations of the non-state-driven rural development pursued by the Christian Fellowship Church are in large-scale logging carried out in collaboration with Asian companies, not in projects of 'sustainable development' more palatable on the environmentally oriented international scene. Indeed, direct liaisons between customary resource owners and foreign companies have been the norm in the Solomon Islands logging boom, with the former licensing the latter to fell timber on customary land in return for royalty payments stipulated in versions of the national government's 'Standard Logging Agreement'.

Western Province, the second most populous province of Solomon Islands, is the most resource-rich part of the nation. Extensive reef-and-lagoon systems provide rich marine harvests for subsistence and commercial purposes (Hviding 1996). The absence of inland settlements from at least the early twentieth century has resulted in vast stands of well-developed rainforest on the islands of New Georgia, Kolobangara, Vangunu, Rendova and Vella Lavella (Bayliss-Smith *et al.* 2003). Thus, in the Western Solomons, timber has been exploited on a large scale by foreign companies since before Solomon Islands' independence in 1978. During the so-called 'logging boom' of the 1990s, timber extraction throughout the Solomons, not least in the western islands, accelerated, as a large number of Asian companies started operations, largely on customary land (Bennett 2000; Kabutaulaka 2001a; Hviding and Bayliss-Smith 2000; Dauvergne 1999; Frazer 1997). Rural areas experienced unprecedented levels of timber royalty income and, predictably, intense conflict among land-owning groups. Although the timber royalties actually paid by logging companies to land-owning groups far from reflect the overseas market value of high-grade tropical hardwood, and logging in Solomon Islands thus mainly benefits the companies that fell and export the timber, the cash economy in the rural Solomons was so modestly developed prior to the 1990s that any royalty funds infused into rural areas were of a scale that seemed unbelievable to most villagers (Hviding in press). Large proportions of timber royalties have gone into the pockets of elite representatives of customary land-owning groups, many of whom reside in Honiara, and many villagers have expressed their grievance at seeing little benefit from having their forests logged. Another pattern adds to such grievances: all too often, people complain that the timber royalties that did actually arrive in the village were wasted by those in power on the purchase of outboard motors, beer and other consumables of limited longevity. Only a small minority of land-owning groups have managed to divert timber royalties into long-term communal investments such as the building of churches or schools.

It is in this volatile situation, where money in the form of royalty payments flows from logging companies to customary land owners, and in the process is all too easily wasted through conspicuous consumption or appropriated by elites in ways that lead to prolonged disputes in the legal system, that the Christian Fellowship Church has developed an alternative. This singular alternative has enabled timber royalties to be accumulated and used to build rural economic and educational infrastructure and to wield political influence beyond the rural sphere. In this there is a strong element of redistribution from centre to peripheries.

The complexity of contested perspectives and unexpected trajectories that surrounds logging in the Solomons, in particular timber-rich New Georgia, makes the recent national logging arena – constituted as it is at the interface of local aspirations and the agendas of Asian transnational capitalism, with the added dimension of Western conservationist NGOs – by far the most influential and issue-generating sector in Solomon Islands political economy (Bennett 2000; Kabutaulaka 2001a; Hviding and Bayliss-Smith 2000). The long-running relationship in north New Georgia between the Christian Fellowship Church and Asian logging companies epitomizes the complexity of these developments, and illustrates the point made by Bruce Knauft (1999:243, with reference to Gewertz and Errington 1997) that Melanesia is notable in the present world for the remarkable ways in which 'the local intersects the global in axiomatically condensed forms'. As I have argued elsewhere (Hviding 2003a), this is a situation of 'compressed globalization', where relatively few actors on the ground engage in a large and varied repertoire of interfaces between the local and the global.

Successive Solomon Islands governments have expressed the importance of looking for ways in which the customary land holdings of rural people can be drawn into larger agendas of development, without alienating the land from its customary owners, or those owners from the nation's ambitions. On 1 September 2005, the *Solomon Star* newspaper ran a summary of a talk by Prime Minister Kemakeza in which he expressed an urgent need to inquire more closely into the interfaces between government policy, RAMSI intervention, and some not necessarily well-known dimensions of rural and national development:

> **PRIME Minister Sir Allan Kemakeza has outlined policy challenges being faced by the current government and Solomon Islands.**
> Addressing a forum of Permanent Secretaries and Under Secretaries yesterday in Honiara, Sir Allan said Solomon Islands is in the 'rebuilding stage and it is important we remind ourselves of the policy challenges we are facing'. Sir Allan said the policy challenges or issues include:
> - How do we sustain and build on the progress that has been achieved so far?
> - Are we building the necessary capacity to ensure that we can look after ourselves and beyond RAMSI?
> - How can we promote and foster respect and tolerance of our diverse cultures and traditions thus strengthen national unity and solidarity? This task is key to ensuring long term peace, stability and harmony in our country.
> - How can we improve service delivery to our people and enhance their participation in the decision making process? To what extent will the proposed Federal structure or political system address this need?
> - Has the Government's bottom up approach to development been really working? If not how can we make it work better for our people? How can we engage our communities in both decision making and development?
> - How can we utilise the advances in information and communications technology to enhance service delivery and ensure that we utilise the opportunities provided by globalisation and trade liberalization.

I suggest that Kemakeza's talk about these policy challenges was informed in part by what he had seen on his visit to and 'field trip' at the headquarters of the Christian Fellowship Church earlier that year.

Despite these calls from the Prime Minister to high government officials for them to examine closely the poorly known dimensions of rural development, close investigations of change-oriented rural movements have remained mostly confined to the pre-independence anthropological literature on the Solomons. Examples of important rural movements in Solomon Islands are not limited to the Christian Fellowship Church, but include the more well-known 'Maasina Rule' in Malaita (Laracy 1983) and the Moro Custom Company in Guadalcanal (Davenport and Coker 1967). However, the perspectives taken by the writers of the time, including a detailed study by Frances Harwood (1971, 1978) of the CFC as a religious revitalization movement, accentuated the apparently millenarian outlook of the movements and the prophetic nature of their leaders, tended to view them as cults, and largely masked their potential for social and economic planning and well-organized business ventures.

'New Life': the emergence of an independent church

Founded in the early 1950s by Methodist catechist Silas Eto (1905–83), the CFC emerged in the remote northern parts of New Georgia as a movement of separatism from the Methodist Mission. Its first beginnings were before the Second World War, when Eto was preaching in his home village of Kolobaghea in Kusaghe. After the war his teachings were gradually steeped in anti-colonial rhetoric, with strong charismatic notions of the true faith and a direct connection to the Holy Spirit. The latter privilege was claimed by Eto as bequeathed to him by the Reverend J.F. Goldie, head of the Methodist Mission in Solomon Islands, Eto's mentor, and a charismatic New Georgian leader in his own right during the first four decades of the twentieth century. A central element in CFC doctrine is that shortly after his death in 1954 the Reverend Goldie revealed himself to Silas Eto in a vision, and transferred his locally recognized spiritual power – true *mana* in New Georgian terms – to Eto, for him to continue as the earthly manifestation of that power. In essence, this transfer consisted of Goldie handing over to Eto a box containing the Holy Spirit.

Not unexpectedly, this fertile combination of Christian and New Georgian beliefs and the spiritual incorporation of Goldie into local cosmology and CFC theology amounted to heresy in the eyes of expatriate Methodist missionaries and their closest local allies. They also worried about Eto's anti-colonialism, and feared the 'Etoism' that was soon rampant in villages of the Roviana and Vonavona lagoons, of Kusaghe and of Kalikolo, nearly all of which had so far been securely Methodist. Eto voiced deep distrust of the political order of the expatriate-controlled mission. However, as for many other Melanesians, his wartime experiences had given him a favourable impression of Americans, and already in 1945 he had written a letter to President Roosevelt to ask for support.

Through the 1950s some 20 villages, or rather land-owning cognatic kin groups which in New Georgia are called *butubutu* (Hviding 2003b), joined

Figure 3 *Rich and diverse decorations in blue/white/red, drawing on Christian imagery, New Georgia traditions, US wartime symbols and more, on a very large church under construction at Kolobaghea, the birthplace of the Holy Mama. Photo: Edvard Hviding, 2010.*

the movement. People in more and more Methodist villages experienced what was seen as 'ecstatic possession' (*taturu*) by the Holy Spirit, and sought the guidance of Silas Eto to interpret their deep emotional experiences. The result was a collective attainment of the essential CFC condition of *taturu* – a state of 'love', 'affection' and 'compassion' – seen as emanating from Silas Eto and Jesus Christ, and being an essential requirement for New Life.[4] The CFC is still spoken of as consisting of 22 constituent villages, meaning the original localities in which the church became established. This number has not been increased as, unlike in its early years, the CFC does not proselytize; but population growth has produced more actual villages. The '22' now refers to those original *butubutu* from which an efficient system of religious community, pooled land holdings and regional leadership was built by the prophet and his associates.

Eto's movement emerged as a separate church in 1960, with its own constitution formally recognized by the colonial government despite protests from the Methodist Mission (Harwood 1971). From not-so-millenarian promises of a 'New Life' of peace, love, unity, social harmony, hard work and cooperative friendly coexistence for his people – founded on prophetic visions involving J.F. Goldie, Jesus, angels, and other spiritual beings as well as 'a beautiful land with many flowers and children'[5] – Silas Eto developed the village of Menakasapa in the Kusaghe area into a large model settlement he named Paradise. As the breakaway movement had grown into an independent church in its own right, Silas Eto had become The Holy Mama – *mama* being in New Georgian languages an affectionate term of address for 'father'. This new title also identified Eto as the true earthly manifestation of the spiritual power (*mana*) on which the CFC is based.

Many Solomon Islanders continued to regard the CFC with suspicion and as not anchored in mainstream Christianity, with its low frequency of formal church services, doctrinal space given to 'heathen' traditions from old New Georgian religion and, most notoriously, its reliance on the ecstatic worship of living humans as godly beings. Yet for his followers, the Holy Mama by and large fulfilled his promise of attainment of a New Life, both in terms of spirituality and the practical challenges of the everyday, including the payment by the church of people's school fees and taxes. With his ability to fuse customary land tenure with the rapidly expanding membership of the church, the Holy Mama carried out land-tenure reform before it had become a policy phrase. He forged a large-scale communal pool of contiguous land holdings in northern and western New Georgia, through which similarly large-scale projects of copra production, primary-school education and financial management could be devised independently of government and expatriate-led missions. For those rural Solomon Islanders who shifted their allegiance from the Methodist Mission to the CFC, New Life, then, implied spectacular spiritual revival as well as massive increase in experienced local control over the conditions for rural life. Notably, New Life also included a significant return to certain practices and morals considered to be of the old times before Christianity.

Grounded in strong doctrines of communalism preached by the Holy Mama, to the extent that the church has overall corporate control over the customary lands and natural resources of the resident *butubutu* in adherent villages, the CFC has since maintained sectarian isolationism and fierce independence from the outside world. Yet the movement has always promoted large economic projects at village level. Huge copra plantations dominated CFC villages from the 1960s well into the 1980s. The era of coconut plantation development was headed by the Holy Mama, using his capacity to direct the management of the land and resources of the constituent *butubutu* of the church. While the customary chiefs and associated leaders of each *butubutu* managed the everyday affairs of people and territory, the Holy Mama's authority transcended intra-*butubutu* leadership and provided him with inter-*butubutu* control of the combined customary territories of all church members. The Holy Mama was knowledgeable in the realms of genealogy and cultural history, and efficiently claimed (and received recognition of) wide personal links of bilateral kinship to a large number of constituent *butubutu*, thus bolstering the legitimacy of his power over land also in terms of ancestral entitlement. These beginnings of a corporate system, in which the Holy Mama's decision-making power encompassed many different but connected local arenas of *butubutu* leadership, outlined the circumstances for the more recent large-scale management of logging operations and forest-plantation development that will be discussed shortly.[6]

Rescuing the rural in times of government collapse

Throughout the 'tension' years when the Solomon Islands economy was at a standstill and government services to rural areas collapsed, the CFC, with a steady and solid income base from timber royalties and interest earned from substantial bank deposits, managed to fill many of the voids created by the collapse of national government and the limited capacities and resources of a fledgling state government. A brief summary of the present range of economic, infrastructural and other enterprises owned and operated by the CFC is instructive: logging on customary land (by Asian companies, mainly Golden Springs International); reforestation of logged land with teak, mahogany, *Eucalyptus* and *Gmelina* intended for export; rice cultivation for import substitution; oil-palm plantations under establishment; copra export involving a Singapore business partner; shipping services around New Georgia; retail

Figure 4   *His Grace, Reverend Ikan Rove KBE, the Spiritual Authority of the CFC, in front of Buckingham Palace before receiving his knighthood, 18 October 2005. Photo: Edvard Hviding.*

stores in the provincial capital (purchased from Chinese); an educational system with 11 primary schools and 2 secondary schools; subsidies to rural clinics and government high schools; organized support to selected provincial and national politicians; domestic and overseas investment, mainly in the form of savings accounts in Australian banks with Solomon Islands offices. On the village level, though, CFC people remain notable in the Western Solomons for their strong and productive subsistence economy.

On this combined background of modernist development agendas, fierce autonomy and sectarian isolationism, the presence and influence of the CFC in the rural areas of the Western Solomons and in the nation continues, although the movement remains a somewhat secretive institution entrenched in the remote parts of northern New Georgia and the more accessible lagoons of Vonavona and Roviana. At the time of the national census in 1999, 8,904 persons in Western Province were counted as CFC followers; just over 14% of the provincial population of 62,313. Thus the CFC is dwarfed in numerical terms by the Methodist United Church and the Seventh-day Adventist Church, the two largest denominations in the province. The movement has remained reclusive in terms of media and unobtrusive vis-à-vis other church denominations, although the latter have continued to regard it with distrust. Its major role in Western Solomons political economy is not well publicized. CFC leaders themselves make a point of being inaccessible to outside visitors, although they represent the church at larger national, provincial or local events such as church jubilees or instalments of high-ranking customary chiefs. CFC villages are also known to be less than hospitable to unannounced visitors. People there are busy and want to carry out their work undisturbed, it is said. So, until the burst of attention from national media in 2005, the CFC and its activities went unnoticed by the Solomon Islands news scene. This is in large measure a conscious strategy by CFC leaders, who scoff at modern inventions such as organizational websites, and who refuse collaboration with foreign non-governmental organizations. They are also careful to minimize connections with aid donors (although some aid of the 'no-strings-attached' type has been accepted from the Republic of China), from a fundamental notion that accepting aid creates customary obligations of reciprocity and the possibility of domination from the aid donor, thus jeopardizing the autonomy of the CFC.

The public image of the CFC in Solomon Islands was considerably improved, and national-level knowledge of the realities of the movement expanded, with the media coverage given in 2005 of the two high-level visits to the CFC headquarters at Duvaha in the Kalikolo area of northern Marovo Lagoon, first by the Governor-General, and then the already mentioned one by the Prime Minister. Further national newspaper and radio attention was given later in that year with the bestowment of a knighthood (for 'services to religion and community') by Queen Elizabeth II to the CFC's hereditary spiritual leader, the Reverend Ikan Rove, who travelled to London with his immediate family and personal secretary for the investiture.[7] Finally, the increasingly visible large-scale development by the CFC over the past decade of large tree plantations on logged customary land, not least their planting of hundreds of thousands of teak trees of potentially great future value, has caught attention in the national search for post-conflict options for rural development.

Melanesian rural development outside government influence, financed through logging by Asian companies, resulting in a knighthood to the spiritual leader of a social movement – the story in summarized form would seem unbelievable to those tuned in to a dismal view of Solomon Islands as a failed state with little economic activity except logging, where rural landowners are the passive, impoverished victims of the ruthless trickery of Asian companies. The CFC, on the other hand, remains dedicated to autonomy and economic independence, promotes and underpins the evolution of traditional chiefly hierarchies and hereditary leadership, worships its own founder as well as his living descendants, and takes care of most aspects of its adherents' life-worlds from a sound financial base of timber royalties. This indigenous church succeeds in looking after its members 'from before they are born till long after they are dead', as is commented locally. One logging operation – and the CFC has over the years managed a great number of them – routinely generates 2–3 million SI$ in royalties to the customary landowners.[8] The secret of the CFC, it is sometimes said by church leaders, is to keep all that money outside of the village economy. The CFC instead runs a complicated system of redistribution in which centrally accumulated wealth from royalties accruing to constituent landowner groups is used to provide educational, health and administrative services to church members and their villages.

'Second Creation': the time of development

When the Holy Mama died in 1983 and was enshrined in the remote village of Tamaneke in the Kalikolo area, his spiritual presence was considered by church members to remain. But the CFC entered several years of relative passivity as matters of succession were sorted out. As it turned out, the Holy Mama's two sons Ikan Rove (b. 1942) and Job Duddley Tausinga (b. 1951) came to attain complementary roles in the continuity of the CFC, connecting the movement firmly to national politics and global economy while retaining solidly local foundations. In this new era, three additional sons of the Holy Mama have fulfilled other central church leadership roles in financial planning, education and community organization. In the written documents of the church as well as in everyday perceptions and speech, the paths followed by the CFC towards the twenty-first century are seen as founded in the Holy Mama's original concept of *Vinahavoro Vinakeke* ('First Creation'), which opened *kolokolo lotu* (Marovo for the 'time of church and worship') and saw the church through its first three decades. The recent remaking of the CFC under the leadership of His Grace the Reverend Ikan Rove, KBE[9] is now referred to by himself and church members as *Vinahavoro Vinakarua* ('Second Creation'), signalling the advent of *kolokolo divelopmen* ('the time of development').

In his capacity as the Spiritual Authority, the Reverend Ikan Rove has remained true to the traditional local origins of the CFC while pursuing strong agendas of rural development. Rove's model of leadership has not simply been effected through generational transfer. Since the Holy Mama is still regarded to have a presence among the people, his successor could neither inherit his title nor take over his personal attributes and strategies. Having inherited from his father the privilege of being recognized as the living manifestation of the spiritual power on which the CFC is based, and in which its followers believe, the Reverend Rove thus has had to forge his own personal approach to this demanding office. His role as the earthly manifestation of the Holy Spirit was devised by him not as a new Holy Mama, but as The Spiritual Authority (or, in the vernacular, *nginirangira magomago*).

Rove is a dedicated performer of his role. His manner of speech ranges from the high-pitched and dramatic to the solemn and ceremonial, and he often punctuates conversations with sudden inquisitive remarks or bursts of humour. While known to supervise large-scale community work by megaphone,[10] he also carries out a lot of manual work on the land, cultivating gardens and plantations, and he elaborates his image as a man of the people by dressing simply, usually only in a lava-lava, and by expressing a constant desire for betel-nuts and tobacco. On the other hand, he remains difficult to reach for most (for outsiders also because he refuses to speak Pijin or English). The respect he commands as the supreme leader of the CFC is such that in the eastern parts of the Roviana Lagoon he is referred to as *tamasa toana*, 'living god', a designation that he himself categorically denies having invented. More simply, at village level the Reverend Rove is called Papa Hope, especially by those for whom the English designation 'Spiritual Authority' is difficult to pronounce or who consider the vernacular equivalent *nginirangira magomago* too awe inspiring.

Unlike in the breakaway years and pioneer decades of building a church, the leadership mission for the CFC from the 1990s has been to consolidate and develop the church and its financial base, in order to promote explicit ideas about 'development' (or, *divelopmen*) and to maintain and expand political strength. This strength is viewed by the Reverend Rove and his associate leaders (mainly his brothers) as expressed most significantly through visible self-sufficiency and autonomy from government, aid donors, NGOs and the like. The CFC's autonomy in this regard also entails the ability to identify and cultivate collaborative outside partners of their own choice: hence the long-standing and complex cooperation with the Indonesian logging company PT Sumber Mas, which in the Solomon Islands operates somewhat reclusively as Golden Springs International (reflecting the Indonesian name). The Golden Springs company has operated in the CFC-controlled areas of New Georgia, as well as in some adjacent areas controlled by Seventh-day Adventist groups, since 1989 (Hviding and Bayliss-Smith 2000:225–38). The arrival of an 'Asian tiger' came as somewhat of a surprise to outside observers at the time (e.g. Frazer 1997:56), given that the CFC people of North New Georgia had, only a few years previously, succeeded in creating so much trouble for the colonial-era logging company of Levers Pacific Timbers that it quit operations in Solomon Islands altogether (Hviding 1996:316–20). To outsiders, then, in the 1989 events it appeared as if a conservation-oriented tribal group suddenly became supporters of large-scale logging. What was not understood was that this apparently mysterious change of attitude and land use among CFC people was founded in ideas about autonomy and political influence over logging operations, and about control over the rural income that logging generates. The main mover of this spectacular leap was the Holy Mama's son, J.D. Tausinga, then the Premier of the Western Province and a long-standing and vociferous opponent to Levers' logging operations (see Tausinga 1992).

Thus as the Reverend Ikan Rove has built his career as Spiritual Authority into a godlike position of regional high chief, combining, as it were, the pre-colonial roles of influential chief and high priest, his younger brother, the Hon. J.D. Tausinga, Member of Parliament for North New Georgia, has developed the CFC's global connections. The university-educated Tausinga is a distinguished national and provincial parliamentarian with a remarkable career as a customary leader, student of law and political science, Provincial Premier (in the 1980s), Member of Parliament (uninterruptedly since 1984), Cabinet Minister (for Natural Resources, Foreign Affairs, Environment, Education and Forestry, as well as periods as Deputy and acting Prime Minister, and leader of opposition) and international businessman. Consistently receiving an overwhelming majority of votes in his CFC-dominated constituency at parliamentary elections (if he is opposed at all, which has rarely happened), Tausinga is considered to be a secure lifetime MP if he so wishes. With his remarkable unbroken parliamentary record and his positions in cabinet and elsewhere, Tausinga is one of the most influential persons in Solomon Islands politics over the years. Appearing as a total contrast to his supremely powerful brother's self-presentation as an ordinary rural man, Tausinga is at ease on urban and international scenes. Fluent in English and the jargons of

Figure 5 *Honourable MP Job D. Tausinga, longest-serving parliamentarian in Solomon Islands. At a ceremony in Government House, November 2010. Photo courtesy of Tom Mountjoy.*

government and politics, he communicates in elaborate and calm speech, and is noted for his ability to infuse complicated analysis with metaphor and humour. He is widely travelled and well-connected in government and business circles, at home and abroad. Tausinga's ideas on economic policy and political organization have a broad range of inspirations, since he is an active reader with a substantial library that includes Greek philosophy, Oriental religions and Marxist economics.

From Tausinga comes a particularly telling summary of development strategy in the form of a discussion paper entitled 'Economic Concept' (Tausinga 2002) presented to a gathering of Western Solomons political and administrative leaders at a time when the Solomon Islands government was bankrupt, defunct and without any rural reach. In 2003, Tausinga shared and discussed this paper with me, pointing out its twofold nature as a general statement for the Western Solomons, but built on the specific CFC model. Indeed Tausinga's Economic Concept paper can be seen as a clear and succinct expression of present-day CFC policy on resource development. Intended as a substantial intellectual input into the development policy of a new state of Western Solomons, it echoes its author's diverse personal experiences:

> The guiding principal of economic concept and plan is encapsulated on the unwritten wisdom of the spirit of the modern world and thus:
> – Resources are not resources until you develop them,
> – Economic developments are not economic development until you have an economic vision
> – Economic vision is not an economic vision until it is translated into an economic concept. (p. 2)

> The exercise we take in identifying the economic opportunities shall encourage both local and foreign investors to participate in commercial activities. (p. 5)

> The policies and legislations that shall attract and regulate the economic and commercial activities must be 'multi-dimensional' in that these policies and legislations must target both indigenous as well as foreign investors (and corporate entities) to engage in these commercial activities (p. 5)

The idea that resources are not resources until you develop them is argued with reference to 'the spirit of the modern world' and may seem drawn from Marxist thought (perhaps not unlikely given Tausinga's education in the 1970s at the University of Papua New Guinea). However, the notion accurately reflects deep-seated New Georgian attitudes that have often come to the forefront as villagers and their leaders have engaged in discussion with conservation organizations over the years (Hviding 1996:56–7, 2003a).

Tausinga's accentuation of the complementary roles of local and foreign investment, and of the need to form corporate entities, defines a significant space between the globalized challenges of today and the old days in which the New Georgia islands were dominated by polities whose predatory approach to inter-island relationships (through warfare, headhunting, tribute, trade and exchange) was geared towards exploiting what was to be found overseas. The incorporation of thoughts, objects, persons and institutions from outside is a foundational strategy of New Georgian ways of relating to wider worlds, as is so common throughout the island Pacific (Hviding 2003c; cf. Hau'ofa 1993). In this sense it is possible to read the development strategy of the CFC, as expressed in Tausinga's discussion paper and as seen on the ground in North New Georgia and Roviana, as a present-day instantiation of long-running socio-political formations characteristic of New Georgia and the Western Solomons more widely.

What is unique today, though, is the convergence between these local ontological frameworks and Asian capitalism. This convergence forms an essential channel for fulfilment of CFC ambition. Such a close fit was never possible in the colonial period, but has similarities in the ways in which chiefs of pre-colonial and early colonial times developed their influence in order to control access to the foreign of the day. The long-term logging operations on CFC lands in northern and western New Georgia by Golden Springs International have also been influential in the decision made by church leadership to start reforestation of logged-out areas in the form of large tree plantations. In fact, both the Spiritual Authority and the Hon. Tausinga visited teak plantations in Malaysia in the late 1990s, and plans were accordingly made to start such developments at home, with (to quote CFC policy documents) 'sustainable enrichment of the land' as the aim.[11] Asian connections have also unfolded in other, more modest ways through the purchase by the CFC of some old Chinese trade stores in the Western Province capital of Gizo. The socio-political significance of the latter development should not be underestimated, as the control over the trade-store sector and other business by the Chinese remains a feature, however contested, of everyday life in the towns of Solomon Islands.[12]

Fellowship, unity and hierarchy: cultural heritage at work

So the CFC and its leaders continue to devise large-scale projects that on the one hand create and maintain rural infrastructure independently of the government, and that on the other hand involve financial scenarios that underwrite the long-term autonomy of the CFC and its activities. Some of the projects under way, especially the large teak plantations, promise to result in very substantial future incomes, unlike anything seen in the form of timber royalties from logging. Meanwhile, the CFC quietly operates its own schools, transport facilities, trade-store networks, rural redistribution and credit systems and other enterprises.

Big as these developments may seem, they are – and this is readily expressed by CFC leaders – seen as ground-level tools for maintaining control over political and economic conditions for simple village life under global pressure (cf. Friedman 1997), subsumed under the all-embracing expression of 'New Life'. I see the concept of New Life as only vaguely millenarian, because CFC doctrines as founded by the Holy Mama and brought into the present by the Spiritual Authority do not focus on life after death, nor on fulfilment of prophetic ambitions in a distant future. What the doctrines do promote is the ideal condition of 'Fellowship'; a respectful, mutually helpful and socially satisfactory state of relationship among living persons within and outside of the church, founded in the Holy Mama's conceptual trinity of 'peace, love, unity' (in the doctrinal Roviana language, *binule, tinataru, kineke*). In 1986, early in my first fieldwork, I visited the secluded village of Tamaneke where traditions of and connections to CFC origins remain particularly strong. With reference to a carved inscription on a house gable, I was instructed in a foundational saying from the early days of the Holy Mama's work:

Keke ghemi, keke mi
One ours, one to us
(i.e. 'all that which is ours is one [not divided]')

An ancient proverb in an inland dialect of the Hoava language, the saying was further specified:

Keke ghemi ninani
One ours [1st PL EXCL] [of] food
(i.e. '[the] food is one [not divided] for all of us [in this companionship')
Keke mi kasiatona
One to us [are] things [which are owned – referring, for example, to a coconut plantation]
(i.e. 'all things owned are one [not divided] for us all')

Among influential groups in the CFC such quaint proverbs in an almost forgotten language amount to rules of life, and as such were invoked and explained by the Holy Mama when during the foundational years he travelled as Silas Eto around New Georgia to assist villagers who had revelatory experiences and sought his guidance. The general implication of the 'rules' presented above is that anyone who lives in a community has an obligation to share, the unwanted alternative being the separation and individualization of every right, property and person, and the severance of customary relationships.

Successful Fellowship, then, is what gives CFC members spiritual blessing in their everyday lives. A concept grounded not in English etymology but in Melanesian social cosmology concerning the substance of social relationships, Fellowship becomes the most important, yet for outsiders by far the most elusive, element in the workings of the Christian Fellowship Church. The lack of emphasis in CFC doctrine and practices on life after death, and the assumption that spiritual fulfilment is reached in life through proper interaction with fellow humans, have interesting parallels in the beliefs of the Moro Movement on Guadalcanal (Hviding and Kabutaulaka n.d.). These observations serve to modify assumptions about the millenarian nature of rural social movements in Melanesia, in favour of a view of them as organized social forces capable of pursuing the attainment of both spiritual and material goals in the immediate present.

The Holy Mama devised an elaborate set of 'laws' referred to as *tinarae*, an important New Georgian concept that approximates the realm of state-sanctioned legislation in that it implies punishment meted out to offenders. Important everyday examples of *tinarae* are anchored in the organizational system of *butubutu* and are similar throughout New Georgia – in and beyond the CFC – in the pragmatic ways in which they regulate, for example, fishing on reefs not controlled by one's own *butubutu* and the individual access to communally held land plots for establishing gardens. The specific *tinarae* of the Holy Mama, however – some written, some unwritten and all maintained by his successor the Reverend Rove – regulate everyday life in more detailed ways. Some are grounded in old New Georgian social etiquette concerning gender, age and hierarchy. The 'laws' stipulate detailed rules for interaction between men, women, boys and girls, and between generations, for marriage and family life, for obligatory participation in communal work under church auspices several days a week, for respectful behaviour towards church authorities, and for customary respect towards chiefs and leaders on the *butubutu* level. Significantly in post-'tension' times, these 'laws' also stipulate that youth who leave school must be usefully employed in service for elders and church (labour-intensive forest plantation development comes in handy here).

The laws of the Holy Mama are generally seen as founded on New Georgian customs and traditions (or *kastom*);[13] indeed, CFC villages are noteworthy in the Western Solomons for their traditionalist orientation on every level, from house construction to food sharing and sexual morality. In

New Georgia the Christian Fellowship Church is both an influential presence and a significant 'other'. Villagers of the Methodist and Seventh-day Adventist churches view life in CFC villages as much more strictly regulated than in their own, and comment on what they see as traditionalist things, such as the prevalence among CFC people of 'leaf houses' built of bush materials and the scarcity among them of children born to unmarried mothers. The Methodist Mission arrived in the Western Solomons in 1902, and the Seventh-day Adventist Mission in 1914. It seems not a little ironic, given this long history of Protestant missions, that villagers of these major denominations will attribute the strict moral codes and unique social cohesion in the CFC to the latter's stronger, and from a certain 'mission perspective' objectionable, orientation to *kastom*. On a more practical side, there is envy expressed in the other denominations at the low intensity of formal worship in the CFC (with only one weekly service, on Sundays), and at the fact that many CFC households have school fees and state taxes covered by church funds.

Among followers of the CFC it is assumed that breach of any of the Holy Mama's laws will provoke punishment from church authorities, such as excommunication or temporary banishment, as well as spiritual sanctions including some grounded in pre-Christian sorcery beliefs. If one criterion of state formation is that of enforcing law, then the CFC with its elaborate disciplinary system, under continuous enforcement by church leadership – to which is added a long record of developing, financing and maintaining rural services of education, health, credit and transport infrastructure – is well on the way to being considered an alternative state-like structure.

I have known, and lived in the villages of, the leaders of the CFC off and on since just after the death of Holy Mama, and am aware that they were somewhat uncomfortable about their inherited powers and privileges. Knowledge of those early days, however, could not prepare me for the explosive later growth, nor allow me to predict today's situation. The most immediately visible fact of the escalation of leadership and cultivation of principles of traditional hierarchy is the way in which the leadership of the CFC is now held in awe by thousands of followers in ways at least equivalent to the respect accorded the Holy Mama, and the way in which the Reverend Rove, in particular, is difficult to gain access to – both because of his itinerant lifestyle, and from the level of etiquette surrounding his person. The offspring of the Holy Mama are respectfully referred to within the CFC as belonging to the *tatamana hope* ('sacred family') – with the Reverend Rove and his own nuclear family seen as particularly sacred, and surrounded by much protocol. For most people in the church (and for outsiders in particular) they are not easily accessible on short notice, and ordinary CFC followers have to keep a respectful distance unless an 'audience' is arranged. The Reverend Rove is, on the one hand, busy on an everyday basis with travelling between villages to carry out inspections and give services, and working in coconut and timber plantations; and on the other, is mindful of his need for time spent undisturbed in order to meditate and meet with a select few associate leaders.

In August 2003, just as RAMSI had entered the country, I commented to my friend Ikan Rove, now the awe-inspiring Spiritual Authority, that the CFC of the twenty-first century stands out through its efficient integration of *butubutu*, land, resources, economy, politics and religion, organizing so many different groups in a large number of places across New Georgia – yet remarkably, under the supreme leadership of one man only. To this he responded: 'It is not good if there are many big men or chiefs. They are not of one mind, their work will not be of one kind, and so all types of work are not going to lead to good results. So it is!' He added that as far as he is concerned, the stature of his present leadership is no more than a repetition of sorts of the status of really big chiefs in the olden days, and that it is in line with the hierarchical principles and regional scope of high chieftainship in pre-colonial New Georgia. 'It was only that the colonial government, and then in turn the national government, prevented us from doing it this way,' he concluded. Then he added that when the government does not deliver, then it is the task of the CFC (which he himself refers to as *Si Efu* – 'CF', 'Church' not being required as reference) to move in and help the rural people. He also reminded me that all the great work carried out by the CFC is actually based on no more than two compulsory days of communal work per week for everyone. The huge coconut plantations still maintained in the vicinity of most CFC villages, and the rapidly expanding network of large forest plantations on logged-out land, attest to the efficiency of this communal work system.

While the political power of the present-day CFC and its corporate social nature extend across a large number of land-holding *butubutu*, and indeed connect to thoroughly modern contexts and channels, it is important not to underestimate the potential contained in the connections of the Holy Mama, and in turn his descendants, to cultural history. The Holy Mama's shrewd handling of bilateral kinship to many *butubutu* around New Georgia was important for building the church as a movement that transcends numerous domains of customary leadership; but it could never have been so successfully accomplished had it not been for certain qualities of some of his recognized ancestors from the Hoava and Vahole peoples. These groups have a reputation for a unique role in the history of the area called Kalikolo, a culturally complex (and timber-rich) zone of confluence between northern New Georgia and the Marovo Lagoon, and between the Marovo and Roviana lagoons. Today centred on the remote but locally famous village of Tamaneke, where the Holy Mama is enshrined, the group (from whose past sorcerers and shamans Silas

Eto claimed strong descent) still maintains its own distinct language. The Hoava language (Davis 2003) has deep and dramatic intonation patterns and is an object of rather fond ridicule around New Georgia among speakers of the dominant Roviana and Marovo languages. It is associated with the Kalikolo district, and is the home language of the Holy Mama and of the Spiritual Authority and his siblings. By implication, Hoava is the foundation language of the CFC. While Roviana is the everyday working language of the CFC, Hoava is used by the Spiritual Authority in high levels of prayer, which boosts the ritual importance of this small language that might under other circumstances have been seen as endangered. The ancient history of the mysterious, respected and quite widely feared Hoava speakers, with significant allusions to supreme spiritual powers of regional scope, has infused the CFC leadership with an added legitimacy of ancestrally derived *mana*. By extension, then, New Life also denotes a re-appreciation of such valuable things from the New Georgian past as have often been discarded by members of other denominations.

In June 2004 the entire membership of the CFC, government dignitaries and leaders of other churches gathered at the large CFC village of Madou in the Vonavona Lagoon for a grand celebration. The occasion was the centennial of the arrival in 1902 of the Methodist Mission and the Reverend J.F. Goldie. As the week-long celebrations opened, no less than fifteen full-size war canoes of the classic New Georgian type, complete with ornamented black hulls, richly decorated tall prows and sterns and traditionally dressed crews, were presented and organized into several days of racing competitions on the lagoon.[14] The Reverend Rove had commissioned one complete war canoe from every CFC village around New Georgia with the labour capacity to make one. There were shortcuts: these were 'mission-style' war canoes, built up from a large dugout hull to which was added prow and stern posts and one or two strakes; but the new strakes were sewn onto the dugout hull in the old fashion and decorations were as authentic as possible. On several occasions since 2004, part or all of the CFC fleet of war canoes have been paddled from their dispersed home villages to gather and appear prominently on the public scene, welcoming national and international government leaders to Gizo, celebrating the Spiritual Authority's knighthood, racing in Gizo harbour for the province's Festival of the Sea in 2006, and being filmed in 2007 by a BBC crew for the high-profile documentary *South Pacific*. The New Georgian war canoe is back on the water, but this time flying the large green and blue flag of the CFC in addition to its traditional decorations. New Life is fused with the olden times (*kolokolo tuari*).

Although the official purpose of the Madou celebrations was to mark the arrival of the Methodist mission, still regarded by the CFC as a point of origin, the week-long event also held other messages for the CFC members and to Solomon Islands at large; most generally, the attainment and resilience of New

Life. What was also celebrated at Madou in 2004, and what formed the basis for the Spiritual Authority's ascension into a Knight of the Most Excellent Order of the British Empire the following year, was the advent of the 'Second Creation' and the firm establishment of *kolokolo divelopmen*. In a striking move, the entire scope of the celebration was materialized by the new fleet of war canoes: a powerful icon of Western Solomons history and pre-colonial times. The extraordinary accomplishments of the 'new' were commemorated by the singular epitome of the 'old' – and the CFC leadership signalled success in the twin ambitions of harnessing the forces of capitalism and modernity, and of connecting to cultural heritage.

'Not as master but as servant': state connections
The essential accomplishment of the Christian Fellowship Church during the 'tension' and the years following was that of rescuing the viability of rural lifestyles by providing infrastructure, finance, leadership and spiritual guidance – in part by taking up the roles that a functioning state would have filled. In this, the CFC of today builds on more than fifty years of combining important elements of New Georgian custom with any foreign or otherwise exogenous elements seen as useful for the greater purposes of New Life and the unity of church followers. Certainly, in the context of the recent government collapse, the CFC may be said to have 'replaced' the state with regard to many of the latter's purposes and roles. It is important to note, however, that the Solomon Islands nation of post-'tension' times has been a scene of much work towards 'reunification' whereby a revitalized state has gained more space also on the rural scene. At no time during the challenges of the past decade has the CFC been entirely separated from the state it appears to have situationally replaced; most evidently since the Hon. J.D. Tausinga has remained Member of Parliament for North New Georgia since 1984 and has been a frequent cabinet minister, including in two successive governments since 2006. As the Reverend Rove expressed it eloquently to me in August 2003, just after the nation had entered its initial post-'tension' stage: 'If the government is not straight, then the CFC will enter into its work in order to put in good order the important tasks, to help the people of the villages!' In this sense the CFC's apparent replacement of the state is actually perceived by church leaders and members as an act of assistance or help (*tinoka*) – a key element in Fellowship as defined by the Holy Mama. So the hard-working people of the CFC assume that their effort 'helps' a trouble-ridden nation, but unlike the more outspoken political ambitions of some Makirans with regard to the state (M. Scott, this volume), the CFC seems largely content with ordering things in its homelands of the Western Solomons. Not that such ordering is independent of relations with government: it is seen as important by village people and leaders alike

that the CFC has a continuous parliamentary presence,[15] whether for influence or for insight, and the movement's leaders are strong supporters of the long-planned national implementation of a federal system wherein the Western Solomons will be a state rather than a province (cf. Scales 2007).

The Governor-General of Solomon Islands, Sir Nathaniel Waena, quite surprisingly visited the CFC headquarters at Duvaha on his tour of Western and Choiseul Provinces in February 2005. The news and associated feature stories from this visit probably amounted to the first major press coverage of the media-shy Christian Fellowship Church since the Holy Mama appeared on the cover of the special Solomon Islands independence issue of the periodical *Pacific Islands Monthly* in 1978 (Chesher 1978). A reporter who was on the Governor-General's tour wrote with enthusiasm about the visions and accomplishments of the Reverend Rove, perhaps reflecting his own surprise at encountering such a success story way down in the remote parts of the 'West':

> ... despite his little formal education background, [Rove] is also a very influential man, not because he can perform miracles but because of his leadership style in treating everybody as equals. He inspired the church's followers by his ability to work, that is physical work in plantations, gardens and many other church's projects as well as conducting church's religious programmes.... Some of the development projects under his care are reforestation, teak and mahogany plantations, copra, cocoa and oil palm plantations. All benefits from these projects are divided communally and not only for the leader himself. These are some of the many things that inspired many followers, and even many professional people including government leaders are inspired by Rev Rove's leadership.
>
> (Kadamana 2005b)

The Governor-General was reported to have publicly praised 'Western rural people' for their prayers:

> He told the people that Solomon Islands would remain a united nation with the influence of the church, pointing out that the churches have played a significant role in reuniting the nation. 'I am sure that with the guidance and contribution from the churches, we will march forward to a better future,' he said. The Governor General also thanked the people ... for electing good and respected leaders to be part of the government's political leadership.... 'I congratulate you for your contribution towards the leadership of this nation and economic development,' he told the people in the two constituencies [of North New Georgia and Ranongga/Simbo].
>
> (Kadamana 2005a)

The Governor-General visited Duvaha and the Reverend Rove in the company of the Hon. Tausinga, and so the praise given by the nation's highest public figure conveniently covered both the rural, non-governmental and the urban, governmental dimensions of the CFC. The local interpretation of this recognition by the Governor-General was appreciative, but quite a few CFC followers also found it logical that the 'great work' (*tinavete gete*) should finally be brought to the attention of the leaders and people of the nation.

The unexpected increase in media attention and national awareness of the work of the CFC was to further intensify during that busy year. Already in May, another visit of the highest level was paid to remote Duvaha. Now it was the Prime Minister who was on a tour of the Western Solomons, and his enthusiastic reaction to what he saw as the Spiritual Authority gave him and his delegation a guided tour was quoted at the beginning of this chapter. Sir Allan seemed to have hit the mark, capturing the unique combination of hard work and large-scale planning, and indicating the financial scope of it all. The CFC leadership, recognizing that the Prime Minister had actually made a detour just to make this 'courtesy call' to Duvaha, took the opportunity to respond to the lavish praise, setting the response in the context of the perceived accomplishment of the Kemakeza government in bringing RAMSI in, and carefully underlining the CFC's loyalty to the government. Under the heading 'CFC hails gov't', the following was reported in the *Solomon Star*:

CHRISTIAN Fellowship Church (CFC) members applaud the government for inviting the Regional Assistance Mission to Solomon Islands (RAMSI) to restore law and order in the country. Speaking during the Prime Minister Sir Allan Kemakeza's courtesy call to the centre one of the elders said CFC greatly welcomed the work of the RAMSI. He said RAMSI has brought back happiness to their community and to the country. 'I thank the government for the accountable leadership,' he said. The elder highlighted that CFC through its prayer has supported the government not as master but as servant. 'We believe very much in spirit of obedience and stands with the government,' he added. He further stated that the presence of RAMSI in the country reaffirms the grounds of confidence in the future. Sir Allan in response congratulates CFC Christians for providing an environment of peace where development can take place. 'I thank you for your spiritual partnership with my government,' he said. Sir Allan calls on to the members of the CFC to work together to ensure law and order is sustained.

(Wate 2005b)

It is tempting to suggest that in the words of the CFC elder, 'prayer' is used as a euphemism for 'great work'. In any event, it must be reassuring for a Prime Minister to be told that a rural social movement, once seen as a deviant cult, in fact supports and prays for his government, promises obedience, and assigns itself the role of servant to the government.[16] Not that the CFC in its contemporary essence is in any way detached from the Solomon Islands government. In August 2010 the Hon. J.D. Tausinga was the first person to be re-elected to parliament for a seventh period. In terms of both the CFC and the nation, Tausinga's scope of 'great work' includes the ambition to be Prime Minister. He nearly made it in April 2006, and before the next election in 2010 he stated in characteristic terms that 'if no one has a strong mind on leading the nation then ... he [was] willing to take on the responsibility' (Solomon Islands Broadcasting Corporation, 18 June 2010).

In order to understand the current world situation with weakened state forms and the breakthrough of globalization processes in the most 'out-of-the-way' places, to use Anna Tsing's expression from her work on the hinterlands of Borneo (Tsing 1993), it is becoming crucial to reassess the existing alternative social regimes that initiate these developments in localized settings. This means taking seriously the continuities of character and viable alternative social formations built into local institutions, and to investigate critically the distinct character of the transformations of society and political economy that arise out of the global challenges. The story of the CFC's accelerating and expanding influence in the Western Solomons throughout years of government disruption, and the strong connections of these accomplishments to both local cultural heritage and global capitalism – and to many dimensions in-between, including the situational replacement of and assistance to the Solomon Islands state – presents an extraordinary, viable alternative. The internal 'unity'[17] (in the doctrinal Roviana language *kineke* or the locational *koa keke*) that secures New Life and underpins the success of the CFC by enabling its leaders to challenge global forces, generate income from them, and intervene (alternatively assist) in nation- and state-building while developing the rural, is founded in local cultural heritage. But this heritage, the recent spectacular revival of war canoes excepted, first and foremost consists of deep, often quiet continuities in New Georgian social scenarios, organizational structures and generalized spiritual beliefs, not 'traditional' objects or specific codified rituals.

The future of *divelopmen*

Finally, a reflection on the present 'time of development' (*kolokolo divelopmen*), which lends itself to a comparison with the Melanesian (Papua New Guinean) concept of 'develop-man' as discussed by Sahlins (2005 [1992]; see also

Robbins and Wardlow 2005). Sahlins makes use of a somewhat contrived but salient interpretation of Tok Pisin *'defelopman'* to suggest a more general type of non-Western model for handling the world capitalist system in ways that promote rather than undermine indigenous cultural practice; a model of cultural appropriation of modernist development and capitalist forces. In a process of 'develop-man', according to Sahlins, indigenous agency is reinforced, not obliterated, by encounters and interactions with capitalism. For the local people it is a process that leads to 'the enrichment of their own ideas of what mankind is all about' (Sahlins 2005:24). The capitalist system is thus not the overpowering force often expected, and local projects may expand in scale and complexity through capitalist connections, at least for some time. Certainly, the CFC's present *kolokolo divelopmen* fits this model well. The CFC model is infused with faith in the local, and in spectacular ways visualizes its own success in forging profitable links between capitalist systems and local cultural heritage, thus fulfilling a particular version of 'Melanesian dreams of social unity' (Lindstrom, this volume).

The CFC story has, in an important sense, only just started. 'Second creation' is unfolding, and one significant future scenario involves the wealth potential developing in the thousands of teak trees now growing in communally held forest plantations across northern and western New Georgia. The question remains whether this communalist organization with its potential for co-ordinated economic effort – and indeed, when government fails, for taking over rural public service sectors such as education, health, transport (and to a significant degree, discipline and law enforcement, thereby providing a substantial alternative state-like form) – represents a model that can be adapted to meet urgent challenges elsewhere in rural Solomon Islands. Indeed, that question is increasingly asked in elite Solomon Islander circles, although timely caution should be expressed in terms of the transfer potential of the 'CFC model' outside of the movement's own historical grounding and cultural circumstances. Whatever the answer about the applicability of the CFC's 'model' may be, the political rise of this movement over the recent decade demonstrates more general patterns in the Melanesian capacity for building large-scale projects in ways that are founded in local social relationships but that may reach far beyond the local – and that in the process may well also encapsulate aspects of external capitalist forces, and challenge, converge with and re-position the state.

Acknowledgements

The background for this chapter is my long engagement with the people of the Western Solomons, in particular the Marovo Lagoon. My gratitude first and foremost is to the people of Marovo, and New Georgia more widely –

villagers not only of the CFC but also of the Seventh-day Adventist Church and the United (Methodist) Church – who have hosted me, fed me, taught me and supported my work in so many ways over so many years. For hospitality and conversation and unique insights into the CFC itself, from the highest level, I express my respectful gratitude to four sons of the Holy Mama: His Grace the Reverend Ikan Rove KBE (the Spiritual Authority), the Hon. Job D. Tausinga, Roosevelt Leti and the late Scriven Peloko. Several other people of CFC's Marovo- and Hoava-speaking Kalikolo area have played a major role in my education. In 1986, Vincent Vaguni first invited me to live at Tamaneke, and our conversation has continued ever since. Aseri Yalangono has been another long-term friend and conversation partner, always ready to give a new interpretation of complicated issues, be they financial, political or theological. To the Reverend Opportunity Kuku, Special Secretary to the Spiritual Authority, I am grateful for illuminating night-time discussions at Duvaha and in London. To Vincent, Aseri and Opportunity, their families and the good people of Tamaneke, Keru and Duvaha, I am grateful for experiencing and discussing life in the CFC, and for insights into the CFC's relationships to the wider world. In the world of academic colleagues, I owe much of my understanding of the CFC outside its heartlands of Kalikolo to Shankar Aswani, with whom I am completing a book-length study of the movement. Daichi Ishimori has also shared his knowledge from fieldwork at Paradise village. Graham Baines, John Barker, Cato Berg, Annelin Eriksen, Jonathan Friedman, Tarcisius Kabutaulaka, Bruce Kapferer, Andrew Lattas, Karen Leivestad, Debra McDougall, Knut Rio and Geoffrey White are colleagues who have illuminated for me a number of comparative aspects concerning the CFC as a religious, social and political movement. Finally, I wish to thank seminar and conference participants in Bergen, St Andrews, Paris, Verona and Honolulu, and students at the University of Bergen, University of Hawai'i, James Cook University and elsewhere, for inspiring discussions on the many occasions at which I have been allowed to present parts of this chapter.

NOTES

1. RAMSI (www.ramsi.org) is the acronym for Regional Assistance Mission to Solomon Islands. Initially invited by the Solomon Islands government and known also as Operation Helpem Fren, RAMSI remains in the Solomons and has grown into a large long-term organization involving Australia, New Zealand and thirteen additional Pacific nations, with a change in focus from armed intervention and the re-establishment of 'law and order' to everyday concerns of policing and civilian assistance to the government (see, e.g., Dinnen 2008).

2. 'Tension' is a widely used local euphemism in Solomon Islands for the years of armed conflict and the associated rural hardships and decay of government and economy. A concept of vernacular usage, 'Tension' (derived, obviously, from the labelling by outside observers of the conflict as 'ethnic tension', cf. Kabutaulaka 2001b) is used simply as a historical reference marker, and is applied in both Solomon Islands Pijin and vernacular languages.

3. I have carried out fieldwork in the Western Solomons for about three years since 1986, with visits over the years varying in length from eighteen months to one week. In this work I continue to live at, and maintain relationships on, two very different localities: the maritime-oriented Seventh-day Adventist village of Chea in central Marovo Lagoon, and the remote, more inland-oriented village of Tamaneke in northern Marovo. The latter is a key place in the history of the CFC. Living for periods with the people of Tamaneke has enabled me to interact with the leaders of the movement on an informal basis and to discuss the history and recent activities of the CFC with them, as well as to experience ordinary life in a number of other CFC villages in the Kalikolo-Kusaghe area. The present work forms part of a larger book-length study of the CFC carried out in collaboration with anthropologist Shankar Aswani, who has lived for extended periods in the villages of the Roviana and Vonavona lagoons, where the majority of the CFC's followers are located (Hviding and Aswani n.d.).

4. A clarification of central vernacular concepts is in order here. Whereas *tataru* (the meaning of which is similar to Polynesian *aloha/talofa*) is the pre-condition for New Life, this rather calm condition of good will and spiritual fulfilment was in the early years invariably a result of an initial ecstatic, trance-like possession referred to as *taturu* in New Georgia. These two widely different terms that are so phonetically similar and so closely connected in the history of the CFC have tended to be confused by outside observers, including Frances Harwood, who used *tataru* for 'possession' in her Ph.D. thesis on the CFC (1971, chapter 5).

5. The quote is from Silas Eto (1967), 'Holy Mama's Autobiography', on deposit in the Harold Scheffler Papers (MSS 0481), Mandeville Special Collections Library, University of California, San Diego.

6. Observations of this inter-*butubutu* system at work during Tension years gave rise to the comment by resource-management scholar Simon Foale (2001:55) that [i]n North New Georgia the Christian Fellowship Church (CFC) in fact doubles as a unique and remarkable system of local government.'

7. The investiture at Buckingham Palace, and other activities of the CFC entourage in London (such as a visit to the storerooms of the British Museum to examine old objects from New Georgia), was documented on film as an extraordinary rich series of cultural encounters (Hviding and Scott 2007).

8. The Solomon Islands Dollar (SI$ or SBD) has in recent years fluctuated in the range of 7–9 SBD to the US Dollar.

9. The title used by Rove after he was knighted in London in 2005. As a senior clergyman, the Reverend, through the investiture as a Knight Commander of the Most Excellent Order of the British Empire, attained the privilege of being entitled 'His Grace', the equivalent of 'Sir' for non-clerical holders of knighthood.

10. In a traveller's account, an example of community work at Duvaha is described whereby a couple of hundred people plant 2,000 trees in less than twenty minutes, supervised over a megaphone by the Reverend Rove (McDonald 2003:14–17). The efficiency of communal work by CFC people is also appreciated by the other denominations: CFC groups are not infrequently hired to clear new garden lands, tidy up overgrown coconut plantations, or even clean and mow rural airfields.

11. Although claims have been made for substantial Australian initiative and assistance in the establishment of these teak plantations (e.g. Makim 2002), in 1999 the CFC actually paid 100,000 Australian Dollars for technical assistance from the University of Queensland (UQ) in setting up teak nurseries. UQ involvement was halted by the coup in June 2000. Subsequent developments have been in local hands.

12. In this regard is important to note the riots following the election for prime minister in April 2006 which targeted Chinese businesses in Honiara. The Hon. Tausinga was a people's favourite in this election, but after some last-minute changes of allegiance among the MPs he lost to the candidate from his neighbouring Marovo constituency, the Hon. Snyder Rini. Peoples' protests against alleged Chinese involvement in the political process followed, with massive destruction of properties in Chinatown and elsewhere in Honiara. See Moore (2006) for an account.

13. *Kastom* has its own conceptual history and, within Melanesian anthropology, its own trajectory of exploratory theoretical debates which do not need to be summarized here. In the Western Solomons, the concept is sparsely used and rendered *kasitomu*. In the Marovo language, for example, the history-conscious concept of *tinavete pa tuari* ('the work of olden days') or the non-historical *hinuhinua* ('habitual ways') are among a range of vernacular substitutes for that range of meanings *kastom* connotes. Being in such large measure a vernacular-based organization, the CFC and its followers rarely invoke the term *kastom/kasitomu* unless the spoken context is Pijin.

14. The considerably more numerous Methodists of the Western Solomons had duly marked the centennial in 2002 (as it were, with celebrations during that time of hardship supported in cash and in kind by the Reverend Rove of the CFC). Given the CFC's origins as a breakaway movement, and the wish to infuse the celebrations with their own quality, it was seen as proper for the CFC to mark the centennial two years later. In any case, the 2004 event clearly communicated how the CFC leaders regard their movement to be in essence of Methodist origins. The Madou celebrations in June 2004 were documented on a film (Aswani and

Haas 2005) that highlights both the canoe races and the key role given in church proceedings to the Reverend J.F. Goldie, amounting to presenting him as an ancestor.

15. At the national election on 4 August 1010, Silas Kerry Vaqara Tausinga (the son of the Hon. Job D. Tausinga) won the important seat for West New Georgia, adjacent to his father's North New Georgia constituency. At 28, he became the youngest ever member of parliament in Solomon Islands. With this political move, the CFC now has the members of parliament for its entire core area.

16. It could, of course, be argued that having treated the visiting Prime Minister and other dignitaries to great food and a well-organized demonstration of spectacular material and organizational accomplishments, the hosts (i.e. the CFC) might have been perceived in Melanesian terms as the true masters of the situation at hand, to whom the guests must be seen as fully subservient. From such a perspective, the speech by the CFC elder would also have had a valuable element of situational clarification for guests who might feel somewhat overpowered, and instant reciprocity was reached by way of mutual praise.

17. The 'unity' promoted by the CFC leaders, their doctrines and their followers represents a more general Melanesian desire and scene for social innovation examined by several other contributors to this volume, as exemplified by the discussion by Lindstrom (this volume) of 'new and innovative social unities'. While chapters by M. Scott and Lindstrom examine different drives towards island-based unity, the CFC has not been much concerned with 'island' as spatial context for its unity. A simple reason for this is the spatially fragmented nature of the New Georgia group of islands. While the CFC has a strong concentration on the island of New Georgia itself, it also has significant presence on a number of other islands in the group. CFC unity, then, amounts to an inter-island network, and although the movement is firmly associated with the Western Solomons (which has its own political history of unity ambitions in relation to the nation, cf. Scales 2007), it must co-exist with the majorities of Methodists and Seventh-day Adventists in that part of Solomon Islands.

BIBLIOGRAPHY

ASPI (Australian Strategic Policy Institute) 2003. *Our Failing Neighbour: Australia and the Future of Solomon Islands.* An ASPI Policy Report. Barton, ACT: Australian Strategic Policy Institute.

Aswani, S. and J. Haas 2005. *The Christian Fellowship Church One Hundredth Year Commemorative Celebration of the Arrival of Methodism to the Western Solomon Islands, June 2004.* Documentary film. In Association with The Anthropology Department, University of California, Santa Barbara, and EthnoVideo Productions.

AusAid 2006. *Solomon Islands: Transitional Country Strategy, 2006 to Mid-2007*. Canberra, ACT: Australian Agency for International Development.

Bayliss-Smith, T., E. Hviding and T.C. Whitmore 2003. 'Rainforest composition and histories of human disturbance in Solomon Islands'. *Ambio* 32:346–52.

Bennett, J.A. 2000. *Pacific Forest: A History of Resource Control and Contest in Solomon Islands, c. 1800–1997*. Cambridge and Leiden: White Horse Press/ Brill Academic Publishers.

Chesher, R.H. 1978. 'Holy Mama, Solomons prophet built a paradise for his people'. *Pacific Islands Monthly* July 1978:18–20.

Dauvergne, P. 1999. 'Corporate power in the forests of the Solomon Islands'. *Pacific Affairs* 71:524–46.

Davenport, W. and G. Coker 1967. 'The Moro Movement of Guadalcanal, British Solomon Islands Protectorate'. *Journal of the Polynesian Society* 76:123–75.

Davis, K. 2003. *A Grammar of the Hoava Language, Western Solomons*. Pacific Linguistics 535. Canberra: Pacific Linguistics, Research School of Pacific and Asian Studies, Australian National University.

Dinnen, S. 2002. 'Winners and losers: politics and disorder in the Solomon Islands 2000–2002'. *Journal of Pacific History* 37(3):285–98.

Dinnen, S. 2008. 'Dilemmas of intervention and the building of state and nation'. In *Politics and State Building in Solomon Islands* (eds) S. Dinnen and S. Firth, 1–38. Canberra: Asia Pacific Press.

Dinnen, S. and S. Firth (eds) 2008. *Politics and State Building in Solomon Islands*. Canberra, ACT: Asia Pacific Press.

Foale, S. 2001. '"Where's our development?" Landowner aspiration and environmentalist agendas in Western Solomon Islands'. *The Asia Pacific Journal of Anthropology* 2(2):144–67.

Fraenkel, J. 2004. *The Manipulation of Custom: From Uprising to Intervention in the Solomon Islands*. Canberra: Australian National University, Pandanus Books.

Frazer, I. 1997. 'The struggle for control of Solomon Islands forests'. *The Contemporary Pacific* 9:44–52.

Friedman, J. 1997. 'Simplifying complexity: assimilating the global in a small paradise'. In *Siting Culture: The Shifting Anthropological Object* (eds) K.F. Olwig and K. Hastrup, 268–291. London: Routledge.

Gewertz, D. and F. Errington 1997. 'Why we return to Papua New Guinea'. *Anthropological Quarterly* 70(3):127–36.

Harwood, F.H. 1971. The Christian Fellowship Church: A revitalization movement in Melanesia. Unpublished Ph.D. thesis, University of Chicago.

Harwood, F.H. 1978. 'Intercultural communication in the Western Solomons: the Methodist Mission and the emergence of the Christian Fellowship Church'. In *Mission, Church, and Sect in Oceania* (eds) J.A Boutilier, D.T. Hughes and S.W. Tiffany, 231–50. ASAO Monograph 6. Lanham: University Press of America.

Hau'ofa, E. 1993. 'Our sea of islands'. In *A New Oceania: Rediscovering Our Sea of Islands* (eds) E. Waddell, V. Naidu and E. Hau'ofa, 2–16. Suva: University of the South Pacific.

Hviding, E. 1996. *Guardians of Marovo Lagoon: Practice, Place, and Politics in Maritime Melanesia.* Pacific Islands Monograph Series, 14. Honolulu: University of Hawai'i Press.

Hviding, E. 2003a. 'Contested rainforests, NGOs and projects of desire in Solomon Islands'. *International Social Science Journal* 55(4):178:439–53.

Hviding, E. 2003b. 'Disentangling the *butubutu* of New Georgia: cognatic kinship in thought and action'. In *Oceanic Socialities and Cultural Forms: Ethnographies of Experience* (eds) I. Hoëm and S. Roalkvam, 71–113. Oxford: Berghahn Books.

Hviding, E. 2003c. 'Between knowledges: Pacific Studies and academic disciplines'. *The Contemporary Pacific* 15:43–73.

Hviding, E. 2005. 'Christian Fellowship Church (Solomon Islands)'. In *Encyclopedia of Religion and Nature* (ed.) Bron Taylor, 306–7. London: Continuum Books.

Hviding, E. (in press). 'Compressed globalization and expanding desires in Marovo Lagoon, Solomon Islands'. In *Returns to the Field: Long-term Ethnographic Research and Contemporary Anthropology* (eds) S. Howell and A. Talle Bloomington: Indiana University Press.

Hviding, E. and S. Aswani n.d. *Rescuing the Rural: The Christian Fellowship Church as a Development Agent in Solomon Islands.* Book under final submission to the East-West Center / Stanford University Press Series "Contemporary Issues in Asia and the Pacific".

Hviding, E. and R. Scott 2007. *New Life in the Old World.* Documentary film. Bergen: University of Bergen and SOT Film.

Hviding, E. and T. Bayliss-Smith 2000. *Islands of Rainforest: Agroforestry, Logging and Ecotourism in Solomon Islands.* Aldershot, UK: Ashgate.

Hviding, E. and T.T. Kabutaulaka n.d. 'Global forces and local movements in Solomon Islands: the Christian Fellowship Church and the Moro Movement compared'. Paper in preparation.

Kabutaulaka, T.T. 2001a. Paths in the jungle: landowners and the struggle for control of Solomon Islands' logging industry. Ph.D. thesis, Australian National University.

Kabutaulaka, T.T. 2001b. 'Beyond ethnicity: the political economy of the Guadalcanal crisis in Solomon Islands'. Working Paper 01/1, State, Society and Government in Melanesia Project, Australian National University.

Kabutaulaka, T.T. 2005. 'Australian foreign policy and the RAMSI intervention in Solomon Islands'. *Contemporary Pacific* 17(2):283–308.

Kadamana, C. 2005a. 'GG praises Western rural people for their prayers'. *Solomon Star*, 24 February.

Kadamana, C. 2005b. 'Lead to serve his people'. *Solomon Star*, 4 March.

Knauft, B.M. 1999. *From Primitive to Postcolonial in Anthropology and Melanesia.* Ann Arbor: University of Michigan Press.

Laracy, H. (ed.) 1983. *Pacific Protest: The Maasina Rule Movement, Solomon Islands 1944–1952.* Suva: University of the South Pacific.

McDonald, R. 2003. *Money Makes You Crazy: Custom and Development in Solomon Islands.* Dunedin: University of Otago Press.

McDougall, D. 2008. 'Religious institutions as alternative structures in post-conflict Solomon Islands? Cases from Western Province'. Discussion Paper 2008/5, State, Society and Governance in Melanesia. Canberra, ACT: Australian National University.

Makim, A. 2002. 'Globalisation, community development, and Melanesia: The North New Georgia Sustainable Forestry and Rural Development Project'. Discussion Paper 2002/1, State, Society and Governance in Melanesia. Canberra, ACT: Australian National University.

Moore, C. 2004. *Happy Isles in Crisis: The Historical Causes for a Failing State in Solomon Islands, 1998–2004.* Canberra, ACT: Asia Pacific Press.

Moore, C. 2005. 'The RAMSI intervention in the Solomon Islands crisis'. *Journal of Pacific Studies* 28:56–77.

Moore, C. 2006. 'No more walkabout long Chinatown: Asian involvement in the Solomon Islands Political Process'. Workshop paper presented to State, Society and Governance in Melanesia Project, Australian National University.

Robbins, J. and H. Wardlow (eds) 2005, *The Making of Global and Local Modernities in Melanesia: Humiliation, Transformation and the Nature of Cultural Change.* Aldershot: Ashgate.

Sahlins, M.D. 2005. 'The economics of Develop-Man in the Pacific'. In *The Making of Global and Local Modernities in Melanesia: Humiliation, Transformtion and the Nature of Cultural Change* (eds) J. Robbins and H. Wardlow, 23–42. Aldershot: Ashgate. Originally published in *RES*, Vol. 21 (1992):13–25.

Scales, I. 2007. 'The coup nobody noticed: the Solomon Islands Western State Movement in 2000'. *Journal of Pacific History* 42:187–209.

Tausinga, J.D. 1992. 'Our land, our choice: development of North New Georgia'. In *Independence, Dependence, Interdependence: The First 10 Years of Solomon Islands Independence* (eds) R. Crocombe and E. Tuza, 55–66. Honiara: University of the South Pacific / Solomon Islands College of Higher Education.

Tausinga, J.D. 2002. 'Economic concept: a discussion paper at leaders' meeting, 2–4 May 2002'. Unpublished paper.

Tsing, A.L. 1993. *In the Realm of the Diamond Queen: Marginality in an Out-of-the-way Place*. Princeton: Princeton University Press.

Tuza, E. 1977. 'Silas Eto of New Georgia'. In *Prophets of Melanesia* (ed.) G.W. Trompf, 65–87. Port Moresby/Suva: Institute of Papua New Guinea Studies/Institute of Pacific Studies, University of the South Pacific.

Western Province 1985. *Strategy for Development. The Resource Development Approach and Policies of the Western Province of Solomon Islands*. Western Solomons Resource Development Paper No. 1. Gizo: Western Provincial Government.

Wate, A. 2005a. 'PM visits CFC projects'. *Solomon Star*, 10 May.

Wate, A. 2005b. 'CFC hails gov't'. *Solomon Star*, 10 May.

CHAPTER 3

Voyaging, cultural heritage and rites of passage

The Hawaiian transformation of Pacific and global space

*

ROLF SCOTT

Introduction

The revitalization of Hawaiian navigation and ocean voyaging has instigated a new era of Polynesian navigation and voyaging across the Pacific region (Finney 1994, 2004, 2007). The practice is now also present in Aoteroa New Zealand, Cook Islands, Tahiti, Tonga and Samoa as well as in the Marshall Islands in Micronesia. This large-scale activity may be described as a social movement based on a certain notion of cultural heritage, one which has been used strategically to reposition and reconstitute Hawaiians within the vastness of global space and time.

Voyaging has changed indigenous Hawaiians' relationship to the non-indigenous population in Hawai'i, including the Hawaiian state. Voyaging has altered the status of Hawaiians with regard to other Polynesians across the Pacific, and the change has also reached a global audience. These transformations are signified most clearly in the prominent role voyaging has in Hawai'i's tourist industry; in the alteration of the history of navigation and archaeology of the Pacific; in the introduction of voyaging into various school curriculums in Hawai'i and elsewhere; in literature and films in general; and in its presence on numerous web sites. As such, voyaging has enabled Hawaiians to take control over their present in order to shape and reshape their past, as well as the future, and so indeed to alter the present, past and future of all Polynesians. Voyaging has thereby been immensely influential in transforming Hawaiians from living as a subdued and dominated indigenous group at the end of the 1960s, towards becoming agents of their own destiny who also set agendas for the way non-Polynesian Hawaiians define themselves.

The transformative substance of these seemingly obvious and radical alterations are, I will argue: the existential, highly ritualized and rite-of-passage qualities of voyaging and navigation and their influence on the creation of realities; the structure-free or liminal and ambiguous quality of ocean space; the way in which voyaging and navigation create references in and transformations of global space; and the equally ritualized ways in which these accomplishments are introduced and incorporated into social life ashore.

Ben Finney, the re-introduction of scientifically based Polynesian voyaging and the Polynesian Voyaging Society

The revitalization of non-Western navigational practices in Hawai'i and subsequently in the wider Pacific region can be understood through three main interwoven story-lines and histories. One began in 1958, when Ben Finney, an American anthropologist studying for his master's degree in Hawai'i, began dreaming about building a canoe and sailing it to Tahiti. In the mid 1960s he built *Nalehia*, a replica of a Hawaiian double-hulled canoe, to test its seaworthiness. One reason for his engagement – other than his culturally inspired scientific interest in ocean exploration and adventure – rested on his wish to disprove the then more-or-less popular acceptance of early Pacific settlement as accidental, not deliberate on a consistent basis (Finney 1979:10–17). In short, the popular argument of the time was that it could not have been possible to navigate such vast ocean distances without the aid of Western navigational instruments (Sharp 1957, 1960, 1963). Certainly, this scope of oceanic voyaging could not have been done with the large but 'flimsily' built and lashed double-hulled canoes portrayed, for example, in some of the graphics from James Cook's exploration of Hawai'i. These were, after all, vessels whose propulsion was ensured by simple crab-claw sails woven of *lauhala* (pandanus), and they even lacked the keels and genoas that would enable them to sail close to, and thereby against, a mostly prevailing trade wind.

Ben Finney's scientifically inclined investigation into the practices of voyaging led him to engage with the white American Tommy Holmes, who was a canoe paddler, a 'water man' as they say in Hawai'i, and Herb Kane, a part-Hawaiian commercial artist raised in the US Midwest who was seeking out his Hawaiian roots. Kane would later become renowned as an artist for his many historical drawings and paintings of a reconstructed Hawaiian past. In 1973 Finney, Holmes and Kane founded the Polynesian Voyaging Society (PVS), of which Finney became the first president. By 1975 they had built and launched the first modern voyaging canoe, which was 62-feet long and named the *Hokule'a* by Kane, after Hawai'i's guiding star, Arcturus.

Although the *Hokulea* is commonly called a replica, this is not quite right. There are no known images of any Hawaiian voyaging canoe (Finney 1979:18–26), and the art of navigation died out in Hawai'i centuries before the first contact with Captain Cook. Rather, the *Hokulea* may be described as an imitation of an idea of what a Hawaiian voyaging canoe might have looked like. Further, its hulls were built of plywood, fibreglass and resin; the sails were of canvas and the lashings of synthetic cordage. The reason for using such modern materials rests on the fact that the PVS lacked the funds and skills to utilize more traditional ones.

In 1974 Finney asked the Micronesian Mau Piailug (1932–2010) to navigate the canoe in a 'traditional' Micronesian way (see Gladwin 1970), without the use of Western maps and navigational instruments. Piailug was an expert ocean navigator from the outer island of Satawal, who had begun learning navigation from his grandfather when sailing out into the ocean away from flat, and thus quickly disappearing, Micronesian atolls. By the age of 11–12, he had received further training from a master navigator of a neighbouring island. Piailug was engaged by the PVS because there were no known Polynesians who knew the art of non-Western navigation, which was also rapidly disappearing in Micronesia.

In 1976 the *Hokulea*, navigated by Mau, captained by the Hawaiian Kawika Kapahuleua and led by Ben Finney, sailed from Hawai'i to Tahiti on a journey that took 34 days, without the use of Western maps and navigational instruments. The magnitude of this accomplishment is indicated by the sheer distance, approximately 4,400 kilometres. This is only about 800 kilometres less than the voyage of Columbus when he departed the Canary Islands for the West Indies. The cultural resonance of the event was signified by the greeting of the canoe by 15,000 people – 16 per cent of the Tahitian population (Miles 1984:161) – who waited for the landing. However, during the endeavour of building, launching and sailing the *Hokulea* it had become quite clear that the idea of trying out a scientific, rationalized practice to substantiate Finney's ideas on voyaging had further contributed to what may be described as an already volatile social situation among the Hawaiian participants in the project. This brings us to the second story-line and history, that of indigenous Hawaiians who were ready for the practice of voyaging to emerge.

The Hawaiian-identity movement prior to voyaging

By the early 1970s, Hawaiians had lost much of their cultural substance, including their land, language and control over their own spatial realm (Herman 1999). The Hawaiian decline begun with the first contact with Captain Cook, and escalated after their European-styled kingdom and nation-state were overthrown by Euro-American businessmen in 1893, annexed by the USA in 1898, and finally incorporated as a state in 1959. Before entering into details on Hawai'i prior to US annexation, I will discuss how the Hawaiian loss of autonomy manifested itself in the 1960s and early 1970s.

The presence of the USA as an imperial power is very obvious in Hawai'i. By 1960, the last year the Hawaiians were counted as a distinct 'racial' group, they were but 1.7 per cent of the population. However, if including the various 'racially mixed' groupings, people defined as having a Hawaiian ancestry numbered in 1975 a total of 150,000 people or 16.7 per cent of the population (Linnekin 1983). Out of these, half were 18 years' old and younger, 62.6 per cent had no recorded income, and the unemployment rate was double that of other groupings in the state. According to an official report in 1980 referring to the 1975 data, this was due to lack of '...basic education, stereotyping and low self-image, and lack of skill training and job readiness orientation'.[1]

It must here be made clear that 'Hawaiians' refers to people defined as the indigenous Polynesian population. A white person will automatically be referred to as a *haole* by all other population groups in Hawai'i, even if he or she has generations of ancestral connections to the islands. 'Hawaiian' and '*haole*' are, in the present, both used to signify opposition to the dominators of the lands.[2] With regard to the non-Hawaiian 'mixed' population, many were introduced to Hawai'i as plantation workers during the growth of the sugar industry in the last decades of the nineteenth century, but the largest numbers arrived after the annexation. This was, of course, due to the continuing need for workers in the sugar industry, the establishment of a military complex and, finally, the development of what was to become an enormous tourist industry.

Thus, among the signs of imperial presence, other than the sheer domination of the islands by non-Hawaiians, is the looming figure of the USA's massive military force (Sai 2007:7), whose purpose is quite obvious: to access the vast and unobstructed ocean space that borders large parts of the world, including potential areas of interest and rival countries. From this perspective, Hawai'i is also a stronghold for possible invaders of the USA, something made very clear when the Japanese bombed Pearl Harbour in 1941. Still, an even more visible sign of the imperial might of the USA is the way in which capitalism manifests itself in the high-rises of Honolulu and the tourist resorts elsewhere in the islands.

Nonetheless, by the late 1960s it had become clear that the long-term cultural decline of Hawaiians, obvious already early in the century, had for decades solidified a presentation of its original population as a culturally and materially poor, as well as stigmatized, group who had not managed the transition into the modern with a substantiated, proud identity. Their hierarchically low status was very visible in various globally distributed media presentations of the time, for example in the three fiction films starring Elvis

Presley and named 'Blue Hawaii' (1961), 'Girls! Girls! Girls!' (1962) and 'Paradise Hawaiian Style' (1965). It was equally present in the famous American TV series 'Hawaii Five-O' (1968–80). All portrayed Hawaiians at best as one-dimensional props with low social status: figuring in sex fantasies, or as servants and entertainers of the white American. It would, therefore, seem as if Hawaiians were reaching a crossroads, where they had a choice of letting themselves become assimilated as free-floating individuals within the liberal, capitalistic society of the USA, where it would seem material wealth was the primary measure; or of trying to constitute a stronger cultural core (Kanahele 1979).

The first significant public sign of frustration, and of what might be described as an early ethnic awareness, appeared in John Dominis Holt's book *On Being Hawaiian* (1964). The topic was the loss of language and culture, and the suppression of Hawaiian identity. These notions emerged in resonance with a more globally conceived movement in which people opposed former authorities and their truths, parallel to the equally global growth of a notion of ethnicity. Ethnicity is here looked upon as a group specific, a modern, positional and politicized form of defining otherness in a global world (Eriksen 2001; Okamura 2008; Aoudè 1999). This development was highly influenced by the expansive increase in global communications and media.

In mainland USA, the opposition to authorities took shape, for example, in the protests against the Vietnam War and the growth of the hippie movement. A significant opposition to authority that were simultaneously highly ethnic in form was the civil rights movement of its black population. Ethnicity was, however, developing in all groups, and many of the Latino, as well as white, citizens of the USA were finding it important to constitute an ethnic identity.

In Hawai'i, the main growth of Hawaiian ethnicity took place in urban settings that consisted largely of young Hawaiians who did not know the Hawaiian language and were separated from the more substantial cultural qualities of rural life. As such, it was natural to gravitate towards a (by then romanticized and public) memory of Hawaiian culture, much of which was rooted in nationalism. Frustrations were further focused by the intellectuals at the University of Hawai'i, who in the late 1960s initiated politicized programmes of ethnic studies and Hawaiian studies. Thus courses in Hawaiian language and Hawaiiana became popular all over the islands (Linnekin 1983:244–5).[3] The music scene would also spring forth as a means of creating identity, and quickly took on a politicized form (Kanahele 1979:3; Lewis 1984).

Running parallel to the wakening ethnic awareness was the fact that crown land, through the Organic Act of 1900, had been ceded to the USA as a trustee, for the 'benefit' of the living conditions of the Hawaiian people.[4] As tourism bloomed and real estate soared in the 1960s, the more militant of the Hawaiian activists would increasingly focus on land as a basis of identity

construction and voice their grievances at having been dispossessed from
territory held in trust by the state. Their agendas would also take the form of
a conscious move towards more marked ethnicity by organizing opposition,
thereby defying authorities as well as dominators, and ultimately the USA.
In the early 1970s this consciousness would erupt into occasional violent
demonstrations. Significant conflict arose when Hawaiians and other tenants
were evicted from the Kalama, Waiahole and Waikane Valleys on Oahu due
to tourist development (McGregor 1989; Nakata 1999). This was followed by a
struggle to re-claim the island of Kaho'olawe, which had been used by the navy
for bombing practices (Linnekin 1983:246–8).

The *Hokule'a* breakthrough

Given the Hawaiians' broad background of general dissatisfaction and
frustration, it is understandable why the creation of the PVS and the building
of the *Hokule'a* turned out to have volatile potential. The canoe took a year
to complete and was both highly visited and a well-discussed topic among
Hawaiians. The 1975 launching took place at the Kualoa Beach Park, a sacred
place in Hawaiian history, and included an elaborate mixture of revived as well
as invented rites and chants (Finney 1979). It was therefore almost inevitable
that different groups would try to use the vessel for their own goals. The first
and most obvious way of doing this was to focus on the fact that the leader of
the PVS was a *haole* from mainland USA.

The opposition to *haole* leadership was probably also inspired by internal
strife within the PVS. Even before the launching of *Hokule'a*, Herb Kane used
his skills as a commercial advertiser and ethnic entrepreneur (see Linnekin
1983:245) to actively promote his own agendas with regard to constructing
his Hawaiian identity and his version of Hawaiian culture, which at the
same time implied an exclusion of Finney and of Tommy Holmes. Kane
and others transformed the canoe through drawings into a graphic symbol,
while instigating modern ethnic ideas about the importance of the voyage for
Hawaiians. Nonetheless, by doing this he gave (as Finney had done through
his rationale of scientific experiments) glimpses into vast Hawaiian spaces,
dimensions beyond the stark reality the Hawaiians were experiencing in the
mid 1970s. To quote Finney (2007:298): 'After we founded the Polynesian
Voyaging Society Herb painted a stunning vision of *Hokule'a* sailing over
the blue ocean which he then reproduced on posters, launching the canoe
into public imagination.' This promotion included presenting *Hokule'a* as the
'Spaceship of our ancestors' and 'the central artefact of Polynesian culture'
(Finney 1979:29). Many would therefore look at Finney's position and doings
as yet another case of the white man stealing part of their culture.

Thus chaos quickly replaced the early optimism and clear-cut goal that had instigated the PVS. The canoe and its original purpose became drawn into a whole range of ethnic and politicized agendas by its crew, as well as by various Hawaiians leaders, who had personal, cultural and nationalistic goals, but whose overall intentions did not necessarily correlate. The intended voyage became further threatened when a film crew from the National Geographic Society arrived. Their purpose, it would seem, was to create a film about a presumed ethnic conflict involving the Hawaiian crew members who wanted to take over the project in order to promote their own ideas of Hawaiianness.

A likely reason for the film crew's focus was that the struggles of ethnic minorities against dominators was (naturally enough) a commonplace thematic, and a reality of the times. However, it is also quite clear that commercial, consumer-oriented television documentaries tend to focus on individual protagonists, often emphasizing a dramatized story-line over truth, and that conflict is acknowledged as an important driving force for a story. In their efforts to capture their envisioned plot, the film-makers exacerbated the problems. 'Actors' were chosen for their good looks (or so it would seem, Finney 1979:74–5), and they were compelled to play out their 'ethnic roles', 'narratives' and 'conflicts' whenever the camera appeared, placing them instantly onto a public stage with a potentially global audience.

The combined force of these troubles almost lead to the end of voyaging. There were several attempts at taking control of the *Hokule'a*, including an initiative to sail her to Kaho'olawe Island and use her as a vessel of protest against the USA. The most dangerous situation occurred on the voyage to Tahiti, when six of the Hawaiian crew tried to sabotage the sail by going on strike, after an ongoing quarrel with a *haole* about the intentions of the voyage. It must be added that the film crew from the National Geographic Society were present on the trip, and continued to force their story of conflict ahead. By the time the *Hokule'a* arrived in Tahiti, Mau Piailug had decided to never return to Hawai'i, and he flew home to Satawal from there. Ben Finney also flew home to Hawai'i from Tahiti. After the *Hokule'a* had returned to Hawai'i by the use of Western navigational methods, there was still a notion among many that voyaging was the property of the Hawaiians, and if they could not do it, then no one should. By now, Finney was physically and emotionally exhausted. The continuing bickering and general problems of cooperation with certain groups of Hawaiians would eventually cause him to step down as the leader of the PVS.

Still, radical change had already been instigated, and took further form in a young part-Hawaiian by the name of (Charles) Nainoa Thompson. Along with many other Hawaiians, Nainoa had followed the building and launching of the

Hokuleʻa, and had also been culturally inspired through deep talks with Kane. After crewing on the return journey from Tahiti and experiencing the ocean and the sky during the day and night for several weeks, his interest finally crystallized into a desire to learn star navigation.

In 1978 the new leaders of the PVS decided to set forth on another journey to Tahiti, during which Nainoa was to try to navigate without the use of Western navigational instruments, in parallel with, and where necessary corrected by, sextant navigation. However, during the planning of this voyage none of the experienced crew from the former voyages were consulted. To make matters worse, the *Hokuleʻa* set sail despite storm warnings (Finney 2007:301). After only hours of sailing, she capsized in the Molokaʻi channel. The shipwreck was followed by the death of a member of the crew – famous waterman Eddie Aikau was lost while trying to paddle a surfboard to land in order to get help. A result of this catastrophe was that the PVS was accused of not having planned and prepared sufficiently for the voyage before departure (Finney 2007; Coast Guard Inquiry 16732/20–78). The future of the voyaging society seemed to be very uncertain.

In 1979, Myron Bennet 'Pinky' Thompson (1924–2001), Nainoa's father, decided to intervene in the situation at the PVS. 'Pinky' Thompson was a highly respected, resourceful, socially engaged and strategic promoter of Hawaiian culture with the experience needed to lead the PVS in troubled times, and also with the ability to rally support from Hawaiians in general. In 1974 he had become a trustee of the Bishop Estate, the richest foundation in Hawaiʻi, and the economic basis of the Hawaiian-only, elitist Kamekameha Schools. For him, a major focus was that children were instigators of change. He quickly found a way to use the Bishop funds, previously primarily for the Kamehameha Schools, for the education of Hawaiian children all over the state.[5] In 1979 he became the leader of the PVS, and he would continue leading and sponsoring the society until his death in 2001, when his son Nainoa took over the post as president. In the same year Mau Piailug was once again engaged, but this time as a teacher. On the *Hokuleʻa*, in 1980, Nainoa Thompson became the first Hawaiian for centuries to navigate and sail to Tahiti and back without the use of maps or Western navigational instruments (Kyselka 1987). This not only indicated that such voyaging and way-finding could have been done in an ancient past; even more importantly, it was a statement that it was possible for an urban Hawaiian to manage such an awesome task in the present.

Voyaging as a rite of passage: Hawaiian voyaging expertise and ritual leadership

Both the 1976 and 1980 voyages from Hawai'i to Tahiti and back are undoubtedly well-defined physical transitions and rites of passage, as well as radical transformations of space and time. A rite of passage is a universal method human beings use to relate to and manage change, as well as a way of reconstituting the alienation inherent in social structure. Thus a rite of passage refers in its basic structure to the phenomenology of orientation, conceptualization, organization and reorganization, and also to the anchoring of one's motion in or through existence.

Arnold Van Gennep (1960 [1909]) was the first person to theorize its dynamics. He describes how the rite of passage is actually made up of a series of rituals that effect separation, transition and incorporation, and by means of which the initiate passes from one status or condition to another. Within the period of transition the initiate has to let go of the departed condition in order to be able to head towards the intended new one. Van Gennep named this phase *limen*, a term that was further elaborated on by Victor Turner, who named it the *liminal* or *liminality* (Turner 1969, 1974).[6] Anything is potentially possible in the *liminal* as it is a highly liberated state which consequently generates heightened ambiguity. Groups passing through *liminality* can experience periods of deep almost spiritual unity, since the social structure associated with social segregation is considerably weakened, sometimes dissolved. Still, when the incorporation and its rites begin, these circumscribe the transition. From this perspective the incorporation and its rites and forms, restrict the possibilities inherent in the liberation that arises in the *liminal*.

The departure from land to sea is a separating process, which continues well out into the ocean space. This is followed by a voyage on the ocean, which is physically, ritually and symbolically structure-free or *liminal* in character, when set in relationship to land and life ashore (Scott 2002). There are social and cultural structures out at sea, but these relate more directly towards maintaining social control on the voyaging vessel and managing life in the 'uncontrollable' elements of the ocean. Finally, I will argue, the voyage begins to be drawn into a new status and condition as it comes closer to its destination, which includes being incorporated back into a land-based existence. I will elaborate on this shortly. For now it is important to underline some differences in emphasis in these two seemingly similar voyages. The most obvious is the way the 1976 voyage, although having definite and Hawaiian cultural goals, emphasized a scientific orientation. The 1980 voyage, on the other hand, although having scientific and explorative goals, emphasized Hawaiian culture.

Another way of viewing these differences is to say that the first voyage needed to include the Hawaiian people and their culture and goals in order for its scientific objectives to stand out as legitimate, both to the scientific community and to Hawaiians; while the second voyage needed to have a scientific and explorative agenda in order to stand out as legitimate to people outside of the Hawaiian context. Importantly, symbolically and otherwise, a Western scientist (and ritual leader) led the first project of the PVS while a Micronesian (ritual leader) navigated the voyage in a non-Western manner to Tahiti, with a crew containing many were *haole*. On the second successful voyage of the PVS, a highly respected urban Hawaiian (and ritual leader) who was an active instigator of cultural change took the reins, and his son (and ritual leader) navigated the voyage in a non-Western manner to Tahiti and back with a mostly Hawaiian crew.[7]

Thus the 1980 voyage did not only link Hawaiians directly to their possible voyaging heritage, but it underlined their worth, capability and capacities in the present. The transformative force of this journey revealed itself also in the fame bestowed on Nainoa and the crew, all of whom gained instant status and prominence in Hawai'i. Nainoa's status quickly took on heroic, even iconic, properties: due to his continuing quest to gain voyaging, navigational, explorative and controlling knowledge over the ocean, as well as of Western and Hawaiian cultural space; through his charismatic but also enigmatic qualities; from his obvious personal transformations through voyaging; and finally because he was willing to teach what he had learned.

The differences in the goals, and results, of these two voyages show that the resurrection of Hawaiian culture on a global scale necessitated Hawaiian leadership and knowledge of non-Western navigation; though also – as exemplified in the 1978 catastrophe – careful planning, strategic vision and a highly conscious relationship to risk. This leads us to the third story of voyaging, in which Hawaiians can be said to have territorialized, re-territorialized, transformed and reconstructed global space.

The Euro-American creation and domination of global and Pacific space, and its influence on Hawai'i

When the *Hokule'a* set sail from Hawai'i to Tahiti, it seemed as if the canoe sailed out into a space that had been created, substantiated and dominated by the Western world for centuries. Before arguing that *Hokule'a* did not, in fact, sail out into a global space defined by the Western world, I need to define global space.

The phenomenological basis of global space is, as I have argued more thoroughly elsewhere, the spherical and grid-based geometrical construction of horizontal and vertical lines named latitude and longitude (Scott 2002, 2007, n.d.). This visual and virtual model of existence, which has been given primary references such as the Prime Meridian of Longitude, the Equator, and a North and South Pole, is the mainframe of Western navigation and spatial coordination. From its introduction in Florence in 1400, it has been used as a basis from which to measure and position individuals, land and places in standardizing, hegemonic ways within a global whole (Scott 2007, 2010; Edgerton 1975; Ptolemais 2000). Thus the individual has become positioned as a point in a coherent, resonating, and thereby individualizing and constantly developing, whole. The centre of global existence became the individual, the centre of the world became Europe, and the margins became the Pacific.

The European exploration of the ocean and their construction of the global empowered them with the privilege and awesome power of embedding the grid with individualized feats, which stood out as additional directives to the grid, and which resonated in the physicality of the global. Most prominently, it made it possible for Europeans to define the spatial as well as temporal qualities of space, and to categorize and name large parts of the world and the cosmos, including natural and cultural systems and inhabitants. The first truly global explorer (and 'ritual leader' in the transformation and construction of global space), Ferdinand Magellan, cemented the European notion of a global grid-defined existence, while revealing the oceanic physicality of 'the far side' which he named the Pacific Ocean. Others would name lands and the people living in this ocean space (such as the Polynesians), as well as many of its other creatures. This prolific naming would also cover natural phenomena such as ocean currents and winds, as well as outer-worldly objects like stars and planets.

When Captain James Cook, cartographer and explorer (as well as cultural representative and ritual leader) arrived in the island group that he 'impudently' named the Sandwich Islands, he circumscribed Hawai'i with a hegemonic global space and time defined, controlled, categorized and to a high degree named by Europeans. This placed Hawai'i and the Polynesians as living in isolation at 'the margins of the global', separated from the rest of existence by an enormous, ambiguous and dangerous barrier of sea space. Meanwhile, and perhaps as a result of contact, Kamehameha I set out to conquer the different Hawaiian Islands, formally establishing the Kingdom of Hawai'i in 1810 (Sahlins 1992; Daws 1989). During Kamehamehas' struggles for sovereignty, and in the remaining years of his reign, he actively set out to transform Hawai'i by incorporating foreign technologies and knowledge. These localized changes took place while the land and its people became incorporated into a European imaginary or mythic understanding of life in their own margins (Smith 1979, 1985; Gillis 2004). Such understandings would find substantial and resonating forms through tales, literature and objects brought back by visitors (Frost 1979; Joppien 1979). Eventually this would also inspire missionaries to travel to Hawai'i. In their quest to convert and save souls, but also to preserve parts of indigenous culture from the degenerative forces of urban life, missionaries would work actively to transform the spatial as well as spiritual realms of the Hawaiians.

In becoming part of global existence, Hawai'i was exposed to diseases previously unknown to its inhabitants and to the influence of capitalism, whose protagonists had for centuries utilized and altered the rationale of the global so as to develop its markets and its ideas of commerce (Wallenstein 1974). The former stands out as the most erosive force to Hawaiian culture in first half of the nineteenth century, while the latter gained increasing momentum as the main transformative dynamic in the second half. Thus, the spatial transformation of Hawai'i and its global orientation went hand in hand with the loss of people (and culture) and the increasingly more substantial influence of capitalism on people's daily lives.

A revolutionary change took place in 1819 with the Hawaiian-initiated overthrow of the *kapu* system, which basically separated their social world from a direct and ordering interaction with the divine forces of a Hawaiian-controlled cosmos (Sahlins 1992; Daws 1989). Following this, in the mid-nineteenth century, land became interlinked with the global grid, as it was redefined into geometrically measured plots that were privatized and commoditized under the Great Mahele (Sahlins 1994; Banner 2005; La Croix and Roumasset 1990). Another major change was the way the Pacific historicity of the Hawaiians became increasingly defined not through its own people, but rather by the words of Western scholars, who set the standards for how one should present the timely or historical aspect of global space (see Friedman 1992). Thus historicity took its form through definite spatial positioning and further rational interpretation of objects, events and their trajectories in a global space-time that was, naturally, subjective from a Western point of view.

Even today there is neither direct archaeological evidence for, nor Western observations or records of, voyaging, other than a simple map drawn for Cook by a Tahitian navigator named Tupaia that gives the rudimentary positioning of various Pacific islands. Furthermore, the oceans of the world have since the time of the ancient Greeks appeared to Europeans and Westerners as areas of chaos, danger, existential drama and ambiguity. It has therefore been difficult for Western land-based intellectuals of the past to discuss in unbiased ways a non-Western 'stone-age' rationale held by individuals who might not necessarily fear the ocean, and who could have set out to sail, deliberately, on flimsy vessels into what the West defines as the 'dangers' of global ocean space.

During the late nineteenth and early twentieth century Europe and the USA dominated both the oceans and the trade of the world, as well as economic life in most of the Polynesian islands of the Pacific. The region was subjected to an increase of Western businessmen, settlers and travelers. Many began to present their own spatially rational, as well as romanticized, views of the area, based on personal experiences in their locally positioned Pacific contexts. Such writings arose in parts through a Euro-American 'bourgeois' need to grasp, identify with, appropriate, control and transform the local spaces and landscapes of the Pacific (including some of its myths) in writings, in artistry, through science, and later on through photography and film (Smith 1985, see Kern 2003; Rio and Scott 2009). One may argue that this constitutes a further development of the globalizing process initiated by Magellan, and that it may also be defined as a continuation of ongoing Euro-American appropriation and definition of Pacific space. Nonetheless, in the air of such romanticism, scholars like Abraham Fornander and Stephenson Percy Smith analyzed myths and genealogies of Polynesians and used these to tell stories of heroic Polynesians with Aryan origins who migrated from Asia to Polynesia in great coordinated fleets (e.g. Fornander 1996, 2009; Percy Smith 2010; see Finney 1963, 1991). Fornander and Percy Smith were thereby also transforming local understandings of origin into a Western rationale that needed to place people, cultures and their 'development' into temporally framed positions and narratives that unfolded in a Western understanding of space-time (see Terrell, Hunt and Gosden 1997).

The simplified and speculative visions of Fornander and Percy Smith would lay the foundation for later serious criticism, particularly in the wake of Thor Heyerdahl's *Kon Tiki* expedition in 1949, which popularized to a global audience his scientifically marginal ideas that the Pacific was settled through the Americas (marginal because many in the scientific community disagreed with his claim that migrants had to sail with, not against, the trade winds). The simple conclusion that did arise after the issue of pre-historic Pacific voyaging had become a global (but mostly Western) debate was that deliberate inter-island voyaging or migration of the Polynesians into the Pacific could not have taken place (Sharpe 1963:122–8; Finney 1963:5, 2007:297). As we have now returned to the argument Finney set out to disprove, it is appropriate to look more closely at the early accomplishments of the Polynesian Voyaging Society, and to revisit my point that on the voyages to Tahiti and back the *Hokule'a* did not, in fact, sail into global space defined by the Western world.

The importance of heritage in reclaiming Polynesian space through voyaging

When *Hokule'a* set sail for Tahiti in 1976 and in 1980, the voyages were similar in form but different in content. The departure rituals for both voyages were similar, in that they had both a private and public form. The private dimension took place between each crew member and their friends and family. Then there were a whole range of official departure rituals. During the 1976 voyage the Hawaiians followed the launching of the canoe by creating a number of departure (or separation) rites, such as chants. These rituals were repeated on the second journey and were later expanded into an official protocol of voyaging.[8] The Hawaiian state would also engage in departure rituals, which included passing the crew through immigration, so that officers symbolically separated the crew from US territory. Other official rituals were instigated by the public focus on the departures and arrivals, and included the visits of reporters, photographers and film producers who visualized, virtualized and globalized the voyage and its symbolism.

A departure from land to sea is dramatic. The canoe departs land-based space for an ocean space devoid of terrestrial solidity and social systems. Life on the ocean is undoubtedly physically, socially and symbolically liminal, something that soon becomes obvious from the reduced impressions and observations of life, and because the ocean, the vessel, the sky, the sun and the stars are in constant motion. It takes days, sometimes weeks, before an individual processes the physical and mental departure from land, while trying to adjust to the motion of the sailing vessel and life at sea. During this time, land and its systems become increasingly distant, but also observable as 'objective' entities that exists far away, enabling the crew member to become increasingly liberated from all that they have left behind. The separation from land-based impressions enhances the sensations, structures (including rituals and symbols) and social relations that take place on board the vessel. Finally, the 'nothingness' of the ocean starts to become filled with its own impressions, as the urbanized crew, who are used to consuming goods of all kinds (see Slater 1997), have to alter their orientation and begin to engage sensually with their immediate natural and cultural surroundings (Scott 2002:106–23). In the 'chaotic' liminality of the powerful ocean, anything is potentially possible. However, in such a fluid domain, the people travelling the ocean will necessarily recreate their reflective and coordinative senses from the basis of the references at hand. This is so in particular for the navigator, who has to relate to the natural and cultural references he uses to orientate in, and control his and the vessel's voyage through, space.

When Western people sail into the liminality of the ocean they do so by relating on a constant basis to their position, which is defined as a point or coordinate within the abstracted global grid of latitude and longitude, which land is set in a positioned relationship to. Ocean maps away from land are in fact nothing but a local section of a global grid on paper. However, this does not mean that the map or the grid are devoid of social and cultural meaning. The global grid is a rational directive which organizes the individual's relationship to global space and to everything that can be positioned in this space, thereby giving the individual access to a coherent, totalizing space-time dynamic beyond the physicality of the body. The point-based position derived from a GPS, or from a sextant and a marine chronometer, is given meaning in the certainty of the global grid, and enables the sailor to orient themselves rationally in a more or less accurate relationship with land, islands, wind, ocean currents and so forth. This enables the Western sailor to know his or her position in place and time, and in relationship to everything else in the same globalized grid, with more or less certainty and accuracy (Scott 2002:117). However, when Western people sail into ocean space, they also acknowledge the fragile and flimsy nature of such a structured global existence and the potential chaos of existence in the ocean. This is underlined as the land-based world and its values and structures acquire the perspective of an ocean-based distance, and because a liminal existence in the fluidity of the ocean negates a sense of progressive time. Thus the crew will, even though their navigation and global coordination constitute globally accurate space-time measurement, experience a strong sense of timelessness, liminality or 'limbo'. This feeling is particular intense during the first part of the voyage, when the crew has no concrete notion of an arrival date due to the unknown character of the voyage, the unpredictability of sailing, and the ocean and weather in general. Nonetheless, when navigating the *Hokule'a* both Mau Piailug and Nainoa Thompson disregarded the global grid and Western navigational instruments and systems – by simply not using them. This was further underlined by intense, and partly spontaneous, ritual practices. The canoe would consequently depart from a notion of coherent, progressive, positional and totalizing Western space-time, and enter into a non-Western space devoid of the directives of the global, including historical time. I will return to this later. For now, let me continue the comparison of the two journeys.

During the 1976 voyage, the (ritual) leader of the project was a *haole*, while the navigator (and ritual leader) of the existential was a Micronesian. Furthermore, the voyage by non-Western navigational means ended in Tahiti, not in Hawai'i. Therefore, although the 1976 voyage may be described as a voyage of rediscovery and was treated to Hawaiian departure rituals, as well as some Hawaiian (but mostly Tahitian) arrival or incorporation rituals, the existential references with regard to heritage pointed at the Western and Micronesian orientations of Finney's scientific approach and Piailug's navigation, and circumscribed the overall goal. As such, the first voyage probably did more for the Polynesians in Tahiti than for the Hawaiians, since the *Hokule'a* became a vessel that returned to a presumed origin – the cultural-historical core of Tahiti. What's more, the Tahitians had a stronger cultural identity, and were not directly involved in the ethnic unrest in Hawai'i that the *Hokule'a* and its crew were caught up in. In other words, if the voyage is looked upon as a rite of passage that included voyaging into a heritage of the past, the Hawaiians were not the main protagonists of the transformation that occurred during the voyage, nor were the main goals Hawaiian.

It is also important to understand that people, when sailing on a relatively structure-free ocean voyage and in a confined space, reveal basic relational structures and personal as well as cultural perspectives and traits. Relational structures, including potential differences, become all the more important as they are enhanced due to the lack of other structures. It is thereby understandable why the Hawaiian and *haole* crew members on the 1976 voyage entered into discussions that led to in intense conflict for the rest of the voyage. The opposition that Finney encountered can also be explained by the Hawaiian crew members seeing him as a representative not only of the US dominators, but also of a scientific rationale that had enabled the dominance in the first place, and whose rhetoric had continued to subdue the Polynesians in various ways. Thus this voyage (although crystallizing significant ideas about Hawaiian voyaging heritage) could only indicate to Hawaiians that it would have been possible for them to have sailed a double-hulled canoe in the past, navigating it over longer distances, even deliberately – without the use of charts and Western navigational instruments.

The 1980 voyage of Nainoa, on the other hand, initiated a totally different process. During this journey the urban navigator was, like Mau Piailug, travelling into an unexplored liminal realm or space mostly devoid of the 'naturalized' homogenous Western notion of space-time. Nainoa's orientations (as a ritual leader), as well as those of the crew, were definitely Hawaiian. In the chaotic ocean space, the only physical references are external heavenly bodies – like the sun, stars and horizon; which closer aspects – like the vessel, the direction and form of swells, the flight of sea birds and the massing of clouds – can be set in a relationship to. Nainoa's task was first to know the navigational (as well as existential) position of his departure point (and voyaging origin) in order to know where home was, and to be able to return there. Thereafter, he would use his knowledge of the position of his departure point, together with external references, to envision an ocean space and notions of duration, and to navigate; while communicating with the vessel's captain, who directed the crew to sail the vessel in the direction indicated by the navigator. The navigator needed to conceptualize not only the ocean space around the vessel and its relationship to the moving sun and stars, but also to cognitively grasp and resonate with the space from here to there – all the way from Hawai'i to Tahiti. The navigator would, therefore, begin to envision a new Hawaiian or Polynesian space, even in the first voyage. To use the words of Nainoa when addressing the early teachings of Piailug:

In November of 1979, Mau ... asked, 'Can you point to the direction of Tahiti?' I pointed. Then he asked, 'Can you see the island?' I was puzzled by the question. Of course I could not actually see the island; it was over 2,200 miles away. But the question was a serious one. I had to consider it carefully. Finally, I said, 'I cannot see the island but I can see an image of the island in my mind.' Mau said, 'Good. Don't ever lose that image or you will be lost.'

(Thompson n.d.)

However, in this ritualistic process the vessel and the manner it is operated on by the crew are also highly significant. The canoe is the ritual vessel that transports and actively transforms its crew, including their relationships to each other and to the natural and cultural world on, and beyond, the physicality of the canoe. As such, it is essential to the well-being of the voyage that the crew manage to form close, harmonious and trustful relationships on an existential level. Furthermore, the crew, like the navigator, reach out into and resonate with the liminal space that encompasses life on the canoe. In so doing, the crew will (particularly if the canoe is run well) conceptualize some sort of individualized ontology in relation to the natural and cultural, while still following the directives of the navigator and captain. The double hull of the canoe, the crab sails and the steering oar are all powerful symbols of Hawaiian heritage, especially so when handled in performative ways by Hawaiians. These generate culture-specific phenomenological signs, as well as directives in the liminal, influencing the way in which voyaging is conceptualized. The crew was plentiful, so as to symbolize Hawaiian unity and migration and to reduce risk, but also because the steering of the voyaging canoe, contrary to Western yachts, demanded collective handling.

Although one may argue that it is impossible to copy ancient Polynesian voyaging, as it has not been practised for centuries, it is still possible to mimic the activity. From this perspective, when sailing the *Hokule'a*, Nainoa, the captain and the crew navigated and sailed in similar ways to their ancestors on a similar vessel, relating to the same ocean, sun, stars, winds, fish, whales and birds. In the timeless, existential and forceful liminality of the ocean, such mimicking generates specific links to a potential Hawaiian oceanic past. When looking at navigation as a rite of passage, the process through which voyaging induces the need to underline a specifically Hawaiian sense of belonging and heritage, as well as the feeling of controlling a destiny, may be likened to both homeopathic and contagious magic (Frazer 2000). Homeopathic, in that voyaging – sailing, the canoe and its symbols, the navigation and the conceptualization of the ocean and the passage, and the reach for a destiny that lays ahead – mimics what it wants to control: Hawaiian heritage. Contagious, in that the navigator and crew have the same blood as their ancestors and sail on the same ocean and breathe the same air, and relate to the same sun, moon, stars etc. All this amounts to a fusion of the voyaging practitioners of the present and the past. As quoted by Nainoa:

> *Hokule'a* is like, is kind of like a window ... you can look through to see
> our past. It's almost as if sailing on *Hokule'a*, you could slice through layers
> of time and look back at who your ancestors were. *Hokule'a* provided a
> tremendous amount of inspiration for not just Hawaiian's, but for all the
> people we met in the south Pacific. It's a tremendous symbol that we all can
> honor and find pride in. Because we're able to see (and experience) how
> much our ancestors were able to do in working with so little.[9]

The entire ritual process – departure, of re-territorializing an existential and forceful space devoid of unmoving references, of mimicking the (presumed) past and re-connecting to it on a ritualized vessel, of being ritually circumscribed by incorporation rituals at arrival – states and instigates a dynamic that opens up a deeper understanding of the processes that generate culture. It also underlines the generative power of rites, and rites of passage specifically, to understand, create and conceptualize existence.

Rite of passage as a virtual-reality machine

In an article on virtuality, Bruce Kapferer looks at the mechanical dimension of ritual and uses the notion of the virtual to explain its resonating, intentional and creative functionality. The virtual, he argues, is a kind of

> ...phantasmagoric space whose dynamics allows for all kinds of potentialities
> of human experience to take shape. As a phantasmagoric space, the virtual
> is a plane of immanence and emergence ... the crucial aspect of ritual
> virtuality is that it is *simultaneously its own reality*, and *an opening up*
> *within ongoing existential realities.*
> > (Kapferer 2006:673; italics added)

Kapferer refers to Deleuze and Guattari's use of 'actuality' to further explain his use of ritual virtuality (Deleuze 1991; Thanem and Linstead 2006).[10] 'Actuality' focuses on the processual aspect of existence. Like Bergson's virtuality (Bergson 2007), it exceeds any attempt of total representation and is chaotic, ungraspable and 'subject to forces that are always extending beyond any human knowledge of them' (Kapferer 2006:674). Further, the 'actual' is also 'the complex mass of singularities of which human being and its own manifold processes of formation are at once part of and continually emergent within' (Kapferer 2006:674).

Kapferer further argues the central point that virtual ritual space is a dimension that enables the individual to conceive of the 'actual', as it slows down some of its 'formational flux' (ibid.). From his perspective, the ritual and the rite of passage is a virtual-reality machine, which 'opens particular moments and sites within the chaosmic flow of human actualities' (Kapferer 2006:674). Thus, Kapferer adds:

> The phantasmagoric space of ritual virtuality may be conceived as a
> space (or a space opened by means of the virtual) whose dynamic not
> only interrupts prior determining processes but also is a space in which
> participants can reimagine (and redirect or reorient) themselves in the
> everyday circumstances of life. (2006:674)

If we follow Kapferer, when controlling the ritual process of their own voyages the Hawaiians enter a liminal ocean space and use the virtual space produced by the ritual of the voyage – including the notion of specific heritage comprising a culturally articulated navigation, the managing of the vessel and the crew – to structurally slow down and make sense of the unlimited, direct and existential force of the actual. This is of course indicated in Nainoa's earlier statement that the *Hokule'a* functions like a window in time. The ritualistic task of voyaging thereby connects the individual tasks of the present to a Polynesian heritage of the past.[11] In the actual (or liminal), then, voyaging is unrestricted by the space-time structure and historicity of Western science. The connection to Hawaiian heritage becomes direct and ontological, which enables the present to circumscribe the past when the past emerges in the present. To use the words of Nainoa when trying to explain a connection between him, his navigation orientation and his surroundings after being lost in the doldrums due to heavy cloud cover:

> And it was almost like, when I just gave up fighting to try to find something
> with my eyes, I just settled down, and then all of a sudden, it was like this
> warmth came over me. It was just solid rain, and the guys steering the
> canoe, they were looking for direction. That put more pressure, because
> that was my first [voyage]. And all of a sudden, when ... I leaned against
> the rail – I felt this warmth come over me, and ... I knew where the moon
> was... And then I directed the canoe with all this total confidence... I turned
> the canoe to this particular direction, got things lined up, felt very, very
> comfortable in this cold, wet, rough environment, and then there was a
> break in the clouds and the moon was there.[12]

This presents Nainoa as a ritual leader who, in a direct intuitive as well as spiritual way, orients and connects the canoe and the crew within the surrounding cultural and natural world – directed, focused and defined by the rite of passage. This is also the moment when Nainoa leaves the past behind and embraces his future by becoming a Hawaiian navigator. The ritualized and performative acts and dynamics of navigating, sailing and managing the vessel through the 'actual-liminal' reorients the existential anchoring of the initiates who participate. New, distinct cultural (heritage-based) references arise from which to draw directives and inspiration. These acquire a potent and multi-vocal meaning because they draw force, or *mana*, as well as multi-vocality, from the unlimited potential of the 'actual' or the 'liminal' of the ocean. From this perspective, Nainoa was not only the first modern person of Polynesian descent to navigate a canoe to Tahiti, but he would also on his return 'rediscover' Hawai'i from a non-Western spatial orientation. Nainoa, the crew and the *Hokule'a* would thereby open up a linkage between Hawai'i and the Hawaiians, in a direct way, to the vast and awesome Polynesian ocean space he and his crew had managed and territorialized. If not replacing the hegemonic global space imposed on Hawai'i by Cook, the Hawaiians did at the very least transform this space and redefine it from their own perspective, as well as adding new dimensions to the global.

Leaving the 'liminality' of the ocean when returning to Hawai'i, the voyagers and their messages were circumscribed by Hawaiian arrival rituals, many of which were spontaneously created, it would seem, in reaction to the perceived potency of voyaging. As such, the incorporation and its rituals had the power to reach back and create a dynamic frame and narrative for the voyage, thereby also making it simpler to grasp. Further, the voyage and voyagers were ritually reincorporated back into a Western grid-based space upon being symbolically incorporated into a state, be it French Polynesia or Hawaiian USA. This was of course followed by the same ritualized media coverage as in the departure. An obvious occurrence of being related to grid-based space takes place when people observe the *Hokule'a* after arrival in any non-Hawaiian port. The voyaging canoe's hull, sails, rudder and crew symbolize a non-Western background, while the flag, the suntan, bleached clothes, bearded faces and rugged looks of the crew also symbolize national belonging, time spent in the ocean, and personal endurance, among other things. The observer will then relate all of this information to the notion of his or her position in this specific port – as a spot on a map and as a virtual and visualized notion enabled by the global grid. The grid makes it further possible to resonate this experience of the local in the global, and vice versa, with a more or less implicit notion of certainty.

Hawaiians have transformed a vast area of global space by voyaging into an ocean without the aid of Western navigational instruments. By doing this, they have re-oriented themselves in the cosmos and reconnected to a Hawaiian ontological core that includes a spiritual, holistic as well as *mana*-filled existence devoid of time, enabling them to re-territorialize a past and link it to a present. It is possible for Hawaiians to travel into the most undefined and uncontrollable element in a global, natural existence, and to control it from their own perspective. Hawaiians are thereby capable of handling all aspects of their own lives in performative, innovative ways, becoming performers on a global arena. The navigators, the voyaging canoes, the crew and the objects of the voyage accumulate force and become powerful agents and symbols of transformation.

The coming of the first Polynesian navigator marked a new era of voyaging and the strategic development of a Hawaiian self-esteem, through the beginning of massive spatial exploration and re-territorialization of the Pacific Ocean. In retrospect, these accomplishments reveal a strategic approach towards creating cultural substance, not only with regard to an oceanic past, but also, and even more so, the present and future. Naturally enough, such strategies correspond well with the art of navigation and the transformative force of a rite of passage. The training of the modern navigator, as well of a ritual leader, is not only about navigating in space, but about how to move a small society that includes navigator, captain and crew over vast distances in space and time on a technological and symbolic vessel, and to get them to their destination in safety. Hawaiian voyaging is, unlike Western long-distance cruising, a collective endeavour[13] in which everyone is allocated a position from which to excel. As such, it is also possible to see how voyaging stands out symbolically as transformative travel not only for ritual leaders and crew, but for an entire nation of Hawaiians.

Pacific navigation as a re-territorializing social movement

The Polynesian Voyaging Society has since its beginnings been engaged in a range of projects combining exploration and promotion, as well as in projects purely promoting the cultural and practical benefits of voyaging. Amongst these have been the training of new master navigators and crew members by developing programmes that include risk analysis and sail training. Both explorations/promotions and navigator/crew training have acted towards substantiating the transformation of ocean space, as well as the more personal and existential transformations of the navigators and crews that participate in voyaging. Promotional tasks include engaging with potential sponsors and, more importantly, giving public talks and educational lectures and presentations of various kinds, as well as organizing educational sailing voyages on a continuous basis. The PVS has, from the early days of Pinky Thompson's leadership, worked actively and specifically towards educating children, continuously developing educational curricula. Nevertheless, the engine that fuels all other activities of the PVS is that of the major expeditions, which have all been led by Nainoa and his close PVS associates (including more recently trained navigators). The names of the expeditions – which, like the 1976 and 1980 voyages may also be defined as rites of passages – clearly state the society's main strategic goals over time.

In 1985–7 the PVS set out on an expedition named 'The Voyage of Rediscovery', which may be described as their third main voyage. This took *Hokule'a* on a 25,000 km journey along what was looked upon as the ancient migratory routes of the Polynesian Triangle, from Hawai'i to the Society Islands, the Cook Islands, New Zealand, Tonga, Samoa, and back via Aitutaki, Tahiti, Rangiroa in the Tuamutu archipelago, and finally to Hawai'i. The expedition indicated not only a rediscovery of and linkage with a past, but also a territorialization of a past and present, reopening this ocean space-time in a modern form and from a specifically Hawaiian perspective. Furthermore, it demonstrated that it could have been possible for ancient voyaging canoes to sail against prevailing winds, from west to east in the Pacific. The easterly trade winds are not as prevailing as many would believe, but are regularly replaced by seasonal westerly blowing winds. The scientific authority of this voyage was further substantiated by the participation and subsequent writings of Ben Finney, who was reincorporated into the PVS. Finney (2004) chronicled and analyzed the efforts. More than anything, this expedition substantiated the awesome symbolic, individualizing (and therefore modern) force of the *Hokule'a*, its crew and its master navigator, Nainoa Thompson, and showed that the PVS had a clear future-oriented agenda.

The *Hokule'a* voyages of the 1970s and 1980s expanded the ocean space for all Polynesians. Thus voyaging contributed towards reorienting not only Polynesians but also other 'indigenous' people of the Pacific, as the grand feats of voyaging enabled many to see themselves in a new and more confident light. It is therefore also arguable that voyaging created the setting for the emergence of texts like Epeli Hau´ofa's influential essay 'Our Sea of Islands' (1993). In that essay he contrasted the term 'Sea of Islands' with 'Islands in the Sea' in order to describe the existential difference between the sea as an element that unites and as one that separates. While the latter idea emphasizes islands as isolated surfaces in a vast ocean far from the centres of power, the former see islands in the totality of their relationships with each other.

In 1992 the *Hokule'a* set out on what was named the 'Voyage for Education', underlining the other important focus of the PVS: the communication of voyaging knowledge to the coming generations. The voyage went to

Rarotonga in the Cook Islands, where the canoe participated in the sixth Pacific Arts Festival, which celebrated the revival of traditional canoe building and navigation in the Pacific. This trip included an educational programme that allowed students in Hawai'i to follow the canoe through daily, live radio reports. This approach was continued and further developed on subsequent voyages.

The 1995 expedition was named 'The Voyaging Family of the Vast Ocean', underlining a focus on spatially uniting the Polynesians of the Pacific. *Hokule'a* set out to sail to the Marquesas Islands, from which some believe early Hawaiian settlers had arrived (with reference to language similarities). The return trip went via Tahiti and Ra'iatea. On this voyage five other canoes joined the *Hokule'a*: the *Hawai'iloa* and *Makali'i* from Hawai'i, the *Te Aurere* from New Zealand and the *Takitumu* and *Te Au o Tonga* from the Cook Islands.

During the summer of that same year, the *Hokule'a* and the *Hawai'iloa* were shipped to Seattle, where *Hokule'a* sailed southbound to San Diego in order to share the *mana* (and legitimacy) of the canoe with Hawaiians, Native Americans and other Americans living there. Meanwhile the *Hawai'iloa* sailed north to Juneau in Alaska in order to visit the land of the Tlingit, Haida, and Tshimshian, who had donated the logs for its hulls because there were no longer any trees suitable for voyaging purposes in Hawai'i.

In 1999–2000 the *Hokule'a* reached the far south-eastern corner of Polynesia, completing its modern exploration of the Polynesian Triangle. This in many ways settled the score with regard to re-territorializing the ocean space that was re-defined after contact with the Western world.

In 2003–4, on a voyage named 'Navigating Change', the *Hokule'a* sailed to the Northwestern Hawaiian Islands to explore the unique natural and cultural resources of this outer archipelago, while stating the potentially important role of these islands in Hawaiian past, present and future. The focus was on the environment, which had always been a major issue for the society, though it had not previously been specifically spotlighted.

In 2007, on an occasion which may be described as the end of an era, the *Hokule'a* sailed to Micronesia and then Japan on a voyage named 'One Ocean, One People'. On the first half of the journey, named 'Ku Holo Mau' ('Sail On, Sail Always, Sail Forever'), the *Hokule'a* was accompanied by the voyaging canoe *Alingano Maisu*. The latter vessel was a gift for Mau Piailug, who was returning to spend the rest of his life on his home island of Satawal. The purpose of the gift was also to revitalize and perpetuate the voyaging traditions of the Micronesian people.

In Satawal, Piailug held – for the first time in 26 years – a Micronesian initiation ceremony for navigators, called the *pwo*. During the ceremony Nainoa Thompson and other prominent Hawaiian navigators, including

Shorty Bertelmann, Chad Paishon, Chad Baybayan and Bruce Blankenfeld, were initiated into the symbolic world of Micronesian navigators. Piailug thereby acknowledged the modern, pan-Pacific status of the Hawaiians by integrating their *mana* into Micronesian navigational heritage, while the Hawaiians were integrated into a navigation genealogy probably unbroken since the first people arrived in Micronesia.

The official purpose of the continuing journey to Japan was to celebrate a century and more of intercultural exchange, and the focus was on school children of all ages. However, the voyage was also symbolic for a reunification with an old friend of the nineteenth-century Hawaiian Nation. This journey was named 'Ku Holo La Komohana' ('Sail On to the Western Sun'). By now, the daily radio reports were joined by web-based diaries and interactive blogs containing photos of the voyage in which people could follow the progress on a map.

Symbolically speaking, this expedition signified that the PVS had achieved what they had set out to do. They had re-territorialized and brought into the modern world the ocean space they lost to the West, they had re-created a past cultural substance, they had spatially united the Polynesians across the Pacific region and, in so doing, they had transformed the ocean and its space from something that separated to something that unites. Thus the PVS had actively repositioned themselves, their people and their cultural contexts in a present global world.

To quote the PVS (n.d.): 'In the years spanning the beginning of voyaging to today more than 525,000 of a population of 1.2 million [in Hawai'i] have participated in our programs of education, research, training and dialogue.' In other words, like the voyagers who ritually mimicked the past in order to control the present and future, people participating physically in the programmes are ritually mimicking the voyagers of recent times, as well as the more ancient past. As an example: in 1996–7 the PVS had a 10-month state-wide voyage, and more than 25,000 school children and community members visited or sailed on the *Hokule'a*.[14]

The story of voyaging has been acclaimed as a major driving force behind what is described as the Polynesian cultural renaissance, and is now part of the curriculum of every school in Hawai'i. The tourist industry presents the story to visitors. Two museums in Hawai'i alone – the Hawai'i Maritime Center in Honolulu and the Imiloa Astronomy Center at Hilo on the Big Island – are dedicated specifically to voyaging. Their exhibitions promote the prevailing notion that the Pacific was consciously and deliberately colonized and crossed by Polynesian navigators and voyagers. Voyaging in Hawai'i has also spread out into more ethnically focused arenas, such as in the navigational initiative instigated by master navigator Chad Babayan on Big Island, in which his particular school activities focus specifically on the ethnic development of Hawaiian culture.

Conclusion

The *Hokule'a* is now Hawai'i's most potent symbol and stands as a metaphor for the directive tasks in voyaging. These tasks are: first, find your position; then use this as a basis for conceptualizing a past that can be used strategically for planning in the present, while envisioning your future goal. Voyaging pertains to all social arenas and ethnicities, ranging from religious goals, to business, family-oriented or individual goals. Anyone who finds it important to navigate into the promise of a prosperous future of self-control may make use of these directives. Further, many of the voyaging crew, including several who are not of Hawaiian descent, have become individualized heroes, celebrities and role models. These individuals underline the transformative success of voyaging and the way in which this practice transforms not only Hawaiians, but everyone. A result is that the *Hokule'a* has become an official state treasure and Nainoa Thompson has been voted the most respected man in Hawai'i.

It seems that voyaging over time has increasingly become a symbolic force for all the people in the Hawaiian Islands. At the very least, this stands out as a strategy for national balancing, which Nainoa and his father Pinky were engaged in since the 1980 voyage – constantly insisting that voyaging should not be limited to indigenous Hawaiians. With this background it seems that the future goal of the PVS is to unite the various ethnic groups in Hawai'i within a frame that defines the islands of Hawai'i as a special territory with many basic values drawing potency from pre-European heritage. This is certainly indicated in the circumnavigation of the globe planned to take place in 2011–14, which will be multi-ethnic and involve 120 crew members and 22 crew changes, with 30 per cent of the crew from other countries.[18] To quote Nainoa Thompson from the press release on the worldwide voyage:

> We expect to see at least four major outcomes – the worldwide voyage will bring awareness of critical issues of sustainability. It will connect cultures around the world – we will learn from one another and forge a path for protecting not only what is uniquely special about Hawai'i's environment, but the Earth's. It will improve how and what we teach our children, and it will create action for change, including training new leaders prepared to make important decisions for our future.[16]

Despite all of this, Hawaiians continue to be materially marginalized. But by comparison to the recent past, they are no longer culturally marginalized and stigmatized. The Hawaiians, and Polynesians in general, are no longer confined by the limitations of their islands, and many are spreading their minds into the vastness of global space. Once again, they have their own spatial dynamics and cultural context to draw inspiration from. History has been rewritten by voyaging. There is no longer any doubt that Polynesians have deliberately set out and colonized the islands they live on, and that there may have been regular voyages between many of the larger cultural centres, though there is still no direct proof of this. However, and perhaps even more importantly, Hawaiians have become a highly influential force in the shaping of the modern Hawaiian state, as active political and cultural agents in the creation of a future Hawai'i.

NOTES

1. Breach of Trust? Native Hawaiian Homelands; A summary of the proceedings of a public forum sponsored by the Hawaiian Advisory Committee to the U.S Commission on Civil Rights. October 1980.

2. *Haole* is a Hawaiian term for foreigner. See Rohrer (2006) and Geshwender *et al.* (1988). For the issue of Hawaiian ethnicity see Okamura (2008).

3. 'Hawaiiana' comprises a selection of performing arts: chanting, weaving feather leis, and the Hula.

4. The 1900 Organic Act: http://www.capitol.hawaii.gov/hrscurrent/Vol01_Ch0001-0042F/03-ORG/ORG_0001.HTM. See http://www.hawaii-nation.org/gis/contents.html

5. http://archives.starbulletin.com/2001/12/26/news/story2.html; http://the.honoluluadvertiser.com/article/2001/Dec/27/ln/ln02a.html; http://pvs.kcc.hawaii.edu/pinkythompson.html.

6. Meaning 'the moment of becoming' or 'the space between worlds'. If subliminal means that which is below the threshold of ordinary consciousness and perception, then the liminal is the point of emergence, the threshold itself.

7. Most of the crew were of mixed backgrounds but could claim a Hawaiian heritage, which was emphasized and made increasingly important and dominant through the voyage.

8. The headings are: 'Departure, Arriving at a new place, Gifting, Sharing, Respect, Departure, Homecoming Chant, Welcome Home Lauau'.

9. In 'Wayfinding, A Pacific Odyssey', http://www.pbs.org/wayfinders/wayfinding3.html.

10. Deleuze and Guattari use the concept 'actuality' to develop Henry Bergsons' notion of the virtual, which he conceptualized as the real albeit intermediate aspects of the immenseness of material existence available to human conception (Bergson 2007). These are of two kinds: the objective virtualized (image of the) universe beyond the perception of the individual, and the subjective (image of

the) universe and its parts, constantly emerging in resonating relationship to the virtuality (or image) of the body.

11. The notion of heritage relates an often undefined understanding of an ancestral existence, and that may include whatever one desires to have it include. Thus Herb Kane has become famous in Hawai'i for portraying a (romantic) vision of voyaging as well as of other historicities that fits well with the (romantic) yearnings of a people longing to see themselves in such imagery.

12. From http://www.pbs.org/wayfinders/wayfinding3.html.

13. The technology on Western long-distance cruising yachts, such as auto-pilots, roller furlongs, GPS, generators etc, focuses on making the yacht manageable for solo sailing. As such, the yacht may be defined as a vessel that idealizes Western individuality.

14. http://pvs.kcc.hawaii.edu/aboutpvs.html.

15. http://archives.starbulletin.com/2008/03/16/news/story02.html; http://pvshawaii. squarespace.com; http://pvshawaii.squarespace.com/voyaging-news/2009/2/27/ hklea-worldwide-voyage-links.html.

16. See the press release at http://www.hokuleawwv.org/sites/default/files/ WWVrelfinal.pdf.

BIBLIOGRAPHY

Aoudè, I.G. (ed.) 1999. The ethnic studies story: politics and social movements in Hawai'i'. *Social Process in Hawai'i* 39.

Banner, S. 2005. 'Preparing to be colonised: land tenure and legal strategy in nineteenth-century Hawaii'. *Law & Society Review* 39:273–314.

Bergson, H. 2007. *Matter and Memory.* New York: Cosimo Classics.

Coast Guard Inquiry, Department of Transportation, United States Coastguard. 16732/20–78.

Daws, G. 1989 [1974]. *Shoal of Time: A History of the Hawaiian Islands.* Honolulu: University of Hawai'i Press.

Deleuze, G. 1991. *Bergsonism.* New York: Zone Books.

Edgerton, S. 1975. *The Renaissance Rediscovery of Linear Perspective.* USA: Harper and Row.

Eriksen, T.H. 2001. 'Ethnic identity, national identity and intergroup conflict. the significance of personal experience'. In *Social Identity, Intergroup Conflict, and Conflict Reduction* (eds) R.D. Ashmore, L. Jussim and D. Wilder, 42–70. Oxford: Oxford University Press.

Finney, B.R. 1963. 'New, non-armchair research'. In *Pacific Navigation and Voyaging* (ed.) B. Finney. Wellington: The Polynesian Society Inc.

Finney, B.R. 1979. *Hokule'a: The Way to Tahiti.* New York: Dodd, Mead & Company.

Finney, B.R. 1991. 'Myth, experiment, and the reinvention of Polynesian voyaging'. *American Anthropologist*, 93(2):383–404.

Finney, B.R. 1994. *Voyage of Rediscovery: A Cultural Odyssey through Polynesia*. Berkeley: University of California Press.

Finney, B.R. 2004. *Sailing in the Wake of the Ancestors: Reviving Polynesian Voyaging*. Honolulu: Bishop Museum Press.

Finney, B.R. 2007. 'Renaissance'. In *VAKA MOANA: Voyages of the Ancestors. The Discovery and Settlement of the Pacific* (ed.) K.R. Howe, 288–333. Honolulu: University of Hawai'i Press.

Fornander, Abraham 1996 [1878]. *The Ancient History of the Hawaiian People to the Times of Kamehameha I.* Honolulu: Mutual Publishing.

Fornander, Abraham 2009 [1877]. *An Account of the Polynesian Race, its Origin and Migrations*. Charleston: Bibliobazaar.

Frazer, J.G. 2000 [1922]. *The Golden Bough*. New York: Bartleby.

Friedman, J.1992. 'Myth, history and political identity'. *Cultural Anthropology* 7(2):194–210.

Frost, A. 1979. 'New geographical perspectives and the emergence of the romantic imagination'. In *Captain James Cook and His Times* (eds) R. Fisher and H. Johnston, 5–19 Seattle: University of Washington Press.

Geschwender, J.A., R. Caroll-Seguin and H. Brill 1988. 'The Portuguese and Haoles of Hawaii: implications for the origin of ethnicity'. *American Sociological Review* 53:515–27.

Gillis, J.R. 2004. *Islands of the Mind. How the Human Mind Created the Atlantic World*. New York: Palgrave Macmillan.

Gladwin, M. 1970. *East is a Big Bird: Navigation and Logic on Puluwat Atoll*. Cambridge, MA: Harvard University Press.

Hau'ofa, E. 1993. 'Our sea of islands'. In *A New Oceania, Rediscovering Our Sea of Islands* (eds) E. Waddell, V. Naidu & E. Hau'ofa, 2–16. Suva: University of the South Pacific.

Herman, R.D.K. 1999. 'The Aloha State: place names and the anti-conquest of Hawaii'. *Annals of the Association of American Geographers*. 89(1):76–102.

Holt, J.D. [1964] 1974. *On Being Hawaiian*. Honolulu: Topgallant Publishing.

Joppien, R. 1979. 'The artistic bequest of Captain Cook's voyages'. In *Captain James Cook and His Times* (eds) R. Fisher and H. Johnston, 187–210. Seattle: University of Washington Press.

Kanahele, G. 1979 *The Hawaiian Renaissance*. kapalama.ksbe.edu/archives/pvsa/primary%202/79%20kanahele/kanahele.htm.

Kapferer, B. 2006. 'Virtuality'. In *Theorizing Rituals, Volume 1: Issues, Topics, Approaches, Concepts* (eds) J. Kreinath, J. Snoek and M. Stausberg, 671–684. Leiden: Brill.

Kern, S. 2003. *The Culture of Time and Space, 1880–1918*. Cambridge, MA: Harvard University Press.

Kyselka, W. 1987. *An Ocean In Mind*. Honolulu: University of Hawai'i Press.

La Croix, J. and J. Roumasset 1990. 'The evolution of private property in nineteenth-century Hawaii'. *The Journal of Economic History* 50(4):829–52.

Lewis, G.H. 1984. 'Da Kine Sound: the function of music as social protest in the new Hawaiian renaissance'. *American Music* 2:38–52.

Linnekin, J. 1983. 'Defining tradition, variations on the Hawaiian Identity'. *American Ethnologist* 10:241–52.

McGregor, D.P. 1989. 'Ho'omau Ke Ea O Ka Lahui Hawai'i: the perpetuation of the Hawaiian People'. In *Ethnicity and Nation-building in the Pacific* (eds) M.C. Howard, 74–97. Tokyo: The United Nations University.

Miles, J.A.R. (ed.) 1984. *Public Health Progress in The Pacific. Geographical Background and Regional Development*. Helmstedt: Geo Wissenschaftliche Gesellschaft.

Nakata, B.1999. 'The Struggle of the Waiàhole-Waikàne Community Association'. *Social Process in Hawa'ii*, 39:60–74.

Okamura, J. 2008. *Ethnicity and Inequality in Hawa'ii*. Philidelphia: Temple Univesity Press.

Percy Smith, Stephenson 2010 [1921]. *Hawaiki: The Original Home of the Maori; with a Sketch of Polynesian History*. Charleston: BiblioBazar.

PVS n.d. http://www.pvs-hawaii.com/about_pvshistory.htm.

Ptolemais, C. 2000. *Geography*. Princeton, Oxford: Princeton University Press.

Rio, K. and Scott, R. 2009. Nordmenn som formet Hawai'i [Norwegians who shaped Hawai'i]. Film. Documentary film, 29 minutes. SOT Film AS, Bergen Museum.

Rohrer, J. 2006. '"Got race?" The production of haole and the distortion of indigeneity in the Rice Decision'. *The Contemporary Pacific* 18(1):1–31.

Sahlins, M. 1992. *Anahulu: The Anthropology and History of the Kingdom of Hawaii. Volume 1*. Chicago: University of Chicago Press.

Sai, K. 2007. A slippery path toward Hawaiian indigeneity. an analysis pertaining to the terminology of indigenous Hawaiian and its use and practice in Hawai'i today. Indigenous Politics Colloquium, Department of Political Science, University of Hawai'i at Manoa, January 30, 2007. http://www2.hawaii. edu/~anu/pdf/Indigeneity.pdf.

Scott, R. 2002. 'Cruising the world as a Western sea nomad'. Cand. Polit. thesis, University of Bergen.

Scott, R. 2007. 'Å posisjonere individet i en global verden'. *Norsk Antropologisk Tidsskrift* 1:46–61.

Scott, R. n.d. 'The photograph and film: cosmological roots, global dynamics and
        impact on individuality'. Forthcoming in *Human Interface between Ritual,
        Theatre and Film.* (eds) B. Kapferer and A. Hobart, Oxford, New York:
        Berghahn Books.

Sharp, A. 1957. *Ancient Voyagers in the Pacific.* Harmondsworth: Penguin Books.

Sharp, A. 1963. *Ancient Voyagers in Polynesia.* Auckland: Longman Paul.

Sharp, A. 1960. *The Discovery of the Pacific Islands.* Oxford: Clarendon Press.

Slater, D. 1997. *Consumer Culture & Modernity.* Cambridge: Polity Press.

Smith, B. 1979. 'Cook's posthumous reputation'. In *Captain James Cook and his Times*
        (eds) R. Fisher and H. Johnson, 159–89. Seattle: University of Washington
        Press.

Smith, B. 1985. *European Visions and the South Pacific 1798–1850.* New Haven: Yale
        University Press.

Terrel, J.E, T.L Hunt and C. Gosden. 1997. 'The dimensions of social life in the
        Pacific'. *Current Anthropology* 38(2):155–95.

Thanem, T. and S. Linstead. 2006. 'The trembling organisation: order, change and the
        philosophy of the virtual'. In *Deleuze and the Social* (eds) M. Fuglesang and
        B. Meier Sørensen, 39–57. Edinburgh: Edinburgh University Press.

Thompson, N. n.d. 'Finding a way: 1974–1980'. Polynesian Voyaging Society's web
        pages at: http://pvs.kcc.hawaii.edu/nainoa80tahiti.html.

Turner, V. 1969. *The Ritual Process: Structure and Anti-Structure.* Chicago: Aldine
        Publishing.

Turner, V. 1974. *Dramas Fields and Metaphors: Symbolic Action in Human Society.*
        Ithaca: Cornell University Press.

Van Gennep, A. 1960 [1909]. *The Rites of Passage.* Chicago: University of Chicago
        Press.

Wallenstein. I. 1974. *The Modern World-System: Capitalist Agriculture and the
        Origins of the European World-Economy in the Sixteenth Century.* New
        York: Academic Press.

Other references

Breach of Trust? Native Hawaiian Homelands; A summary of the proceedings of a
        public forum sponsored by the Hawaiian Advisory Committee to the U.S
        Commission on Civil Rights. October 1980.

Coast Guard Inquiry, Department of Transportation, United States Coastguard.
        16732/20–78. 11 April 1978 and various letters between the Investigating
        officer, and the PVS.

An interview with Nainoa Thompson in 'Wayfinding, a Pacific odyssey'. http://www.
        pbs.org/wayfinders/wayfinding3.html.

CHAPTER 4

Nan Madol on Pohnpei

The future of its past

✳

DAVID HANLON

Introduction

This is a prefatory essay for a larger project that, through fieldwork and archival investigation, will examine the complex, contested and colonially affected site of Nan Madol on the island of Pohnpei in the Eastern Caroline group of the larger Micronesian geographical area; a site whose past may yet inspire a future that offers local and alternative possibilities to reigning assumptions about governance, development and political stability. A consideration of Nan Madol complements this volume's focus on the vitality of cultural practices and properties, and their potential for inspiring social movements that seek to reconfigure the imbalance and inequity that characterize contemporary life in many areas of Oceania. A consideration of locally grounded responses to larger global and neocolonial processes is particularly needed for a part of the region considered by many to be near totally and fatally 'Americanized' (Gale 1979).

An archaeology of Nan Madol and it representations[1]

Nan Madol is a truly impressive site. It abuts Temwen Island and lies just off the south-eastern coast of the main island of Pohnpei in the modern-day municipality or chiefdom of Madolenihmw. There is the immediate complex of ruins at Nan Madol, and the larger area of Deleur of which Nan Madol was a part. Deleur, an older name for the core area of what became Madolenihmw, covers 18 square miles with Nan Madol as its southern boundary. Those who ruled from Nan Madol would do so through the title of Saudeleur or 'Lord of Deleur'.

Figure 1 *Nan Dauwas. Image courtesy of J. Stephen Athens, International Archaeological Institute, Inc., Honolulu, Hawai'i.*

The main complex of Nan Madol consists of 93 artificial islets and linking channels built on the reef adjoining Temwen Island.[2] Immense columns of prismatic basalt rock, quarried from various locations on the island, provided the foundations and walls for Nan Madol's islets. The individual islets varied in size, internal structural complexity and architectural style. The name Nan Madol translates as 'in the space between things', and refers most immediately to the intricate network of tidal channels and waterways which border the inner islets, and which provided a means of communication and travel for their occupants.

Local histories suggest that Nan Madol was divided into two separate sections: Madol Powe and Madol Pah. Madol Powe or 'Upper Madol' covers the north-eastern half of the complex and included priestly residences and sites associated with ritual activity. Nan Dauwas is the best known of Madol Powe's islets because of its prominent location, its impressive size and multiple construction features. Madol Pah or 'Lower Madol' is made up of islets in the south-western half of the complex that served more secular purposes. Of these, Pahn Kadira is perhaps the most notable: L-shaped, it covers an area of nearly 13,000 square meters, has 39 significant features and 98 sub-features, and is understood as the residence of the Saudeleur, the ruler of Nan Madol. Pahn Kadira is similar in construction style to Nan Dauwas, but smaller in

Figure 2 *The central burial vault at Nan Dauwas. Image courtesy of J. Stephen Athens, International Archaeological Institute, Honolulu, Hawai'i.*

scale. Archaeologists speculate that the variation in layout and architectural complexity of the islets, which includes the quantity and size of basalt prisms, may represent differences in functions, construction periods or the status of the occupants (Athens 1980; Ayres, Haun and Mauricio 1983; Bath 1984b).

Earliest human habitation of the Nan Madol area dates to about 1 AD. Drawing from ceramic-bearing deposits taken from the tidal zone under the fill of Nan Madol's artificial islets, archaeologists believe the first occupation consisted of stilt-houses of the Lapita type situated over the flat reef. Additional archaeological work indicates that the building of megalithic structures at Nan Madol began in 900 AD, and intensified during a 400-year period from 1200 to 1600 AD (Kirch 2000). This megalithic construction is associated in the island's histories with the arrival of a foreign party from Katau Peidi (or 'Downwind Katau') led by two men, Ohlosihpa and Ohlosohpa (Bernart 1977; Hadley 1981). Nan Madol, then, is a site created by people from elsewhere, whose presence and ambitions initially elicited enormous and possibly cooperative labour from the inhabitants of Pohnpei, then later tribute and ultimately resistance.

The language used to describe Nan Madol by nineteenth- and early twentieth-century observers ranged from the sensational to the near-scientific (Hanlon 1990). Early voyagers used adjectives like 'awesome', 'remarkable', 'massive', 'mysterious', 'ghostly' and 'stupendous' to characterize the site. Later accounts employed such words as 'Cyclopean' and 'megalithic'. The analogies inspired by Nan Madol also varied. Some saw a 'deserted Venice' or a 'fortified town' with well laid-out streets, while others wrote of haunted castles, sacred altars, deadly cold dungeons and abandoned courts. Comparisons were made with the ancient ruins of Egypt, Mexico, Stonehenge and the Andes. More scientific observers described Nan Madol in terms of lines, angles, prisms and geometric shapes. Later attempts at more exact representations produced somewhat different, more nearly perfect forms. Western instruments of measurement, such as the compass, the tape measure and measuring rods gave neatness, precision, regularity and symmetry to Nan Madol's rough shapes. In short, Nan Madol was measured by outlanders in ways that belied its actual layout and design. Perhaps the need to render familiar a strange complex of megalithic structures led to those simplified representations. What intrigued most early commentators on Nan Madol, however, was not only its size, but the identity of its builders. Speculation on their origins ranged from locations in Asia to South-East Asia to outer space.

At first glance, the earliest written descriptions of Nan Madol seem a collection of sensational travellers' tales, self-serving accounts by missionaries and colonial apologists, and inaccurate scientific treatises. But when seen in a larger context, they reveal Nan Madol as something far more than a complex of ruins about which outsiders innocently mused. In a sense, different groups of Euro-Americans appropriated Nan Madol to serve as a powerful symbol that justified their presence and purposes in the Pacific. In the twentieth century, those who saw degeneration and decline between Nan Madol's builders and more contemporary residents of Pohnpei Island prescribed development as a medicine for social advancement and material betterment. Outlander attempts to appropriate Nan Madol continue through a programme of cultural resource management that has gone by the name of historic preservation in the American-affiliated areas of contemporary Oceania.

The possibilities of Nan Madol as a cultural property that suggests political alternatives for future governance will need to overcome not only a century and a quarter of different colonial regimes, but the histories that those regimes have constructed about the larger area called Micronesia.[3] Much of the written history of this region is rendered through a litany of periods, beginning with first encounters, and then moving on to the Spanish,

Figure 3   *1910 map of Nan Madol, by the German ethnographer Paul Hambruch. Image courtesy of J. Stephen Athens, International Archaeological Institute, Inc., Honolulu, Hawai'i.*

Plan von Nān Mátol. Ponpe. Mātólénim. August 1910.

German, Japanese, British, Australian and American colonial periods. The deeper, pre-contact pasts receive only cursory comment, if they receive any acknowledgement at all. The temporal markers of this all-too-common kind of history are Magellan's landing at Guam in 1521 and the establishment of formal colonial rule over the Caroline Islands by Spain in 1885. The pasts of these islands prior to contact with the West are assumed to be forgotten, buried under sand and sea, and irretrievably lost. Europeans and Americans loom as the catalysts of change, and the most appropriate subjects around which to organize the more recent, accessible and documented past.

However, as intimated earlier, there exists a substantial body of transcribed and translated oral histories of Nan Madol that describe its construction, development and decline (Bernart 1977; Hadley 1981; Hambruch 1932, 1936). These are partial, often ambiguous and sometimes conflicting histories that are difficult to date or sequence, and that are referenced to individuals, places, practices and events not easily aligned with cultural memories and current language usage.[4] They reflect the particular interests, experiences and perspectives of those who told, retold and now retell them. These histories are largely gendered male in both their content and in the identity of those who narrate or have narrated them. Care needs to be taken, then, in assessing this evidence; but they are histories, nonetheless. The multiple and contested histories of this incredible site speak of the foreign identity of its builders, the system of political and religious rule established there, the assertion of that rule over Pohnpei proper, and the varying responses from different areas of the island that included a complex mix of acquiescence, adaptation, appropriation and resistance.

Nan Madol's relationship to the larger island of Pohnpei certainly varied. Local histories suggest that Nan Madol's founders were a foreign people who eventually intermarried with Pohnpeians in the Deleur area. In what is today the chiefdom and municipality of Kiti on the island's western side, there is Sapwtakai, a site whose layout and structure mimic those of Nan Madol but on a smaller scale (Bath 1984a). Whether Sapwtakai was a complex in alliance with Nan Madol remains unclear. Again, histories of Nan Madol suggest increasing demands and requirements imposed upon the island from Nan Madol (Bernart 1977; Hadley 1981; Hambruch 1936; Hanlon 1988).

The collapse of the Saudeleur's rule at Nan Madol involved invaders from a place called Katau. They were led by Isohkelekel, the son of the Pohnpeian thunder god Nahnsapwe and a Katauan woman.[5] Assisted by local allies, this party of warriors engaged the Saudeleur's forces and their Pohnpeian supporters. The ruling clan of Madolenihmw, the Dipwenpahnmei, traces its lineage from Nan Madol through the new form of chiefly rule established by Isohkelekel, the conqueror of Nan Madol, who took the title of *nahnmwarki*.

Figure 4 *An aerial view of Nan Madol. Image courtesy of J. Stephen Athens, International Archaeological Institute, Inc., Honolulu, Hawai'i.*

For Madolenihmw and the Dipwenpahnmei, then, the ties to Nan Madol are particularly deep.

The adoption of the *nahnmwarki* system of chiefly rule by other, later chiefdoms also link those parts of the island to Nan Madol and its history. One generalization for a project that focuses on studies of cultural heritage and political innovation in the area called Micronesia concerns the differential relationships to an object, a place or a practice within a set group of people. As noted in the introductory chapter to this volume, the term 'invention of tradition' pales against the need for an historical as well as ethnographic sensibility to the study of cultural heritage as it relates to political innovation and social movements (see also Jolly 1992).

Later histories, changing demographics and affected landscapes

In the time Nan Madol has endured as a cultural property, perhaps even a cultural force, much has happened. Since the abandonment of Nan Madol sometime in the late eighteenth or early nineteenth century (Campbell 1836), the island of Pohnpei has experienced epidemics, consequent depopulation, four different colonial regimes, localized rebellions against two of those regimes, world war, modernization, development and inclusion in the Federated States of Micronesia (FSM), a self-governing entity in free association with the United States.

Movement, migration and forced relocation would be features of colonial times (Hezel 1995, 2001). The typhoon of 1905 led the German colonial government to transport displaced Mortlockese Islanders to the chiefdom of Sokehs on Pohnpei; people from the relatively nearby atolls and islands of Sapwuahfik, Mwoakilloa, Nukuoro, Pingelap and Kapingamarangi would make their way to Pohnpei in the immediate decades after the Second World War in search of education, opportunity and the physical and material resources of an island that was now serving again as the regional administrative centre for another colonial power. According to the 2000 FSM census, the total population of Pohnpei Island is 31,540, of which 25,737, or roughly 82 per cent, identify themselves as ethnically Pohnpeian. The balance of the island's population consists of people from the other islands within Pohnpei State and from the other states of the Federated States of Micronesia. There are also small expatriate populations from the larger Pacific region, and from Asia and North America, whose members work for the FSM government, foreign embassies, regional and international organizations, the local college and outside business interests. Not surprisingly, Pohnpei's physical and material landscapes have changed dramatically in recent decades.

The word 'state' figures prominently in any discussion of Pohnpei's present and the ways in which that present is linked to its past. Though Pohnpei is one of the four states that make up the Federated States of Micronesia, its relationship to the FSM national government has been a strained one. The island did not prove particularly gracious in offering a home to the national government (Hanlon and Eperiam 1988). Jobs, improved incomes and the development of local infrastructure did not quell concerns about increased numbers of non-Pohnpeians on the island. Pohnpei's local constitutional ban (1984) on the ownership of land by non-Pohnpeians conflicted with provisions in the national constitution that allow FSM citizens to own land in any of the four states.

Concerns over states' rights and worries about the disturbance to the constitutionally based, representational balance in the FSM Congress posed by the possible, but as yet unrealized, recognition of a fifth and Chuukese state bothered elected representatives of the other three FSM states. There was, too, the 1990 constitutional convention and the variety of issues it raised regarding states' power, the distribution of national revenues, the roles of traditional chiefs and procedures for secession (Petersen 1994). A second constitutional convention in 2001 addressed many of the same issues, but again with none of the offered amendments to the existing constitution being approved in a national referendum. Interestingly, the government of the FSM is headquartered at Palikir in the north-western municipality or chiefdom of Sokehs, near the site of a large rock mound that local histories identify as having originally been a pile of chicken manure left behind by the Saudeleur's rooster during one of its reconnaissance tours around the island. This historical geography metaphorically reflects the sentiments of some Pohnpeians who regard the FSM government as foreign, intrusive and disrespectful.

The stakes for different states in the preservation of Nan Madol

The FSM and Pohnpei state governments clash over numerous jurisdictional issues, including historic preservation or cultural resource management programmes. There has been competition between the FSM and Pohnpei State historic preservation offices over administrative authority for Nan Madol. This jurisdictional conflict is complicated further by continuing claims to Nan Madol from the *nahnmwarki*, or paramount chief, of Madolenihmw, and from a local family on Temwen Island who claim agricultural usage rights over Nan Madol on the basis of a deed issued by the German colonial government in the early twentieth century.[6] There is another actor, another set of states in play here – the United States of America – to which Pohnpei and the rest of the FSM are affiliated and allied through a compact of free association. In what some might understand as the ultimate colonial act, Nan Madol is listed on the United States National Register of Historic Places (http://www.nps.gov/history/nr/about.htm). There is a history here worth noting that underscores Guido Pigliasco's cautions in this collection of essays about the dangers resulting from the legal codification of culture by state and metropolitan agencies.

The United States administered Micronesia – Kiribati and Nauru excepted – as the UN Trust Territory of the Pacific Islands from 1947 until 1986. In 1974, the US Congress amended the National Historic Preservation Act of 1966 to include the Trust Territory as a 'state' for purposes of the act (King 2006). This allowed the Trust Territory to receive grants from the US National Park Service that administered the historic preservation programme. The amendment stipulated that actions undertaken, assisted or permitted by the United States government in the Trust Territory are subject to section 106 of the National Historic Preservation Act. Section 106 requires any US government-supported project to be reviewed and assessed to ensure that there will be no harm done to historic properties eligible for inclusion on the National Register. Such a review includes the identification of historic properties, an assessment of the project's effects upon them, and the issuance of a clearance or a directive on the mitigation of determined harmful effects.

The 1974 ruling came at an auspicious time, when the Trust Territory government was about to initiate a major improvement programme to be undertaken by the US Navy and the Army Corps of Engineers. Much of the archaeological research at Nan Madol during the late 1970s and 1980s was contracted with funds provided to meet the requirements of the 1974 amendment to the National Historic Preservation Act. What plagued most efforts during the start up of the programme was a basic incompatibility between what the National Park Service valued and what was important to most Micronesians. Second World War structures and sites, for example, hold powerful significance for many Americans, given the United States' extensive involvement in the Pacific theatre. For the people on whose lands and seas the war was fought, the meanings and memories are decidedly different (Poyer 1992).

Reflecting back on his efforts to establish a US-funded historic preservation programme in the Trust Territory while on assignment from the US National Park Service's Interagency Archaeological Services Division, Thomas King wrote in November 2006 that Micronesians are profoundly interested in their cultural properties, but not as esoteric monuments, tourist sites or national monuments trumpeted by politicians, archaeologists, historians and cultural resource management specialists. These properties hold tremendous significance because of their on-going place in people's daily lives, and in their beliefs about themselves, their ancestors and their environment. King recognized that cultural properties, places, landscapes, seascapes and objects do not lie outside of the rest of culture: they are part of a complex of daily activities, spiritual beliefs and esoteric knowledge that is at once rooted in the past but not adverse to change. In short, they hold a place in an ongoing cultural life that helps inform and maintain a distinct and definable identity. King's observation resonates strongly with the words of Willie Bongmatur on the importance of locality that open the first chapter of this volume.

The establishment of the FSM government in free association with the United States has not meant an independent or more culturally sensitive programme of historic preservation (O'Neill and Spennemann 2006). While there is now a FSM national historic preservation programme, state offices and supporting legislation, most funding continues to come from Historic Preservation Fund grants provided by the US National Park Service, as approved and authorized by the Compact of Free Association with the United States. The funds are subject to the terms and conditions of approval outlined by the afore-mentioned 1966 legislation and its 1974 amendment for Micronesia. As King noted, the result is an incredible amount of frustration with bureaucratic requirements that are seemingly endless, unnecessarily complex and time consuming, and that direct precious resources away from any substantive, locally meaningful cultural heritage work. Donor-imposed rules for project selection, management and reporting mean more bureaucracy than preservation. Preservation programmes in the FSM are largely dependent on Historic Preservation Fund grants. Such dependency means that this limited funding is allocated to projects that are acceptable to external donors. Historic preservation in the FSM and elsewhere in Micronesia is thus driven by the preferences of the United States government as articulated and administered by its National Park Service.

Nan Madol stands as an exception to this pattern, but not for the better. While Pohnpei is now one of the Federated States of Micronesia, Nan Madol, as noted earlier, has been placed on the US National Register of Historic Places and designated a National Historic Landmark. This occurred back in December of 1974. In the interests of clarity, the National Register of Historic Places is administered by the US National Park Service within the Department of the Interior and was authorized by the National Historic Preservation Act of 1966. Its purpose is 'to coordinate and support public and private efforts to identify, evaluate, and preserve historic and archaeological resources' (http://www.nps. gov/history/nr/about.htm). Properties listed in the Register include districts, sites, buildings, structures and objects that are significant in American history, architecture, archaeology, engineering and culture. Of the 80,000 listings that make up the National Register, over 2,400 are designated as National Historic Landmarks by the Secretary of the Interior because of their importance to all Americans. Nan Madol is one of those landmarks designated as important to all Americans, whether or not they know it. This fact relates to my earlier point about the continued appropriation of Nan Madol by external forces, and for purposes that justify the presence and activities of those forces. In short, the externally determined need for the preservation of Nan Madol requires its formal colonization. This is an old story in the Pacific.

Nan Madol's more recent past

Nan Madol has not been easily or totally subdued, however. It has continued to exert a presence and to impact events on Pohnpei even after its abandonment. The 1910 collapse of one of the corners of Pahn Kadira built by the master stoneworker Kideumanien of Sokehs is said to have foreshadowed the collapse of the chiefdom of Sokehs, as a consequence of its revolt against German colonial authority in that same year (Ehrlich 1978; Hadley 1981). The failed revolt led to the execution of fourteen of its leaders and the banishment to Palau of its surviving 426 residents. The disturbance of a chiefly burial site at Pehi en Kitel by the German governor Viktor Berg in 1907 is said to have led to his death soon after (Hadley 1981).

In more recent decades, Nan Madol has proven a site of contestation between Pohnpeians and those who colonized them and, in the process, sought to define their cultural heritage and the ways in which its preservation might be effected. In 1950, J.R. Bass, the Civil Administrator for the Trust Territory of the Pacific Islands acting on behalf of the High Commissioner, issued a proclamation designating all historical remains and works from pre-contact times to be the property of the people of the Trust Territory as a whole.[7] As such, Nan Madol was declared to be under the jurisdiction of the Trust Territory government. With a territory-wide law code yet to be enacted, immediate responsibility for the preservation and protection of pre-contact sites and artefacts fell to the district administrator and the appropriate local municipal government.[8] The district administrator for Pohnpei, called 'Ponape' for most of the Trust Territory period, thus assumed administrative responsibility for the site and was assisted in his supervisory duties by the Madolenihmw municipal council. Time would pass, but the proclamation did not go unchallenged. In 1968, then Nahnmwarki of Madolenihmw, Samuel Hadley, vigorously protested the Trust Territory government's claim and solicited the assistance of the recently formed Congress of Micronesia in reasserting what he and many others believed to be his rightful title to jurisdiction over Nan Madol.

That same year, a committee of Pohnpeians appointed by Deputy High Commissioner Martin Mangan and drawn largely from the Ponape District Legislature and Madolenihmw municipality held a series of public meetings to take testimony from all parties concerned. The committee issued a final report that underscored the historical significance of Nan Madol as the place 'where Ponapean customs originated'.[9] Members were unanimous in their recommendations that the right of ownership to Nan Madol be vested solely with the Nahnmwarki of Madolenihmw and that the Trust Territory government relinquish all claims to jurisdiction over the site. Officials at Trust Territory headquarters on Saipan and in the district office on Pohnpei sought a compromise that designated Nan Madol as a Micronesian heritage site under the joint trusteeship of the High Commissioner and the Nahnmwarki of Madolenihmw. The effort at compromise proved short lived. The Trust Territory Attorney General's Office reviewed the proposed compromise and found it in violation of established legal practice that held Nan Madol to be a part of unclaimed public land previously administered by the German and Japanese colonial administrations. Jurisdiction over all public land on Pohnpei and in the other five administrative districts of the Trust Territory, argued the Attorney General's office, had legally passed to the United States as a result of the 1947 United Nations Trusteeship Agreement.[10] Jurisdictional authority over Nan Madol, wrote the authors of the opinion, could not be shared or transferred.

The Nahnmwarki of Madolenihmw also opposed any compromise over Nan Madol. In a letter to High Commissioner Edward Johnston dated 18 September 1973, Hadley stated his objection to an aerial survey of Nan Madol then being requested as part of a larger project to accelerate the mapping of the island, and facilitate related programmes involving homesteading and infrastructure development.[11] The Nahnmwarki wrote that no aerial survey or any other government-sponsored activity could take place until fundamental questions over the ownership of Nan Madol were resolved. He denied all claims of ownership or jurisdiction by the Trust Territory government, and added that Nan Madol had been entrusted to the holders of the title of *nahnmwarki*, who had exercised control over the site for centuries on behalf of their people. Things did not end there, however. Disputes over the jurisdiction of Nan Madol persisted through the final decades of the Trust Territory, and have been complicated of late by preservation laws enacted as part of the law code of the Federated States of Micronesia. Its legal status remains unresolved, and may become even more contested pending the outcome of a possible application by the FSM's National Archives and Cultural and Historic Preservation Office to have UNESCO declare Nan Madol a World Heritage site.

Pohnpeians also proved skilled at making use of other institutional resources and practices. The 1974 amendment to the National Historic Preservation Act that allowed for the inclusion of the Trust Territory under the Act authorized the creation of local historic preservation committees. The Ponape District Historic Preservation Committee proved quite effective in representing local interests in matters involving the protection and preservation of historical properties and objects. The committee, for example, protested promptly any and all unauthorized visits to Nan Madol, and monitored all reports of tourist development plans for the site.[12]

In 1980, the committee entered into a then seventeen-year-old dispute concerning the return of artefacts removed from Nan Madol in 1963 by a three-member team of archaeologists and anthropologists sent by the Smithsonian Institution in Washington, D.C. Working through the Trust Territory Historic Preservation Office, the committee insisted on the long overdue return of the artefacts in several written communications to Smithsonian officials.[13] While the Smithsonian rejected all requests on the grounds of the minimal quantity and significance of the artefacts, yet-to-be-performed analyses and contractual obligations to the researchers,[14] the Ponape State Historic Preservation Committee proved persistent and increasingly adamant in its insistence that the artefacts be returned. As with the dispute over jurisdiction and ownership of Nan Madol, efforts to win the repatriation of artefacts taken from the site in 1963 have gone unresolved. Nonetheless, Pohnpeian efforts to reclaim Nan Madol by using the institutional procedures available to them can be likened to more aggressive forms of the political protocols and diplomatic etiquette that Rosita Henry (this volume) writes about in her chapter on Aboriginal and Torres Islander dance performances in Australia.

Nan Madol as a cultural force for an alternative future

The questions to which the preceding pages have been a preface are these: how might Nan Madol and its past inspire alternative imaginings or possibilities for Pohnpei's future? More particularly, and in line with the themes of this volume, how might Nan Madol as a historically significant cultural property promote expanded perceptions of cultural heritage and the emergence of new political forms in response to the challenges of the global political economy? Some have argued that Nan Madol is best understood as a centre of religious power and ritual that exerted considerable, sometimes forceful, influence over the life of the island (Kirch 2000); others see in Pohnpei's relationship to Nan Madol the continuity of larger historical and cultural patterns involving cultural borrowing and creative adaptation (Hanlon 1988). Paul Rainbird (2004) argues that Nan Madol attests to the link between genealogy and power. Much of the archaeological work on Pohnpei assumes Nan Madol to be the product of an evolutionary trend toward political centralization on the island (Bath and Athens 1990). Glenn Peterson (1990), however, argues that for contemporary Pohnpeians, Nan Madol exists as a symbol that warns against foreign domination and centralized control, and urges instead the search for good local government.

Pohnpeians have always guarded their autonomy against foreign encroachment. They fought Spanish incursion on several occasions between 1887 and 1899, and remain the only Oceanic people to have forcefully driven a European colonizer from their land and into the surrounding sea. German efforts to develop the island economically by reforming its land-tenure system, and thus undermining the basis of chiefly power and privilege, contributed to the rebellion of the chiefdom of Sokehs in 1910. Following the suppression of the rebellion, there developed at least three secret societies on the island that the German administration accused of promoting sedition (Hezel 1995:141). The Typhoon Society and the United States Company were two whose members, it was said, engaged in ritual practices such as scarification, the eating of raw lizards and sexual promiscuity. The German administration, moved quickly against these societies: twenty-one of their members were arrested and exiled to New Guinea. These instances of resistance, however, were not island-wide in character, but rather sectional. Their study should not be romanticized. As Marshall Sahlins (2008) has reminded us, the interplay between autochthony and alterity is always a complex and fraught engagement, and can result in unexpected turns and twists. Still, there is a history here of cultural persistence and survival that requires recognition.

In more recent times, Pohnpeians have resorted to less violent means to protect their island and preserve their identity. They have become more unified in their appropriation of foreign tools and methods as a way to deflect, or at least manage as best they can, those forces that seek to dominate them. Pohnpeians have certainly proven adept at using laws, institutional resources and even bureaucratic processes to protect Nan Madol from those who seek either to exploit it or to protect it through their own very particular culturally informed understandings of heritage and preservation. In so doing, they remind us of the intimate triadic relationship involving history, identity and autonomy. If Nan Madol is ultimately the place 'where Ponapean customs originated', then an understanding of its importance to the island's future as well as its past is crucial. Pohnpeians' 1983 vote against the Compact of Free Association with the United States, their unease as a citizens of the Federated States of Micronesia and their recurrent talk of secession from the FSM all suggest a society that continues to look for its own way in the context of lessons learned from its past. In this sense, the futures of Nan Madol and the island of Pohnpei are as inextricably linked as their pasts.

As indicated earlier, Pohnpeians' relationships to Nan Madol differ along clan, sectional and gendered lines. Most Pohnpeians, however, continue to regard Nan Madol with a great deal of respect, reverence and silence. Nan Madol is not explicitly referenced in dialogues over governance or negotiations between the FSM and US governments. It is nonetheless there; it persists and endures. In understanding the future of its past, we might consider Nan Madol not as a set of ruins but as an active, sacred site that lives on in the active consciousness of modern-day Pohnpeians. If Petersen is correct, Nan Madol's history, among other lessons, offers a cautionary tale about the need for local autonomy and control in the areas of government and development. In short, Nan Madol, as it has in the past, may well inspire a reconfiguration of political arrangements and alliances, as Pohnpeians persist as a people in an increasingly globalized but still neo-colonial world marked by the rapid movement and flow of ideas, technologies and material goods.

NOTES

1. This section borrows from previously presented work. Please see David Hanlon, 'Histories of the before: Lelu, Nan Madol, and deep time'. In *Changing Contexts – Shifting Meanings; Transformations of Cultural Traditions in Oceania* (ed.) Elfriede Herman, Honolulu: University of Hawai'i Press, forthcoming.

2. This archaeological survey and description of the Nan Madol area draws from the works of Athens 1980, 1981, 1990, 1995; Ayres 1990; Ayres and Haun 1985; Ayres, Haun and Mauricio 1983; Bryson 1989; Hambruch 1932 and 1936; Kirch 2000 and Rainbird 2004.

3. See, for example, Hezel 1983.

4. Glenn Petersen (1990) critiques these histories in his *Lost in the Weeds: Theme and Variation in Pohnpei Political Mythology*.

5. There is considerable debate about the exact location and identity of Katau. Fischer, Risenberg and Whiting (1977) identify Katau with the island of Kosrae in the histories of Nan Madol's downfall. Goodenough (1986) argues that Katau or Kachaw is a generic, pan-Micronesian term that refers to the other or sky world, and is not the name of any specific island or place.

6. A history of this continuing conflict can be found in 'Correspondence, Reports and Documents Relative to the Ownership, Historical Background, Maintenance and Preservation of Nan Madol, Madolenihmw, Pohnpei , German Deed Included, 1967–1981', United States Trust Territory of the Pacific Islands Archives (TTA), reel no. 2101, frame no. 0149. A copy of this microfilmed archive is housed with the University of Hawai'i at Mānoa's Hamilton Library.

7. A copy of this two-page proclamation can be found in TTA, reel no. 2101, frame no. 0149.

8. During the Trust Territory period, the different islands and island groups were divided for administrative purposes into six districts: the Marianas, the Marshalls, Palau, Ponape (Pohnpei), Truk (Chuuk), and Yap. Each district was further divided into municipalities that were usually based on local divisions and boundaries. On Pohnpei, these divisions mirrored the five separate chiefdoms, with separate municipalities also established for the six outer islands included in the district.

9. See Special Nan Madol Committee, 'Report and Recommendations on the Legal Status and Future Disposition of Nan Madol', 2 August 1968, TTA, reel no. 0445, frame no. 0115.

10. See Stanton and Miyamoto to Kurtz, Attorney General's Opinion 35–71, 2 September 1971, TTA, reel no. 2101, frame no. 0149.

11. See Hadley to Johnston, 10 September 1973, TTA, reel no. 2101, frame no. 0149.

12. See letters from Kostka to King, 10 March 1980; Cordy to Nakazawa, 4 April 1980; and King to Iriarte, 17 April 1980, contained in 'Non Contract Correspondence Related to Restoration of Nan Madol. Much Historical Data, 1967–1982' TTA, reel no. 5033, item no. 0141.

13. See Iriarte and Kostka to Nakayama, 2 October 1980; Iriarte and Kostka to Santos, 2 October 1980; Russell to Ripley, 29 October 1980; King to Pettet, 3 December 1980, TTA, reel no. 2010, item no. 0149.

14. Ubelaker to Ayres, 4 May 1981, TTA, reel no. 2101, frame no. 0149.

Bibliography

Athens, J.S. 1980. *Archaeological Investigations at Nan Madol: Islet Maps and Artifacts.* Guam: Pacific Studies Institute.

Athens, J.S. 1981. *The Discovery and Archaeological Investigations of Nan Madol, Ponape, Eastern Caroline Islands: An Annotated Bibliography.* Revised ed. Micronesian Archaeological Survey Report 3. Saipan: Trust Territory Historic Preservation Office, Saipan.

Athens, J.S. 1990. 'Nan Madol pottery'. In *Recent Advances in Micronesian Archaeology* (ed.) R.L. Hunter-Anderson, 17–32. A Special Issue of *Micronesica*. Supplement no. 2. Mangilao: University of Guam Press.

Athens, J.S. 1995. *Landscape Archaeology: Prehistoric Settlement, Subsistence, and Environment of Kosrae, Eastern Caroline Islands, Micronesia. Archaeological Data Recovery Investigations for the Kosrae Wastewater Project.* Honolulu: International Archaeological Research Institute, Inc.

Ayres, W.S. 1990. 'Pohnpei's position in eastern Micronesian Prehistory'. In *Recent Advances in Micronesian Archaeology* (ed.) R.L. Hunter-Anderson, 187–212. A Special Issue of *Micronesica.* Supplement no. 2. Mangilao: University of Guam Press.

Ayres, W.S. and Alan E. Haun. 1985. 'Archaeological perspectives on food production in eastern Micronesia'. In *Prehistoric Intensive Agriculture in the Tropics* (ed.) I.S. Farrington, 455–73. B.A.R. International Series 232. Oxford: British Archaeological Reports.

Ayres, W.S., A.E. Haun and Rufino Mauricio. 1983. *Nan Madol Archaeology: 1981 Survey and Excavations*. Report submitted by the Pacific Studies Institute, Guam, to the Historic Preservation Committee, Ponape State, Federated States of Micronesia, and the Historic Preservation Program, Trust Territory of the Pacific Islands, Saipan.

Bath, J.E. 1984a. *Sapwtakai: Archaeologoical Survey and Testing*. Micronesian Archaeology Survey Report 14. Saipan: Trust Territory Historic Preservation Committee.

Bath, J.E. 1984b. 'A Tale of Two Cities: An Evaluation of Political Evolution in the Eastern Caroline Islands of Micronesia Since A.D. 1000'. Ph.D. dissertation, University of Hawai'i at Manoa.

Bath, J.E. and J. Stephen Athens. 1990. 'Prehistoric social complexity on Pohnpei: the *Saudeleur* to *Nahnmwarki* transformation'. In *Recent Advances in Micronesian Archaeology* (ed.) R.E. Hunter-Anderson, 275–290. A Special Issue of *Micronesica*. Supplement no. 2. Mangilao: University of Guam Press.

Bernart, L. 1977. *The Book of Luelen*. (eds and trans.) J.L. Fischer, S.H. Riesenberg, and M.G. Whiting. Pacific History Series 8. Honolulu: University Press of Hawai'i.

Bryson, R.U. 1989. 'Ceramics and spatial archaeology at Nan Madol, Pohnpei'. Ph.D. dissertation, University of Oregon.

Campbell, Dr. 1836. 'Island of Ascension'. *The Colonist* (New South Wales) 2(78):22 June 1836; reprinted in R.G. Ward (ed.) 1967, *American Activities in the Central Pacific, 1790–1870*:126–39.

Ehrlich, P.M. 1978. 'These are the clothes of men: "Ponape Island and German colonial rule, 1899–1914"'. Ph.D. dissertation, State University of New York at Stony Brook.

Federated States of Micronesia Government. 2002. *The 2000 Federated States of Micronesia Census of Population and Housing. Pohnpei State Census Report*. Pohnpei Branch Statistics Office, Division of Statistics, Department of Economic Affairs, Kolonia, Pohnpei.

Fischer, J.L., S.H. Riesenberg and M.G. Whiting, (eds and trans.) 1977. *Annotations to the Book of Luelen*. Pacific History Series 9. Honolulu: University Press of Hawai'i.

Gale, R. 1979. *The Americanization of Micronesia: A Study in the Consolidation of U.S. Rule in the Pacific*. Washington, DC: University Press of America,

Goodenough, W.H. 1986. 'Sky word and this world: the place of Kachaw in Micronesian cosmology'. *American Anthropologist* 88:551–68.

Hadley, M. 1981. 'A history of Nan Madol'. Manuscript translated and edited by P.M. Ehrlich. Copy in author's possession.

Hambruch, P. 1932. *Ponape. Ergebnisse der Südsee Expedition, 1908–1910.* Vol. 1.
    G. Thilenius (ed.), II, Ethnographie, B, Mikronesien, Bd. 7. Hamburg:
    Friederchsen, DeGruyter und Co.

Hambruch, P. 1936. *Ponape. Ergebnisse der Südsee Expedition,1908–1910.* Vol. 3.
    G. Thilenius, ed., II, Ethnographie, B, Mikronesien, Bd. 7. Hamburg:
    Friederchsen, DeGruyter und Co.

Hanlon, D. 1988. *Upon a Stone Altar: A History of the Island of Pohnpei to 1890.*
    Pacific Islands Monograph Series 5. Honolulu: University of Hawai'i Press.

Hanlon, D. 1990. '"The pleasure of speculation and conjecture": early Euro-American
    visions of Nan Madol and their relevance to post-modern archaeological
    investigations'. In *Recent Advances in Micronesian Archaeology* (ed.) R.L
    Hunter-Anderson, 99–116. A Special Issue of *Micronesica.* Supplement
    no. 2. Mangilao: University of Guam Press.

Hanlon, D. In press. 'Histories of the before: Lelu, Nan Madol, and deep time'. In
    *Changing Contexts – Shifting Meanings: Transformations of Cultural
    Traditions in Oceania* (ed.) E. Hermann. Honolulu: University of Hawai'i
    Press.

Hanlon, D.L. and W. Eperiam. 1988. 'The Federated States of Micronesia: unifying
    the remnants'. In *Micronesian Politics.* Suva: Institute of Pacific Studies of
    the University of the South Pacific.

Hezel, F.X. 1983. *The First Taint of Civilization: A History of the Caroline and
    Marshall Islands in Pre-Colonial Days, 1521–1885.* Pacific Islands
    Monograph Series 1. Honolulu: University of Hawai'i Press.

Hezel, F.X. 1995. *Strangers in Their Own Land: A Century of Colonial Rule in the
    Caroline and Marshall Islands.* Pacific Islands Monograph Series 13.
    Honolulu: University of Hawai'i Press.

Hezel, F.X. 2001. *The New Shape of Old Cultures: A Half Century of Social Change in
    Micronesia.* Honolulu: University of Hawai'i Press.

Jolly, M. 1992. 'Specters of inauthenticity'. *The Contemporary Pacific* 4(2):49–72.

King, T.F. 2006. 'How Micronesia changed the U.S. Historic Preservation Program
    and the importance of keeping it from changing back'. *Micronesian Journal
    of the Humanities and Social Sciences* 5(1/2):505–16.

Kirch, P.V. 2000. *On the Road of the Winds: An Archaeological History of the Pacific
    Islands before European Contact.* Berkeley: University of California Press.

O'Neill, J.G. and D.H.R. Spennemann. 2006. 'A review of historic preservation
    funding in Micronesia, 1986–2003'. *Micronesian Journal of the Humanities
    and Social Sciences* 5(1/2):580–91.

Petersen, G. 1990. *Lost in the Weeds: Theme and Variation in Pohnpei Political
    Mythology.* Occasional Paper 35. Honolulu: Center for Pacific Islands
    Studies, University of Hawai'i at Manoa.

Petersen, G. 1994. 'The Federated States of Micronesia's 1990 Constitutional
        Convention: calm before the storm?' *The Contemporary Pacific* 6(2):337–69.

Pohnpei (State) Government. 1984. *The Constitution of Pohnpei*. Copy in Hamilton
        Library, University of Hawai'i at Manoa.

Poyer, L. 1992. 'Defining history across cultures: insider and outsider contrasts'. *Isla:
        A Journal of Micronesian Studies* 1(1):73–89.

Rainbird, P. 2004. *The Archaeology of Micronesia*. Cambridge World Archaeology
        Series. Cambridge: Cambridge University Press.

Sahlins, M. 2008. 'Autochthony and alterity: Malayo-Polynesian cosmographies of
        the marvelous'. Raymond Firth Memorial Lecture. 7th Conference of the
        European Society for Oceanists. Universita di Verona, Italy. 10–12 July.

United States. Department of the Interior, National Park Service. "Welcome to the
        National Register of Historic Places." http://www.nps.gov/history/nr/about.
        htm.

United States. Trust Territory of the Pacific Islands Archives. Microfilmed Records of
        the Trust Territory Government, 1952–1986. Honolulu, Hamilton Library
        at the University of Hawai` at Manoa.

CHAPTER 5

From *kastam* to *kalsa*?

Leadership, cultural heritage and modernization
in Manus Province, Papua New Guinea[1]

✳

STEFFEN DALSGAARD AND TON OTTO

Changes in leadership practices often provide a good indication of changing value orientations in a society. Aspiring leaders often wish to explore new resources of power and authority, including concepts of culture and heritage, and through their practice they may themselves become important agents of change. In this chapter we focus on the actions of one particular man in order to investigate how concepts of tradition are in a process of change in Manus Province, Papua New Guinea: from primarily referring to exchangeable intellectual property (*kastam* in Manus Tok Pisin) to articulating the inalienable property that defines group identity (cultural heritage or *kalsa*).

Soanin Kilangit, from Baluan Island, is not of *lapan* birth (traditional inheritable leadership status), but over a span of 20 years he has become a significant leader in Baluan affairs. Today he personifies innovations in political practice, changes in conceptualizations of culture, and transformations of both traditional and modern forms of leadership. Soanin has headed a Port Moresby based dancing group of Baluan emigrants. As a returning migrant he has initiated one of the largest culture shows in living Baluan memory; and he contested the Manus Open Seat in the 2007 Parliamentary Election and the election for the Balopa[2] Local Level Government presidency in 2008. By positioning himself in a discourse about *kalsa* rather than *kastam*, he fuels a transformation of local concepts of traditional practices such as dancing, singing and canoe making: from being part of exchange relations between persons and descent groups, these traditional practices become 'heritage' to which every Baluan person has rights of access.

In this chapter, we show how Soanin presents 'Baluan culture' as a unifying whole that can attract resources and processes of modernization from the outside – from other Manus groups, the government, tourists and even the visiting anthropologists. However, while promoting *kalsa* he also gets caught in the demands from the sphere of *kastam*, showing how these different concepts refer to different domains of action and valuation. The case of Soanin Kilangit contributes to the other discussions in this volume by showing how (political) struggles can be intrinsic to defining culture as heritage. Such a struggle is here disclosed in a framework of conflicting elite and grassroots aspirations to status as well as self-determination. Heritage (*kalsa*) becomes a resource for political agency, democratic processes and self-reliance, as *kastam* has been in the past (see M. Scott, this volume).

Kastam and *kalsa*

Within the last few decades, 'cultural heritage' has become a hotly debated topic in scholarly circles (e.g. Cole 1985; Handler 1988; Linnekin and Poyer 1990; Kirshenblatt-Gimblett 1998; Lowenthal 1998; Olwig 1999; Rowlands 2002; Brown 2003; Kaneff and King 2004; Harrison 2006; Burton 2007; Bunten 2008). In this guise, however, the relevance of the application of the concept itself has not always been questioned, and in particular in relation to Melanesian discussions of tradition and culture, it has mostly been applied as an 'etic' rather than 'emic' concept without enquiry into if, and in that case how, 'heritage' may differ from these local conceptions. For instance, the concept of *kastam* has in a Baluan and Manus context referred on the one hand to actual traditional ceremonies as *kastam* work (in Baluan language *puron*), and on the other hand more generally to a moral sphere of tradition understood as 'the way of the ancestors' (Otto 1991, 1992b). These local conceptualizations have to a degree overlapped with notions of 'culture' or 'heritage', but they have foremost implied an emphasis on exchange, mutuality and relationality, which is also what has been noted about other local conceptualizations of tradition in PNG (e.g. Mosko 2002; Leach 2003).

A different group of scholars have generally taken similar concepts of *kastam* to refer to an approximation of a conceptualization of 'culture' or 'heritage' sponsored by elites (e.g. Babadzan 1988; Keesing 1989) even if that conceptualization of traditional practices was regarded primarily as an inauthentic 'invention' rather than a 'true connection' to the past (see Babadzan 1988; Hanson 1989; Jolly 1992). That there are overlaps and contrasts between understandings of *kastam* and other similar concepts is not new. Yet, it is only recently that this understanding has been objectified in Baluan as a category in its own terms, when people like Soanin Kilangit have begun to ascribe to traditional cultural practices the label of being 'culture' or 'heritage', expressed with the Tok Pisin word *kalsa*. Having two terms within the broad field of cultural concepts opens the potential for articulating differences, something we will explore in this chapter.

Notions of *kastam* have historically developed in Melanesian societies in contrast to other concepts referring to the morality of social practices (Tonkinson 1982, 1993; Foster 1995b). Otto (1991, 1992a, in press) details the origin of *kastam* in Manus in relation to the emerging semantic domains of *gavman* (modern political system and development) and *lotu* (church). The bifurcation of notions of tradition into *kastam* and *kalsa* is, as mentioned, very recent, and is an example of the way the development of cultural traditions is closely linked to local agency that is both facilitating and facilitated by these traditions (Otto and Pedersen 2005). Let us map out the differences between the Baluan 'grassroots' conceptualizations of *kastam* and *kalsa* as they have become apparent during the past few years. Implied in the contemporary notion of *kastam*[3] is that traditional practices are perceived as transactable 'objects', owned by the patrilineal descent groups, but controlled by the *lapan* (traditional leader) of the group in question. Baluan examples could comprise particular ceremonial content, such as the use of a specific 'design', or could be knowledge of how to craft a particular item in a specific way. The way these practices have come into the possession of a descent group is acknowledged, but they are not regarded as created by it. Typically they are acquired at some stage, and then come to be a defining part of the group's identity. Access to the use of such traditional practices can be given to other groups or single persons in exchange, or they may be 'stolen', as a practice that could be 'mimed' or 'copied' without consent of those claiming ownership (cf. Harrison 2006). As the notion of *kastam* developed, it implied an orientation towards the past and the ways of the ancestors, for legitimacy and moral value (Otto 1992a and 1992b). Defined as such, the meaning ascribed to *kastam* paralleled that of the notion of *pasin* ('way' or 'fashion'), which was a common way of expressing (stereotypical) differentiation in the past (cf. Schwartz 1993).

In contrast to *kastam*, the notion of *kalsa* is aimed at uniting larger groups at the level of the village or the 'ethnic group' (e.g. Baluan), and it regards traditional practices as the cultural heritage of everyone in those groups. In this regard, the performance of traditional practices is 'self-celebratory', as a way for these groups to show, and perceive of themselves, as such. Traditional practices become something akin to cultural 'brands' (cf. Harrison 2006; Foster 2008), and the focus is not on the distinct way of performing mortuary ceremonies or bride prices, but on the performance of dance, music and art-styles detached from their traditional use on ceremonial occasions. Such practices are, under *kalsa*, conceived differently, as resources, and they are also performed with the intention of attracting income and generating exchange with the outside world. The notion of *kalsa* and the focus on popular cultural performances is thus one that aims at attracting processes of development and modernization from external institutions (such as the provincial government and the national tourist authorities), and of course by attracting tourists themselves, and as such it is, in contrast to *kastam*, focused on the present but also orientated towards future progress. Since everyone has access to traditional resources when they are defined as *kalsa*, these resources are no longer in control of the *lapan* by virtue of their traditional positions, but rather are controlled by the cultural innovators who have been at the forefront of commercial dancing groups: people like Soanin.

Soanin Kilangit

Soanin Kilangit embodies most, if not all, of the changes implied in our analysis. After the first government school on Baluan had been established in Lipan village in 1951, education was eagerly embraced by large numbers of people there.[4] Soanin was one of the first Baluan people to go through a regular school programme and to continue his education outside of Manus. Where the previous generations of migrants had primarily worked as plantation labourers, ships' crews or policemen (see Carrier and Carrier 1989; Otto 1991), Soanin's generation was the first to emigrate to gain secondary and tertiary education, and to take up work based on that education. Gaining adulthood coincided for Soanin's generation with PNG's preparations for independence, where initiatives like the introduction of locals into the administration to replace expatriate public servants were paramount (e.g. Pokawin 1992; Denoon 2005). Soanin's first education was as teacher, but he took employment as a welfare officer and had different postings in Wau, Madang and, later, Goroka. In several of these postings, he replaced Australian officers as part of the process of localization of the public service. After Goroka, he went back to college and received training as a social worker. In the early 1980s he applied for and got a teaching position at the Administrative College of Papua New Guinea in Waigani, where he remained until he was made redundant in 2006 after 40 years of residing away from Baluan. As a teacher at 'Adcol', as the Administrative College was known, Soanin was in touch with the education of several generations of public servants, which in 2007 he was hoping to turn into an advantage for his election campaign.

While living in Port Moresby, Soanin had been involved in organizing Manus people for dance performances since his time in university. In 1993, on the occasion of the 25th anniversary of PNG's electricity company, Elcom (today PNG Power), he became one of the initiators and key organizers of a dancing group of Baluan migrants with the name of 'Paluai Sooksook'.[5] Paluai Sooksook quickly became a success in Port Moresby and presented

Baluan, and indirectly Manus, dance throughout PNG and on some occasions even overseas. Over the years they have performed in Australia (1995, 2000, 2005), South Korea (1996), and France, Spain and Switzerland (2004). Paluai Sooksook became the breeding ground for new perspectives on traditional practices and the meaning that was attributed to them in various contexts. The dancing was seen as an entrepreneurial and commercial exercise, because the group was paid for their performances at Port Moresby hotels and at official occasions. The overseas trips were primarily done for the sake of experience, as they did not generate additional income, the payment being in the form of travel, accommodation and pocket money. But the dance troupe also had traditional roots, as it was maintained by a core group of Baluan people who were closely related to each other, and almost all stemmed from Lipan. People on Baluan have criticized Soanin for spoiling their *kastam* by performing dances that were not the cultural property of his own lineage. He defended himself by saying that he never 'brought the culture out', and that Paluai Sooksook has been making its own version of dances, which therefore were owned by others. The motto of the group was 'progress through culture', referring to both personal development and economic gain.

When dancing performances began to become popular in the years after independence, critics argued that Manus groups should be authentic; and there were even government initiatives trying to define and control cultural expressions such as those in dances (Dalsgaard 2007, 2009). In an interview, Soanin argued that if they had stuck strictly to the original authentic dances, then they would be just like another well-known dancing group from the Manus mainland, Tedukile, which only had four dances. Paluai Sooksook, on the other hand, could do a hundred, and he argued that their performances would never get boring and that they could show different things to different audiences. The group worked on the choreography of the dances, for example by dancing in strict lines and by increasing the tempo of the beats. They also produced medleys, and were generally eager to find out what worked with an audience and what did not.

Although Soanin had not lived permanently in Baluan since he went to school, he always retained contact with his kin on the island, making an effort to return at least every other year, as the final payments of his employment contract allowed him to. On his return visits he often took part in *kastam* ceremonies (bride prices, mortuary rituals) and contributed as was expected of a person with a regular income from working outside of Manus. His wife is also from Lipan, and with the help of his brothers and his affines he built the largest house on Baluan. Through his continual involvement in island affairs and family networks, Soanin was upon his retirement in a much better position to take up a leading role than many others who had returned from their wage-labour experiences empty-handed and without having kept in touch with their relatives to pay 'customary dues' over the years.

The festival

Soanin was the principal initiator and organizer of the Balopa Cultural Festival, which ran from 27 December 2007 until 1 January 2007. He promoted the idea, mobilized people and applied for funding. As Soanin first moved to Baluan in the course of 2006, he was dependent on a number of people on the island to assist him in organizing the local population. The main local organizer was Soanin's brother-in-law, Mela Popeu, himself a returned migrant worker with a higher-education background who had left behind a well-paid job as a surveyor some ten years previously. During the festival Mela performed the role of master of ceremonies most of the time, as a clear indication of his prominent role in the festival. In addition to the two brothers-in-law and their families, a number of local *lapans* put their weight behind the festival and were active in the preparations, such as practising dancing, carving dancing poles, making gardens and inviting other villages. As Soanin and Mela had already organized a minor version of the festival at independence celebrations in September 2005, the air was filled with expectation. This first festival was called Balopa Mini Cultural Festival, and several new ideas were tried out, most prominently the use of a stage for the dancers. Soanin explained that this was a combination of the traditional Baluan dancing pole (*sinal*) and the Western theatre stage, which the Port Moresby based dancing group had observed during their Europe tour in 2004.

As a central motto for the festival, the organizers had chosen 'unity through culture'. This was clearly in line with an earlier motto 'progress through culture' that Paluai Sooksook had worked with. Soanin later explained to us that they wanted the local people to take development in their own hands instead of waiting for handouts from the government. One part of this was to keep traditional culture alive by giving young people a motivation to practise and learn from their elders. This was not meant as pure preservation, as the culture was changing simultaneously with the incorporation of new elements. Paluai Sooksook, for example, were changing elements of their dances on the basis of the impressions they received during their international tours. The enthusiasm generated by the festival would create a feeling of identity, unity and motivation for action. In addition, the revival of culture as traditional dance and performance was seen as an important means for attracting tourists to the island. In the application for funds the organizers wrote: 'Tourism remains the only untapped goldmine for 42,000 Manusians which include 4,000 Balopa people'. The authors of this chapter were invited, so as to make a film and assist with spreading the news about the festival.

The festival itself had a number of elements which made it very different from traditional ceremonies (*kastam*), even though it was looked at with a *kastam* perspective by many participants, as we will see. The programme of the festival built on similar events organized elsewhere and included an interesting mix of Western influences and traditional practices. The opening ceremony included – in addition to the obligatory speeches – a dance on the dancing pole performed by a leading *lapan* while addressing the people present. It also presented all the dancing groups on the festival ground in front of the stage. The following days were filled with traditional dances performed by dancing groups taking part in a competition for the best act. A jury had been appointed, and they also judged the other elements of the festival's programme: queen quest, choir singing (mostly religious), string bands, traditional songs, drama, display of traditional houses, canoe races. The queen quest was based on the concept of a Western beauty contest, in which local girls were dressed in traditional finery and had to perform a dance, a catwalk and a speech. Soanin told us that it was also inspired by the local tradition of dressing up the bride at a wedding ceremony. All participating girls, who were between 14 and 18 years old, expressed their pride of their culture and many emphasized the importance of attracting tourists to the island. The closing ceremony comprised the distribution of prize money (all participating groups received something), speeches and a presentation of all participants in their traditional dresses.

The Balopa Cultural Festival presented numerous scenes and themes relevant to this chapter. These include the dances, the rhythms, the crafting and sale of artefacts, the participation of the 'anthropological tourists'. For the sake of clarity and focus, however, we will deal only with the relationship between the main initiator of the festival, Soanin, and the local traditional leaders, the *lapans* of Baluan and, especially, Lipan, the village where the festival took place. In the initiatory stages of preparing for the festival, several of these *lapans* had been included in the decision making and had been giving their advice regarding specific arrangements, or had been carving drums and dancing poles for the occasion. When the event drew near, though, several of them came to feel marginalized, and they decided to pull out before the festival began. Only those most closely related to Soanin and most directly involved remained, such as the chairman of the organizing committee (Mela) and the highest-ranking *lapan* of Lipan, who had been member of Paluai Sooksook when he lived in Port Moresby and who was given the honour of speaking from the *mui* (special type of dancing pole) at the opening ceremony (Sapulai Papi).

Here we want to focus on one of those elder *lapans*, Pokowei Paril, who had pulled out, but was persuaded to participate nonetheless. On the day before the opening of the festival there was a ceremony in which contributors of funding were presented and handed over their contributions. As part of the ceremony, Pokowei had been asked to cut and distribute the betel nuts, as is customary in any traditional ceremony of importance (*kastam*). He had agreed to do this and gave branches of the bundle to the contributors of money and to the participating clans and villages. However, the next day Pokowei slipped and fell during his morning routine of going to the coast for his toilet. He hurt his knee badly and was unable to walk to the festival grounds at the sports field. Pokowei was convinced that his accident was a punishment for participating in the festival despite the boycott levelled by several of the other *lapans* – delivered by the ancestral spirits because of the negative feelings that his participation had evoked. Even when his knee had improved and Pokowei was able to move around again, he did not go to the festival, although he much regretted not being able to see the dances and other attractive programme elements. This example shows how participation in the festival (as *kalsa*) constituted a risk to the traditional leaders. This was because some felt that the festival was not held according to *kastam* principles and could not therefore be endorsed by several of the *lapans*. The discontent resulted partly from the way decisions had been taken, ignoring *lapan* consultation and advice, and partly from accusations that Soanin had not obtained proper permission to do traditional dances his descent group did not own. The next example will further show the contradictions that arose between a subjectivized regime of *kastam* as beliefs, rules and norms (cf. Akin 2004) and the festival as *kalsa* detached from traditional obligations.

During the festival large numbers of people from other islands (Lou and Pak in particular) were camping near the festival ground and, as organizer and host, Soanin was expected to help provide food for them. Since food was running low, Soanin wanted to send his boat to Lou, where there were stocks to be collected, and he had asked a distant kinsman, John Malai, from Pam Island next to Baluan, for help in finding petrol for the trip. John was the chairman of the provincial Culture and Tourism Board, and Soanin expected him to have access to money in his role as a government representative. Malai had demanded that Soanin first produced receipts for the expenses that he had already incurred. This angered Soanin, and he hit John on the brow. It was unheard of that a host should attack his guest; what is more , John was a guest who was a kinsman and classificatory, albeit distant, 'father'.

Interviewing John about the incident later, it was our impression that he had not had any money. The Culture and Tourism Board rarely held meetings, did not have a budget, and much of the work John did was to write a plan for the development of tourism in Manus.[6] Any government funding would have to come from the MPs representing Manus or from the Manus Provincial Administration, which had already contributed to the festival through the Governor of Manus.[7] The incident thus seems to stem from expectations as to the resources available to someone claiming government authority clashing with expectations as to accountability. For Soanin, the incident was one that led some people to doubt his abilities as a leader. Impulsive aggression was not seen as a good thing, and as someone later said to one of the authors, when Soanin had been nominated for the National Parliamentary Election, 'What will it look like if he [Soanin] goes to parliament and punches someone there?' Such an act would reflect badly on Manus and Baluan in particular.

The day after the incident, some of the kin who where related both to Soanin and John arranged a *ponpon* – a traditional 'sorry' ceremony meant to mediate in a conflict. Some of the traditional leaders asked Soanin to submit himself to this and to apologize to John publicly, which involved the presentation of a considerable amount of gifts (a pig, money and cloth) and an oral apology. Hitting one's kinsman was a violation of *kastam* (in this case customary rules of hospitality and expectations of the organizer of a *kastam* ceremony), and Soanin was thus forced to agree to the terms of the *ponpon* if he wanted the festival (here considered as his '*puron*' or *kastam* event) to continue. In other cases, such a dispute would likely have ended in a court case involving the local village magistrate or the court in Lorengau, but since the matter was of great importance to the success of the festival and the name of Baluan, some of Soanin's and John's mutual relatives stepped in, an action that worked as a confirmation of the role of the traditional leaders and the importance of *kastam* in general.

The issue of accountability that led to the fight was also mentioned as a general issue after the festival. At the festival opening, several contributors and financial sponsors had been publicly named and their contributions of money displayed publicly on the stage. When the time came for the handing over of prizes during the closing ceremony, the total amount of money presented here was believed by some people to be smaller than the total given by the sponsors. These people were now speculating that Soanin had put the difference in his own pocket. Allegedly, Soanin had used some of the money from the sponsors to cover his own food and petrol expenses, which he claimed had run up to several thousand Kina. People now argued like John, that if Soanin had spent money organizing the festival, he should have kept the receipts. In other words, it was the lack of public display of Soanin's own contribution that confused people and led to suspicion. It was a violation of the implicit rules of *kastam*. The example shows that the festival, although not formally classified as *puron*, was still evaluated in terms of *kastam*. As in *puron* ceremonies, the organizer was expected to stand up first and present his contribution publicly. In conversations Soanin readily admitted to comparisons between the festival and a *puron*, but he had clearly underestimated the implications of this blending of *kastam* and *kalsa* perspectives. In various ways he was held accountable for not following the rules of *kastam*, even though, in his view, the culture festival was something different. People judged his behaviour as that of a *lapan* – even though on hereditary grounds he was not one – and expected him to live up to the concomitant standards of generosity and public display. Soanin definitely had the intention of helping his fellow islanders, but he also wanted to maintain a clear division between his own resources and those put into the festival. One of Soanin's sons had presented 3,000 Kina as a gift to the festival on behalf of the whole Port Moresby based dancing group, but Soanin wished to be compensated for the many smaller expenses he had incurred in running his boat and transporting people and food free of charge. In this attempt to separate his private economic sphere from the public festival event, we see the emergence of a different kind of personhood – that of the Western possessive individual (Macpherson 1962; Martin 2007; Sykes 2007). This type of personhood articulates well with the new notion of *kalsa* as cultural heritage, but runs into conflicts of legitimacy when considered from a *kastam* perspective.

The elections

The notion of *kalsa* exhibited during the cultural festival also came to have instrumental value to Soanin in his attempt to contest the National Parliamentary Election, but it was not without difficulties as an innovative political tool, as *kastam* values were also here paramount to people's evaluations of leadership. In May 2007, less than five months after the conclusion of the festival, Soanin was nominated for the election. During the festival we had already tried to find out whether he had any intention of contesting. He did not deny it, and gave the appearance of being interested, but neither did he confirm outright that he would.

In the weeks up to the nomination period for the election, Soanin and a group of kin and supporters had toured Manus seeking out relatives in other parts of the province in order to elicit their support for his candidacy and in order to present himself in places where he was not well known. Interestingly, Soanin presented this to us as a strategy that consciously followed the rules of *kastam*. On the day of the nomination, Soanin and a large group of supporters had gathered at the house of his brother-in-law, Jim Paliau, a few hundred metres from the office of the Electoral Commission in Lorengau. The majority of the group that was with him consisted of Baluan people, many of whom were his relatives; but other parts of Manus were also represented, in particular the islands of Lou and Pam, which along with Baluan make up the area of the Balopa Local Level Government (LLG).[8] Among the group from Pam was the President of Balopa LLG, John Micah, giving Soanin the air of being the preferred candidate for this part of Manus. Also in the procession was Sapulai Papi, considered by many as, genealogically, the highest ranking *lapan* of Lipan, Soanin's home village.

At the house of Jim Paliau, Soanin and his group waited for the right moment to move in order to get the most attention and the biggest crowd of spectators for their nomination procession. When they saw that the procession of the candidates for the National Alliance (NA) party was on its way, they decided to intercept them and make it to the Electoral Commission office ahead of them in order to hijack their crowd. The NA's candidates were the former Governor of Manus, Stephen Pokawin, and a former independent member, Memel Pohei, both of whom commanded large numbers of supporters and could attract big crowds.

While waiting, Soanin was given various 'traditional' artefacts to decorate him for the occasion. He wore a headband or 'crown' made of beads and dogs' teeth, the use of which is usually restricted to those who are lapan.[9] He had been given permission to do this by the head of his descent group, and the senior lapan of his home village took part in the procession, therewith endorsing Soanin's candidacy and use of dog's teeth. Someone had also given Soanin an obsidian spear and his own immediate kin had made a large plaited bag, which he carried across his torso. The bag had been filled with betel nuts, *kambang* (coral lime) and a small amount of money (20 Kina). Someone had also sprayed a little bit of *kambang* on Soanin's face. He told us that these decorations were gestures of a 'celebratory' nature – all meant as adornment to make him look nice – and he commented that the money was probably for his 'good luck'. Underneath the decorations he had worn his European style clothing (a shirt and long trousers), indicating their ambivalent, that is, not fully *kastam*, nature. Attention and excitement were also the purpose of the group of dancers and the *garamut* (log-drum) ensemble that accompanied the procession. The *garamuts* were carried on the back of a large truck, where also some dancers performed as they went along. While Soanin was inside the Electoral Commission's office, the group was performing various beats and dances outside to entertain the crowd. As mentioned above, performance of culture has been one of Soanin's 'trademarks' as one of the organizers of the well-known and popular Port Moresby based dance group Paluai Sooksook. In his campaign speeches, when talking about his work with the group, he mentioned them as breaking 'world records': they were performing the 'fastest leg dances on the planet' and constructing the 'biggest *garamut* on the planet', and he emphasized that this work had been done by ordinary people, implying that ordinary people could achieve great things.

The above account indicates Soanin's understanding of the importance of traditional cultural elements in the nomination event. Their purpose is to enthuse people and draw attention, and their performance is available to everyone in Manus. This breaks with the understanding that knowledge of dancing and *garamut* (both rhythms and construction of the instruments) is restricted and owned by individual descent groups. This change links to the long-term effect of Soanin's influence, which was possibly strengthened by the visit of an ethnomusicologist (Tony Lewis of Sydney Conservatorium of Music), who advocated and facilitated for young men outside the owning lineages to be taught specialized skills relating to *garamut*. However, other candidates for the election had stressed other meanings of similar decorations and practices employed during their nominations. Their *kambang* was meant to protect them against attacks from people with evil intent. The bag was a gift that would display who the candidate's supporters were, where he came from, and that he was a man who had resources, something expressed also in the bag's contents (distribution of betel nuts in the past had been the privilege of *lapan*, traditional leaders). One might add that distribution of money increasingly seems to signify in the same way – he who distributes money manifests himself as a leader.[10]

In other words, the significance of the decorations and the procession was in most likelihood interpreted differently by the different participants. Soanin's interpretation of what went on related to his perspective on tradition as *kalsa* and as evoking excitement. Others could interpret the event as not just evoking excitement (which indeed specific practices and decorations related to traditional rhythms and dances might be seen as doing), but as also emphasizing the relations that supported their candidacy. That is, decorations and performances were displays of one's relational and cultural identity, and one's social status as holding the support of many relations and relatives. Soanin's interpretation could be seen as a conscious avoidance of these issues as they are related to rights over traditional cultural practices. By not acknowledging *kastam*, but referring to these elements as *kalsa* (as he had done with the cultural festival), he could dissociate himself from obligations to kin. As we will discuss below, Soanin's failure to do better in the election may to some extent be caused by a tendency to neglect exchange obligations and a failure to live up to expectations of generosity from a leader.

Even though Soanin had the endorsement of the President of Balopa, this did not automatically do away with competition from other candidates, since local politics is quite a volatile affair. The support of one leader may automatically result in being shunned by that man's rivals. Apart from Soanin, there were seven others who had direct links to Balopa either as natives or by having a fosterage relationship. This led to frustrations for several of these candidates, as they had to share what was already a scarce resource: the number of voters in Balopa being less than the average for LLGs in Manus, thus giving candidates from that LLG a weaker starting point for their endeavours. Generally Manus people talk about a candidate's home area as his *asbasket* – the bottom of his basket. This is seen as the most important 'base vote' and should ensure that he is 'in the game' (see Pokawin and Rooney 1996). It is important to give potential voters the impression that the candidate has the support of his own area and is a serious contender not only when the counting commences, but throughout the campaigning.[11] This is thus the concrete aspect to the importance of carrying betel nuts and money in the bottom of one's basket.

In the end, Soanin turned out to be the most popular candidate in Balopa and in Baluan (he received 389 votes out of 1,196 formal votes cast in Balopa). But he had also met resistance, and some of his campaigning had been misunderstood or perhaps deliberately turned against him. After the incident during the cultural festival, Soanin had agreed to do a sorry ceremony (*ponpon*). The election results and the way people spoke about Soanin, particularly in the period leading up to the LLG election in 2008, showed that another *ponpon*, or some similar show of repentance, could have been further help, because people had increasingly begun to have doubts about Soanin's leadership. Especially after he had lost in the 2007 election and then declared that he wanted to try the LLG election in 2008, people started saying that Soanin only got attention because voters had heard of Paluai Sooksook and wanted to watch them perform. While he still had several strong supporters among his close kin and associates, a number of interrelated criticisms were heard over and over again among other Baluan people. As far as we know, no one confronted Soanin directly with these, but he heard about most of them from kin as they circulated as gossip.

Most significantly, Soanin was criticized for not helping people. The large boat that he had purchased upon his return to Baluan had been employed as a passenger boat and he charged people for transporting them and their goods to town. The price had been a little higher than the normal fare if getting a lift. Furthermore, he charged extra per kg of cargo. Soanin had seen the boat as a way to help Baluan people by providing transport to town, but he was now accused of earning money from Baluan people when he should instead be providing a (free or at least cheap) service. People found it wrong that he had money and now wanted to finance his campaigning and lifestyle with their money. Soanin was regarded as a city person and as still having a city-person's lifestyle, having nearly forgotten what life is like in the village. This conviction was reinforced by the way he spoke – often using English or Tok Pisin words even when speaking the local language.

Soanin was regarded as very knowledgeable because of his education and experience in Port Moresby, but that also led to high expectations. Hence, people started asking why he had not done more for Baluan. Whereas Soanin preferred to compare himself with a legendary big man of the past (i.e. Soanin regarded the festival as the biggest thing that had happened in Baluan since that big man), others rather compared him with the late ward councillor of Lipan, a humble man, who had spent a lot of time and energy on attracting AusAID funding for water tanks to the village – and was said to have died from the stressful anxieties related to this feat. The late councillor had accomplished this regardless of his scant education and living most of his life in Lipan; Soanin, despite his knowledge and position, had no comparable achievements.[12]

Finally, Soanin was also accused of trying to 'force' people to vote for him. One story was that he threatened the people in the neighbouring village of Mouk, saying that he could send them off their land. When one of the authors spoke to Soanin, he got the impression that he had tried to tell the Mouk that they should be grateful, since they have the land they live on thanks to his ancestors; but a different message was communicated, and spread like a wildfire.[13] What was heard from Soanin himself, was that he would charge people more for using his boat if he did not win the election. In other words, Soanin was ready to lay the blame for a failed election result on people who were actually likely to have supported him.

In spite of these criticisms, which focused on Soanin's failure to live up to some of the *kastam* expectations of a traditional leader – especially reciprocity, generosity and non-aggressiveness – there is no doubt that Soanin was regarded as a big and important man. We should also emphasize that he scored well in some respects, especially regarding his skill and drive in organizing big public events. As a comment on his decision to contest the LLG presidency, some had said that it looked 'wrong' for him to contest the lower level LLG after having failed the parliamentary election. The criticism of Soanin may have been expressed to us for numerous reasons. While some genuinely worried about the quality of leadership, others were perhaps looking for excuses for voting for others that they felt more obliged to. Soanin remains an influential man in Baluan affairs, and his initiatives have often sparked enthusiasm and pride among those participating.

Conclusion

In this chapter we have shown how a returned migrant worker has played a significant role as an agent of change on his native island. In his attempts to have an impact on local affairs, Soanin Kilangit tapped into a semantic change in the local understanding of traditional practices, and his own activities contributed to this change. Understanding tradition as *kalsa* rather than as *kastam* had far reaching consequences for people's notions of social relations, personhood and the ownership of culture. Soanin employed *kalsa* as a resource for uniting people, rather than as something that defined differences between descent groups. He saw culture as something that could energize people and provide them with initiative and knowledge to make money in a situation where other economic means of development were very limited. By setting an example of how culture could be used by an internationally successful dancing group (Paluai Sooksook), he hoped to show a way of achieving progress to the people of Baluan and other Manus islands. The organization of the Balopa Cultural Festival was both an implementation of this strategy and a way to build up local support for his political aspirations. However, organizing such a big event had many parallels with traditional public exchanges and was considered by many people as a mega-size *kastam* ceremony, something Soanin did not object to. As a result of this merging of concepts and perspectives, Soanin's acts were also judged on the basis of internalized *kastam* values and rules, which sometimes would clash with his own understanding of traditional practices as *kalsa*. In particular, Soanin would be held accountable for kin obligations and traditional property relations that he did not consider equally valid in the context of the festival. In other words, Soanin's attempts to furnish unity were at odds with values of reciprocity and generosity – or unity established through personal exchange and 'partibility' (see Lindstrom, this volume).

A similar blending of conflicting perspectives occurred during the nomination for the elections, where Soanin emphasized the power of *kalsa* to unite and excite, rather than to divide and limit access to traditional resources. However, by being seen as not acknowledging certain traditional 'debts' and obligations, he was prone to criticism of lacking the generosity and humbleness required according to *kastam*. This no doubt contributed to his disappointing result in the elections. Soanin was of course aware of the criticisms, and defended himself against allegations that he used *kalsa* to make money. He told us that these ideas originated from a deep-rooted cargo-cult mentality, in which people expected to be given things without effort and initiative. He wanted to give the less wealthy islanders knowledge and opportunities to improve their own lives, but he could not hand out money and services without being able to renew his own resources. In these differences of perspective and judgement a deep-seated contradiction between two types of morality emerges. According to *kastam* ideas, Soanin should feel obliged to continue supporting poorer kin and exchange relations, even though this would drain his resources. In the long run, he would be able to call upon them to help him in return. Soanin, however, wanted to be able to close off his personal economic sphere from these demands, so as to be able to support his closest family. In that sense his perspective comes close to a Western type of possessive individualism (Sykes 2007). *Kalsa* is something that unites and develops the whole community, but it does not limit the individual's rights to use tradition, nor does it force the individual to share in the same way as *kastam* does.

The bifurcation of the local perspective on tradition into one of *kastam* versus *kalsa* is the product of choices made by social agents like Soanin, but it is simultaneously a structural phenomenon made possible by global changes, like the spread of Western notions of cultural heritage and individual personhood. Therefore similar transformations have been observed elsewhere, albeit with different local expressions of the notions of culture involved (Harrison 2006, especially chapter 5; Martin 2007). The concept of culture that is now gaining force is built on a concept of cultural heritage that is inalienably owned by a group, which is defined by this possession. This is in line with some earlier uses of *kastam* as ancestral traditions – or the PNG or Melanesian Way – that have paved the way for notions of the nation characterized by a distinguishable cultural identity (Narokobi 1983; Babadzan 1988 and 2000; Foster 1995a; Otto and Thomas 1997). However, concepts of culture as exchangeable property owned by small groups which control access are still strongly alive, and notions and rules of objectified *kastam* have become internalized through the increasing weight that traditional practices have received in the past 30–40 years (cf. Akin 2004). The conflicts of value and judgement described in this chapter thus illustrate the ongoing development and employment of notions of tradition and heritage in Manus societies and politics.

NOTES

1. The research for this chapter was carried out as part of the project 'Globalisation in past and present', part of the Galathea 3 expedition under the auspices of the Danish Expedition Foundation. It is Galathea 3 contribution no. P53. The research was funded by Bikuben Fonden, the Faculty of Humanities at the University of Aarhus, Carlsbergs Mindelegat for Brygger J.C. Jacobsen, and an EliteResearch travel stipend from the Danish Ministry for Science, Technology and Innovation. We would like to thank the organizers and the participants of the ESfO panel for the discussions, and the other participants in our Galathea 3 project, of whom Christian Suhr Nielsen especially has contributed to this piece. Finally, we are grateful to all those Manus people, from Baluan in particular, who hosted us, helped us and generally have allowed us to be part of their lives, and to Soanin Kilangit for inviting us to participate in and document the cultural developments we write about here. Both authors contributed equally to the chapter.

2. Balopa is the Local Level Government formed by the islands of Baluan, Lou and Pam.

3. As elsewhere, *kastam* is a comparatively recent term, and earlier 'culture-concepts' were phrased in terms of the Tok Pisin *pasin* or in Baluan language *nurunan*. The word *kastam* gains currency in Manus around the mid 1970s (see Otto 1991:243).

4. Until then, it was only a minority who had the chance of attending mission schools (see Otto 1991:191).

5. Literally 'Baluan Dancing' – originally it was spelled Paluai Suksuk.

6. At the time of fieldwork he had not received any response from the government on the plan he had proposed.

7. In addition, an amount was promised by the chairman of the government committee that oversaw the funding held by the MP from the Manus Open Electorate.

8. Linguistically and culturally, Pam and Baluan can be classified as one group, and Lou is closely related.

9. He also wore that dogs' teeth crown on the photo for his election poster and on the candidate poster that voters would see at the polling stations.

10. In a similar vein, some commented that the obsidian spear would signify the *kastam* of Soanin's descent group as warriors. One of Soanin's in-laws said that in a way his aggressiveness (evidenced in the punch on John Malai during the Festival) was Soanin's *pasin* – it was the cultural 'trait' of his kin.

11. Much more deserves to be said about this than we can cover here. Since most government funding is handed out by MPs, it is important to establish an exchange relationship with them, and what is then better than to confront them with a 'you owe me for my vote' request. Hence no one wants to vote for someone who is not likely to win the election, unless you are somehow obliged to that person in the first place.

12. That evaluation may not be totally fair. One of the authors witnessed Soanin take part in initiating the original planning of the submission for funding for water tanks, which took place in Baluan over Christmas in 2002–3.

13. The Mouk people were invited to settle at their present location in 1946 when Paliau Maloat gained the land from the traditional owners in order to facilitate his reforms (see Otto 1991 and 1992b).

BIBLIOGRAPHY

Akin, D. 2004. 'Ancestral vigilance and the corrective conscience: kastom as culture in a Melanesian society'. *Anthropological Theory* 4(3):299–324.

Babadzan, A. 1988. '*Kastom* and nation-building in the South Pacific'. In *Ethnicities and Nations*, (eds) R. Guidieri, F. Pellizzi and S. Tambiah. Houston, Rothko Chapel, 199–228. Huston, Austin: University of Texas Press.

Babadzan, A. 2000. 'Anthropology, nationalism and "the invention of tradition"'. *Anthropological Forum* 10(2):131–55.

Brown, M. 2003. *Who Owns Native Culture?* Cambridge (Mass.): Harvard University Press.

Bunten, A.C. 2008. 'Sharing culture or selling out? Developing the commodified persona in the heritage industry'. *American Ethnologist* 35(3):380–95.

Burton, J. 2007. 'The anthropology of personal identity: intellectual property rights issues in Papua New Guinea, West Papua and Australia'. *The Australian Journal of Anthropology* 18(1):40–55.

Carrier, J. and A. Carrier 1989. *Wage, Trade, and Exchange in Melanesia.* Berkeley: University of California Press.

Cole, D. 1985. *Captured Heritage: The Scramble for Northwest Coast Artifacts.* Seattle: University of Washington Press.

Dalsgaard, S. 2007. 'Revendiquer sa culture: nouvelle définitions et propriété des pratiques culturelles dans la Province de Manus (Papouasie Nouvelle-Guinée)'. *Journal de la Société des Océanistes* 125(2):229–36.

Dalsgaard, S. 2009. 'Claiming culture: new definitions and ownership of cultural practices in Manus Province, Papua New Guinea'. *The Asia Pacific Journal of Anthropology* 10(1):20–32.

Denoon, D. 2005. *A Trial Separation: Australia and the Decolonisation of Papua New Guinea.* Canberra: Pandanus Books.

Foster, R. (ed.) 1995a. *Nation Making. Emergent Identities in Postcolonial Melanesia.* Ann Arbor: University of Michigan Press.

Foster, R. 1995b. *Social Reproduction and History in Melanesia.* Cambridge: Cambridge University Press.

Foster, R. 2008. 'Commodity, brands, love and kula'. *Anthropological Theory* 8(1):9–25.

Handler, R. 1988. *Nationalism and the Politics of Culture in Quebec.* Madison: University of Wisconsin Press.

Hanson, A. 1989. 'The making of the Maori: culture invention and its logic'. *American Anthropologist* 91(4):890–902.

Harrison, S. 2006. *Fracturing Resemblances: Identity and Mimetic Conflict in Melanesia and the West.* New York: Berghahn Books.

Jolly, M. 1992. 'Specters of inauthenticity'. *The Contemporary Pacific* 4(1):49–72.

Kaneff, D. and A. King 2004. 'Introduction: owning culture'. *Focaal* 44:3–19.

Keesing, R. 1989. 'Creating the past: custom and identity in the contemporary Pacific'. *The Contemporary Pacific* 1(1):19–42.

Kirshenblatt-Gimblett, B. 1998. *Destination Culture: Tourism, Museums, and Heritage.* Berkeley: University of California Press.

Leach, J. 2003. 'Owning creativity'. *Journal of Material Culture* 8(2):123–43.

Linnekin, J. and L. Poyer (eds). 1990. *Cultural Identity and Ethnicity in the Pacific.* Honolulu: University of Hawai'i Press.

Lowenthal, D. 1998. *The Heritage Crusade and the Spoils of History.* Cambridge: Cambridge University Press.

Macpherson, C. B. 1962. *The Political Theory of Possessive Individualism: Hobbes to Locke.* Oxford: Oxford University Press.

Martin, K. 2007. 'Your own buai you must buy: the ideology of possessive individualism in Papua New Guinea'. *Anthropological Forum* 17(3):285–98.

Mosko, M. 2002. 'Totem and transaction: the objectification of "tradition" among North Mekeo'. *Oceania* 73(2):89–109.

Narokobi, B. 1983. *The Melanesian Way.* Boroko: Institute of Papua New Guinea Studies.

Olwig, K. F. 1999. 'The burden of heritage: claiming a place for a West Indian culture'. *American Ethnologist* 26(2):370–88.

Otto, T. 1991. The Politics of Tradition in Baluan. Ph.D. Thesis, The Australian National University. Centre for Pacific Studies: Nijmegen.

Otto, T. 1992a. 'The Paliau Movement in Manus and the objectification of tradition'. *History and Anthropology* 5(3–4):427–54.

Otto, T. 1992b. 'The ways of kastam: tradition as category and practice in a Manus Village'. *Oceania* 62(4):264–83.

Otto, T. (In press). 'Inventing traditions and remembering the past in Manus'. In *Changing context – Shifting meanings: Transformations of Cultural Traditions in Oceania* (ed.) E. Hermann. Honolulu: University of Hawai'i Press.

Otto, T. and P. Pedersen 2005. 'Disentangling traditions: culture, agency and power'. In *Tradition and Agency* (eds) T. Otto and P. Pedersen, 11–49. Aarhus: Aarhus University Press.

Otto, T. and N. Thomas, Eds. 1997. *Narratives of Nation in the South Pacific.* Amsterdam: Harwood Academic Publishers.

Pokawin, S. and N. Rooney 1996. 'Manus: reign of subtlety over deception of hospitality'. In *The 1992 Papua New Guinea Election: Change and Continuity in Electoral Politics* (ed.) Y. Saffu, 23:122–43. Canberra, Research School of Pacific and Asian Studies: Australian National University.

Pokawin, S.P. 1992. 'Papua New Guinea: post-colonial experiences of Australian public administration'. *Australian Journal of Public Administration* 51(2):169–75.

Rowlands, M. 2002. 'Heritage and cultural property'. In *The Material Culture Reader* (ed.) V. Buchli, 105–14. Oxford: Berg.

Schwartz, T. 1993. 'Kastom, "custom", and culture: conspicuous culture and culture-constructs'. *Anthropological Forum* 6(4):515–40.

Sykes, K. (ed.) 2007. Interrogating individuals: the critique of possessive individualism in the Western Pacific. Special Issue of *Anthropological Forum.*

Tonkinson, R. 1982. 'Introduction: *kastom* in Melanesia'. *Mankind* 13:302–5.

Tonkinson, R. 1993. 'Understanding "tradition" – ten years on.' *Anthropological Forum* 6(4):597–606.

CHAPTER 6

The rise of the Pleiades

The quest for identity and the politics of tradition in French Polynesia

✳

GUILLAUME ALÉVÊQUE

Introduction

Until recently, discussing 'cultural heritage' in Tahiti was the prerogative of politicians, intellectuals, artists and clergymen, who between them monopolized claims of identity and tradition. Their public discourse often reflects Tahiti's past as an idealized 'golden age', while the day-to-day relationship of the people with this past presents a more ambiguous reality. In fact, everything that may appear as a relic of the pagan past in a Christian present is treated with suspicion, and sometimes threatens to involve ghosts, curses and sorcery. Nevertheless, a grassroots movement founded in various non-profit organizations and engaged in environmental claims and identity issues has tried to revitalize the past and enhance the status of the ancestors. Members of the movement organize ceremonies, largely filled with pre-Christian references, in the hope of achieving a general cultural awakening. These non-profit organizations have become politically influential, and now play a major role in cultural life.

Through a description of contemporary Tahitian representations of culture and their associated past relations, the purpose of this chapter is to analyse the issues involved in the acting out of Māʻohi ethnicity in French Polynesia. I will begin by examining how people have represented themselves in colonial and post-colonial Tahiti, before focusing specifically on the elaboration of ceremonies by the cultural movement and its relations with local government.

Representing the self in colonial Tahiti

Polynesians have been confronted with a Westernized imaginary of themselves for more than two centuries. This imaginary has long been taken for granted in their way of representing the self, even though it had been imposed by colonial otherness. The issues surrounding this representation have evolved, nevertheless, and an analysis of these changes may help us to understand how Tahitians define both culture and heritage today.

Until the emergence of the *renouveau culturel* movement in the 1970s and the assertion of Māʻohi identity,[1] practices referring to the pre-Christian past were never a public matter, except during the Tiurei. The Tiurei, meaning July in the Tahitian language, was staged for the first time in 1880 on the initiative of the French protectorate, a few months before annexation. The original purpose was the celebration of the French national day on 14 July, and the expression in songs and dances of the local population's patriotic attachment to France. The Tiurei then became the authorized space for practices prohibited or restricted by the church since the 1820s. The importance of this celebration increased and the villages rapidly concentrated their artistic and craft efforts on parades and other kinds of competitions. Even so, the objective of staging ethnic identity did not appear before the 1950s (Stevenson 1996). In fact, the colonial administration, in encouraging such representation of the self through a patriotic expression of folklore, unwittingly allowed the existence of a space referring to the past – in symbolic opposition to Christian day-to-day life.

In this colonial society, people were ashamed of the pagan past and of the sins of their pagan ancestors. Tahitians actually internalized, in part, the racism of European colonialism. They saw themselves as lesser Christians because they were Polynesians. During the Tiurei, however, being Polynesian was not lived out as a negative identity. This was viewed as a time of symbolic inversion, and may be considered a form of carnival. The Tiurei, as a colonial construction, seems to have been included in the representations of the Po, which refers to the past, paganism and the night – in opposition to the Christian light. The Tiurei was the only time for the Po to be publicly referred to, perhaps because as a celebration and a representation of the self imagined from the outside, the Tiurei made the necessary detachment possible. It was also a time of accepted transgressions: the parish choirs could sing, in public, themes they dared not sing in other circumstances, and dancing was tolerated despite the disapproval of the church. Thus, the Tiurei became the time of unvoiced evocations, a time to conjure up the past and the ancestors.

With the *renouveau culturel* movement the Tiurei received a new dimension of protest. In the 1970s, under the influence of young intellectuals and artists like Henry Hiro and Turo Raapoto, cultural claims were made with the aim of defining Māʻohi ethnicity. This was a new change in the relationship to the past and the representation of culture which needed to be rediscovered and preserved, and to the identity thereby affirmed. The Tiurei, as the only space for exhibiting the social relation with the past, subsequently became the privileged space for showing these new claims through artistic expressions and new practices such as 'cultural reconstructions'.

The new activities associated with the Tiurei, such as fire-walking, were soon considered to be traditional. With the *renouveau culturel* movement, the symbolic inversion – the carnival aspect of the celebration – was no longer connected to Christianity, but instead to colonization. This is significant in the context of viewing the 'cultural reconstructions' as ambiguous staged settings of pre-Christian ceremonies. The fact that cultural reconstructions often represented the coronation of the King and Queen of Tahiti reveals an ironic carnival inversion in its display of Tahitian sovereignty during French National Day celebrations. These reconstructions disappeared after the Tiurei became the Heiva in 1985 and no longer was associated with 14 July, but to 29 June, which was the newly established Autonomy Day.

From the beginning of colonization through to the demands of decolonization, the representation of the self in French Polynesia has moved from the expression of a Polynesian Christian identity, through an imposed exhibition of ethnic folklore, to the full staging of Māʻohi ethnicity.

The new legitimacy related to the autonomy adopted in 1985 institutionalized the *renouveau culturel* movement and funded the local heritage policy (Stevenson 1996). In fact, under the pressure of the movement, cultural institutions were created during the 1980s in a context where the representation of the self in Tahiti progressively lost its transgressive dimension, alongside associated collective cultural demands. Protest has re-emerged today, however, in the form of a grassroots movement organized in 'cultural associations'.

New ceremonies for a cultural awakening

Haururu, or 'Together in Peace', was created in 1994, and is the most important and active of these Tahitian non-profit organizations. It was initially established by the residents of Papenoo, a village located on the north shore of Tahiti, who desired to promote 'ecological progress' in their district. This organization (or 'association') gradually moved up the Papenoo valley to attend to three archaeological sites, and to keep an eye on the environmental consequences of the electricity company's activities and its dams. They also built a village in this valley, close to the largest archaeological site, Fare Hape, which may currently accommodate eighty people and receives school groups during cultural weeks.

Until 2000, Haururu's members performed annual 'folklore' shows to awaken curiosity about past Tahitian civilization. They have now substituted these shows with 'ceremonies'. According to the Haururu, and to the other organizations of the movement, ceremonies are 'more real'[2] than shows, and have a true spiritual and sacred aspect. Members also explain that they do not want to 'act culture' any more, but 'live' it, since culture cannot be limited by art and must express itself day-by-day as a way of life. The members of these organizations have been engaged in an individual and collective quest for identity and have developed alternative ways of representing the self (on the group level). However, as we will see, these practices are less an affirmation of an ethnicity than a questioning of the Māʻohi way of life.

The first ceremony created by Haururu was a welcoming ceremony using cultural protocol to receive important Tahitian or foreign guests. In 2003 they began to organize the Pleiades rising (*Matarii i nia*) and setting (*Matarii i raro*) celebrations[2] in order to honour and share the astronomic and environmental knowledge of their ancestors with fellow Tahitians. Initially, Haururu members had hoped to extend the Matarii celebrations to all of French Polynesia over the next ten years. Five years later, in 2008, the celebration was staged by Haururu in eight of twelve districts in Tahiti, as well as on the islands of Moorea, Huahine, Raiatea and Tubuai by other cultural organizations. In 2006, a successful attempt had been made to convince the president of French Polynesian to organize an official Matarii celebration. These Matarii celebrations brought legitimacy to the Haururu, developing and improving its public relations with the Tahitian people, and enabling it to become a major actor in cultural life. Finally, in addition to these public ceremonies, the Haururu's members created more 'private' ceremonies in the valley in collaboration with three related organizations. These they referred to as the 'awakening' and 'putting to sleep' of the *unu* (which are carved wooden boards). All the ceremonies involve dances, songs, kava ceremonies and *pii*, an invocation inviting gods/ancestors/nature spirits to join the ceremony. A cultural ceremony always ends with the conjuring of the ancestors to engage in interaction of a temporary nature, as people and ancestors do not belong to the same world. The cultural associations accept that ancestors are truly invoked during their ceremonies, and as such have to be properly dealt with. Indeed, such ceremonies involve a new interaction with the ancestors, and in this sense also a new process of ritualization.

The first ceremony performed in public was a ceremony of welcome in 2000, when the Haururu invited a traditional Hawaiian dance foundation to Fare Hape. Initially, this ceremony was created to compensate for the absence of a Tahitian welcoming protocol, but it has since been progressively evolved, and its significance has become increasingly complex.

The ceremony began in the morning at the mouth of the Papenoo River, where hosts and guests had an official meeting accompanied by dances and songs. They then made an offering to the sea, and the Hawaiians sang in honour of the sea gods. Until this day, the Haururu members consider this practice to be Hawaiian, but they are still curious to find out if it was indeed a general Polynesian practice. Secondly, sea water was taken for another offering at the first archaeological site in the valley. Located six kilometres from the sea, the site is considered by Haururu members as the principal gateway between the lower and upper valleys. Sea water is offered in front of the *ahu* (the altar of a *marae*, the ancient place of worship) in order to ask the ancestors' permission to enter the valley. This is accompanied by specific songs and dances created and performed by Haururu members and dance troupes connected with the movement. In the past, sea water was mainly used to invest somebody or something with sacredness (Oliver 1974:108–9), however this was not the organization's sole purpose. According to the Haururu, salt was a valuable merchandise in the commerce between the people of the shore and those of the upper valley and, therefore, sea water is today an adequate gift in exchange for permission to enter the territory.

Eighteen kilometres further on, instead of entering the main area (Fare Hape village) by road, participants stopped their four-wheel drive vehicle and took a trail leading to a river. Here, some young men of the parish made an *āorero* (a traditional speech) in honour of the god Tane. During this *āorero*, the group had to cross the small river in order to purify their minds and to leave behind all negativity and stress coming from the modern world. Before noon, guests presented themselves at another *marae*, where a shrub was planted to symbolize their adoption by the valley.

After a traditional lunch, a kava ceremony introduced a *nati* ('weaving') ceremony. For the association members, a kava ceremony signifies an egalitarian gathering with the scope to sanctify a common decision made under the eyes of the ancestors.[3] In this case, the kava ritual sanctified the connections between hosts and guests, connections materialized by the *nati* ceremony, during which a few people attached themselves symbolically to the *taura tupuna*. This 'ancestral rope' is an artefact woven from coconut-palm bark and represents the octopus as a mythic Polynesian figure. Each tentacle belongs to a member of the Haururu and represents his or her genealogy. A few tentacles belong to other non-profit organizations linked with the Haururu, and on others, members recorded the significant dates of the association's history. The head of the octopus, a cone made of plaits twisted together, represents the common origin of the Polynesian lineages. This artefact is a modern form adapted from an *aide mémoire* exhibited in the Tahiti Museum. Little is known about its use in the past (von den

Steinen 1925:64–6; Handy 1923:342), however Haururu members believe that great pagan priests used it to record the history and genealogies of the chiefs' families. For them, being attached to this ancestral rope is a great honour, as it symbolizes the relationship between members and their reconciliation with their ancestors.

This is a strongly emotional ritual that ends with both hosts and guests crying and kissing each other. The evening is devoted to a 'cultural sharing' party, during which each group of guests and hosts gives a song or a dance to the other group. Nowadays, however, this ceremony is organized in its entirety only once or twice a year, in order to establish bonds between local people and non-profit organizations working for shared purposes of ecology, culture or education. In the case of a simple guest reception, they now perform the water offering only in connection with the planting of shrubs.

This ceremony presents us with two major aspects of the character of these 'associations'. First, it represents the necessity for cultural organizations to stage Tahitian identity, to demonstrate the place of Tahitian culture in Polynesia, and to show its similarities and differences with other Polynesian archipelagos such as Hawai'i or New Zealand. The ceremony stages ethnicity within the scene of Polynesian unity (cf. R. Scott, this volume) and gives visibility to their own views of Tahitian culture, rather than those of the Western imaginary. Second, the ceremony converts informal relationships into social community relationships, sanctified by the kava ritual and materialized by the *nati* ceremony. The process of engendering a community reveals social as well as political issues, and the ceremony is used to create a network of similar associations in French Polynesia and beyond. For the Hawaiians I encountered, the ceremony is like an identity pilgrimage, since they consider Fare Hape to be the centre of Tahiti and the birthplace of the Hawaiian fire-goddess Pele.

In 2003, Haururu instituted the already mentioned celebration of the Pleiades constellation, Matarii. This is performed twice a year according to the ancient ritual calendar, once in November on the first day that the constellation is visible, and again when the Pleiades leave the sky. *Matarii i nia* marks the coming of gods who fertilize the land, and *Matarii i raro* marks the beginning of the season of restraint and the departure of the gods.[4] Matarii is a public ceremony which takes place on the beach at sunset, whereas all the other ceremonies take place in the valley. People sing and dance in honour of the ancestors, a kava ceremony takes place with offerings to the sea, and finally a buffet is served. In some places the local parish also joins the ceremony. During the Matarii celebrations orators explain the meaning of each part of the ceremony, demonstrating that the ancestors were not in fact 'barbarians' but possessed knowledge, wisdom and complex spirituality, and enjoyed a better way of life, in harmony with their island. This ceremony is the association's main instrument for public relations, in that it demonstrates the movement's network and allows access to the media. It is also a time for its members to increase cultural awareness, and it is the only ceremony readily accessible to non-participants. Matarii is sometimes considered to be the least sacred, with Haururu members defining it as a celebration rather than a ceremony.

In order to materialize the return of the gods and to organize a more private ceremony than Matarii, the organization added the ceremony of *unu* in 2006. A week before the rise of the Pleiades, they erected the *unu* on the *marae*, and then removed them in a silent ceremony in May. These *unu* statues represent *tāura*, ancestral animals regarded as family guardian spirits or protectors. Nowadays in French Polynesia, many families have forgotten the *tāura* associated with their name. But as a family emblem, the *tāura* have begun to fan people's interest, and they are now becoming a favourite tattoo model. Looking for their own *tāura* is also an important aspect of people's personal genealogical research. When the *unu* are erected in the *marae*, the ceremonial participants related to the *tāura* represented on the statues are brought into contact with the narration of their genealogy in a traditional way.

As representations of ethnicity, these ceremonies seem not altogether different from the Heiva, or so-called *kastom* festivals in Melanesia. This type of ceremony became a political issue when associations began to consider their practices as an alternative definition of Mā'ohi identity, in contrast to artistic shows and heritage activities. I will now examine how members mobilize the local sphere of cultural representations and the underlying relation to the past.

How to deal with the past and the ancestors: culture, religion, folklore and sorcery

All the above-mentioned ceremonies seem to be conceived from the associations' definition of culture as a concept in contrast to 'folklore' and 'religion'. This contrast between culture and folklore is related to the desire to perform 'real' ceremonies. This involves a great deal of bibliographic research in order to legitimize practices as authentically Tahitian. Such work is not sufficient, however, as authenticity appears to be more reliably linked to the meaning of the practice, and to the involvement of the participants, than to its form. Members do not want to copy practices of the ancient society which no longer have any meaning today, other than as mere 'folk events'. Their aim is not to perform a ritual exactly like it may have been performed previously, but to discover what is 'essentially' Tahitian, through the combination of what is known about ancient society and what is relevant today. Consequently, association members' quest for identity and cultural authenticity implies and requires reinterpretation. Haururu members justify their right of interpretation on the basis that they consider their sources unreliable, that all historical accounts are European, and that Europeans could not really understand Tahitian culture. Reading between the lines is deemed necessary, and even if Haururu members actively seek information about ancient Tahitian society, they also claim the freedom of interpreting history with the aim of finding their roots and reviving their culture.

In fact, none of these cultural ceremonies have proven links with any pre-Christian practice. There is no proof that the ancient Tahitians even drank kava as a ritual practice. Similarly, the *unu*'s function is subject to speculation, and there are no accounts of rituals associated with it or of a connection to the *tāura*. In the view of the cultural movement, the kava ceremony is important nowadays not only because it shows Tahitians as Polynesians, but also because Tahitians need to develop community. Erecting *unu* symbolizes individual and collective quests for roots, identity and reconciliation with the ancestors, rather than whatever they used to symbolize. 'Real' ceremonies also assume interaction with the ancestors and cannot use any detachment processes such as artistic licence (which prevents the presence of the ancestors).

Cultural ceremonies are also imagined from an opposition between culture and religion. This is an ambiguous opposition, referring simultaneously to pagan religion and to Christianity. According to the organizations of this movement, all ancient ceremonies were religious, while today they perform cultural ceremonies (except in the case of the Matarii celebration, which they say has always been a cultural ceremony, not unlike New Year's Eve). Members of the cultural organizations stress this important distinction between cultural and religious practices for the following reasons. First, they consider that religion divides people, whereas culture is about sharing. Culture belongs to all Tahitians, and ceremonies related to it cannot refer to religion because not all Tahitians (and not all members of the associations) are part of the same church denomination. This is perhaps heritage from the French representation of republican secularism. People may belong to a church, but they may express it only in the appropriate space and at the appropriate time. A significant number of members of the cultural associations are teachers in the French national educational system, which is a historic vector of secularism. Second, Tahitian society has inherited from its history a negative vision of its own past and its pagan ancestors. Consequently, members of cultural associations are also afraid of being considered pagans or sorcerers, because their practices refer to the past and to ancestors, without the usual procedures of detachment such as artistic licence.

In French Polynesia, certain diseases are regarded as spiritual or as caused by the spirits of the dead. These are sometimes regarded as manipulations of sorcerers, but are often interpreted as the consequence of family ghosts being angry. In the latter case, the family needs to identify the ghost and determine why it cannot find peace, and then exorcize it. In the worst cases the cause of a spiritual disease is a pagan spirit, which is deemed more dangerous and powerful since its existence is beyond the Christian God's kingdom, and its soul was never saved.[5] The pagan spirit is an impersonal threat, unlike the other two kinds of spiritual aggression. If this kind of threat is nowadays no longer a collective but an individual issue, interacting with the past still involves finding a reason for misfortune. Therefore, in Tahiti and the Society Islands today, everything that refers to the pre-Christian past is still regarded as a potential spiritual threat. As a consequence, most Tahitians avoid facing situations that may create interaction with a spirit – including encounters with old ruins and artefacts.

Herein lies the ambiguity of the relationship to the ancestors that the members of the movement would like to remove. They consider it to be a demonization of Polynesian culture by the churches. Today, some pastors in the Māʻohi Protestant church are engaged in an internal debate surrounding the 'Tahitianization' of the service, with the introduction of songs, ukuleles and *orero*, and the substitution of coconut water for wine. These pastors consider Tahitian gods to represent a different form of God's power, and see cultural ceremonies to represent Tahitian ways of honouring Him. However, for the majority of the population, reservations about pre-Christian practices remain, and cultural associations act and speak very carefully, since suspicions of sorcery could compromise the reconciliation with the ancestors and the cultural awakening they desire. Moreover, the way they act and speak is not only influenced by a fear that people may understand it as folklore or paganism, but also by the members' own apprehensions about interacting with ancestors.

Owing to this fear of contact with dangerous spirits, even Haururu members did not enter the *marae* during ceremonies until 2006. Rituals were instead performed just in front of them. Members generally consider Tahitian gods to be powerful heroes, as ancestor spirits with *mana*. Thus, even if ancestor spirits are not evil, the fear of sorcery still remains, as some people may, intentionally or unwittingly, influence spirits – and association members cannot be sure of the consequences of their actions. Even if associations themselves point out that spirits are not evil and must be honoured as ancestors, interacting with these powerful spirits of the nineteenth century can still be a truly daunting experience. Ancient rituals are considered too strong, dangerous and complex, and members cannot foresee the consequences of a mistake or of a misunderstanding of historical data. Hence, when members perform a new ceremony, they begin on a smaller scale, and if nothing untoward happens, they enlarge and improve it. In this way, they introduce some spiritual protection in their ceremonies, as exemplified by the river crossing during the ceremony of welcome. This protects the group against animosity coming from the outside, but also clears the mind of 'negativity' – which refers to all the bad feelings coming from within the participants: jealousy, anger, frustration and so forth – which would otherwise have a detrimental influence on the ceremony and the interaction with ancestors' spirits.

Therefore, members of the cultural movement do not see themselves as totally in control of the consequences of the ceremonies, and on occasions certain undesirable effects appear. For example, on 21 March 2008 Haururu performed for the first time a ceremony for the equinox and for the World Water Day. All day long they made flower offerings in the rivers of the valley, and at sunset they drank kava and conversed about astronomy, myths and symbols referring to the water element. Two months later, observing the unusually low levels of the rivers, they worried about mistakes they might have made, and concluded that their offerings could have caused this unwanted effect.

Throughout the cultural ceremonies, members of this movement experiment with a forgotten culture and try to gain an understanding of it. From the Haururu perspective, interacting with ancestors should be an important part of a Tahitian way of life that needs to be slowly re-established. This movement reveals a new relationship with the past, in which culture appears as esotericism, and the quest for identity is apprehended as initiation. This past is difficult to conceive of, as there are so few traditions connecting it to the present. Indeed, members and representatives from the Ministry of Culture, museums, artists etc., consider that certain people are 'in the culture', as distinct from the rest of the population. This is not normative, and does not lead to hierarchy in the cultural associations, nor is it explicitly a part of their discourse. It is, however, a representation based upon the disparities between the state of Tahitian culture in the present and that of ancient times.

Present-day society is widely judged to be in cultural decline – acculturated to the West; whereas the ancestors, it is believed, could live totally immersed in their culture without the restrictions of the churches and Western modernity. For the members of the movement, rediscovering Tahitian culture is a matter of climbing cultural steps, without knowing where they will lead. In the past, people could live 'freely in their culture', and during the cultural ceremonies people may aim to rediscover this state. The presence of Tahitian ancestors' spirits – regarded as better repositories of culture than books – makes the ceremonies 'sacred' and 'allows culture to be felt'. In this sense, culture is not a matter of knowledge (which for association members is seen as the Western way); it is something you have to 'feel with your guts'. It appears that ceremonies are the appropriate time to 'feel' culture. The thrill felt by participants during the ritual is perceived as the experiencing of a communion with the ancestors, and as the sharing of the 'real' culture this communion allows. The experience of 'feeling culture' improves people's understanding and helps them in their quest for identity. However, the achievement of identity and collective reconciliation with the ancestors appears a very slow processes. People who seem advanced in their quest – but not necessarily the most influential members – must not progress too rapidly if they want to avoid becoming disconnected from society. Even if members, especially the elders, have become gradually more confident with their ancestors, they want to maintain ceremonies with different degrees of understanding. Nobody is on the same step along the path, and consequently the common purpose of a global awakening prevails over individual self-realization. Members of the movement know that their practices may easily be suspected of sorcery or that they may be misunderstood by people who are not 'in the culture', as they say, and this may compromise their desire for a cultural awakening.

The crypto-Christian religiosity associated with the ancestors has not been eliminated by their revalorization. Despite the movement's general discourse regarding the ceremonies as being 'anything but religious', this religiosity is a central ambiguity they try to hide behind the term 'spirituality'. Members of the associations do not all have the same attitude to this religiosity, but ceremonies have to be consensual. The tensions sometimes resulting from their divergences reinforce their belief that religion divides people.

The initiation quest for identity appears as a path between the porous frontiers of 'religion' and 'folklore', but these people cannot accept being considered as worshippers or folklore performers. The principal threat to the potential success of associations is that they are increasingly seen as actors of heritage. Since their actions are nowadays accepted by most Polynesians, their ceremonies tend to be seen as traditional rather than politically militant.

Cultural ceremonies and intangible cultura heritage policy

After thirteen years of leadership under the autonomist Gaston Flosse, Oscar Temaru became the first separatist President of French Polynesia in May 2004. However, the separatists had no time to implement the Taui, or 'change', as promised, for the election was deemed invalid in October 2004. After a new election was organized, the separatists won again in March 2005. From 2004 to 2009 a political crisis affected French Polynesia, with nine successive governments. Society, cultural organizations included, expected the changes promised by the separatist party, because they seemed more aware about ecological and cultural issues than the autonomists. In actual fact, the separatists have for the last twenty years adopted a nationalist discourse based

on a valorization of Tahitian ethnicity and culture. Consequently, in 2005, only
a few weeks after his re-election, Oscar Temaru accepted Haururu's invitation
to come to the valley at Fare Hape for two days of cultural meetings. They
convinced him that it was unfair that there was no real Tahitian national day,
while Christians have Christmas and the Chinese community has its New
Year festivities. The government responded by letting the Minister of Tourism
organize the first official celebration of Matarii in November 2006.

However, all but two small organizations refused to participate in
this celebration. The refusal was explained by two arguments. First, the
government handed the project to a marketing agency belonging to the
Ministry of Tourism, Te Heiva Nui, which organizes all major cultural events
in Tahiti. The movement blamed the government for changing the nature of
this Matarii celebration and turning it into a folklore project void of cultural
significance. The fact that the government only organized a *Matarii i nia*
celebration (the opening of wet season) and not a *Matarii i raro* (its closing)
also demonstrated this. Therefore, an epic show taking place in a theatre was
seen as inappropriate, since real and meaningful cultural exchanges required
intimacy and involvement. People must actively participate in celebrations,
and should not be mere spectators. From the point of view of the cultural
associations, official celebrations enacted as shows lack the necessary sacred
aspect. Consequently, association members fear that their own Matarii
celebration could also be seen by people as a folklore performance. Second, Te
Heiva Nui had chosen former members of the Haururu for the performance,
people who were on poor terms with other members but who worked in a
governmental cultural institution. Hence, the official celebrations and the
associations' ceremonies did not take place on the same day. In November
2007 and 2008 the government tried to take these arguments into account,
and the celebration was less elaborate as an entertainment spectacle.
Nevertheless, criticisms remained.

The government's way of taking over these ceremonies reveals a different
perspective on cultural heritage from that of the non-profit organizations.
Whereas the latter desire cultural awakening, the government is testing a
new heritage policy. In fact, in 2001 the government created the Service de la
Culture et du Patrimoine, a merging of the departments of archaeology and
ethnology of the Centre Polynésien des Sciences Humaines with the Service
de la Culture, an exclusively administrative institution up until that point.
The new entity has since been directly managed by the Ministry, whereas
the Centre Polynésien des Sciences Humaines had a great deal of freedom in
research and programming of events. This policy was strengthened in 2003
with the creation of the aforementioned Te Heiva Nui, which was to manage
all the great cultural, artistic and sports entertainments including the Heiva.

Before this, the Heiva was organized in collaboration with several artistic organizations. Today, a large part of the government budget for culture goes to Te Heiva Nui, so when the government decided to organize the *Matarii i nia* celebration, the project was lead by Te Heiva Nui and the Service de la Culture.

Tahitian separatists are looking for traditions to exhibit, as there are no collective practices which consecrate Tahitian ethnicity, such as the New Year's Eve ceremony for the Chinese community. Traditions classified as 'intangible cultural heritage' are political actions which show and glorify an immemorial ethnic unity. The separatist party was involved in a symbolic nation-making process (symbolic, because in its status, French Polynesia is a country under the sovereignty of France, and so not a nation), and this influenced their cultural policy. The initial project was to propose a Mā'ohi celebration related to the pre-colonial past, replacing both the pre-existing Autonomy Day, celebrated by the previous majority (because in the view of the separatists, the Autonomy Day was too closely affiliated to the autonomist party to represent all Tahitians), and the Heritage Days. The *Matarii i nia* celebration therefore had to compete with the Heiva linked to Autonomy Day. Separatists wanted a more authentically Polynesian Heiva related to pre-Christian culture in spite of the colonial history. Owing to the government's instability, Autonomy Day has since been re-established, and in the current context of political alliance, *Matarii i nia* is no longer a priority, though it is still part of the present heritage policy.

In addition to these cultural events organized by the government during the *Matarii i nia* in November 2007, a ceremony was held to honour Tahiti as the earth mother, according to a myth showing the island as a fish.[6] Songs, dances and a traditional invocation of the gods were performed. This part was organized by the president of a smaller non-profit organization, Te Hivarereata, which has close ties with the separatist movement. He has stated that his organization is 'based on worship, not culture'. This differentiation removes the common ambiguous distinction, used by other associations, between honouring ancestors and praying to pagan gods. Te Hivarereata adopts a religious approach to cultural heritage, which seems to have made the separatists uncomfortable. As a result, during the invocation of the pagan gods in 2007 (performed at sea, without spectators), some of the organizers secretly stayed ashore and recited Christian prayers, hoping that these pagan activities would not make God angry. Like cultural-heritage performances, the official ceremonies honour the memory of the ancestors, not the ancestors themselves; unlike cultural movements, their protocol refuses any interaction with the ancestors. Official Matarii celebrations appear as a glorification of cultural heritage, but as the separatist party is strongly Christian (even with a Christian cross on their ballot paper), it is reluctant to accept ancient practices even if it has acknowledged the 'traditional' culture being used to give substance to the ethnic and nationalist discourse.

This use of tradition is also significant in another ceremony organized during the separatist presidency. In March 2006 the government organized 'Birth Days' during which a human placenta was buried in the garden of the presidential palace. In French Polynesia, placenta burial is a strong tradition, but mainly in the form of a family ritual concerning kinship and land. It represents the link between a child and its family's land (Saura 2003). Parents plant a tree, and its fruits are meant to feed the child during its lifetime. The secret family name is also given to this tree. Burying an anonymous placenta in a public place is a new interpretation of this tradition, symbolizing that Tahiti belongs to all Tahitians, and not to France. In this particular case, the separatists gave new meaning to a private ritual, but for members of cultural movements it seemed eccentric to radically reinterpret an on-going tradition that continues to have both social and spiritual meaning. According to them, the 'Birth Day' ceremony is a distortion deriving from Western ways of thinking, adopted by the dominant mixed-race class of people ever present in political life. The way in which politicians deal with tradition and culture is considered by the members of the movement as part of the decline of Tahitian society – a decline against which they fight.

Both non-profit organizations and local government organize cultural events in order to stage ethnicity, but their purposes differ on crucial points. Since the emergence of the *renouveau culturel* movement, politicians have adopted cultural and ethnic discourses in their demands for decolonization. This heritage-focused policy is an affirmation of identity, an acting out of the statement 'We are Mā'ohi!'. It is first and foremost a nation-against-state claim, but more generally it amounts to a political form of otherness that looks for wider recognition, including that gained by meeting the demands for classification by UNESCO and tourism policy. Staging ethnicity is a way to reclaim the representation of the self in a place where Westerners have imposed their mythic version of a lost paradise for more than two centuries.

If members of the associations generally agree on the necessity of this type of external recognition, they do not accept the way heritage policy is using culture. It demonstrates for them a Western way of dealing with culture, not the Tahitian way they endeavour to recover. They liken this to speaking Tahitian with a French syntax. Cultural ceremonies are an alternative way both for staging identity and for challenging its official manifestations. Through their ceremonies, members asked: 'What is it to be Mā'ohi?' and 'How can we be truly Mā'ohi?'. This is not a question related to identity alone, but refers to the social space.

Cultural non-profit organizations as alternative political movements do not represent the aspirations of the whole society, but those of a particular social group. Indeed, the majority of cultural associations' members belong to the Tahitian middle-class that has been emerging for the last thirty years (Robineau 1984). They are Christians, essentially Protestants, and live in semi-urban areas. The leaders of the movements are mostly teachers, because they are the ones who know a lot about ancient Tahitian society, and are generally influential people in the semi-urban areas.

In Tahiti the middle-class has been emerging at the same time as the *renouveau culturel* movement in a period of great social transformation, with the opening up of the territory, the generalization of the wage system and a general turn to an economy of consumption. The colonial system has not only implied an absence of sovereignty, but also a particular social order. With the progressive autonomy of the territory, the emerging middle-class's demands are no longer recognized by the politicians' nationalist point of view. So, they take over the representation of the self as a collective expression of social change: what they want, and what they would like to recover.

The semi-urban area is the zone where social change has been most visible in the last twenty years, and where the traditional community based on family and parish life seems to have been progressively disappearing. Protestantism, as the main denomination in Tahiti, has become less influential with the strong proselytism of Mormons, Adventists and Jehovah's Witnesses, and with immigration from Catholic archipelagos like the Marquesas. Families and villages are thus more divided today than ever before. In this context, cultural associations aim to sustain a form of community life they consider to be in opposition to modern Western individualism. Moreover, deep in the valleys, in places which seem to be outside the reach of modernity, these associations have created and kept alive community bonds. This helps one to understand why ceremonies like kava drinking or the ritual of *nati* are so important for them. The kava ceremony implies sharing among humans and with the ancestors, and the *nati* ceremony materializes members' bonds. Culture, therefore, represents an immemorial identity shared by all Tahitians; religion, on the other hand has tended to divide them.

Conclusion

Cultural claims have a number of interconnected dimensions in the context of Tahitian cultural movements: a search for identity, for collective experiences and a social panacea in which ceremonies are a means of personal development; group communion; public relations; and political action. For part of the middle-class who try to maintain a community life that is no longer provided by the churches, ceremonies therefore represent an attempt to find a Tahitian way to express identity. These intentions stand in direct relation, as well as in contrast, to the cultural policy of local government, which is engaged in a symbolic nation-making process with ethnic claims based on the glorification of Tahitian identity through cultural heritage.

This chapter has shown the complexity of the representation of the self in French Polynesia, involving political claims in a changing society, crypto-Christian religiosity and the reshaping of past relations with the ancestors, within a particular definition of culture. These kinds of practices, often seen as cultural festivals, may be analyzed through ritual theory, although this is rarely done – perhaps since anthropologists more easily identify rituals as derived from stable or persistent phenomena, rather than from manifestations of social change.[7]

I argue here that cultural ceremonies entail 'ritual condensation' as conceptualized by Houseman and Severi (1994) with regard to the Naven (a male rite of passage in the Iatmul society of New Guinea) and defined as:

> The simultaneous enactment of nominally contrary modes of relationship:
> affirmations of identity are at the same time testimonies of difference,
> displays of authority are also demonstrations of subordination, the presence
> of persons or other beings is at once corroborated and denied, secrets are
> simultaneous dissimulated and revealed, and so forth.
>
> (Houseman 2004:76)

In the case of an analysis of rituals of social change the question could be: can the network of relationships acted out in a ritual generate, for example, male identity in a Melanesian society through a similar process as the attempts to create Mā'ohi identity in contemporary Tahiti?

This question proposes some interesting scenarios for the analysis of the particular status of terms like 'culture' and 'modernity' in the rituals. In view of social change, members of the Tahitian cultural associations perceive modernity as a threat to society. Modernity appears to be a vector of 'chaos' (Kapferer 2004), and society needs to be healed. This is the purpose of the cultural associations' political demands and ecologically oriented actions, as well as of their rituals. Cultural ceremonies reveal a specific religiosity associated with 'culture'. Such 'culture', experimented on by a group's communion with ancestors, enhances Mā'ohi identity and acts constructively on chaotic modernity.

Acknowledgements

I would like to thank Laurent Dousset, Deborah Pope and Claire Grant-Leroy for their valuable remarks and advice, and also the editors who have greatly improved the clarity of this work.

NOTES

1. Before this period the term Māʻohi was not an ethnonym but an adjective meaning 'local' or 'from here'. It is a floating identity, sometimes referring to a pan-archipelago identity in nationalist terms, including other identities, and is not fully accepted. In centre/periphery dynamics it is more commonly used in Tahiti than in other archipelagos, where people prefer their own ethnonym.

2. For Matarii rituals in ancient Tahitian society, see Moerenhout 1835 and Babadzan 1993.

3. There is no question of rank involved, and women can participate – in contrast with most former observations about kava ceremonies in Polynesia (see for example, Newell 1974 and Sahlins 1985).

4. Note the close similarity between the Matarii and the well-known Hawaiian *makahiki*, including the latter's significant role also in Hawaiian cultural revival.

5. This summarizes the traditional view of sorcery analysed 30 years ago by Babadzan in the Australes (Babadzan 1983).

6. This myth of origin, which characterizes each district as a part of fish anatomy, is the only one representing Tahitian unity. It is one of the most commonly used myths in identity claims (like the myth representing the Marquesas as a house with an island for each part), because it can justify an ethnic unity, used today in political and identity discourses.

7. There are exceptions, of course. See, for example, Firth 1967; Turner 1974; Robbins 2008.

BIBLIOGRAPHY

Babadzan, A. 1983. *Naissance d'une Tradition*. Paris: ORSTOM.

Babadzan, A. 1993. *Les Dépouilles des Dieux*. Paris: MSH.

Firth, R. 1967. *The Work of the Gods in Tikopia*. London, New York: Humanities Press.

Handy, H.S.C. 1923. *The Native Culture in the Marquesas*. Honolulu: Bishop Museum.

Houseman, M. 2004. 'The red and the black'. *Social Analysis* 48(2):75–95.

Houseman, M. and C. Severi 1998. *Naven or the Other Self. A Relational Approach to Ritual Action*. Leiden: Brill Publications.

Kapferer, B. 2004. 'Ritual Dynamics and Virtual Practice'. *Social Analysis* 48(2):35–54.

Moerenhout, J.A. 1835. *Voyages aux îles du Grand Océan.* Paris: A. Bertrand.

Newel, W.H. 1974.'Kava ceremony in Tonga'. *Journal of the Polynesian Society* 56:364–477.

Oliver, D. 1974. *Ancient Tahitian Society.* Honolulu: Bishop Museum.

Robbins, J. 2008 'Conversion, hierarchy, and cultural change: value and syncretism in the globalization of pentecostal and charismatic christianity'. In *Hierarchy: Persistence and Transformation in Social Formations* (eds) K. Rio and O.H. Smedal, 65–88. New York: Berghahn.

Robineau, C. 1984. *Tradition et Modernité aux Iles de la Société.* Paris: ORSTOM.

Sahlins, M. 1985. *Islands of History.* Chicago: University of Chicago Press.

Saura, B. 2003. *Entre Nature et Culture.* Papeete: Haere po.

Steinen, K. von den, 1925. *Die Marquesaner und ihre Kunst.* Berlin: D. Reimer.

Stevenson, K. 1996. 'Heiva: continuity and change of a Tahitian celebration'. *Contemporary Pacific* 2(2):255–78.

Turner, V. 1974. *Dramas, Fields, and Metaphors.* London: Cornell University Press.

CHAPTER 7

Dancing diplomacy

Performance and the politics of protocol in Australia

✳

ROSITA HENRY

Building an understanding of the complex nexus between social movements, cultural heritage and the state in Oceania requires attention to the intangible dimensions of heritage expressed in public events. This chapter explores how Indigenous Australians are productively harnessing the performative power of cultural heritage beyond, but also in engagement with, the state. I provide a comparative analysis of three different performance events that reveal how, in the service of diplomacy, Aboriginal and Torres Strait Islander Australians employ 'the human body as a moving agent in a spatially organized world of meaning' (Farnell 2001:7). I define diplomacy as a form of political engagement in which the participants employ various performance tactics of etiquette, to announce whatever claims are at stake and with the intention of avoiding open conflict. As Judith Martin writes in a paper entitled 'A philosophy of etiquette':

> Etiquette does not operate on the encounter-group theory of social
> harmony, which believes that conflict can be resolved through the frank
> expression of everyone's every thought and feeling. Rather, it recognizes that
> people may sincerely harbour a great many thoughts and feelings that, if
> expressed, would cause social disharmony.
>
> (Martin 1993:352)

I offer vignettes of dance performances at three different events: local, regional and national. My aim is to show how dance operates as political protocol, or as a form of etiquette in diplomacy, to convey messages that are all the more powerful because they remain unspoken and to announce sentiments that are all the more strongly conveyed because they are veiled. It is its very ephemeral qualities and intangibility that lend this power to dance. Through moving their bodies in dance, people bring fraught socio-political relationships into the limelight and attempt to mediate exchanges between estranged or alienated parties. I emphasize here the notion of movement and of cultural heritage as including 'culturally elaborated ways of attending to and with one's body in surroundings that include the embodied presence of others' (Csordas 1993:139). As Rolf Scott (this volume) in his discussion of the revitalization of Hawaiian navigation shows, while '[t]he double hull of the canoe, the crab sails and the steering oar are all powerful symbols of Hawaiian heritage', their political efficacy lies in the way they are collectively performed by Hawaiians as moving agents. It is in the dynamic act of navigating and voyaging itself that the power of heritage lies.

My understanding combines a semiotic with a phenomenological approach. I treat dance as a form of political strategy that can only be fully comprehended through symbolic analysis as well as aesthetic experience. What dance communicates is partially understandable through consideration of its affects; fuller appreciation must also extend to symbolic value. Dance is about feeling, but it is also about meaning. We understand the meaning of dance through feeling and we feel dance through understanding what it might mean. The events under consideration are at a local level, a birthday celebration on Thursday Island (Torres Strait); at a regional level, a cultural festival in Cape York (Queensland); and, at a national level, the opening of parliament in Canberra (Australia) on 12 February 2008.

A birthday party on Thursday Island

On 29 September 2007, I was invited to a birthday party on Thursday Island in the Torres Strait. It was a joint eightieth-birthday celebration for twin sisters, Ina and Cessa, of the renowned Torres Strait Islander singing group, The Mills Sisters.[1] The party was organized in a community hall in the main street of the town. There were tables laden with food, cooked and contributed by family and friends. The containers of food were labelled with the name of the contributor and the contents. Dishes included dugong, turtle cooked in its own blood, deer curry, fried rice, damper, stir-fried chicken, and sweet potato and pumpkin cooked in a variety of ways. After the meal there were speeches, and then guests went home to shower and rest while the tables were rearranged to make room for the night's programme of dance and so that the performers would face the table at which the birthday party sat in pride of place.

The dances consisted of rehearsed performances of *ailan dans* by a number of different dance teams, generally representing different islands in the Torres Strait. According to Mabo (1984), this style of dance was developed by Islanders from different Torres Strait islands at a two-week workshop

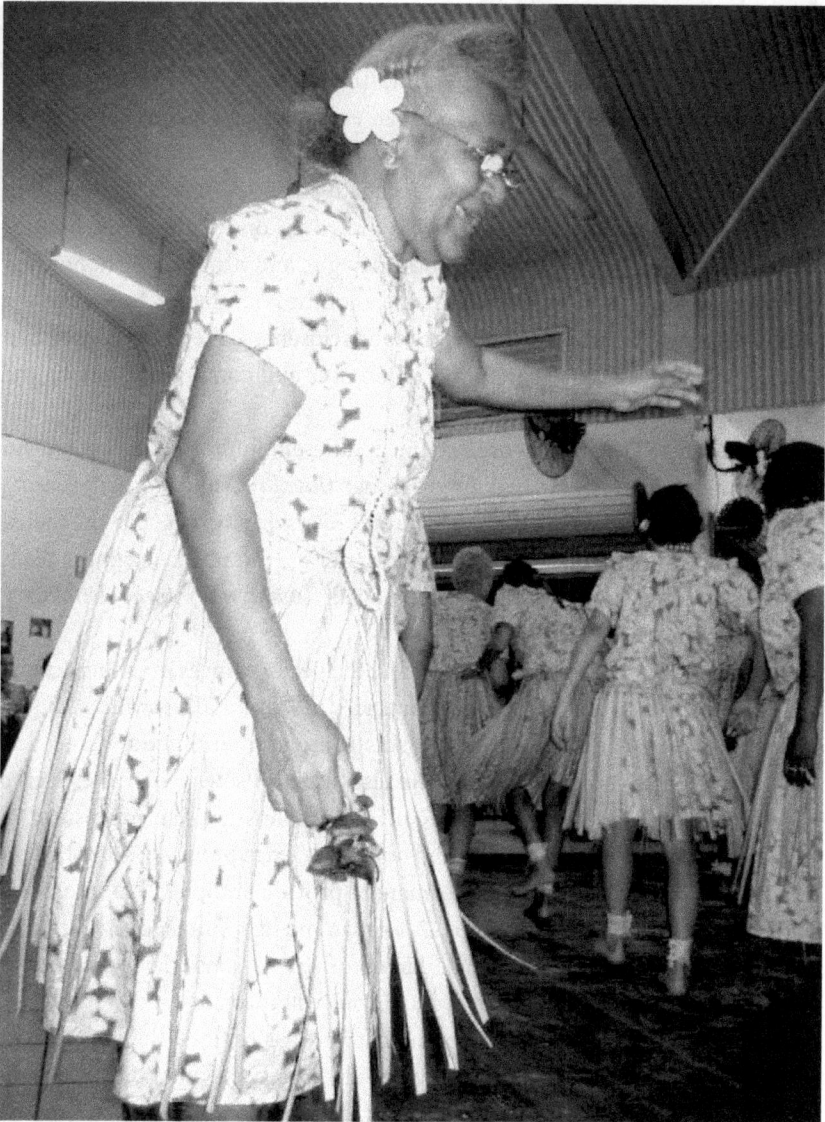

Figure 1 *Ruth Neru Doolah dancing at the Thursday Island birthday celebration for her twin sisters, 29 September 2007. Photo: Rosita Henry.*

about ninety years ago on Mabuaig island, while their pearling luggers were sheltering from the weather (see also Fuary 1991:267). The style is based on *taibobo*, a form of dance introduced to the Torres Strait by Rotuman Islanders (Mabo 1984). *Ailan dans* contrasts with an earlier style, which islanders refer to as *prapa dans* (Lahn 2004:75).[2]

The birthday celebration was an intimate small-community celebration among kin and friends who were well known to one another. The dance performances were both a form of birthday gift and a means of honouring and paying tribute to these well-loved elders of the community. Yet, while the dances displayed relatedness and communal closeness, they also constituted a diplomatic articulation of divisions, differences and competition among the participants.[3]

Each dance group was dressed in a different uniform marking team identity, men wearing plain, coloured sarongs (*lavalava*) and women wearing patterned island dresses with coconut-frond overskirts. Except for the Saibai Island dancers, who had much more ornate and complex leggings, team members wore simple white cotton anklets (*makamak*) (see also Fuary 1991:267; Lahn 2004:74).

I highlight the observation that, during the performances, members of the audience jumped up and sprayed the dancers' shoulders and legs with perfume or dusted them with talcum powder. This is a common practice associated with Torres Strait Island dance and is also found elsewhere in the Pacific (Liep 1994; Hereniko 1995). Fuary (1991:269) explains it as an expression of 'audience appreciation and delight' and notes that 'extra perfume is lavished on certain kin'. Indeed, the dance performances provide an opportunity to mark publicly particular kin relationships. A woman might spontaneously jump up and briefly dance close to her male kin (brothers or sons). Fuary (1991:275) notes that 'Sometimes she will not dance, but will instead stand close to her kinsman and hold a lantern or a torch nearby, so as to draw the attention of the audience to his performance, of which she as a kinswoman is immensely proud.' According to Beckett (pers. comm. 17 June 2008) in his day (1960s) 'they held up a kerosene pressure-lamp over the dancer'.

Such observations refer to invitations for spectators to see the dancers under the light, to hearken to the stamping of their feet and the sound of their seed rattles and bamboo-stick clappers, and also to smell the performance of these dancers. Corporeal experiences of sight, sound and smell enable the constitution and mediation of intersubjective relations. The anointing of the dancers with sweet-smelling powder and perfume is a practice that echoes other cultural practices in the Torres Strait, revealing the experiential importance of the sense of smell in constituting and mediating relationships among persons, persons and spirits, and among groups. Some time after death, the belongings of a deceased are usually distributed among kin. Fuary (1991:307) cites Lui, who noted that the clothes of a deceased were distributed 'so that the smell of the deceased was dissipated' and would not bring sickness and death to his wife and children. The spirit of a relative or friend may appear to a person in the form of a sweet smell and Beckett (pers. comm. 17 June 2008) has observed islanders dusting talcum powder onto a grave site.[4] It appears that Liep's (1994:70) argument for the Massim area in Melanesia applies also to the Torres Strait: '[B]aby powder has been appropriated into a symbolic context of colours, smells and tactile qualities employed in a discourse of life and death, youth and old age, success and failure.'

In addition to jumping up and perfuming the dancers, there is another practice that according to Beckett (pers. comm. 17 June 2008) can be observed all over Torres Strait in one form or another: 'Women, mainly older women, and occasionally older men do a funny dance, while serious dancing is going on. The dancers are not supposed to respond.' This intervention, he notes, can be: 'just to make people happy with no particular dancer in mind' or a means of 'celebrating the dance of a favourite son or brother, or nephew – probably a new or particularly skilled dancer' (see also Beckett 1987:2).

This form of intercession in the choreographed dance by members of the participant audience is known as *kaythian* (Fuary 1991:271) in the Western Torres Strait language. A woman will spontaneously join the dance team of men and perform in a comic or exaggerated way in front of one or more of them. According to Fuary (1991:272), a woman will generally do this to her sister's husband and notes that 'the physical avoidance and physical restraint which obtains between cross-sex affines in everyday life is temporarily allowed to disintegrate.' The performance constitutes a kind of practice of diplomacy, I argue, in that it provides a means for the mediation of potential tensions between gender categories and also categories of kin, particularly affines, as well as mediating actual relationships of estrangement and alienation between kin groups. Such performances, in which social boundaries that are maintained on other occasions are collapsed, are much appreciated by the participant audience, who in this local community context are well aware of the nuances and the nature of the relationships at stake. Their particular inter-corporeal aesthetic experience of the performance is flavoured by their ability to understand what the comic, sexually charged frolicking of the women, and other ribald interventions from the participant audience, symbolically represent in terms of the specific nature of the relationships being spotlighted.

During the performances of different teams at the birthday party, such burlesque or exaggerated cavorting by women occurred several times, to the delight of the participant audience, which responded with much laughter. One instance particularly stood out. In this case, a woman meandered on to the dance floor with a plate of food. She danced sensuously in front of the men, flourishing the dish, and then sat herself immediately before one of them and proceeded to eat with delicate deliberation. In the mean time, the man continued to dance and maintained studious inattention to her performance. Beckett (pers. comm. 17 June 2008) has never seen a routine with a plate of food in his field experience. Fuary (pers. comm) has also not observed this particular routine, but she has observed similar ones between women and their brother-in-laws. She has also observed mothers jokingly pretending to breastfeed in front of their sons, and suggests that in this way they highlight the reciprocities entailed in that relationship, but also reduce the dancer to, and remind him of, his most basic bodily processes and dependencies.[5] Another anthropological interpretation might be that such life-cycle events allow for performances in which social hierarchies are inverted, so that, as Hereniko (1995:77) writes in relation to clowning at Rotuman weddings,

> ... relations of complementarity that are conflict prone – between chief
> and commoner, between male and female, and between kin groups –
> are inverted and re-examined. The wedding context, like the plays of
> the western world, provides a frame in which forces that are potentially
> threatening to the well-being of its members can be acted out and diffused,
> displaced, or resolved in a safe arena.

The spontaneity of the women's interventions at the Torres Strait birthday party challenged the rehearsed choreography and equanimity of the trained row of dancers.[6] Structured roles, autonomous social statuses and idealized bodily states were momentarily exposed for what they are: part of a socially constructed smokescreen that hides the fact that the dancers remain dependent slaves to physical demands. Yet, as Suzanne Langer (1953:349) writes, 'the fact that the rhythm of comedy is the basic rhythm of life does not mean that biological existence is the "deeper meaning" of all its themes'. For Langer, 'the essential comic feeling' is what she calls 'felt life' or 'felt vitality' – 'the sentient aspect of organic unity, growth, and self-preservation' (ibid.:350) and laughter is 'a culmination of feeling – the crest of a wave of felt vitality' (ibid.:340). It is this felt vitality, I argue, that lends power to the dance as a tactic of persuasion.

The Laura Aboriginal Dance and Cultural Festival

The second event I will describe is a performance that I observed at the Laura Aboriginal Dance and Cultural Festival in Cape York, Australia. The festival brings together, every two years, Aboriginal people from Cape York communities and, occasionally, invited dance teams from other parts of Australia.

Figure 2 *Injinoo Dancers on the Dance Ground at the Laura Aboriginal Dance and Cultural Festival, Cape York. Photo: Rosita Henry..*

I first witnessed the dance performance I describe here at the 2005 Festival and it was repeated at the 2007 Festival. What struck me as significant about this particular performance was that this dance was a deliberate combination of Islander-style dancing and Aboriginal-style 'shake-a-leg', whereas the two styles of dance are otherwise kept quite separate and there is a heavy emphasis on the fidelity of the different dance traditions. In fact, before the performance the leader self-consciously announced that the young men and boys in the Aboriginal dance group from Injinoo at the tip of Cape York were actually of mixed Aboriginal and Islander heritage, and that in their dance they would celebrate both sides. This is all the more noteworthy because there had been tensions over the inclusion of Torres Strait Islander dance teams in what is considered to be an essentially Aboriginal Festival, and whether they should be permitted to participate as a matter of course or whether they should perform only if invited as special guests.

Relationships among the five mainland communities at the tip of Cape York have been delicate over the years. The community at Injinoo was established in the early twentieth century 'as an Aboriginal response to the drastic effects of European presence in the region' (Greer 1995:161). The four other communities did not come into being until after the Second World War. Two of the communities, Bamaga and Seisia, were founded by Torres Strait Islanders who relocated from Saibai Island in 1946/7, due to concerns over sea-level rise (Saibai is a swampy island only 1 metre above sea level). Historically, relations between Aboriginal and Torres Strait Islander people have been peaceful but fraught, particularly with regard to jockeying for dominance in, and control of, community councils and associated resources. The changing context of state bureaucratic structures and processes has done little to ease the tensions.

In 2007, while visiting Injinoo in relation to another project, I took the opportunity to ask one of the senior dance leaders about the performance I had witnessed at the Laura Festival. He laughed and said that they had been a dance short, and so, during the festival itself, while practising behind the scene on the banks of the Laura River, they spontaneously created the new dance performance, building on a dance/song that was already well known to the team members. The melody itself, he said, was composed about forty or fifty years ago as part of the creation of an island-style dance. It was an island-style song, but the lyrics were actually from an Aboriginal language of the mainland. In fact, he said, the words were provided by an Aboriginal man from Doomadgee, in the gulf region south of Cape York, and were in the language of that area. He then laughingly said that the song was actually a love-magic song, but that neither the dancers, nor he, knew what the words themselves meant.[7] Moreover, he gleefully admitted, the elders had not told the younger boys that they were actually singing and dancing love magic out there on the festival ground.

The syncretic or hybrid nature of this dance/song, with its mainland Aboriginal lyrics and its islander-style dance rhythms was considered by the dance leaders/elders to provide a perfect base for choreographic license in the context of the festival. The dance leaders drew on this well-known community dance-song to choreograph a new dance of diplomacy, one which performatively spotlighted the different identity categories, while at the same time mediating or bridging political differences between Aboriginal and Islander in Cape York through embodied identification with both.

The opening of Parliament House

My third vignette is the indigenous 'welcome-to-country' ceremony at the opening of the Australian House of Parliament on 12 February 2008, before the newly elected representatives were sworn in as members of the 42nd Parliament. This event exemplifies how heritage, as a construct that serves the state, can at the same time provide a means of unsettling state interests. David Hanlon (this volume) supplies a comparative example in his account of Nan Madol on the island of Pohnpei in Micronesia. While, on the one hand, state recognition of Nan Madol as a heritage site has resulted in its 'formal colonization', on the other hand, Pohnpeians have themselves 'proven adept' at using state laws, resources and processes to protect the site in line with 'their own very particular, culturally informed understandings of heritage and preservation'.

The welcome-to-country ceremony took place the day before the government made its historic Apology to the Stolen Generations of Indigenous Australians. I doubt whether the significance of this ceremony on the eve of the Apology has been fully appreciated within the flurry of media focus on the next day's events, and amid the attention given to scrutiny of the words in the statement. With this welcome-to-country ceremony, for the first time in Australia's history, Indigenous Australians were able to act as a nation to retrospectively welcome representatives of other nations to their country. Through this performance of political protocol, they were able to claim priority in the right to authorize shared access to Australia's resources.

This was the very first time that the Australian parliament had opened with such a ceremony. The leader was Aboriginal elder Matilda House-Williams, who acted also as the interpreter of the symbolism of each of its elements for the unversed. She explained the event by noting that: 'A welcome to country acknowledges our people and pays respect to our ancestors' spirits who've created the lands.' She added that 'For thousands of years our people have observed this protocol, it is a good and honest and a decent and human act to reach out and make sure everyone has a place and is welcome.'

The 45-minute dance performance was choreographed by Marilyn Miller, National Indigenous Dance Co-ordinator of Ausdance's 'Treading the Pathways' programme, who also choreographed the formal greeting by Matilda House-Williams of the Prime Minister and her procession with him to the dais. Miller contracted sixteen performers from around Australia, representing the wider indigenous community, to perform her creation.[8]

Matilda House-Williams interpreted the symbolic value of the performance for the audience by noting that it represented: 'The hope of a united nation through reconciliation, we can join together the people of the oldest-living culture in the world and with others, who have come from all over the globe and who continue to come'. A key element of the ceremony involved the handing of a message stick to the Australian Prime Minister, Mr Rudd. The symbolic value of the message stick was explained as follows: 'The message stick is a means of communication used by our people for thousands of years that tells the story of our coming together'.

But I wish to stress that the choreography of the dance performance itself was not subject to such interpretation. It was left to the audience to understand the significance of the dance, and the audience here was not just those who happened to be invited to attend the opening of parliament, but the Australian nation and the international community, via new media technology. In fact, my own understanding of the event comes not from 'being there', but from the visual representations on television and distributed to the international community via the internet on YouTube.[9] In Australia, and elsewhere in Oceania, cultural heritage is indeed a state project, an expression of state effects that 'never obtain solely through national institutions or in governmental sites' (Trouillot 2001:126). However, cultural heritage is also actively and strategically employed at the grassroots, sometimes against the state. Guillaume Alévèque (this volume) describes conflict that developed when agents of the state in French Polynesia attempted to appropriate, for their 'symbolic nation-making' project, public rituals that had originally been organized and performed at the grassroots as part of a Tahitian social movement aiming to achieve collective 'cultural awakening' beyond the state. Similar tensions are evident in Australia regarding appropriation of Aboriginal welcome-to-country ceremonies in the service of a nation-state-building agenda.

However Aboriginal Australians have themselves employed the concept of heritage as a political means for engaging with the state. This has been described by a number of anthropologists, particularly with reference to public performances involving dance (Greer and Henry 1999; Magowan 2000; Henry 2000 and 2008). Often such performances are interpreted as a form of political resistance/protest against the state. Tamisari (2007:40) argues that the impact and success of such productions 'cannot entirely be understood as Indigenous political strategies in the narrow sense of the term'. She proposes instead that they should be understood as 'a performative tactic, a struggle that, forced to play in the territory of the enemy takes advantage of any opportunity to announce itself and confront' (ibid.:40). The invitation to perform the welcome ceremony in the Member's Hall at the opening of Parliament House indeed provided such an opportunity. Yet, I suggest, the ceremony can also be read differently, that is, in terms of the expressive art of diplomacy. While not conducted between two states, but between an encompassed people and the state, the welcome ceremony is an example *par excellence* of diplomacy as defined by Der Derian (1987:110–11), that is, a 'mediation of mutual estrangements' that 'presupposes a system of reciprocal orientations' for the sake of 'self-preservation in an alien environment'. In heralding the official apology on behalf of the nation by Prime Minister Kevin Rudd that was to take place in parliament the next day, the welcome ceremony gave 'sensuous form to the signs of a desired reconciliation' (Cohen, Dwyer and Ginters 2008:79). The political efficacy of the performance can be judged by its success in enabling non-Indigenous Australians to secure a sense of authentic belonging and legitimacy in place, through feeling welcomed to the country by the original inhabitants. Yet, the ceremony could also be read as an assertion by Indigenous Australians of their right to authorize the very functioning of the state itself.

The sensory and the ideational

The three events I have described can be compared and contrasted in numerous ways and for many purposes, but my main aim here is to highlight how ethnographic understandings about the efficacy of cultural performances in local contexts can be applied to better understand the role of cultural heritage in state contexts. A focus on apparently simple events at the grassroots, such as a small community birthday party or a regional dance festival, can reveal much about the power of similar performances when, as cultural heritage, they are employed in the workspace of nation and state.

For example, in their analysis of the 2007 Balopa Cultural Festival in Manus Province, Papua New Guinea, Dalsgaard and Otto (this volume) describe how the main festival organizer, a local man who was not a traditional leader by birth, attempted to transcend local *kastam* criteria for leadership by harnessing the concept of *kalsa* (translated as heritage) to the festival and to other events associated with his nomination as a candidate for the National Parliamentary Elections. Nevertheless, while he 'employed *kalsa* as a resource for uniting people' in preference to *kastam*, which defines 'differences between descent groups', it could be argued that his case was actually served by the tension between these two concepts and by the ambiguity inherent in local interpretations of the performances as *kastam* or as *kalsa*. This is relevant to my argument regarding the efficacy of dance performances as diplomacy, i.e. that their efficacy lies in their power to veil tensions and to convey messages that must remain unspoken in order to allow for effective social interaction and delicate political negotiation and persuasion. In other words, diplomacy requires the performative means to conceal as much as to reveal.

Comparative analysis of the three Australian events reveals differences in the amount of verbal explanation of the dance performances supplied to each audience. The welcome-to-country ceremony required detailed exegesis for a national and international audience, while the Injinoo dance performance required only a brief introductory announcement for the sake of the regional Cape York audience. In further contrast, at the local community birthday party on Thursday Island, the comic dance interventions of the women required no exegesis at all; nor were the dance teams announced. These participants did not require any interpreter; they personally knew each dancer, how each dance team was socially constituted, how the dancers in the teams were related to one another, and what to expect in terms of their performances. In this context, I argue, the dance performances are understood via attention to their phenomenal surface; meanings are conveyed through sensory experience. Participants' sensory experiences of the dance are mediated by their personal relationships with the dancers, their comfortable interactive knowledge of the dances/songs themselves (evoking familiar memories of many similar past events) and their cultural understanding of the 'movement conventions' (Kaeppler 2001:41).

Adrienne Kaeppler (ibid.) argues that 'Dance like language, communicates, and therefore those who do not know the movement conventions will not have communicative competence and will not be able to understand what is being conveyed both visibly and invisibly.' Nevertheless, in relation to the three events that I have described, what are important for understanding their significance are not so much the movement conventions themselves, as the history and politics of relationships at stake in these encounters. Moreover, meaning is not merely a matter of understanding cultural symbols. Dance conveys meaning, even to outsiders, via the sensory experience of the performance and the embodied experience of 'felt vitality' (Langer 1953:340), and this is what lends dance its particular efficacy in the practice of diplomacy in intercultural contexts.

The three performances engage their participant audiences differently. All three events, the local, the regional and the national, carry sensory and as well as ideological meanings, but they can be arranged along a continuum according to their relative dependence on each of these modalities of consciousness. I am here influenced by the ideas of Victor Turner (1967) concerning the polarization of meaning in dominant symbols. I locate the Torres Strait birthday party at the sensory pole of meaning, where somatic understandings, resulting from sensory modes of attention reign supreme; while the national welcome-to-country ceremony in Canberra is at the ideological pole, where solemn exegesis of key symbols to a distant audience is required (an audience that would/could not dream of intervening in the choreographed performance in the way the participants at the birthday party felt free to do). From the sensory to the ideational, from sensibility to intelligibility, the three events capture the range of ways that meaning can be conveyed through performance and political agency can be asserted.

As a number of authors in this book have shown, understanding the performative dimensions of cultural heritage is crucial for comprehending how grassroots social movements in Oceania creatively work the political space between nation and state. An appreciation of the power of performance as diplomacy, indeed of diplomacy itself as a form of heritage practice, fosters insights into the nature of political innovation and alternative nation-making processes in Oceania today. Successful diplomacy, however, whether it is interpersonal, inter-group or in relation to the affairs of the state, requires subtle and skilful manoeuvring between, and harnessing of, both sense and sensibility, symbolic meaning and aesthetic experience.

NOTES

1. Ina Titasey and Cessa Nakata began performing their unique blend of island, blues and contemporary songs in 1975, with their younger sister, the late Rita Fell-Tyrell. The Mills Sisters have been widely acclaimed nationally and internationally.

2. One possible contrast is that *ailan dans* is 'presentational', while *prapa dans* could be classed as 'representational' (see Keali'inohomoku 2001:35).

3. See also Mabo and Beckett (2000:166), who note: 'The teams that follow one another onto the dancing ground are implicitly competing with one another.'

4. Liep (1994:68) distinguishes three main contexts of use of baby powder in Melanesia: firstly, in funeral rites where it may be sprinkled onto the corpse or the grave; secondly, in rites of passage ending 'social death'; and, thirdly, 'when honouring guests, feting visitors, praising a winning team or celebrating dancers'.

5. For a comparative discussion in relation to female clowns in Rotuma, see Hereniko 1995, and in relation to carnival performances among the Heiltsuk of the central Northwest Coast, Canada, see Harkin 1996.

6. Beckett (1972:3) notes that island dances were 'never spontaneous: with each song went a set of movements which had been put together by a choreographer'.

7. It is not unusual that island-dance song words are understood by neither dancers nor singers. Mabo and Beckett (2000:166) note: 'Most songs have only the most

general reference, for example to the movements of sea and sky, with no attempt to convey a narrative message ... the meaning is considered unimportant.'

8. Performers: Henrietta Baird (Sydney/Kuranda, QLD), Rochelle (Shellie) Bin-Garape (Cairns, QLD), Albert David (Sydney/TSI), Glen Doyle (NSW), Matthew Doyle (NSW), Jeanette Fabila (QLD), Ryuichi Fujimura (NSW), Paul House (ACT), Arnold Marika (Yirrkala, NT), Peggy Misi (Cairns/TSI), Djakapurra Munyarryun (Yirrkala, NT), Dennis Newie (TSI), Rosealee Pearson (Sydney/Yirrkala, NT), Micqaela Pryce (Cairns, QLD), Patricia (Rita) Pryce (Cairns/TSI), Vicki Van-Hout (Sydney, NSW), Rachael Wallis (Nhulunbuy, NT).

9. http://www.youtube.com/watch?v=R1JwyxNh3Ak.

BIBLIOGRAPHY

Beckett, J. 1972. *Traditional Music of Torres Strait* (with musical analysis and transcription by T.A. Jones). Canberra: Australian Institute of Aboriginal Studies.

Beckett, J. 1987. *Torres Strait Islanders: Custom and Colonialism*. Cambridge University Press: Cambridge.

Buckland, T.J. 2006. *Dancing from Past to Present: Nation, Culture, Identities*. Madison: the University of Wisconsin Press

Cohen, M. P. Dwyer and L. Ginters. 2008. 'Performing "Sorry Business": reconciliation and redressive action'. In *Victor Turner and Contemporary Cultural Performance* (ed.) G. St John, 76–93. New York and Oxford: Berghahn Books.

Csordas, T.J. 1993. 'Somatic modes of attention'. *Cultural Anthropology* 8(2):135–56

Der Dorian, J. 1987. *On Diplomacy: A Genealogy of Western Estrangement*. Oxford: Basil Blackwell.

Farnell, B. 2001. *Human Action Signs in Cultural Context: The Visible and Invisible in Movement and Dance*. Lanham, Maryland & London: The Scarecrow Press.

Fuary, M. 1991. In So Many Words: An Ethnography of Life and Identity on Yam Island, Torres Strait. Ph.D. thesis, Department of Anthropology and Archaeology, James Cook University, Townsville.

Greer, S. and Henry R. 1996. 'The politics of heritage: the case of the Kuranda Skyrail'. In *Heritage and Native Title: Anthropological and Legal Perspectives* (eds) J. Finlayson and A. Jackson-Nakano, 16–27. Canberra: AIATSIS.

Greer, S. 1995. 'The Accidental Heritage: Archaeology and Identity in Northern Cape York'. Ph.D. thesis, Department of Anthropology and Archaeology, James Cook University, Townsville.

Harkin, M. 1996. 'Carnival and authority: Heiltsuk cultural models of power'. *Ethos* 24(2):281–313.

Henry, R. 2008. 'Performing tradition: the poetic politics of indigenous cultural festivals'. In *The State and the Arts: Articulating Power and Subversion* (ed.) J. Kapferer, 52–69. New York & Oxford: Berghahn Books.

Henry, R. 2000. 'Dancing into being: The Tjapukai Aboriginal Cultural Park and the Laura Dance Festival'. *The Australian Journal of Anthropology* 11(3):322–32.

Hereniko, V. 1995. *Woven Gods: Female Clowns and Power in Rotuma*. Honolulu: University of Hawai'i Press.

Kaeppler, A. 2001. 'Visible and invisible in Hawaiian dance'. In *Human Action Signs in Cultural Context: the Visible and Invisible in Movement and Dance* (ed.) B. Farnell, 31–42. Lanham, Maryland & London: The Scarecrow Press.

Keali'inohomoku, J. 2001. 'Signatures embodied in dance: their transformative power'. In *Traditionalism and Modernity in the Music and Dance of Oceania* (ed.) H.R. Lawrence, 33–44. Oceania Monograph 52. Sydney: University of Sydney.

Lahn, J. 2004. '"Living in the light" and island dance: morality and temporality in Warraber Christianities'. In *Woven Histories, Dancing Lives: Torres Strait Islander Identity, Culture and History* (ed.) R. Davis, 73–89. Canberra: Aboriginal Studies Press.

Langer, S. 1953. *Feeling and Form: A Theory of Art Developed from Philosophy in a New Key*. London: Routledge & Kegan Paul.

Liep, J. 1994. 'Recontextualization of a consumer good: the ritual use of Johnson's Baby Powder in Melanesia'. In *European Imagery and Colonial History in the Pacific* (eds) T. van Meijl and P. van der Grijp, 64–75. Nijmegen Studies in Development and Cultural Change, v.19. Saarbrücken: Verlag für Entwicklungspolitik Breitenbach GmbH.

Mabo, E.K. 1984. 'Music of the Torres Strait'. *Black Voices* 1(1):33–6.

Mabo, E.K. and J. Beckett. 2000. 'Dancing in Torres Strait'. In *The Oxford Companion to Aboriginal Art and Culture* (eds) S. Kleinert and M. Neale, 165–9. South Melbourne: Oxford University Press.

Magowan, F. 2000. 'Dancing with a difference: reconfiguring the poetic politics of Aboriginal ritual as national spectacle'. *The Australian Journal of Anthropology* 12:308–21.

Martin, J. 1993. 'A philosophy of etiquette'. *Proceedings of the American Philosophical Society* 137(3):350–6.

Tamisari, F. 2007. 'The art of the encounter: the cheek, drama and subterfuge of performative tactics'. In *The Revenge of the Genres: Australian Contemporary Art* (eds) G. Leroux and L. Strivay, Stavelot, Belgium: Ainu Production.

Trouillot, M.R. 2001. 'The Anthropology of the state in the age of globalization: close encounters of the deceptive kind'. *Current Anthropology* 42(1):125–38.

Turner, V. 1967. *The Forest of Symbols: Aspects of Ndembu Ritual*. Ithaca: Cornell University Press.

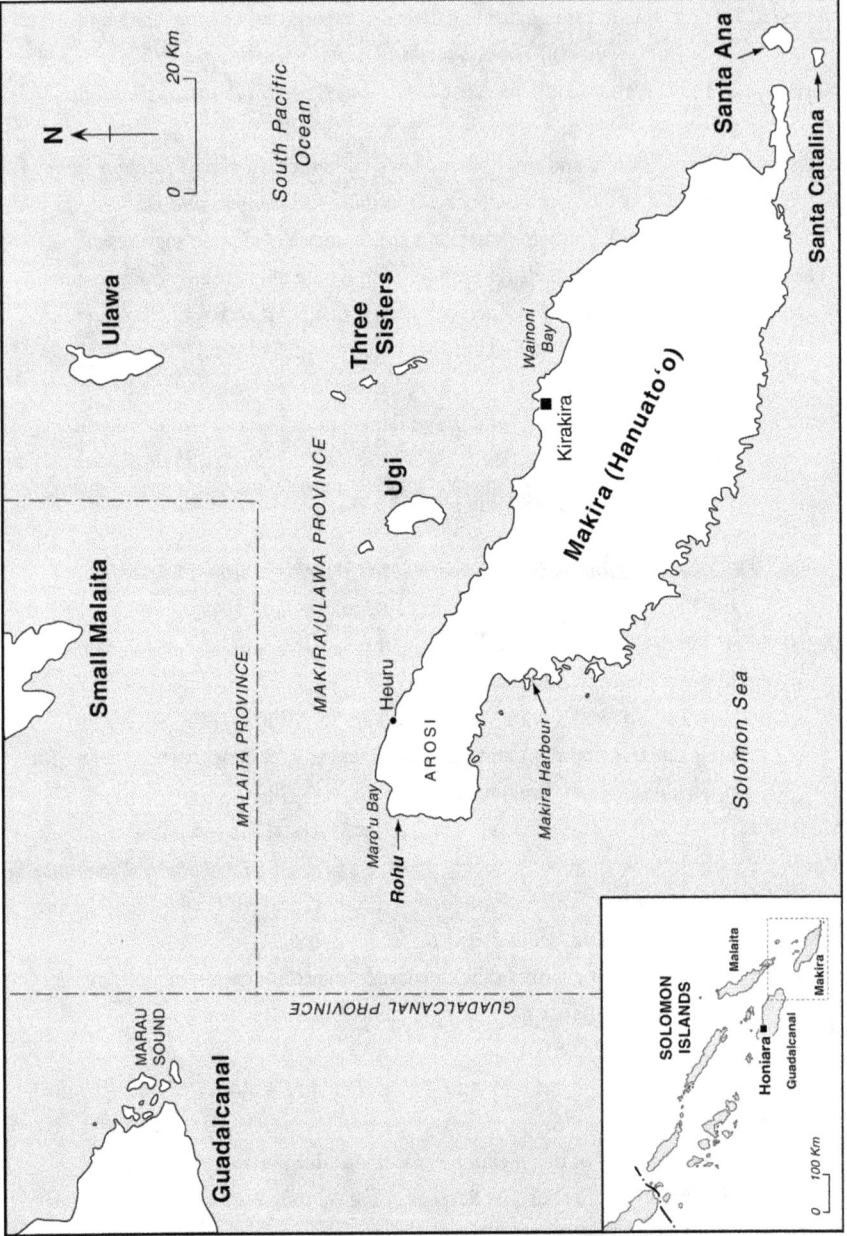

Figure 1 *The island of Makira in south-east Solomon Islands*

CHAPTER 8

The Makiran underground army

Kastom *mysticism and ontology politics*

in south-east Solomon Islands

✳

Michael W. Scott

Calls for a Makiran state and the state of being Makiran
On 4 August 2007, the following news brief appeared in the *Solomon Times Online* under the headline 'Kirakira Residents Awaiting "Mystery Army"':

> It has been reported that the residents of Kira Kira town have been
> waiting, for the past few days, for the appearance of a platoon believed to
> be a secret army trained in the jungles of Makira by specialized Western
> military personnels [*sic*]. Sources from Kira Kira told the SIBC [Solomon
> Islands Broadcasting Corporation] that the army was to have been part
> of celebrations to mark the provinces [*sic*] Second Appointed Day. The
> source from Kira Kira stated that the belief of a secret provincial army has
> been actively promoted by senior citizens of the provincial town, including
> Provincial Assembly Members ... Makira Ulawa Province has been, over the
> past few years, calling for independence from the rest of Solomon Islands.
> It is still unclear whether this idea of a secret army has anything to do with
> its desire to secede ... [R]esidents are eagerly anticipating the arrival of the
> secret platoon, which is said to be on the 17th August. The 17th August
> is also the Province's 'Chief's Empowerment Day'. The Makira-Ulawa
> provincial government has moved the celebrations of its Second Appointed
> Day to August 17th to coincide with the event.
>
> (Sao 2007)

With the aim of investigating earlier rumours and accounts of this same 'secret army', I conducted a total of ten months of field research in 2003 and 2006 on the island of Makira, the southern-most large island in the

Solomons archipelago. Building on my 1992–3 doctoral research, I worked primarily in the linguistically and administratively defined area known as Arosi at the north-west end of Makira, but also east of Arosi in the Makira/ Ulawa provincial centre at Kirakira and in the national capital, Honiara, on Guadalcanal. Recurrent themes I encountered included the idea that the army is stationed underground in a subterranean base, the 'door' to which is located at Rohu on the north-west coast of Arosi; that the army is equipped with super-normal technology devised by Euro-Americans with the aid of dwarf-like Makiran autochthons called *kakamora*; that together the army and the *kakamora* are the guardians of a pure Makiran language and *kastom* (tradition or custom) that has become obscured and depleted among Makirans in the surface world; that Solomon Mamaloni, the deceased Arosi-born former Prime Minister of Solomon Islands, is still alive and in communication with the army, preparing to lead it above ground; and that this emergence will bring prosperity, the restoration of true Makiran *kastom*, and political autonomy for Makira.

I found also that different Makirans engage with the figure of the underground army in different ways and at different times. A small number of Arosi, some of whom I was able to interview, say they have visited the underground and have there received revelatory instruction about a momentous imminent future for Makira. One man, for example, described how white Americans had contacted him in his gardening area and led him, by means imperceptible to his bemused senses, into a vast monolithic complex he supposed was the underground. Another man confided that he had once stumbled inside after treading inadvertently on a crocodile's tooth, causing a hidden point of access suddenly to open up before him. The accounts I gathered from such initiates, although by no means consonant in every way, share a consistent claim: they assert that the army, in accordance with a divine plan, wills for Makira to become autonomous as either a federal state or an independent nation that will be governed by the restored true Makiran *kastom* held in trust by the army and the *kakamora*. When this occurs, abundant resources and wealth will come out from and flow to the island and provide the foundation for Makiran development and regional ascendancy.

Having been privileged with this esoteric knowledge, initiates often feel compelled to seek out potentially receptive auditors, such as clergy, family members, earnest truth-seekers or anthropologists, with whom they might share what they have seen and learned in order to help Makirans prepare for what is to come. Even so, however, they also feel, as one man put it, as if under a 'taboo' not to 'spoil' the army by talking indiscreetly or lightly about it to just anyone. These Arosi are in dialogue with the army as an agent that makes demands on them and catches them up in an already transpiring process of *kastom* resurgence. They experience the army as drawing them into a movement that, if not yet a popular movement, is literally a groundswell, the unfolding of an irresistible force, a divine plan for Makira that is at work in their island and in all Makirans whether or not they will or recognize it.

Despite the burdens of discretion borne by initiates, their experiences and attempts to understand and communicate them are often the sources – usually at many hands' remove – of what other Arosi have heard and repeat about the underground army. But for this uninitiated majority, who say they are simply perplexed and uncertain about what they have heard, the army is not a consistent focus of attention. Some are intermittently motivated to look into the matter, to question others about what they have heard or seen, even to attempt to make contact with army personnel. Such interest in and inclination to give credence to the notion of the underground varies greatly, not only from person to person, but with respect to particular individuals over time. Mirroring the ways in which the army itself is expected to behave, talk about it tends to emerge during times of uncertainty or transition – such as the run-up to the Chiefs Empowerment Day described in the news brief quoted above – but recedes back underground during periods of relative regularity.

Given this diversity and fluctuation of orientations, no single interpretation can exhaustively analyse the Makiran underground army or even isolate what it most fundamentally is about. It invites and rewards multiple angles of contemplation and interrogation both from Solomon Islanders and from international researchers. With this irreducibility in mind, in this chapter I work towards a fuller explication of the opening news brief by examining the figure of the underground army as a clear example of how 'local cultural heritage' in the Pacific continues to be 'a central element in political innovation in and beyond the local' (Rio and Hviding, this volume). Specifically, I explore how the figure of the underground has become a site at which some Makirans are encountering what they experience as Makiran *kastom* – translatable as a 'local cultural heritage' (cf. Lindstrom, this volume) – in ways that are informing political innovations and aspirations for alternatives to the current Solomon Islands state, especially aspirations for greater Makiran self-determination. In so doing, I present ethnographic data that co-develop three interwoven theses. Although not treated strictly in sequence, these theses may be summarized as follows.

First, I argue that the underground army is a recent figuration of the ways in which some Arosi experience what they call the *ringeringe auhenua* (autochthonous way/custom; Pijin, *kastom lo*) of Makira, not only as a set of values and practices, but also – even primarily – as an essential quality intrinsic to a socially emergent pan-Makiran category of being. Makiran *kastom*, and the underground as one of its many images, are coming to signify the agency –

the power (*mena*) – of a distinctive Makiran ontology. For many Makirans this *kastom* is apprehended less as an object or possession than as an alienated self, a past and obscured but nevertheless still present and recoverable Makiran character and efficacy within a continuity of being that encompasses the island, its truly autochthonous people, and its inherent nature or way. Within this insular continuity of being, the relationship between the Makiran person and Makiran *kastom* is therefore non-dual; the latter is always both self and other to the former, eternally internal and renewable even while historically externalized and subject to depletion (cf. R. Scott, this volume).

Second, I argue that this newer Makiran category of being, with its singular insular Makiran *kastom*, is forming up in the likeness of, even while tending to rupture, older matrilineally defined categories, each with its territory-specific *kastom*. Increasing Arosi consciousness of pan-Makiran being and *kastom* must be understood, in fact, as constituting a transformation of Arosi models of ontology that both produces a scaled-up analogue to an Arosi matrilineage and has the potential to subordinate matrilineal difference to a higher unity.[1]

This higher Makiran unity is coming into being among and in mutually determining relationships with diverse but sociologically comparable processes of region or island-based ontology consciousness in neighbouring Solomon Islands contexts (cf. Allen 2009; Scales 2007; White 2001). Accordingly, my third thesis is that, as part of this semiotics, the figure of the underground is a referent through which some Makirans imagine and articulate – not simply what anthropologists have sometimes critiqued as a strategic *kastom* politics in which elements of a *kastom* repertoire are selectively and opportunistically deployed (e.g. Keesing 1989; Tonkinson 1993) – but, more accurately, a *kastom* ontology with an attendant ontology politics. By this I mean a political theory according to which legitimate power in Makira, especially the power to understand and administer Makiran *kastom*, must be inborn (not simply acquired), and is thus, according to some, the rightful province of genuine Makirans only. Such a theory can give rise, furthermore, to what I will term a *kastom* mysticism, the goal of which is similar in some respects to the goal of reunion with divinity, conceived of as a higher self, explicit in many religious and philosophical versions of metaphysical monism. Here, however, the goal is sympathetic insight into *kastom* through reconnection with the core essence of the island as a greater essential self. Understanding themselves to be potential conduits of the greater *kastom* in which they inhere, some Makirans are seeking to be guided and to guide other Makirans by accessing the *kastom* within – both within the underground and within themselves. Their hope is to establish a Makiran state founded on the state of being Makiran, to realize true Makiran-ness as the fulfilment of an ontological condition that is simultaneously a divinely ordained destiny (for discussion of comparable processes among some Malaitans, see Kabutaulaka 2001).

For the ongoing anthropological enquiry into the relationship between *kastom* and agency (e.g. Otto and Pedersen 2005), the relevant resulting observation is that many Makirans do not experience themselves as free agents in relationship to the traditions of their island. *Kastom* is not something these Makirans know as a finite cultural heritage they own or over which they exercise full control. Even efforts at *kastom* recovery and codification cannot wholly capture it, and it is never alienable. Makirans may lose *kastom*, but *kastom* cannot lose them. It enfolds them and calls them back, revealing itself not only *to* them but also *in* them as part of their very natures as Makirans. What Daniel de Coppet's (1985:81) consultant, Aliki Nono'ohimae Eerehau, said of land among the 'Are'are of central and southern Malaita applies to *kastom* among Arosi: *kastom* owns people. The agency of the Makiran person and the agency encountered as *kastom* are two sides of the same ontological coin, in internal dialogue with one another through – among other points of reference – the figure of the underground.

As I conclude, however, this does not mean that there are no strategic operators on Makira employing *kastom* rhetoric to advance personal or local community interests. Rather, it suggests that even the obvious political manipulation of an icon of the force of *kastom* – such as the underground army – may sometimes also be an attempt to respond to a perceived vocation from that force. Calculated appeals to the notion of the underground may, at the same time, be the results of complex existential processes of working out the demands and promises of being Makiran and how best to lead Makira by following its dictates. Returning to the situation reported in the *Solomon Times Online* for 4 August 2007, I examine the case of one particular Makiran politician whose career illustrates this point. Strongly implicated in the fostering of expectations that celebration of a Chiefs Empowerment Day would occasion an epiphany of the underground, this politician and his activities challenge analytical attempts to distinguish between a strategic *kastom* operator and a *kastom* mystic. His discourse and aims, I show, are exemplary of how political innovations in Solomon Islands involve the movement of local cultural heritage back and forth, not only between the seeming opposites of instrumentalist and essentialist orientations, but also between the similarly elided spatial and processual opposites of centre and periphery, state and grassroots, top-down and bottom-up.

From matrilineal ancestors to the underground army of the 'Motherland'

Among Arosi the idea that Makira is the site of a secret and extraordinary subterranean army is both old and new. Constituted as the colonial and neo-colonial transformations of many antecedent transformations of Arosi ideas about the power of autochthony, the underground army has long been a familiar element within a cumulative and dynamic modern Makiran folklore.

In its fully militarized form, the notion that a prodigious power somehow inheres within the island of Makira seems to have originated in the context of Maasina Rule, a post-Second World War socio-political movement prevalent in the central and south-east Solomons c.1944–52.[2] On Makira, Maasina Rule had entailed rumours that Americans fighting in the Pacific had established a modern 'town' in a vast hollowed-out cavern inside the island. These Americans, according to some rumours, were not foreigners, but the descendants of Makiran women taken away by Euro-American explorers and labour traders in the sixteenth and nineteenth centuries (Scott 2007a:105–29; 2008). At the height of the movement, some Arosi had hoped that these returning matrilineal cousins would assist Solomon Islanders to end British rule and achieve development and prosperity.

When I first conducted fieldwork in Arosi in the early 1990s, most people had dismissed these older rumours of an underground town – as well as other aspects of Maasina Rule – as having been misguided. I was surprised, therefore, when I returned in 2003 to find many people eager to discuss fresh rumours of what they termed a 'security force' said to come and go through a 'door' in the limestone cliffs at Rohu on the north-west end of the island. Alleged evidence of its activities included nightly sorties over Makira by small low-flying aircraft between 1999 and 2002; glimpses in the bush and at Rohu of unknown people in military uniform; eerie lights coming from offshore and under the sea; passing submarines – some camouflaged as large marine animals – and a mysterious ship bearing the word 'Motherland' that seemed to be keeping the island under surveillance.

Some people furthermore suggested that this security force might be operating in league with beings known as *kakamora* (alternatively, *pwapwaronga* or *pwapwaangora*). Arosi folk tales and purported eyewitness testimonies describe *kakamora* as small autochthonous people unique to Makira who live in caves and sinkholes and possess incredible physical strength, keen senses, and all-knowing wisdom (Fox 1924:138–47). Some narratives suggest a link between *kakamora* and the preservation of the material integrity of Makira. In the most well-known tale about them, they prop up the western end of the island when it is about to sink (Fox 1924:290); in another, they construct a sea wall to prevent inundation (Scott 2008:143–6 and 157). They also figure in at least one Arosi matrilineage origin narrative. All such narratives entail claims to autochthony through matrilineal descent from diverse phenomena said to have originated with the island. One example, which I have analysed more fully elsewhere (Scott 2007a:139–41), identifies a progenitor as having been a *kakamora*. In all of these representations, *kakamora* personify and reiterate the claim made in the Arosi name for Makira – Hanuato'o – which means 'The Strong Island'. Brought into relationship with renewed rumours about the underground army, however, these motifs appear to be undergoing reproductive reinterpretation in assertions that it is the *kakamora* who have taught the underground army its advanced military technology and have endowed it with their own super-normal attributes: omniscience, the ability to become invisible, and the prophylactic powers intrinsic to their autochthony.

In retrospect, I ought not to have been surprised by these reframings of the idea of the underground. In many respects, they make good moral and mythic Arosi sense as responses to the so-called 'ethnic tension', the period of civil conflict that disrupted Solomon Islands between 1998 and 2003 (Dinnen 2002; Fraenkel 2004; Kabutaulaka 2002; Moore 2004). Among the many causes of this conflict – which was localized mainly in and around Honiara – were disputes between those who see themselves as customary landowners on Guadalcanal and those they see as usurpers, especially economic migrants from the island of Malaita. The escalation of these disputes into coup, armed combat and murder – conjoined with regional concerns about possible terrorist infiltration in an 'unstable' situation – resulted in the intervention of the Australia-led Regional Assistance Mission to Solomon Islands (RAMSI) in July 2003, a mission that remains in place today (Dinnen 2008; Kabutaulaka 2005; Moore 2007).

As onlookers to these events, my Arosi consultants have tended to sympathize with Guadalcanal land-claimants and to stereotype Malaitans negatively as inherently aggressive and grasping of both government positions and other people's land and resources (cf. Dureau 1998; Gray 2002; Kabutaulaka 2001; Keesing 1994; Scales 2007). With the disruption of central-government services and the breakdown of law and order that occurred during the 'tension', many Makirans experienced a heightened sense of vulnerability to the kinds of encroachments and depredations they believed Malaitans were perpetrating nearby on Guadalcanal and might soon bring to Makira. In this context, the old idea of a secret subterranean realm acquired new relevance as the domain of a security force, the purpose of which is to protect Makira from precisely this type of threat.

But the Maasina Rule era rumour of a modern American town flourishing inside the island is not the only figure of power in the land informing current elaborations of the Makiran underground army. Equally important are Arosi assumptions about ancestors and their relationship to the Christian God, matrilineal land and *kastom*. It is chiefly as a scaled-up transformation of these assumptions, in fact, that the army acquires its character as a figure of a pan-Makiran *kastom* integral to a pan-Makiran ontology.[3]

Arosi experience their matrilineages as the bearers of autonomously arising, ontologically discrete categories of being. Arosi representations of primordiality depict diverse autochthonous phenomena – rocks, snakes, birds, spirits of the land, *kakamora* and other quasi-human beings – as existing independently in the island. In their initial condition, these originary entities lived in pre-social isolation from one another. Through processes of transformation and interrelation, they produced fully human beings whose activities of reproduction, place-making and exchange gave rise to the diverse Makiran matrilineages emplaced in their theoretically unique and mutually exclusive territories. Despite these transformations and ongoing relationships, however, Arosi assert that each matrilineage – figured as an ever-extending umbilical cord – constitutes the unbroken continuation of a single, pure and autochthonous category of being.

A corollary to this Arosi experience of Makiran matrilineages as poly-ontological is an experience of Makiran *kastom* as territory-specific and thus likewise fundamentally plural. According to closely guarded genealogically ordered narratives, each matrilineage shaped and was shaped by the land that became its territory. Such narratives tell how lineage ancestors established villages, cleared areas for making gardens, planted or tended fruit and nut trees, and enshrined the bones of their dead. As these lineage pioneers came into mutually eliciting and defining relationships with the land and everything in it – especially a cumulative body of ancestors – they received, divined and innovated the precepts and practices now thought of as the *ringeringe auhenua*, the *kastom* of each lineage in its land.[4] Conditioned by a contingent matrilineal history, each territory-specific *kastom* entails distinguishing elements: conventions for rapport with ancestors; practical and verbal taboos associated with specific locales; and a repertoire of personal names linking people to places etc. These differences in *ringeringe* manifest the ontological differences thought to persist among the Makiran matrilineages, understood as transformations of an original plurality of island beings.

With their representations of both matrilineal ontology and *kastom* as fundamentally plural, Arosi accounts of how fully humanized and territorialized matrilineages came into being furthermore imply an ongoing relationship between *kastom* and agency, within which agency is always both categorical and personal. Being an integral dimension of each ontological category, *kastom* may find expression in its category as a whole or in any of its parts. The territory-specific *ringeringe* of each matrilineage thus transpires continuously as the category acts upon itself via the fundamentally consubstantial agents of territorial land, local non-ancestral powers, plants, animals, ancestral pioneers and the dead. These interactions parse and re-parse *ringeringe* as unique categorical character into *ringeringe* as tradition (knowable precepts, institutions, figural designs, practices etc.), while simultaneously defining certain ancestors as those who, by their personal agency, innovated specific elements of heritage (names, shrines, locales, dances, taboos). Socially transmissible *ringeringe* is not the work of autonomous individuals, it is the product of a complex synergy among diversely manifesting agents within each category, whose interactions (encounters, events, dreams, divinatory communications) and relations with other categories transmute essential categorical properties into propositions for living and cultural forms.[5]

All of that said, however, it is also the case that Arosi interpretations of Christianity are among a number of colonial and neo-colonial factors that clearly have the potential to subordinate these essential matrilineal, territorial and *kastom* differences to more encompassing levels of ontological unity. They often do so, however, in ways that reposition these older, still socially relevant, differences as secondary rather than primary aspects of being (Scott 2005).

Arosi adhere to three main Christian denominations, and there remain today only a few elderly people who were not born into Christianity as their most immediate ancestral religion. Those living in the former Council Area still commonly referred to as Arosi 1 in the north and east are primarily Anglican, while most people in the former Council Area known as Arosi 2 in the south and west belong to the South Sea Evangelical Church (SSEC). Seventh-day Adventists (SDA) constitute a small minority cross-cutting this main denominational and former geopolitical divide.[6]

Apart from the SDA minority (see note 7 below), most Arosi – both laypeople and clergy – have long been at work on ethno-theological projects of rapprochement between their understandings of the pre-Christian past and Christianity (Scott 2005 and 2007a:301–26). Often asserting not merely consonance but virtual identity between the core content of *kastom* and the divine revelation contained in biblical religion, these projects regularly represent the God of the Bible as the true source of the *ringeringe* (way/ custom) of each matrilineage in its land. Implicit in Arosi discourses about such *ringeringe* is the claim that, whereas God revealed his will to Israel and Euro-Americans through Moses and the prophets, the Incarnation and the apostolic tradition, he gave the Makiran matrilineages equal access to knowledge of his will through endemic qualities, powers and allegorical messages placed in their territories (cf. Rose 1996:41–2).

Such claims to separate but equal *kastom* revelations can, however, seem to imply that – local variations not withstanding – each territory-specific *kastom* duplicates all others in at least some respects, if each is the repository of God's eternal universal way. Some Arosi make this explicit, saying that God mediated his *ringeringe* to Makirans, not through a code of norms and practices handed down from on high, but through Makira as a whole in the form of an essential, primordial, indelible quality – 'a good way of living' (*baronga goro*) – that inheres in all things that have arisen in Makira, including the autochthonous progenitors themselves. This Makira-specific 'good way of living' is thus the common inheritance of all autochthonous matrilineages, and, relative to it, the plurality of territory-specific *kastom* can begin to appear epiphenomenal.

In tension with Arosi representations of multiple and ontologically disparate autochthonous categories, this interpretation can suggest that, just as the island and autochthony convey a common core *kastom*, they may also convey a common core ontology as well. Few Arosi attend to this tension, however, or to the fact that the notion of an island-wide good way of living can subordinate territory-specific *kastom* to higher levels of insular and universal *kastom*. Rather, many articulate ethno-theological constructions according to which God both placed his way in the island *and* made the matrilineages the special caretakers of distinctive versions of this way in their territories. In these both/and understandings, the plurality of territory-specific *kastom* is subtly encompassed within nested scales of divine revelation, but it is not lost.

Most non-SDA ethno-theological constructions portray the ancestral powers respected in the pre-Christian past as having been God's deputies, whose primary role was to make known and enforce lineage and territory-specific *ringeringe* through various signs, including retribution for infractions. Today many Arosi continue to regard these ancestors, known as *adaro*, as powerful moral agents enshrined in the land, who will defend the persons and customary privileges of their descendants vis-à-vis strangers in their territory. Even in the early 1990s some people described these ancestral presences to me in military or para-military terms, explaining that they operate like radar systems or immigration control officers to police their territories and protect their descendants from potentially usurping or violating encroachments. *Adaro*, in other words, manifest *kastom* as the unique, God-given nature and efficacy of each matrilineal category in its territory.

It is important to emphasize that Arosi do not appear to conceive of the underground army as made up of, related to, or working in conjunction with ancestral *adaro*. Furthermore, although many Arosi expect *adaro* to be active in the land, I have never heard Arosi describe ancestors as carrying on an afterlife existence underground (but see Fox 1924:234 and 285). Nevertheless, analytically speaking, since the height of the 'tension' it has been as if Arosi are re-imagining the Maasina Rule era idea of an underground town and its inhabitants as the insular-level analogue to their ancestral, territory-specific *adaro*. As these powers are to their respective territories, the underground army is a guardian entity policing the integrity of Makira – conceptualized as 'Motherland' – and the rights of true Makirans within a nation-state undergoing crisis and its aftermath.

But the army is more than a border patrol. Like the *adaro*, it is a source of, as well as the force behind, a distinctive way of life that is not merely the 'law of the land' but the law *in* the land. It is a bearer of *kastom*, according to accounts I garnered, in three related ways at once: it is the embodiment of true Makiran *kastom* because its personnel, like the *kakamora* with whom they are allied, enact and model true Makiran *kastom* in their language and behaviour; it is the physical locus of true Makiran *kastom* as a power concentrated at the core of the island; and it is the means by which true Makiran *kastom* will be restored to the surface. It is, in other words, a figure of *kastom* as a manifestation of the unique, God-given nature and efficacy of the island of Makira as a whole.[7]

This situation is both similar to and different from the one David Akin (2005) describes as prevalent – also since Maasina Rule – among the mountain Kwaio of Malaita, who have adamantly rejected Christianity. In an incisive contribution to recent debates on *kastom* and 'the invention of tradition', Akin analyses the processes whereby *kastom* discourses have reconfigured Kwaio relations with their ancestors, demonstrating that *kastom* is cultural: the transformer and the transformed (cf. Sahlins 1999). He shows how *kastom* discourses preoccupied with codifying taboos regulating women's bodily functions – a generic scale of *kastom* impinging on every household and an apt symbolic site at which mountain Kwaio as an embattled social body seek to regulate their boundaries with others – has foregrounded a generic category of pan-mountain Kwaio ancestors not previously salient in Kwaio moral consciousness:

> In the past, there was no conception of a single 'Kwaio religion' across the area. Rather, distinctive composites of ancestral spirits and their taboos distinguished individuals and communities across the region, highlighting diversity, division, and structures of complex cross-cutting linkages rather than any overall unity. They still do this. But today 'The Ancestors' as an undifferentiated group have also come to symbolize the whole of mountain Kwaio society, a social entity that had no conscious existence as such until the colonial era.
>
> (Akin 2005:199; cf. Burt 1982 and 1994:215; Naitoro 1993:130–2)

Rather than as ancestors, who remain for Arosi icons of essential matrilineal and territorial difference, Arosi figure the character and active power of pan-Makiran *kastom* as an underground army. But despite this difference, as with 'The Ancestors' in relation to the mountain Kwaio, it might well be said that this army 'symbolizes' an insular Makiran identity, an identity that may have had little or no 'conscious existence as such until the colonial era' and that is still very much in the making within the social and political dynamics of the neo-colonial multi-ethnic nation-state (cf. Keesing 1989:21). At the same time, however, from the point of view of those Arosi who engage with it, the image of the army offers more than a Makiran identity to be worn before others. It suggests a living *kastom* that is increasingly presumed to arise from their literal ground of being – underpinning their still important but now potentially subordinated matrilineal selves – even as it impinges on them as an overarching insular power with which they interact.

Kastom politics as ontology politics

This is to say that, within the incipient category of Makiran-ness, the relationship between *kastom* and agency is developing as a scaled-up analogue to the relationship between territory-specific *ringeringe* and agency long modelled as operative within each matrilineal category. For many Arosi today, Makiran *kastom* is part of the essential nature of all true Makirans; it is a power that inheres in them in the same way that it inheres in all things autochthonous to their island: stones, endemic species, non-ancestral 'wild' *adaro*, apical ancestral entities, *kakamora* and, now, the underground. At any time, therefore, Makiran *kastom* may become manifest through the agency of any of these forms, at any of these interactive and co-conditioning scales.

Most Makirans presume that the *kastom* active in them is essentially other vis-à-vis the multiple forms of *kastom* active in people from other islands or regions; some Makirans furthermore presume that their distinctive *kastom* entails – even demands – a *kastom* politics that is, more fundamentally, an ontology politics. This can consist in two key assumptions: first, that any truly autochthonous person of the island, regardless of his or her mastery of *kastom* as received tradition, has the potential to become an authoritative source of a living, renewable *kastom*; and second, that such a person is to be preferred – indeed, *is* preferred *by* the island – to hold, or at least discern who should hold, positions of power impinging on Makira. Such confidence in an essential affinity between a true person of the island and Makiran *kastom* does not depend on engagement with the figure of the underground, however. It informs other *kastom* revival discourses and initiatives as well. Accordingly, in this section I elaborate how this political theory is evident both beyond and in relation to ideas about the underground in ways that are shaping Arosi participation in democratic processes at every level of government.

The most explicit formulations of a Makiran politics of ontology that I encountered arose in connection with the imminent implementation of a political innovation known as the New Community Governance Regime 2006 (cf. Alasia 2008:140). This Regime, in brief, comprises a set of ordinances for the creation and coordination of a complex range of village, ward and provincial councils, authorities and programmes. Among other things, it provides for every electoral ward to empower a Ward Council of Chiefs and to send one Ward Chief to serve on a Great Council of Chiefs in an advisory capacity to the existing Provincial Assembly. It was the inauguration of this Regime, in fact, that stood directly behind the preparations for a Chiefs Empowerment Day referred to in the *Solomon Times Online* news brief quoted above.

Ontology politics came to the surface when people, who to my knowledge have no particular interest in the figure of the underground, shared their views on how this Regime should be put into practice. One man, for example, expressed to me his concern that the people put forward to serve on the Ward Councils of Chiefs prescribed by the Regime ought exclusively to be *sae auhenua*, people who can trace their descent from the putatively autochthonous matrilineages of the island. Ideally, they should be like him: 'true' (*ha'amori*) – by which he meant descended from such exogamous matrilineages through both mother and father. This man has been making a study of *kastom* with older Arosi for many years and is a clerk on a local 'custom court' that is attempting to recruit younger members and train them in *kastom* knowledge. Yet for him, such acquired knowledge alone cannot qualify one to judge *kastom* matters. Only a *sae auhenua*, he said, has the gentle, accommodating and mild disposition necessary to respect, understand and uphold Makiran *kastom* properly.[8] Similarly, another man, who spoke at a village workshop devoted to explaining how the Regime would work (see further discussion of this meeting below), argued that the Great Council of Chiefs ought to have veto power over acts of the Provincial Assembly on the following grounds:

> We want to bring back to life the *auhenua* [autochthonous] government. So
> if the Provincial Assembly passes a bill that does not follow the will of the
> island, the Great Council of Chiefs should have veto power. These [chiefs]
> are the *auhenua* of the island.

This idea that an *auhenua* person can be a conduit of 'the will of the island' constitutes, I suggest, a kind of *kastom* mysticism – a term I employ, not in a pejorative or dismissive sense, but in a specific analytical sense to denote an orientation to *kastom* as integral to one's own being. Makiran *kastom* mysticism is literal identity politics: the political privileging of one who enjoys identity of being with Makira. The concept of the true person of the island, in other words, is as much a figure of the agency of *kastom* as the underground or *kakamora*. Such a person is another site, at the most intimate scale, where *kastom* lies hidden but can never die out. Because *kastom* is a quality and a way of being that was instilled by God in the island at its inception, it pervades all things Makiran and is always potentially available for fresh elicitations and personal epiphanies (cf. Bonnemaison 1994:322–3).[9]

Clearly, the figure of the underground army is neither indispensable to nor definitive of the Makiran mystical quest for reunion with lost *kastom*. Rather, as a figure nearly congruent with the scale of the island as a whole, it is a point of reference through which Makirans can experience *kastom* as an encompassing stream of being in which they live and move and have their being, and which lives and moves and has its being in them. The army is both out there to be encountered and viscerally, intuitively linked to the true Makiran by virtue of this continuous closed ontological loop. An apt Arosi paraphrasing of a mystical reading of Luke 17:21 might be 'the underground is within you.'

To illustrate this point and further develop what I mean by *kastom* mysticism, I turn now to the case of one Arosi man who told me that he is considering standing for election to the national parliament in order to serve what he understands to be the underground army's peace-making agenda. Identifying himself as 'a true person of Makira', he suggested that his political ambitions are inspired by a sense of vocation from God and Makira, mediated through the agency of the underground with which he hopes eventually to communicate. My interlocutor in this instance was a young Anglican in his thirties from north-east Arosi who had been working for seven years in Honiara when I met and interviewed him there.

Our conversation took place on the evening of what has become known as 'Black Tuesday' – 18 April 2006 – the day Honiara's Chinatown was burned and looted following the announcement of a new national government (Alasia 2008; Allen 2008; Kabutaulaka and Kabutaulaka 2007). In this context, which seemed to threaten a return to violent civil 'tension', this man confided his conviction that Makira holds the answer to the problem of civil discord in Solomon Islands. 'We people of Makira can sort out the lasting peace in Solomon Islands', he said. 'Makira can do that. I believe this strongly, because we people of Makira are peacemakers.'

When I asked him how Makira could bring peace, he began circuitously to approach the topic of the underground. Eventually he answered that on Makira 'we have a strange thing, like a *mamaani usuri* (a handed-down account of supposed actual events); people call it *bahai nai ano* (the underground).' Then he cautioned:

> [B]ut it is very sensitive, Scott. It is very sensitive, as I've told you. It is my
> culture [*kalsa*], it is my culture, it is our security. So when I like to tell the
> whole story I don't feel comfortable, because it is an international global
> base and I think it stands ready for things to come in the future.

The future this man anticipates is 'another tension', 'another crisis'. But there will not be 'another RAMSI to come', he predicted. Rather, 'there is a peacemaker already here in Solomon Islands' that will be more efficacious than RAMSI; the underground army will emerge and succeed finally in bringing order to Solomon Islands.

The army will succeed, he suggested, because it has harnessed the power of the true Makiran *kastom* that is synonymous with the *kakamora*. 'I think they use the *kakamora*.' he said. 'That's the only power they're using.' He soon went on to equate the *kakamora* with the 'culture' of Makira: 'I say Makira is a special island. Most provinces have their own culture, but we Makirans have *kakamora*.' They 'hold the real *kastom* of Makira.' It is this man's theory that the white people in the underground are Europeans who have 'adopted' this culture. Like the *kakamora*, therefore, they are now endowed with special abilities. They are in control of 'strong power'. They can 'disappear and appear'. And they have become 'very wise'; they know the true Makiran *kastom* that alone, according to this man, can end disputes and bring lasting peace to the Solomons.

Before this can happen, however, a leader who is 'truly from Makira' must prepare the island for its role as peacemaker by helping Makirans recover their true *kastom*. The Europeans in the underground have adopted true Makiran *kastom*, and now – as this man put it – 'it becomes active to them'. Then he added: 'But not to us, because we have a different culture; we don't know *kastom*. We're all over the place now. So, we have to go back to the original culture which they live according to.' If Makirans return to their *kastom*, he claimed, it will become a source of power for them as well; they will become like the underground army and the *kakamora*. Makira will then be ready to take its rightful place as benevolent leader and peace-keeping 'Motherland' to the rest of the Solomons.

To this end, this man contemplates whether he might be the leader Makira requires, even though he acknowledges that he is not well versed in Makiran *kastom*. 'I'm very young and I want to learn *kastom*,' he told me, 'but I can't, because I have a job.' He is very disturbed by his own theory that

Europeans working with the *kakamora* in the underground have accessed the power of this *kastom*, while he and other Makirans have lost it. At the same time, however, he credits himself as 'a person of Makira' with special powers of insight and prognostication, and seems to regard being 'truly from Makira' as the chief asset he needs in order to lead Makira to *kastom* revival. Moreover, the *kastom* revival he envisions will rely not only on the knowledge of 'old people', many of whom have 'lost the original culture', but also on the experiences of younger Makirans – such as a cousin of his, to whom, he says, the powers at work in the underground are already revealing *kastom* anew. Thus, in spite of his youth and ignorance, and on the strength of such signs of spontaneous renewal, he intends, he told me, to seek a seat in parliament at the next general election and to campaign on a platform of *kastom* restoration.

His plans were still in the making, however. He was not yet sure what the underground wanted him to do. He was looking for 'evidence', for a sign from the underground that his interpretation of the situation in the Solomons is correct. He said he wanted to return to Makira first to look into it, literally, and seemed confident that the army would admit him. 'It will show me a signal directly, and then I'll know what to do and how to go about it.'

In the months prior to my interview with this man, I had been resident in Arosi during the campaigning and polling for the 5 April 2006 general election that eventuated in 'Black Tuesday'. In that context, too, I found that the figure of the underground was a focus for *kastom* mysticism underpinning some people's participation in democratic processes, but with significantly different potential implications for ontology politics. Attending campaign events and speaking with voters, I learned that some Arosi were reading the platforms of various candidates in terms of their own speculations and hopes regarding the underground. But these voters were scrutinizing candidates not so much for their supposed Makiran ontology quotient, as for signs that they might – either with or without their own knowledge – be instruments of the underground's larger purposes. Their *kastom* mysticism lay not in insisting that their future MP be a true person of the island (or in aspiring to stand for office themselves), but in taking it upon themselves to discern signs of who might be the army's chosen means of advancing the destiny of Makira. They looked for supposed allegorical correspondences between aspects of various candidates or their rhetoric and elements of well-known Arosi folk tales, interpretations of Arosi place names, distinctive Makiran landmarks such as caves associated with the *kakamora* or the many distinctive limestone formations suggestive of meaningful forms in the vicinity of the 'door' to the underground at Rohu. Some voters, for example, understood the terms of one candidate's agenda for *kastom* revitalization as containing messages that, if elected, the candidate would work to advance the time when the original *kastom* of Makira preserved by the *kakamora* would re-emerge.

Such acceptance of the possibility that someone whose Makiran ontology might be cast into doubt could nevertheless serve the underground army and the cause of Makiran *kastom* doubtlessly owes something to biblical narratives that depict God making use of the nations to further his plans for Israel (e.g. Isaiah 45:1–7). At the same time, this approach to choosing a leader likewise appears consonant with ethnographic evidence and ongoing understandings regarding how chiefs were chosen in the past (Fox 1924:181–90; cf. Scott 2000 and 2007a:75–82). A traditional chief exercised authority over a polity comprising multiple exogamous matrilineages, but situated on land putatively held by the *burunga i auhenua*, the one matrilineage uniquely autochthonous to that particular territory. But such a chief was not necessarily a member of the matrilineage on whose land he managed inter-lineage sociality. His authority to administer the *ringeringe auhenua* of that place rested on an analogous presupposition that the *burunga i auhenua*, as agents of their specific *ringeringe*, could anoint a non-*auhenua* chief who would follow the will of their land for the benefit of everyone settled in it.

Additionally, beyond the context of the ballot box, evidence that the figure of the underground is mediating *kastom* mysticism in Arosi political life is also legible in the expectations with which some Makirans, as reported in the *Solomon Times Online*, awaited the Chiefs Empowerment Day in August 2007. The anticipation surrounding this event suggests that some *kastom* mystics were operating with the assumption that the army will respond to political measures that realize elements of its *kastom* restoration and regional-autonomy agenda for Makira. Again, this perspective looks familiar; it resembles some forms of biblical Messianism. Just as some forms of biblical Messianism assert that the Messiah will come only after human beings have actively prepared the way by returning to strict observance of God's law, so some Makirans appear to regard the raising of *kastom*, especially the empowerment of chiefs, to be incumbent on human agency as a necessary precondition for the epiphany of the army. As the Chiefs Empowerment Day drew near, some people seemed, in fact, to entertain the possibility that the simple act of installing neo-customary leaders could summon forth the agents of the underground. But more fundamentally, this perspective is consistent with an ontology politics according to which the Makiran person and the underground army can work in tandem as different modalities of a unified category of being qua field of agency to bring about the resurgence of Makiran *kastom*. By giving political allegiance to those policies that promise to 'bring back to life the *auhenua* government' – wherever and by whomever they may be initiated – the Makiran *kastom* mystic can quietly understand her or himself to be hastening the advent of the army and the fulfilment of Makiran destiny.

Politician J: the underground army across centre and periphery

Shortly after it appeared, the news item quoted at the opening of this chapter prompted several unverifiable assertions, posted to an online platform, that a certain well-known Arosi politician had been among those 'senior citizens' who had actively promoted 'belief' in a 'secret provincial army'. It is not my aim here to prove these assertions true or false. Rather, by examining data from my field research that tend towards affirmation of these assertions, my aim is to offer a concluding case study of a person whose instrumentalist, yet perhaps equally essentialist, engagement with the figure of the underground appears to be motivating political innovations that are impinging on the configuration of the Solomon Islands nation-state. Highlighting recent phases in the career of this politician – whom I call Politician J – I trace how he has tacked back and forth between national and grassroots politics, enlisting the centre to facilitate the goals of the periphery and working from the top down to allow Makiran *kastom* gradually to emerge, quite literally, from the ground up.

Politician J stood for a seat in the Solomon Islands national parliament in the 2000 West Makira by-election that followed the death of Solomon S. Mamaloni (1943–2000) and again in the general election of 2001. *Ex post facto* data that I collected in 2003 pertaining to these elections indicate that Politician J and his supporters campaigned on a platform that closely associated Politician J with the underground army. Regarding who exactly articulated these associations – Politician J himself or only his supporters – I heard conflicting accounts. One of my Arosi consultants said he had heard Politician J openly claim to be able to tap into the power of the underground. Another consultant, however – a man who says that Politician J and his supporters had frequently solicited him for his vote – told me that, although Politician J did not make overt references to the underground, his supporters did so regularly in one-on-one asides to voters. When I interviewed some of these same supporters, their accounts of what they had said corroborated on many points the accounts of those whose votes they had been seeking to secure.

Some of this politician's supporters, for example, had likened Mamaloni and their candidate to Moses and Joshua (hence, 'Politician J') as men whose successive leadership would bring Makira out of the crisis of the civil 'tension' – understood as a period of bondage under Malaitans equivalent to the bondage of Israel in Egypt – and into peaceful prosperity as a Promised Land.[10] While he was in office, they had said, Mamaloni had smuggled money and weapons to the underground as a 'preparation' that would serve as a defence against Malaitan encroachment and a foundation for Makiran development. They had furthermore intimated that Mamaloni is not really dead, but has gone to the underground where he sits enthroned as 'King Solomon' at the head of the army. The implication was that, just as Joshua had succeeded Moses, Politician J, if elected, would succeed Mamaloni and, garnering the stored wealth of the 'preparation', establish 'Makira State' as the 'Motherland' from which blessings would flow to the whole Solomons archipelago.

After a brief period in national office, Politician J next secured election to the Makira/Ulawa Provincial Assembly, where he became one of the principal architects of the previously mentioned New Community Governance Regime 2006. While the Regime was still in the process of development and approval, the newly elected Prime Minister, Manasseh Sogavare, launched his 'Bottom-Up Approach', a policy designed to involve grassroots communities in governance and development through the devolution of 'powers, functions and decision making to the periphery' (Sogavare 2006; see also Alasia 2008:137; Kabutaulaka and Kabutaulaka 2007:602). As indicated above, the New Community Governance Regime allowed for local communities to revive traditional forms of leadership and customary practices by means of a two-tiered system of chiefs' councils comprising multiple Ward Councils of Chiefs feeding a single Great Council of Chiefs with direct access to the Provincial Assembly. While seeking support for the Regime, Politician J and others had explicitly promoted it as in line with Sogavare's national policy.[11] Then, throughout mid to late 2006, once the Regime had been slated for 'gazetting' and was about to be implemented, Politician J, together with another prominent provincial politician, made a tour of their constituencies and held a series of workshops to explain this 'bottom-up' scheme to grassroots elders and village leaders.

I attended one such workshop in the north-west Arosi village of Heuru in September 2006. The meeting was chaired by Politician J's associate. He opened with an explanation of how the Regime was – among other things – a framework for allowing communities to identify 'traditional leaders' according to their own criteria and for positioning these leaders as a 'consultative link' between the people and the Provincial Assembly. The purpose of this scheme, he said, was to 'make *kastom* grow back so that our identity will always be here, and then we will look for development'. Referring to a diagram chalked on a blackboard, he laid out the basic structure of the Regime. Speaking of the Ward Councils of Chiefs, he elaborated that their 'most important' work would be to 'coordinate genealogies and the *kastom* belonging to the ward, to straighten lineage and tribal rights, revive good *kastom*, and write every *kastom*, even if it isn't a good one, because it reflects our identity'. As for the Great Council of Chiefs, it would have only an advisory function vis-à-vis the

Provincial Assembly. He acknowledged that the plan was not 'perfect', but indicated that the chiefs would 'later be given more responsibilities and more entitlements'.

A day-long discussion ensued. Then, acting as vice-chair, Politician J stood up and offered a closing statement that amounted to the reportage of a portentous sign. He observed that, 'one of our leaders for this vision' died 'on the third day … after the announcement [of the Regime] had been made'. But before he died, the leader had made this pronouncement: 'I go now, but what is taking place … is what I wanted. Children work to see its fruition'. Intensifying this message, Politician J concluded with: 'So we have to nurture and mature it to see its fruits'.

With these remarks, Politician J was, I suggest, indirectly referring back to and developing remarks made by another workshop participant. Spokesmen for the participants from the two electoral wards involved had just given their summary responses to the workshop, and in this context a leading man from one ward had said:

> It is a historic day for us…. It has been the cry of our forefathers. Maasina
> Rule isn't something to make fun of; it was the beginning of what this
> workshop is about. But the colonial government stamped down on them,
> and some of our relatives died in prison. I want to pay tribute to them.
> Thank you for coming to do the workshop. We highly value this workshop.

The phrase 'the cry of our forefathers' functioned subtly to compare the Maasina Rule period, in which some movement leaders were imprisoned, to the period of Israel's bondage in Egypt (cf. Exodus 3:7 and 6:5). When the speaker then paid tribute to these leaders, this parallelism suggested that, like Moses and other prophets of Israel, they had foreseen and laid the foundations for liberating transformations that would come only after they were gone. Heightening this theme, Politician J's closing remarks implicitly cast the leader who had recently died as the last prophet of the Maasina Rule era, whose death and blessing of the future marked the closing of an old era of preparation and looked forward to a new era of fruition.[12] Like Moses (Deuteronomy 33–4) and Simeon (Luke 2:25–35), this leader stands at the threshold of fulfilment, glimpsing it and commending it to the care of others before making his exit. Reiterating the same providential history narrated in his supporters' construal of himself as Joshua in relationship to Mamaloni as Moses, Politician J was presenting himself and the other architects of the Regime as heirs to the vision of the Maasina Rule leaders, ready to take Makira into the next phase of a divinely ordained destiny.

Such a providential reading of events, alone, is not proof that Politician J hopes that the underground army will intervene to secure the destiny of Makira. It is possible that he was simply seeking to encourage popular take-up of the Regime by infusing it with a sense of sacred gravitas. At the same time, however, he would have been aware that some listeners would make a connection between this providential reading of history and expectations about the underground army. He was addressing 'those who have ears to hear' and inviting them to read the underground into his remarks. It is significant, I think, that when I spoke with him during a break in the workshop, he told me that he hopes one day to take a higher degree; his proposed thesis topic, he said, is 'the wisdom of the *kakamora*'.

Almost a year later, the imminent crowning, via a Chiefs Empowerment Day, of what Politician J had termed 'this vision' briefly brought national attention to Makira, not only as the locus of strange rumours, but also as the seat of one of many sporadically active secessionist movements in Solomon Islands and beyond. 'Makira Ulawa Province has been, over the past few years, calling for independence from the rest of Solomon Islands', writes Ralph Sao (2007). 'It is still unclear', he continues, 'whether this idea of a secret army has anything to do with its desire to secede'. But what exactly is unclear to this journalist? Astutely, Sao seems to suspect a connection between a secret provincial army and the Makiran will to secede. Might such an otherwise logical connection be rendered unclear because the expectation that the army will arrive on the occasion of the installation of neo-customary chiefs seems so inappropriate? Is it not the case, Sao may be assuming, that such concessions to local *kastom* are supposed to strengthen national cohesion, not dismantle it? Why would a secessionist army appear just at the moment of local *kastom* recognition?

There is indeed something wrong with this picture according to the wisdom that has guided much of the national response to local autonomy movements. As in other Melanesian contexts, in Solomon Islands, calls for independence from several island groups go back to the period of preparation for decolonization and have continued intermittently (Premdas, Steeves and Larmour 1983; Standish 1979). Such calls were renewed during the crisis of the civil 'tension' at the turn of the millennium, and a number of provinces, including Makira/Ulawa, declared their intentions to secede from the nation-state. In response to these centrifugal pulls, the national government has sought to contain regional autonomy movements by expediting previously proposed plans to implement a federal system with various forms of devolved government (Moore 2004:156–60; Nanau 2002; Scales 2007:204–9).

But the seeming misfit between expectations of a secessionist army in conjunction with such devolution measures, supports the view that this model of opposite-tending central and peripheral pulls and goals, while accurate to some extent, does not tell the whole story. In this instance, it might appear that state- and elite-sanctioned initiatives to strengthen the nation-state by reviving 'traditional' chiefship – conceived of as a primordially unifying pan-Solomons cultural heritage with local variations (LiPuma 1997; cf. Babadzan 1988:211) – inadvertently revealed that some Makirans thought reformation of specifically Makiran forms of chiefship might, to the contrary, mobilize the Makiran underground army to lead their province to independence. As the trajectory of Politician J confirms, however, it is impossible to separate the national from the provincial agendas at work here, or even the provincial-level agendas from those of 'grassroots' communities (cf. White 1997). The centres of government often include people from village communities – such as Politician J – some of whom may have sought power in the centres precisely in order to further visions of separatism informed by local elements and icons of *kastom* – such as the figure of the underground army – in the name of visions of greater national cohesion through federalism or the creation of laws and institutions that respect *kastom* plurality. Seemingly top-down, stabilizing, ideologically 'secular' agendas can conveniently camouflage – and more importantly may better be understood as having been shaped by – grassroots agendas with literally eccentric aims.

The pathways and policies of Politician J appear to constitute this reality. The political innovation of the New Community Governance Regime 2006 and the rumours that preceded the Chiefs Empowerment Day to which it gave rise were the outcomes, I suggest, of just such a complex mix of representations and objectives. They were the products of a partially hidden, partially revealed ontology politics that is enlisting the state in the quests of local *kastom* mystics, while inscribing the quests of local *kastom* mystics on the state.

Acknowledgments

This chapter is based on research carried out in 1992–3, 2003 and 2006. I thank the Wenner-Gren Foundation for Anthropological Research, the London School of Economics and Political Science, and the Social and Economic Research Council of the UK (Grant No.: RES-000-23-1170) for their generous support. An earlier version of the paper was presented in the session 'Cultural Heritage and Political Innovation' at the Seventh Conference of the European Society for Oceanists, Verona, Italy, July 2008. I thank the session participants for their constructive engagement with the paper and especially the session organizers and editors of this volume, Edvard Hviding and Knut Rio. I am also grateful to Debra McDougall, Krista Ovist, Harry Walker and the anonymous reviewer of this volume, all of whose observations and suggestions were invaluable for the development of this chapter. Thanks also to Mina Moshkeri Upton for producing the map at short notice. My main debt is to the people of Makira who have given me such generous research assistance and hospitality.

NOTES

1. There appear to be many parallels between this transformation and the emergence of a distinction between *kalsa* and *kastam* in Manus Province (Papua New Guinea), as analysed by Dalsgaard and Otto (this volume). Although I do not detect a similar differential use of the Solomon Islands Pijin terms *kalsa* and *kastom* among Arosi, there is nevertheless a tension, comparable to that between *kalsa* and *kastam* in Manus, between invocations of pan-Makiran *kastom* and the demands of matrilineal and territory-specific *kastom*. I would emphasize, however, that the ongoing tension in Arosi lies as much between two experiences of ontology as 'between two types of morality'.

2. For accounts and analyses of Maasina Rule, see Burt 1994; Keesing 1978; Laracy 1983; Naitoro 1993; Scott 2007a.

3. The following paragraphs build on the analysis of the relationship among land, lineages, and ontology as laid out in Scott 2007a; cf. 2007b.

4. Arosi use the Arosi word *ringeringe* and the Pijin word *kastom* interchangeably. By my observation, however, people of north and east Arosi tend to prefer *ringeringe*, while people of south and west Arosi are perhaps more likely to say *kastom*, even in Arosi language speech.

5. It is within this level of the matrilineal and territory-specific category of being that the model of the Melanesian person as 'fractal' (e.g. Wagner 1991) or as a 'partible' 'dividual' (e.g. Strathern 1988) undergoing constant processes of 'decomposition' (e.g. Mosko 1992) is most unambiguously applicable to Arosi sociality. Despite evidence of the increasing social relevance of a pan-Makiran ontological category, however, it should not be assumed without qualification that Arosi view their matrilineal and territory-specific categories as similarly precipitated out of an always already composite pleroma of relationships. Rather, within the recent ethnographic past at least, Arosi poly-ontology has tended to put the primordial categorical parts before any socio-cosmic completeness (see Scott 2007a and b).

6. Arosi began accepting the Anglican Christianity of the Melanesian Mission in the 1850s. The South Sea Evangelical Mission (now SSEC) established its first school in Arosi in the early 1900s. Arosi SDA consultants recalled that men from the western Solomons and Guadalcanal introduced their denomination to Arosi in the mid to late 1930s.

7. There is an important exception to this assertion. In Arosi 2 I interviewed a locally well-known SDA woman, who says she has been approached by the underground army and that it is the army of Satan. As I hope to explore elsewhere, this inversion of the moral value assigned to the army may be correlated with the fact that, relative to their Anglican and SSEC neighbours, most SDA Arosi maintain a negative orientation towards *kastom* and many things associated with the pre-Christian past. Accordingly, this woman experiences the army as trying to 'get her', or win her for Satan, much as she sees aspects of *kastom* as pre-Christian error with which Satan formerly deceived her ancestors and into which she might be tempted to lapse.

8. The distinction made here between Makiran *kastom* as a received body of traditions and Makiran *kastom* as a general moral quality or disposition should not be read as the anthropological distinction between *kastom* as knowledge (Gegeo 1994) and *kastom* as 'contentless symbol' (Keesing 1982:299). Several of my consultants differentiated between *kastom* as various forms of transmissible knowledge and *kastom* as 'good character' or 'a good way of being'. They tended, furthermore, to treat the latter as an indispensable underpinning to the former.

9. According to lineage origin narratives I learned in the early 1990s, *kakamora* are simply one among several types of originary beings. Yet contemporary Arosi discourses appear increasingly to assimilate all apical progenitors to shape-shifting *kakamora* under alternative forms (e.g. rocks, snakes, endemic species), implying that all true Makirans are in some sense the descendants of *kakamora*. Given this conflation of originary beings into the one autochthonous Makiran category of *kakamora*, it could be said that, for Makirans, the new insular *kastom* mysticism is about getting in touch with your inner *kakamora*.

10. This comparison of Mamaloni to Moses reflects the unparalleled local importance of Mamaloni as an Arosi person who achieved national and international prominence. Before Solomon Islands became independent in 1978, he served as the first Chief Minister (1974–6); after independence, he was Prime Minister for three periods (1981–4, 1989–93, 1994–7). At the time of his death in January 2000, he was one of only two people to have held the seat for West Makira since the formation of the constituency. Not all Arosi view Mamaloni in this unequivocally positive light, yet even those critical or ambivalent about him reflect on his career as something phenomenal and indicative of larger forces at work with as yet uncertain consequences for Makira.

11. This intertwining of national and provincial initiatives also marked the eventual celebration of the Chiefs Empowerment Day on 17 August 2007. By invitation from the province, Sogavare attended the celebration, at which he commended the provincial government's initiative as 'the essence of sustainable development that is driven from bottom-up' (Solomon Islands Government 2007). At this event Sogavare himself was installed as an honorary paramount chief of Makira

(Solomon Islands Broadcasting Corporation 2007). It is possible that some Makirans, contemplating these proceedings, interpreted Sogavare's words and participation as tantamount to signs of approbation from the underground army, despite its failure to materialize. It is widely known that Sogavare claims to have had conversation with Mamaloni since Mamaloni's death in 2000 (Sasako 2001 and 2007). Many Makirans take this as evidence in support of the theory that Mamaloni is not really dead, and some may furthermore speculate that Sogavare's supposed meeting with the post-mortem Mamaloni indicates that Sogavare – although an SDA member from Choiseul – is an instrument of the army's agenda.

12. I was unable to confirm the identity of this recently deceased leader, but it is likely that it was either Talman Mona'aro, who died on 13 July 2006, or Kerehote, who died on 27 August 2006. Both men were among those Makiran Maasina Rule leaders, alluded to earlier in the workshop, who had been imprisoned in Honiara during the movement. Mona'aro had furthermore been injured in a notorious truck accident that killed two of his fellow Makiran inmates en route to a prison-labour site on 24 December 1949; a third Makiran died later owing to complications arising from his injuries.

BIBLIOGRAPHY

Akin, D.W. 2005. 'Ancestral vigilance and the corrective conscience in Kwaio: *kastom* as culture in a Melanesian society'. In *The Making of Global and Local Modernities in Melanesia* (eds) J. Robbins and H. Wardlow, 183–206. Burlington, VT: Ashgate.

Alasia, S. 2008. 'Rainbows across the mountains: the first post-RAMSI general election'. In *Politics and State Building in Solomon Islands* (eds) S. Dinnen and S. Firth, 119–47. Canberra: Asia Pacific Press.

Allen, M.G. 2008. 'Politics of disorder: the social unrest in Honiara'. In *Politics and State Building in Solomon Islands* (eds) S. Dinnen and S. Firth, 39–63. Canberra: Asia Pacific Press.

Allen, M.G. 2009. 'Resisting RAMSI: intervention, identity and symbolism in Solomon Islands'. *Oceania* 79(1):1–17.

Babadzan, A. 1988. '*Kastom* and nation-building in the South Pacific'. In *Ethnicities and Nations: Processes of Interethnic Relations in Latin America, Southeast Asia, and the Pacific* (eds) R. Guidieri, F. Pellizi, and S.J. Tambiah, 199–228. Houston, TX: Rothko Chapel and University of Texas Press.

Bonnemaison, J. 1994. *The Tree and the Canoe: History and Ethnogeography of Tanna*. Trans. J. Pénot-Demetry. Honolulu: University Hawai'i.

Burt, B. 1982. '*Kastom*, Christianity and the first ancestor of the Kwara'ae of Malaita'. *Mankind* 13(4):374–99.

Burt, B. 1994. *Tradition and Christianity: The Colonial Transformation of a Solomon Islands Society*. New York: Harwood Academic Publishers.

Coppet, D. de. 1985. '...land owns people'. In *Contexts and Levels: Anthropological Essays on Hierarchy* (eds) R.H. Barnes, D. de Coppet, and R.J. Parkin, 78–90. Oxford: Anthropological Society.

Dinnen, S. 2002. 'Winners and losers: politics and disorder in the Solomon Islands 2000–2002'. *Journal of Pacific History* 37(3):285–98.

Dinnen, S. 2008. 'Dilemmas of intervention and the building of state and nation'. In *Politics and State Building in Solomon Islands* (eds) S. Dinnen and S. Firth, 1–38. Canberra: Asia Pacific Press.

Dureau, C. 1998. 'Decreed affinities: nationhood and the Western Solomon Islands'. *Journal of Pacific History* 33(2):197–220.

Fox, C.E. 1924. *The Threshold of the Pacific: An Account of the Social Organization, Magic and Religion of the People of San Cristoval in the Solomon Islands*. London: Kegan Paul, Trench, and Trubner.

Fraenkel, J. 2004. *The Manipulation of Custom: From Uprising to Intervention in the Solomon Islands*. Canberra: Pandanus Books, Research School of Pacific and Asian Studies, Australian National University.

Gegeo, D.W. 1994. '*Kastom nao stretem iumi*: views from Kwara'ae on cultural policy in Melanesia'. In *Culture, Kastom, Tradition: Developing Cultural Policy in Melanesia* (eds) L. Lindstrom and G.M. White, 43–54. Suva, Fiji: University of the South Pacific.

Gray, G. 2002. 'Habuna momoruqu (the blood of my island): violence and the Guadalcanal uprising in Solomon Islands'. State, Society and Governance in Melanesia Project, Working Papers 2002 Series. Research School of Pacific and Asian Studies, Australian National University, Canberra.

Kabutaulaka, T.T. 2001. 'Beyond ethnicity: the political economy of the Guadalcanal crisis in Solomon Islands'. State, Society and Governance in Melanesia Project, Working Paper 01/1. Research School of Pacific and Asian Studies, Australian National University, Canberra.

Kabutaulaka, T.T. 2002. *A Weak State and the Solomon Islands Peace Process*. East-West Center Working Papers, Pacific Islands Development Series No. 14. Center for Pacific Islands Studies, University of Hawai'i at Mānoa.

Kabutaulaka, T.T. 2005. 'Australian foreign policy and the RAMSI intervention in Solomon Islands'. *Contemporary Pacific* 17(2):283–308.

Kabutaulaka, T.T., and L. Kabutaulaka. 2007. 'Political reviews, Melanesia in review: issues and events, 2006: Solomon Islands'. *Contemporary Pacific* 19(2):597–605.

Keesing, R.M. 1978. 'Politico-religious movements and anti-colonialism on Malaita: Maasina Rule in historical perspective'. *Oceania* 48(4):241–61 and 49(1):46–73.

Keesing, R.M. 1982. 'Kastom in Melanesia: an overview'. *Mankind* 13(4):297–301.

Keesing, R.M. 1989. 'Creating the past: custom and identity in the contemporary Pacific'. *Contemporary Pacific* 1(1):19–42.

Keesing, R.M. 1994. 'Colonial and counter-colonial discourse in Melanesia'. *Critique of Anthropology* 14(1):41–58.

Laracy, H.M. (ed.) 1983. *Pacific Protest: The Maasina Rule Movement, Solomon Islands, 1944–1952*. Suva, Fiji: University of the South Pacific.

Lindstrom, L. 2008. 'Melanesian *Kastom* and its transformations'. *Anthropological Forum* 18(2):161–78.

LiPuma, E. 1997. 'History, identity and encompassment: nation-making in the Solomon Islands'. *Identities* 4(2):213–44.

Moore, C.R. 2004. *Happy Isles in Crisis: The Historical Causes for a Failing State in Solomon Islands, 1998–2004*. Canberra: Asia Pacific Press.

Moore, C.R 2007. '*Helpem fren*: the Solomon Islands, 2003–2007'. *Journal of Pacific History* 42(2):141–64.

Mosko, M.S. 1992. 'Motherless sons: "divine kings" and "partible persons" in Melanesia and Polynesia'. *Man* (N.S.) 27(4):693–717.

Naitoro, J. 1993. The Politics of Development in 'Are'are, Malaita. Master's thesis, University of Otago, New Zealand.

Nanau, G.L. 2002. 'Uniting the fragments: Solomon Islands constitutional reforms'. *Development Bulletin* 60 (December):17–20.

Otto, T., and P. Pedersen. 2005. *Tradition and Agency: Tracing Cultural Continuity and Invention*. Aarhus: Aarhus University Press.

Premdas, R.R., J.S. Steeves and P. Larmour. 1983. 'The Western Breakaway Movement'. In *Solomon Islands Politics* (eds) P. Larmour with S. Tarua, 164–195. Suva, Fiji: University of the South Pacific.

Rose, D.B. 1996. *Nourishing Terrains: Australian Aboriginal Views of Landscape and Wilderness*. Canberra: Australian Heritage Commission.

Sahlins, M. 1999. 'Two or three things that I know about culture'. *Journal of the Royal Anthropological Institute* 5(3):399–421.

Sao, R. 2007. 'Kira Kira residents awaiting "mystery army"'. *Solomon Times Online*, 4 August. http://www.solomontimes.com/news.aspx?nwID=477 (accessed 4 August 2007).

Sasako, A. 2001. 'Rebuilding a battered Solomon Islands'. Paper presented at the Solomon Islands Workshop: Building Peace and Stability, October 24–26. State, Society and Governance in Melanesia Project, Research School of Pacific and Asian Studies. Australian National University, Canberra.

Sasako, A. 2007. 'Fortune tellers: a key player in govt decisions?' *Islands Business*. http://www.islandsbusiness.com (accessed 8 July 2007).

Scales, I. 2007. 'The coup nobody noticed: the Solomon Islands Western State Movement in 2000'. *Journal of Pacific History* 42(2):187–209.

Scott, M.W. 2000. 'Ignorance is cosmos; knowledge is chaos: articulating a
        cosmological polarity in the Solomon Islands'. *Social Analysis* 44(2):56–83.

Scott, M.W. 2005. '"I was like Abraham": notes on the anthropology of Christianity
        from the Solomon Islands'. *Ethnos* 70(1):101–25.

Scott, M.W. 2007a. *The Severed Snake: Matrilineages, Making Place, and a
        Melanesian Christianity in Southeast Solomon Islands.* Durham, NC:
        Carolina Academic Press.

Scott, M.W. 2007b. 'Neither 'New Melanesian History' nor 'New Melanesian
        Ethnography': recovering emplaced matrilineages in southeast Solomon
        Islands'. *Oceania* 77(3):337–54.

Scott, M.W. 2008. 'Proto-people and precedence: encompassing Euroamericans
        through narratives of 'first contact' in Solomon Islands'. In *Exchange and
        Sacrifice* (eds) P.J. Stewart and A. Strathern, 140–76. Durham, NC: Carolina
        Academic Press.

Sogavare, M. 2006. 'Speech to launch the policy framework doment [*sic*] of The
        Grand Coalition for Change Government'. 24 May. http://www.parliament.
        gov.sb (accessed 13 March 2010).

Solomon Islands Broadcasting Corporation. 2007. 'Online news brief, Prime Minister
        installed as Paramount Chief'. August 18. http://www.sibconline.com.sb/
        main.asp (accessed 18 August 2007).

Solomon Islands Government. 2007. 'Press Release: Sogavare congratulates Makira/
        Ulawa Province'. *Scoop Independent News*, 20 August. http://www.scoop.
        co.nz/stories/WO0708/S00526.htm (accessed 30 August 2007).

Standish, B. 1979. *Provincial Government in Papua New Guinea: Early Lessons
        from Chimbu.* Boroko, Papua New Guinea: Institute of Applied Social and
        Economic Research.

Strathern, M. 1988. *The Gender of the Gift: Problems with Women and Problems with
        Society in Melanesia.* Berkeley: University of California Press.

Tonkinson, R. 1993. 'Understanding 'tradition' – ten years on'. *Anthropological Forum*
        6(4):597–606.

Wagner, R. 1991. 'The fractal person'. In *Big Men and Great Men: Personifications
        of Power in Melanesia* (eds) M. Godelier and M. Strathern, 159–73.
        Cambridge: Cambridge University Press.

White, G.M. 1997. 'The discourse of chiefs: notes on a Melanesian society'. In *Chiefs
        Today: Traditional Pacific Leadership and the Postcolonial State* (eds) G.M.
        White and L. Lindstrom, 229–52. Stanford: Stanford University Press.

White, G.M. 2001. 'Native and nations: identity formation in postcolonial Melanesia'.
        In *Places and Politics in an Age of Globalization* (eds) R. Prazniak and A.
        Dirlik, 139–66. Oxford: Rowman and Littlefield Publishers.

CHAPTER 9

High chief, *waetman* and the codification of ritual objects in Vanuatu[1]

✳

KNUT M. RIO

Cultural heritage – now it's there, now it's not

In this chapter I describe a historical process of codification of *kastom* that took place in the social terrain between local chiefs in North Ambrym and the colonial district agents in the 1960s. In line with several other contributions to this volume, I explore how the concept of *kastom* has in many ways served as an ideal appropriation of 'cultural heritage' – a concept that was indeed at the core of the colonizers' experience of native life. I situate that encounter between concepts inside the social movement that led to the Independence of Vanuatu in 1980, and aim to highlight how the contemporary discussion about 'intellectual property rights' was already anticipated in the controversies between the North Ambrym chiefs at that point.

These events can be situated in a long trajectory of inter-cultural encounters, each of which plays out the field of cultural heritage as a paradoxical, ambiguous and troublesome terrain. If we look at Felix Speiser's remarkable volume *Ethnographiphsche Materialen aus den Neuen Hebriden und den Banks-Iseln* (1923), we are able to trace some of this confusion back to the very first encounters between social scientists and 'natives'. Speiser reported in this book what he considered the stock of cultural heritage in the archipelago around his visit in 1910–12, and he also brought back a big collection of artefacts from Vanuatu to Switzerland in order to illustrate the objective character of this heritage. Early in his account he states that '[t]he ethnographical conditions have hardly changed since Cook's visit' (1996:10). This provided his rationale for collecting the remains of these pre-colonial ethnographic conditions of the New Hebrides.

We need to take into account how this idea of uninterrupted, perpetual culture was the paradoxical impression of probably every one of the numerous visitors – whalers, sandalwood dealers, labour traders, missionaries, adventurers and government officials – who travelled to the archipelago in the years since Cook's visit in July 1774. The idea still seems current, as seen in today's blogs and advertisements about 'expeditions' to the 'authentic islands' of Vanuatu. In much popular imagination these were, and still are, unchangeable islands.

As Speiser described the ethnology of Vanuatu, he constructed an image of life in the islands put together from his own observations and accounts by missionaries and government officials. Speiser's report produced a typological description of a functioning traditional society. Lists were made of constructed cultural differences in a detailed account that located all kinds of habits on the same level. This produced a strange list of behavioural cultural heritage: in some islands people were having sex lying down, in other islands they did it 'a posteriori' (1996:66); in Malekula garden fences were made from bamboo canes, in Tanna fences were made from reeds (1996:132); in Santo pitfalls were used for hunting, in Malo and Banks they used pig snares (1996:140); when they ate people in Tanna, the genitals, palms of hands and soles of feet were the most popular morsels, whereas in Northern Pentecost they would prefer the heart, the brain and the feet (1996:217–18); on Ambae men would inherit their father's garden land, whereas in Pentecost they inherited through the matrilineage (1996:298); on Erromango chieftainship was hereditary from father to son, whereas in the northern islands the ritual hierarchy meant that men who acquired the highest ritual ranks became chiefs (1996:304). This is just a random selection of the resulting contrasts in Speiser's mass of categorical information. This manner of piling up observed features created a 'virtual' system of cultural practices, which in turn could be used to create more general ideas about cultural continuities or discontinuities between the islands. The approach resulted in the ethnographic book becoming a museum-like storage room of lived practices. We see how cultural heritage was already a firmly established concept in the activity of these first ethnographers.

But the other side to this paradoxical logic of cultural heritage is that life in these islands was always just about to change. This was already the impression of the first explorers, as today, with the prophecies of impoverishment and instability with the global tide of market forces rushing in over the archipelago. This assumption also guided Bernard Deacon's work in the 1920s, as seen in the telling title *Malekula: A Vanishing People in the South Pacific* (1934). In Speiser's writings, this perception underlies almost every observation. He writes:

The reference here is to the gradual debasement of natives' intellectual heritage such as is caused by the intercourse between the two races. The inferiority of its own culture is inevitably recognized by a weaker race in confrontation with a stronger one, and the greater the difference between the two cultures and the longer the superior one neglects to absorb the inferior into itself or to replace its lost intellectual heritage by another, the more rapidly the weaker race is demoralized

(Speiser 1996:49)

This quote serves as an accurate description of the ontological assumptions of cultural heritage and intellectual property, as modelled on an essentialist racial and Euro-glorifying distinction that has survived until today. Even in UNESCO's report *Our Creative Diversity* there is a taste of the same logic of dominant versus dominated cultures (see also Eriksen 2001:139), as seen in statements such as 'development has meant the loss of identity, sense of community and personal meaning' (UNESCO 1996:15). In Speiser's account, predictions are made of a process of humiliation and moral self-critique, from the realization that one's own intellectual heritage is hard to replace with another. As commented by Strathern and Hirsch (2004:1), 'it is not often that people actually claim other people's ancestors'.

As a result of this process of humiliation, Speiser further predicts that '[i]n this way ["the white man"] undermined the respect in which the chiefs were held because he sapped the mainstay of their authority – belief in their power' (1996:49). He lists a range of already visible consequences: people were losing faith in magic and taboos, the sacrifice of valuable pigs was becoming available to anyone who brought back earnings from the plantations, 'every other man was now a chief', people lost their sense of belonging to tribe or family, the system of customary law was breaking down, 'every man's hand was against every other', 'individualism was rife', and there was sexual promiscuity and collapse of morality.

However, the work of the ethnographer in this early era of globalization was not to carry the idea about intellectual heritage as debased into any analysis of cause and effect. Demise was instead taken for granted, as a physical reaction in the clash of cultures, and energy was turned towards collecting what was being lost. Objects were collected and categorized as material appendices to the collection of observed social categorizations of habits and practices. It has been claimed that when Speiser was back in Switzerland he regretted that he had spent most of his time in Melanesia collecting things, while he had not sufficiently 'got to grips with the minds of the people' (Gosden and Knowles 2001:125).

So, in the space of just a few pages, Speiser vacillates between the following positions: 'The ethnographical conditions have hardly changed since Cook's visit' (1996:10) and 'The indirect result of the penetration of European civilization are: Demoralization and mutual extermination, low birth rate, hopelessness, apathy, debauchery' (1996:50). The local culture of island life was intact, but would soon be lost, because humiliation was total in the face of Western culture (for a different view on Malekula, see Harrison 1936). Paradoxically, it was in this situation, when the idea was widespread among colonial personnel as well as indigenous populations that culture was on the verge of being lost, that concepts of *kastom* and the protection of cultural heritage began to take form. Cultural heritage was discovered and rescued in one and the same instant (Thomas 1997).

It must also be remembered that these types of books and collections were only artefacts of a social field that contained so much more; they were the particular type of cultural encounter that colonialism represented. Thus, contrary to Speiser's prophecy of the debasement of natives' intellectual heritage, we might think about the colonial presence as being a venue for desired change and for an unexpected flourishing of cultural heritage. While colonialism in Melanesia, as elsewhere, appropriated labour and installed discipline and punishment, it also created an arena for exploration and exploitation of opportunities by islanders themselves, as a way out of a demoralizing situation of depopulation and the disruption of relationships and infrastructure across the seas that colonialism had to some degree caused (see also Campbell 1997). That islanders could serve the colonizers by conveying their knowledge about tradition, and even create their own legislation around cultural heritage claims and rights, must be acknowledged as the kind of empowerment it indeed was.

I thus propose a historical argument about the nation-building of Vanuatu. When the colonialist project had managed to install in people a vision of the New Hebrides as to some degree a functioning state, with its own form of legislation, justice and policing of people's lives, the colonial subjects could also expand on this and actually envision an independent nation (see also Rio 2011). In this process cultural heritage, as articulated in the encounter between colonialists and islanders, became instrumental. The emerging nation was directly shaped around the continual colonial focus on cultural heritage – its power, its value or its loss. At the peak of the independence movement the nation was then ready to look at itself as a possessive individual, i.e. with a distinctive culture of its own and the right to autonomously handle this culture as an object (see Lipuma 1998; Harrison 2006:ch. 5)

Cultural heritage and *kastom*

Hence, we need to consider the other side of the story when reading books like Speiser's, and we should also acknowledge the way *kastom* was designed to intersect with some of the most important expectations of the colonial personnel (Lindstrom 1993). To the internal social life of the New Hebrides Anglo-French condominium that was established in 1906, we must also add encounters with the colonial officers, or district agents, as ingredients to the formative process of concepts and behaviours.

It soon became clear that what was really at issue in this inter-cultural dialogue was the 'power' of *kastom* (see Lindstrom and White 1993). In Vanuatu, it was demonstrated to visitors how the realm of the men's ceremonial life – in Ambrym the *mel* (men's house), the *harl* (ceremonial ground) and the *feangkon* (the taboo fire of the ritual hierarchy) – held the power over life, growth and reproduction. Death through witchcraft or sorcery was rampant in the early colonial period (Rio 2002), and as the population was decimated by terrible diseases and musket warfare, the dialogue with white travellers centred on exactly that domain of power – the power to kill, to heal, to foretell and to interact with ancestral spirits. In this dialogue, the *waetman* colonialists of government or church were exposed to the influences of the powerful high men and enthralled with their ritual hierarchy, their engagement in the world of ancestors and their secret magical remedies and wisdom (see Rio 2005).

I suggest that when the high men were talking about *kastom* to white men, it was a way of wrapping up local relations in a pedagogy of mystery. The secrecy and enigmatic character of this talk itself gave the contact with the government representatives a flavour of power, an effect made even more potent by the fact that whites always tried to figure out *kastom*. They were asking questions about how it worked, what its rules were, where it had come from originally, and whether it was being lost. In this dialogue *kastom* was made into a parcel that wrapped up the power of certain men or lineages, and thereby the production and reproduction of island life. It was in this dialogue that the colonialists began to think about 'cultural heritage'. The cultural history museums of the Western world were the answer to this sudden reflection: that culture could be conserved through taking and attributing value to its most cultural of objects. In the same moment, the islanders began to understand that these white men were actually searching for something deeper in their engagement with them: truth, power and authenticity.

A claim can be made that *kastom* became a social movement that took this Western discourse on cultural or intellectual heritage and invested its questions into local concerns (Lindstrom 1993). This meant setting it free from its Western anchorage of preservation and nostalgia for a lost past, and transforming it according to Melanesians' own preferences for how to deal with objects, ceremonial and belonging. Of course, this move was hidden from the district agents, the plantation managers and the missionaries, who at this point often believed that what they saw before them was a fight between modern and traditional, Christian and Pagan, or rationality and mysticism – what Geoffrey White (1993:493) has called 'our own complacent, oppositional rhetoric of tradition'. In fact, what the islanders laid out with their *kastom* concept was a bit like the *pidik* of the Barok of New Ireland as described by Roy Wagner (1986): a 'consensual image' and mystery constructed to engage the subjects in finding ways to open it up and thus reveal its inner components.

The concept of *kastom* in the colonial New Hebrides hence revealed the ability of the high men to create society through ceremonial and exchange, but concealed their secret ways of becoming successful. It revealed the dangers of sorcery, but concealed the true power of the church as a remedy against it. It revealed a stock of powerful objects and practices, but concealed their true origins. In short, the distinction between *kastom* and *skul* (Bislama for 'church' or 'Christianity') left the white man ignorant about the complexity of the relationship between them, by only demonstrating the conflicts. Anything that was seen to be part of the power of high men could be put into *kastom*: a man, an island, a house, a talk, a walk, a song, magic etc. Stating to a white man that 'this is our *kastom*' or 'I am *kastom*' amounted to expressing their view of themselves as a principle of the totality of local powers. For this kind of talk, influential men were often rewarded with the Assessor title and friendship with the colonial agents. The Assessors became paramount chiefs and councillors to the district agents on issues to do with their respective districts (Guiart 1949; Rodman 1983 and 1985; Philibert 1983).

As Thomas (1993) has pointed out, modernist white agents in Melanesia were especially seeking totalizing concepts; and the concept of *kastom* stuck with them, triggering their imagination. With regard to the Melanesian way of imagining part-whole relations (Strathern 1992), where parts and wholes capture different stages in a social process oscillating between containment and objectification, we can see that these views are easily convertible. *Kastom* was set out by local high men as a fractal, wherein all parts were at the same time wholes. The colonialists understood them as totalities, but in another sense. They exchanged *kastom* for Western concepts like 'culture', 'tradition' or 'community' that could not be broken down into parts at all. Therefore they were trapped in the imagined existence of a social whole, and, most importantly, this trap was devised by the high men that produced this imagined whole for them.

The colonial movement, as represented by the District Agents on a personal level, became heavily entangled with this sphere of high men in North Ambrym. They were utterly fascinated with the powers they imagined the 'chiefs' to have. Beyond the political rivalry of *kastom* and *skul*, they came to acknowledge the chiefs as knowledgeable and respectful, and on Ambrym this led to a process whereby the chiefs were attributed traditional authenticity. From the colonialists' point of view, the pagans had something that the Christians had 'lost' and therefore 'lacked': authentic ritual practices and beliefs. This was again related to the ambiguous character of *kastom*, and so the Ambrym high men had managed to trap the white man through the enigma of 'traditional rights'.

I shall now consider an important process in the formation of the concept of *kastom* on Ambrym: the configuration of rights to carvings and ritual insignia. The state effort of 'substantivization' or 'naming' (see Thomas 1992 and 1993) of such rights became important in the relation between chiefs and District Agents in the 1960s, and this in turn became crucial to the nationalist discourse of *kastom* during the time of the independence movement. In an important article about this process in recent decades on Ambrym, Haidy Geismar (2005) has pointed to the crucial agency of the Ambrymese themselves in shaping the concept of 'intellectual property rights'. For other places in Melanesia it has been pointed out how *kastom* came to exist in opposition to commercialism and 'business' (Foster 1992). This was not the case on Ambrym, where *kastom* was in fact rapidly turned into business, creating a close alliance between the *kastom* people and progressive trade that has lasted until today. To give some insight into the issues of this period we shall look at the reports that the British District Agent (BDA), Mr Wilkins, made about North Ambrym after his island tours in the 1960s. While the British DA had most of his responsibilities in the western part of North Ambrym, his French counterpart was mostly associated with the French-speaking community around Olal and the north-eastern parts of the island. In the 1960s, both District Agents became part of a large campaign launched by the high chief Tainmal to gain a monopoly on everything related to *kastom*, most importantly traditional carving designs. The distinct carvings of Ambrym, such as the *atingting* standing drums, the *mage* ritual effigies, the *atata* pig-killing clubs and the *rom* dancing masks, as well as various other carvings related to the sphere of male hierarchy, had already been sought after by European collectors for over a hundred years.

The record of commercial *kastom*

Commodore Goodenough, a senior Royal Navy officer operating in New Hebrides waters around 1870, mentions in his journal that he bought an old and rotten *mage* statue on Ambrym (Goodenough 1876). He paid for it with two knives. Goodenough arrived just as the people were getting ready for a *mage* ceremony of male ritual initiation, and obviously they were unwilling to sell him the new *mage* and the pig-killing club that they were going to use for the ceremony. Thirty years later, around 1900, Frater's comments (1922) seem to indicate that the sale of carvings had somewhat accelerated on Ambrym:

> Two ethnologists, one from Switzerland and the other from America, visited Ambrim, and in the course of their scientific investigations, bought up from the natives large numbers of heathen images and curios of all kinds, for which they offered big prices. The people parted with their best and most finely-carved images
>
> (Frater 1922:126).

The comment that they presented 'finely-carved images' for sale might suggest that people had made these carvings especially for trade with white visitors. Carvings made for ceremonial purposes, or even clubs made for fighting, were often not 'finely-carved', and that the objects were presented in 'large numbers' also indicates that they had been brought into another domain than that of rare ceremonial purposes. From this and other sources (see Speiser 1913; Lamb 1905) we can assume that by the turn of the century carvings had replaced food as a medium for trade with white people. The traveller categories of explorer and pioneer missionary were now being replaced by adventurers and colonial administrative personnel (see Douglas 1996). Slowly, carvings came to be presented for sale to white visitors instead of food, as these new types of travellers brought their own food supplies. Instead, they were interested in taking home souvenirs as evidence of their remote travel destinations.

Ambrym people were among the first in the New Hebrides to adapt to this increased demand for customary products, and rapidly started to bring forward things from their men's houses. While food had been an important communal substance with a potential to transform and extend white travellers into relational entities, carvings were the highly personal status requirements of high men. Carvings served as emblems in status ceremonies; they stood to demarcate one's rank and personal achievements in the various ritual cycles. Through the *mage* cycle, a man became part of the *mage* community and had ownership in the carved design itself. The same was true for the *rom* and many other status designs. The pig-killing club called *atata* was an emblem of participation in a pig-killing ceremony for maternal or affinal relatives, and only people who had killed pigs for their mother or wife could make such clubs. Like the origin stories of places and genealogies, these rights were about having access to the social history of the designs –to be able to control and thus be part of its 'beginning' (*tangbarite*) and further trajectory. At the *mage* men's house, the men were divided after rank into distinct fires (*feangkon* – taboo fire) on which they cooked their food. In the *rom* community this order of the *mage* could be reversed, and low men of the *mage* could initiate high men into the secrets of the *rom* imagery. Thus, men could engage in a multitude of communities or lodges and accordingly decorate themselves with multiple emblems and statuses (Deacon 1934; Bonnemaison *et al.* 1996). So it was the carvings – materializations of membership and ownership in diverse male communities – that came to be exchanged for white man's money. This was an important element in the privileged position Ambrym high men achieved through their contact with white people. Men who could offer carvings were those who were already highly decorated locally. They now gained a monopoly on trade with white visitors.

This situation must already have been an important element as the division between *skul* and *kastom* emerged. Through this prestigious exchange, *kastom* came to be perceived as highly valued among white men, which further strengthened the link between the local high men and the visiting white men. This naturally impacted the value attributed to money on Ambrym, which at first was associated with the morality of Christian values, but later was monopolized by the high men of the ritual hierarchy along with other Western influences.

Chiefs as personifications of *kastom*

The commercialization of the Ambrym arts probably had several ups and downs during the first decades of the Condominium, but by 1960 carving on Ambrym had turned into a veritable industry. Tourists were coming in on a more regular basis, the District Agents brought in British and French government associates to see the islands, and there was a general trend towards appreciating native artistic expressions (Douglas 1996). It was at this time that the manufacturing of carvings for sale to tourists took off, on the initiative of just a few men. They were the major cultural brokers of North Ambrym in their respective districts, of which they were all assessors, and they were already well connected to the field of the white man. The first report by the BDA on this industrialization is revealing:

> A visit was paid to Tainmal's village (Fanla). Not wishing to offend pagan
> sensibilities we refrained from suggesting that they should hand over
> supposedly sacred objects planted on the dancing ground, and enquired
> whether facsimiles could be made. This respect for custom was ludicrously
> inappropriate: it transpired that the dancing ground is in fact a shop-
> window, and at the rustle of a sufficient number of banknotes Tainmal's
> son Tofor would uproot slit gongs and statues from the ground – later to
> be replaced from factory or stock. Although the objects were not actually

tagged with f.a.b. prices they were obviously controlled and there was no discount to be had for government. Mr. Woodward acquired an excellent 11' slit-gong and a three-fern carving at £50 a-piece.

(Extract from touring notes, Central District no. 2, 6 September 1961)

The most remarkable aspect of this comment is perhaps the BDA's respect for the Fanla people's 'sacred objects', and that it came as a surprise to him that the trade was going on. But the same sense of surprise was demonstrated to me in 2000, by tourists who came up to Fanla and were shocked that there were price tags on ceremonial art. The image of the 'noble savage' runs strong among Western tourists, and in encounters like this it gives rise to a veritable self-deception about the state of the world.

The Christian villages on Ambrym had abandoned the carving practices involved in ceremonial life at an early stage, along with other aspects of *kastom*. In the new situation of commercial interest in carvings, the Christians therefore had little to offer white visitors. Hence, in order to get involved in this important emergent field of social and economic relations, they had to negotiate for rights with the pagans who were still producing carvings. The situation became awkward, as people who did not take part in the ceremonial communities now wanted to carve and sell ritual carvings to the white people. The Christian villages had taken an interest in the sale of artefacts, but without initiation through secret ceremonies and thus taking part in the authentic *kastom* legitimacy of the carvings. They argued, however, that they had inherited the rights from their fathers, who had been initiated. Almost all Christians could in one way or another trace their genealogy to some ancestor who had been initiated, but to the *kastom* people this was not enough. If this argument had become legitimate, the sacred status of the secret communities would have been endangered for the pagans, and they resisted with all their means of sorcery and political negotiation.

I believe this political situation and controversy amounted to an innovation that arose from the special situation of *kastom* abandonment and carving commercialism – inside the field of relations that the colonial administration represented. It was also part of the politics of authority. The Christian leaders still had much of their legitimacy from their ancestors, and this was upheld inside this international field of argument. The pagan chiefs, meanwhile, were the only men who still kept performing ceremonies and attending ritual ranks, and they tried to keep the rights to carving designs closely connected to the ceremonies and pig-killings. The argument was that it was very costly to engage in the ritual economy, and that the income of carvings was a kind of reward for these expenses. The front runner of the pagan resistance was the renowned chief Tainmal of Fanla village. He had acquired the highest rank of *mal* in the ritual hierarchy, and was in every respect a powerful man. His many wives, his abundance of magical means for creating wealth around himself, and his power of both foreseeing events and planning strategically gave him a unique position in this historical situation. He was the highest authority in matters of tradition, and if anyone were to be initiated into *kastom,* if there were suspicions of homicidal sorcery, or if there was to be a staging of ritual performance, Tainmal would always have a hand in it. Since he was the holder of all rights, he introduced the idea that he should get some percentage of all carving sales. In 1966, this battle between *skul* and *kastom* interests was developing into a tense situation, and a meeting was held in an attempt to resolve it:

> **Chiefs' meeting at Fona.**
> Chief Tainmal and son Tofor are annoyed that people are cutting for sale artefacts which their forebearers were not sufficiently graded to cut. Chiefs Wilfred and David Bule had prepared a document agreeing to a 10% tribute payable to Tainmal on all sales. Magam particularly was opposed to this. Provisionally agreed after heated discussion that would only cut artefacts in accordance with their grades but that there would be no "tribute" to Tainmal. A further meeting to be held to ratify this.
> (D.K. Wilkins, Touring Notes 1966)

At this point the people of pagan villages had become aware that the Christian villages had started to produce *kastom* carvings and that they benefited from the sales. The most prominent in this practice was Willy Tasso in Fonah village. Tainmal was discontented with this development, because Willy Tasso had not himself paid grades in the *mage,* and had converted to Christianity. He was leaning on his ancestors, whom he claimed had paid appropriately for the rights to various high carvings. Before the meeting Wilkins refers to, Tainmal had challenged Tasso by taking off his own penis wrapper and throwing it at him. By this act he was challenging him to put on this symbol of *kastom* if he was going to pretend to be a *kastom* man and cut carvings. This made Tasso so afraid that he agreed to Tainmal's proposal for 'royalties' to be paid to him on carving income. Chief Willy from Magam had opposed this proposal from Tainmal. In his opinion Tainmal was being unreasonable in claiming to have unprecedented powers as the only real *kastom* man left on Ambrym. According to Chief Willy, there were several other men who had in fact achieved the high grades, and many men indeed were descendants of *mal* genealogies. Therefore, he could not accept Tainmal's monopoly on carving rights. The question of rights had by then become exclusively a question of genealogy, since *kastom* for the *skul* majority had become a matter of history. After this meeting the issue receded, and Tainmal seemed to have the upper hand. People were afraid to oppose him, and he had the traditional authority in the eye's of the government. Later the same year, a formal agreement between the chiefs was declared on the National Radio:

> In North Ambrym, the custom chiefs have now agreed that the local craftsmen may make only those artefacts which are appropriate to their grade in the custom society. The chiefs have found that with the increased business in artefacts, some of which are being exported, some local craftsmen have been making masks, images and slit gongs of a type which should only be made by people of a higher rank. Now, anyone breaking the new regulation will be fined. The senior custom chief in North Ambrym is Chief Tainmal of Fanla village whose duty it is to levy these fines.
>
> (M.J. Leach, Information officer, 6 February 1967)

So, although the pagan chief Tainmal did not succeed in gaining direct monetary benefits from the carving business, he managed to use his charismatic powers over the District Agents so as to be appointed 'chief of chiefs', against the protests of the Christian chiefs. The British DA was here demonstrating his sense of goodwill towards the imagined customary system of rights. He had accepted the concept as it was laid out for them by Chief Tainmal. This comment later appeared in a letter from the British High Commissioner to the District Agent:

> I am interested in these matters mainly because I should like to see the art of this area preserved from degradation as a result of commercial abuse. As you are aware, and as Guiart has been able to observe for some years, there is quite a danger that traditional forms will be corrupted by bogus external influences. Following discussions with me, Tom Layng suggested to Tainmal and Tofor that they should exercise a kind of "quality control" over the artefacts being made by the non-customs people, e.g. the Fonah Co-operative, the object being to ensure that the materials, design and colours were authentic and that workmanship was good. I am told that they readily acceded to this suggestion and that it is acceptable to the co-operative. I hope the arrangement will work but have doubts that it will be effective if there is no financial gain in it for Tofor and his father.
>
> (Wilkins 1967)

Further developments were followed closely, and on his next trip to North Ambrym District Agent Wilkins noted:

Artefacts – despite French District Agent's efforts to oppose the chiefs'
agreement: the agreement that artefacts be made by those interested in
accordance with their grades is being adhered to. Enormous numbers of
black palm images are being exported by Tainmal (Fanla) through the
Tuikakau (counted 20 at the passage during my visit). And the pagan villages
of Neuha and Ranhor (above Olal) through Beguex (trading with Burn
Phillips). Latter is paying about £4 – to £10 cash for them apparently and
holds payment until he has adequate stocks of wine at hand. Alleged by
the Mission Villages that proceeds are being spent almost entirely on wine.
Stacks of empty bottles in the villages indicate this. The Magam region is
concerned about a market for its products as apparently neither Begeaux
nor Tuikakau is interested, and Fonah has more than sufficient on hand.
Every able bodied man now appears to have artefacts for sale. Magam
region wishes to present a blackpalm image or slitgong to HM the Queen.
Explained that this might pose problems but I would find out.

(Touring notes, 16–21 March 1967)

Apparently Tainmal had already reached an agreement with the other
chiefs on Ambrym that there should now be a strict discipline involved in the
carving industry: state discipline, executed by Tainmal himself in his capacity
as assessor. The carving of artefacts should follow either one's own rank or
that of one's father's. This of course meant that a lot of people gained rights
that they had not had previously, when men without rights themselves could
not make carvings at all. The further effect was that Tainmal had taken control
over the carving industry, as the highest ranked man at the time. Tainmal was
the authority in this game, personally involved in all graded initiations and
carvings. Therefore, people also hesitated about claiming the rights of their
ancestors, since the bringing back of the image would also immediately bring
back the things that were attached to the grading; especially the inherent
sorcery and the relation to Tainmal and his son, Tofor. Later in 1967, District
Agent D.K.H. Dale commented in a letter that 'Tainmal's chaps are doing
a rowing trade – I gather they sold to the COOP and Tena Francklen over
$A 2400.00 worth of artefacts' (Letter from BDA to the British Residency,
November 1967). Further, when other people tried to sell things it often
provoked Tainmal and Tofor. They decided which designs were public and
which had restrictions, as demonstrated in this comment:

> Tofor and Tainmal allege chiefs rule over cutting artefacts relevant to grades
> reached being disregarded – Tofor quoted two gongs carved with hands.
> Chiefs to examine and consider appointment of artefacts inspector ... to
> control the standard of artefacts offered for sale.
>
> (BDA Touring notes, 5–16 January 1968)

The slit gongs with hands had been designed for specific ceremonial purposes and ritual circumstances, and were seen as unfit for public sale. A special non-specified slit gong design had been developed for sale to outsiders, while the specified designs were excluded from this arena. The whole process led to numerous incidents in which Tofor acted as a judge as to who held rights and who did not. Being feared for his magical abilities and sorcery, he was taken seriously:

> While at Ranon, Tofor, Mr. Tainmal's son, reported to me that Bule Tabit
> of Wou did not compensate him for selling an image, he said Tabit has
> sold one to a Frenchman without his permission. According to their own
> custom Tabit's father didn't have the right to make one like that, he ought
> to give something to Tofor and his father. Tabit had no right to sell this type
> of image, only the people who reached the grade in custom called *tainmal*
> are permitted to. Tabit is in Santo at present, he (Tofor) asks us to send a
> message to him and ask him to go back to Ambrym as soon as possible to
> fix this business with him and his father in custom or otherwise he must be
> taken to the cell. He said if he were to punish Tabit in custom Tabit ought to
> compensate him with two tusked pigs, if not Tabit would be killed.
>
> (BDA touring notes, 9–14 September 1968)

The most interesting part here is how Tofor now involves the District Agents in his own allegations of breaches of customary law. In the documents and correspondences of District Agents from 1960 onwards, we see that as the pagan chief Tofor took over the business from his father, he increasingly engaged the District Agents in his own agenda. By 1968 he had also taken over the post of being colonial assessor from his father, and he was simultaneously tending his career in the *mage* ritual society. Towards the end of 1968, Tofor charged two leading figures of Linbul village with 'disregarding observance of customary rite'. A village court was set up and the British District Agent was present. Tofor presented his case as follows:

> I am the son of a Mal (High Chief) Tainmal of Fanla village. On June 21st,
> 1968 I observed a custom, called Meleunketlam (small chief) meaning
> that I am embarking of the first signs of becoming a Meleun. The ritual is

to be observed for five days with no noise (whispering only allowed) and disturbance. On the night of 21st I killed two pigs for the night feast and my people started the beating of the gongs until dawn when I had two other tusked pigs butchered, and a live one given to the Lokbaro Natin (2nd highest chief to a Mal) who is responsible for the whole show.

(Report of the BDA, no date)

He was then questioned about the ritual by the BDA, who apparently took the opportunity to try to learn something about how the *mage* worked:

Question: Why did your people beat the gongs?

Answer: To let neighbouring villages and others further away know that I am observing this custom which I had already verbally displayed by messages to them, so that they may not disturb me, as I shall want absolute silence, to pay *mage* and ask for power to the image (a black palm one) planted by the Lokbaro.

Question: Is it right that a Mal only has the right to restore you to the position of Meleunkatlam?

Answer: Yes it is true, however the only Mal here is my father and because I am his son he cannot undertake it until when I am a Lokbaro and ready to be Mal, but he assisted me in some ways.

Question: How often are such feasts and customs observed?

Answer: When I have enough pigs. It will be quite some times before I can hold a feast again as the pigs have all been consumed. I have to kill many pigs and observe and obey customary rites before I can be a Mal. These people of mine who beat the gongs from eve till dawn were paid with a tusk pig. The planting of the black palm image is called Makenepul (hole in which the statue stands) and from the image I get my power. The Meleunkatalam and Makenepul rite cost me eight live pigs to be paid to the Lokbaro, the rest of the pigs eaten not counted. Women and children when I start to observe this custom do not stay in the village but went far out in the bush and made temporary huts to live until the five days passed. Then they return to their individual houses. The reason for this is that children make too much noise and women if present in such customs bring bad omen to whoever is observing such a custom. The men are not allowed to work but are to stay quietly at home and cook their food. When the last day is up I will mark a small area in the main route in the vicinity and imitate planting yams and that is the sign to everyone that the ritual has come to an end and everyone does as he pleases. I lodge complaint against elder Philip and Assessor Isaac because they broke the custom by making noises. I did not fulfil what I had been doing and this made me very angry, also my father and men in the village, because these people of all people who are my next door neighbours should do this to me, knowing well what was going on. According to custom if anyone breaks such law is automatically butchered, and some of my people who had broken the custom because of Philip and Isaak have been punished and they have given me a tusk pig. I insist that they be punished without delay

(Report of the BDA, no date)

In the next statement, Elder Philip from Linbul admitted that he had been up in the plantations to cut copra on that day with a crew of his. One of them had 'made faces' and they had all laughed loudly. They had also chopped wood for the copra-dryer. He added however that he saw no wrong in doing this, since 'I don't believe in such customs and I am an elder of the SDA church at Linbul village, and I don't want to know any of those heathen customs by Tainmal and his son'. Assessor Isaac, who was also charged with making noise in his garden, defended himself by claiming that he thought Tofor's ceremony was finished since he had seen people coming down from Fanla to attend church that same morning.

After the discussion and examination ended, the court, in addition to the BDA consisting of Assessor Willy of Magam village and Chief Wilfred of Fonah, declared their decision: Elder Philip should have finished his work in the plantation before the ceremony started and should not have been laughing and making noise. Elder Philip and Joseph knew what Tofor was doing, and should not have disturbed the ceremony: 'They would not have liked it if he came down to make noise during their church service in Linbul.' They were sentenced to pay Tofor the sum of $20, or a pig, in compensation.

Tofor had thereby managed to build up *kastom* as an equal alternative to church ceremonies, and through his influence over the District Agents, managed to enforce this disciplining authority of the whole colonial apparatus on the Christian population. His rhetoric was of course even more powerful than the church rhetoric. Not only did he claim that he had the democratic right to uphold his way of life, but he also had legitimacy among the District Agents from his claim that this was the original way of life on Ambrym. Around this time, Tofor had built up a reputation as the most powerful man on Ambrym. In another touring note, Wilkins commented sarcastically that:

Figure 1   *Ceremonial killing of pigs in the village of Fanla, North Ambrym, 1960s. Holding the rope of the pig is young Tofor, and behind him is his father Tainmal with his hands covered in pig's tusks. (With permission of the Vanuatu Cultural Centre.)*

> Tofor of Fanla now proposes to build an airstrip at Fanla and wants to start immediately – this is part of the Napoleonic image build-up and I told him that it was essential that he did not do anything until the aviation advisors had decided where on north Ambrym a strip was eventually to be built...
>
> (BDA touring notes, 10–15 October 1969)

As the ultimate confirmation of this 'Napoleonic' imagery, in 1970 a huge standing drum was given as a gift from Tofor to the Queen of Great Britain, hence accomplishing what the Magam people and Chief Willy had been trying to do for years. After a great deal of correspondence between Ambrym, Port Vila and London, the drum was picked up by the Royal Ship *Britannia* on one of its journeys to the colonies. The drum was about 12-feet high and weighed at least two tons. People in Ranon and Fanla can still vividly remember the hauling of the big log through the forest and down to the sea, accompanied by *kastom* songs and dances on the way and a ceremonial feast of food-distribution to those taking part. The drum today stands proudly in the University of Cambridge's Museum of Archaeology and Anthropology.

As we see, the people of North Ambrym were at this time well aware of the value of their cultural heritage – not only carvings, but also dances, magic and 'culture' generally – and through the DAs they tried to make the most of it.

Upscaling *kastom* for national performances

Chief Tofor was a child of these historical circumstances, and came to master them with perfection. He was among the few who kept on performing costly rituals and pig-killings into the 1960s and 1970s. These performances were no longer just local events; Tofor made his ritual performances national, even international events. Around the time of the incident with the noise of the Linbul people, the BDA wrote about North Ambrym:

> Tofor of Fanla asked if he could perform custom dances around the islands
> in the group and whether he could be sponsored by the government. AAO
> told him that this comes like a major undertaking which will involve money
> and transport, therefore the best solution is the Chamber of Commerce in
> Vila. AAO told Tofor that FDA will be informed on this and will let him
> know whether this item of interest could be realised, by the government or
> the Chamber of Commerce. Tofor said that if what he has suggested comes
> to realisation the gains will be split 50-50 with the sponsor.
>
> (Touring notes, 6 June 1968)

At this point, Tofor apparently wanted to broaden his audiences and the scale of his ritual performances. At the same time other high men – like Nagriamel leader Jimmy Stevens on Santo and National Party leader Walter Lini on Pentecost, who became leaders of the independence movement – were broadening their scale of rhetorical performance by suddenly addressing the whole of the New Hebrides, no longer just their home islands and regions. In a sense, Tofor was doing the same thing, but within his own medium of power, notably the ritual-status ceremonies of Ambrym. Tofor was ready to create an overarching ritual stage for the whole New Hebrides. The idea of the Nagriamel movement was based on the same idea. Jimmy Stevens wanted to build a nationwide graded society with its main men's house under the big banyan tree in the constructed village of Fanafo in Santo, and for a while this almost worked, as it was sponsored by American capitalist forces as well as political supporters in Fiji (Tabani 2008). Tofor, however, was working outside of these political formations. He wanted to widen the reach of his renown and powers, and later in 1968 he came up with another idea:

> Tofor T. of Fanla raised with us the possibility of sending a custom dance troupe to Australia. It is difficult to dampen his enthusiasm but possibly something could be done to entertain tourists at Vila. I said I would take up with the Chamber of Commerce or Andre Lancome.
>
> (Touring notes, December 1968)

If Tofor's initiative had come through, he could have ended up as some kind of 'Wild man of Borneo' in circus-like circumstances in Australia. Away from his ceremonial ground in Ambrym, in the eyes of foreigners, Tofor could easily have been seen as an entrepreneur who wanted to make money in a familiar Western sense. He was drinking heavily, and it could have seemed as if he was only trying to finance this expensive habit. This was probably to some degree true, but the logic of his actions did after all arise from Ambrym circumstances, not European ones.

The idea of expanding the Ambrym framework for ritual performances would have been inconceivable among Ambrym chiefs only twenty years earlier, when this was still an arena for the high men to create power among themselves through internal activity. Tofor now found that there were no more high men on Ambrym – apart from his father – to create this power internally, and so he opened it up and turned its focus towards the exteriority beyond Ambrym. Such an initiative would once have triggered violent forces of sorcery and ancestor-related terror. Now the idea had become possible: as *kastom* was perceived to be dead on most islands, exposure to Ambrym *kastom* would no longer be harmful. Tofor, however, probably underestimated the fear of Ambrym sorcery on other islands, and his island tour never happened. He did, however, perform ceremonies in Port Vila, and I have heard many stories about the consequences of this. At one point the Ambrym men were giving a performance where they offered to teach people from other islands how to beat rhythms on the Ambrym standing drums. The pagans had built up a complete Ambrym dancing ground in Port Vila, with drums and flowers brought in from Ambrym. A man from the island of Tongoa wanted to learn about these things, since he felt that they had no *kastom* left on Tongoa. He stayed with the Fanla group the whole day to learn the rhythms. His wife became worried about him when it was getting dark, and tried to drag him off. Although he was completely obsessed by the drumming, she managed to get him along. As they walked home, he tried to convince her that he should go back to the Ambrym *nasara*,[2] but she resisted and brought him home. The next day he walked around normally, but constantly talking about Ambrym. That night, he suddenly died. This triggered the suspicion that he had been killed by the Ambrym men the day before, and that he had been walking around in a trance after they had taken out his intestines and replaced them with magic herbs. This story was told to me by a man from Tongoa in Port Vila, and it accurately reflects the urban status of Ambrym *kastom*.

In every report of the BDA over these years there is mention of Tofor. Tofor was now an assessor and had therefore much to do with the BDA's visits to Ambrym. This does not mean, however, that he distanced himself from the village life of kinship involvement and gardening. In another report of the BDA we read about a court in which Tofor is also involved:

> Wayarkon is the first wife and she wishes to divorce Tintin who is obviously paying too much attention to his second wife. Tintin has the reputation for drinking heavily and has beaten up both wives from time to time. The matter was discussed at length and it was agreed that Wayarkon would return to Tintin on condition that he provided her with the necessities of life and treated her decently, also that he gave up alcohol ... Note that Tofor of Fanla is anxious for divorce proceedings to take place so that he can claim Wayarkon as his third wife: Wayarkon was previously bought by Tainmal for Tofor's elder (deceased) brother but was subsequently taken without payment by Tintin.
>
> (Touring notes, February 1969)

Evidently from these comments and others, Tofor led his life as a high chief in Fanla, taking numerous wives to increase his potency and productivity, while engaging in the field of international trade and government relations. However, unlike the high men who were to engage in the political movement in the next decade, like his north Ambrym rival Chief Willie Bongmatur, who became a regional leader of the National Party in the 1970s, Tofor never converted to town life, to monogamy or to official political positions.

In October 1969 Tofor went through another grading ceremony, for the *meleun* grade he had started the previous year by being initiated into the *Meleungetlam*. The British District Agent D.K. Wilkins was present in Fanla for the event, along with thirty other Europeans. He commented that 'the attendance by the Ambrym people themselves, although a fair number, was surprisingly poor' (BDA 1969). The white spectators were charged $8 each to take photographs during the session. Tofor always notified the District Agents or people from the Vanuatu Cultural Centre so that they could take place in the audience along with tourists and other visitors. This is a typical report of such an event:

At Olal, Tofor was holding one extraordinary custom ritual not seen on Ambrym for a long time. This is 'the shooting' of his mother. It requires him to point the gun at his mother and fire the bullets wheezing just above her head. I was told that a long time ago they shot to kill. Tofor will pay his mother's relatives £1,000.

(BDA Tangarasi, Lakatoro, no date)

These events, produced in the circumstances of cameras and a widely international audience, were the new and powerful arenas for Ambrym rituals. Although the immediate focus of Tofor's rituals were the production and reproduction of kinship locally (Patterson 1981), he transformed them into something else.

The totalization of 'white man'

With regard to Sahlins' structures of conjuncture, what is discussed here is another aspect of the 'totalizing moment' in the course of events (Sahlins 1991). The Condominium governments had represented an 'event' in the developments of the Ambrym community. The District Agents were sent to Ambrym so that they might learn about local relationships in order to intervene in them. This had immediately turned them in the direction of the ongoing conflict between Christians and pagans. They had become entangled in the politics of the enigmatic concept of *kastom*, and they had let themselves be rolled up in the agendas of Tainmal and, later, of Tofor. Now Tofor was using his power within the extensive space of the *kastom* concept, not only to create a particular law and resultant discipline, but also in order to reach out to a much larger community and embrace 'white man'. From within Ambrym ceremonial, he created an image of *kastom* in the nostalgic sense, delivering a concept that many people accepted as the image of authentic culture.

It was this particular social space that Tofor came to take up, in a position between local power and international power – building a national authority that was complementary to the other contemporary national movements of Nagriamel and the Vanua'aku Party. At times, Tofor had his own personal white apprentices staying with him, and he had them indulge in local ways. Anthropologist Jean Guiart spent time with Tofor (then Tainmal's young son) in 1949 (Guiart 1951); anthropologist Mary Patterson saw much of him in the 1960s for her Ph.D. fieldwork; and in the 1970s Kai Muller, writing for *National Geographic Magazine*, was living with Tofor in Fanla as his personal pupil in the ways of *kastom*. Tofor shared many of his secrets with Muller, and even introduced him into the *mage* society. Later, in the 1980s, Tonkinese businessman Dihn Van Than, Vanuatu's leading entrepreneur, became Tofor's personal friend, and Tofor led him to take grades in the *mage* society. Kirk

Huffman of the Vanuatu Cultural Centre was also closely attached to Tofor, and was an important man for documenting and recording Tofor's ceremonial and knowledge. Huffman told me that when Tofor was imprisoned for murder in Port Vila after shooting his main rival in North Ambrym with his rifle, it caused a lot of problems. First, Tofor could not eat food prepared by other people, since he was a man of the 'taboo fire'. The prison manager therefore allowed Tofor into the kitchen to cook his own food, but this caused general unrest among the other prisoners, as they were afraid that Tofor would poison their food. The situation irritated Tofor so much that he escaped from prison. He walked right down to Kirk Huffman at the Vanuatu Cultural Centre and sat down in his office. When the police finally came to get him back to the prison cell, Tofor said to them that they had no rights there in the 'house of *kastom*', and that this was his domain. After a lengthy discussion between the police, Tofor and Kirk Huffman, an agreement was made to facilitate Tofor's stay in Port Vila outside of prison (Kirk Huffman, pers. comm. 1995).

The society of high men on Ambrym had indeed become too small for Tofor. When in the 1990s he attended the high rank of *mal* in Ambrym ranked society, he simultaneously stepped away from the Ambrym scene and became more and more involved with the powerful spheres of Santo Town and Port Vila. During the periods of my own fieldwork, from 1995 until his death in 1999, Tofor was a continual presence, always suspected of sorcery even though he was never around. When he introduced his brothers Bongmeleun and Magekon into the rank of *mage ne hiwir*, the performance and pig-killing was staged for the Vanuatu Cultural Centre, and the whole spectacle, with its big effigy and raised platform, was afterwards set up in the National Museum.

On Ambrym, the *mage* grading system had lost its importance as an important reproductive institution, and with the new order and denial of ritual hierarchy that came with the post-colonial Christian state-formation, Tofor's power also faded. Both on Ambrym and in Port Vila, he became more and more of a mythical character, an icon of authenticity. Already in a report from a tour of North Ambrym in 1975, the BDA mentioned a widespread rumour that Tofor had not been his old self after he had gone through a ritual that included inserting wooden nails into his head with a hammer. Another rumour had it that 'Tofor is not strictly speaking a chief, because he was suckled by his mother at birth, rather than being put immediately on a diet of yams as a true chief should be' (BDA Report, December 1975).

These rumours can be seen as a turning point in Tofor's influence. Things had started to turn against him, just as things were now turning against the colonial regime. Cultural heritage had been the axis around which all these developments had revolved, and even the fall of chiefly authority was legitimated through cultural heritage. But at this point, cultural heritage was also completely transformed, as a new arena for making claims about rights, genealogies, belonging and kinship – the outcome of a century-long process in the field of interaction between chiefs and colonial administration.

Emergent new concepts of *kastom* and nation

From a close study of available documents it becomes clear that the colonial era was a period when the decisive agency and execution of cultural policy lay in the hands of the chiefs as cultural authorities. They came to control, or at least have a hand in, all the activities and issues that the District Agents involved themselves in. However, during the intense period of *politik* (the political struggle between Nagriamel and the Vanua'aku Party) and the growth of the independence movement in the 1970s,[3] pagan chiefs became more and more distanced from power. Along with the District Agents and the plantation owners, the high men suddenly found themselves on the sideline of what was happening. This process was in a sense a continuation of the development that we saw with the carving industry. Christian leaders, like Chief Willy on Ambrym and Walter Lini on Pentecost, were suddenly talking about *kastom* in a new way. It became part of a nationalist rhetoric, and had come to mean the 'culture' of Vanuatu.

In the book *Vanuatu*, published on the request of Prime Minister Walter Lini at Independence in 1980, it is explained that

> there is something which allows us to say without hesitation that custom
> and culture are alive in our country and this is the language, which is the
> pillar and foundation of any society, used by every man, woman and child to
> communicate, all day, every day, for every activity in life.
>
> (Lini 1980:55)

Whereas the ritual hierarchy and *kastom* had previously been the ground for social reproduction, this kind of democratic rhetoric suddenly brought *kastom* into the grasp of the ni-Vanuatu Christian leaders, and expanded it to include certain unifying principles of the islands of the nation, such as bride-payments, circumcision ceremonies, funeral ceremonies and food-sharing. The Christian leaders, who had been fighting *kastom* back in the islands, were now turning it to their own advantage and using it in the national, urban discourse of independence. Thus, Chief Willie Bongmatur of North Ambrym came to stand beside Vanuatu's first Prime Minister, Walter Lini, to raise the independence flag. Chief Willie Bongmatur also became the first President of the National Council of Chiefs, the national institution for deciding issues related to customary law (Bolton 1998). Back on Ambrym, he had for a long time been in a conflict with Tainmal and Tofor over claims to rights in *kastom*. But this quarrel was now swept away by the new rhetoric of freedom and independence, with Chief Willy among those who set the standards for the concept of '*kastom* landowner' that emerged. Now everyone who could demonstrate descent connections to localities through origin stories and genealogy acquired rights over the colonial lands and plantations. The Vanua'aku Party, which won ground over the traditionalist Nagriamel movement, based its victory on the values of the Anglican and Methodist Churches in Vanuatu. Taking inspiration from the nostalgia of 'traditional culture' and 'primitive art' that had been developing since the early twentieth century, the Vanua'aku Party had, however, come to appropriate the symbols of *kastom*, and, furthermore, came to praise the essentials of *kastom* as a reproductive social framework. Chief Willy, who led the fight on Ambrym against the secrecy and sorcery of the *mage* society, now engaged in a long list of pig-killings to demonstrate his kinship relations.

This development as independence loomed came to mean total defeat for the high men of the *mage* ritual hierarchy on Ambrym. I do not think Tofor had seen this coming. At the peak of the period of *politik*, Chief Tofor bitterly addressed the French High Commissioner for support:

> For the Resident High Commissioner,
> Just a small word to advertise that I have a French School in Fanla. Before,
> we were friends, now we are enemies. You know why! In the New Hebrides,
> there used to be two things, now there are three. It is the third that divides
> us. Me, I do not like politics, I am under the law of custom. I am opposed
> to what is about to happen to the New Hebrides. The Chief Bong Bunlap
> of Pentecost agrees with me over these problems. I have been to see Bong
> Bunlap, on the 31-03-77 on the island of Pentecost. When the people go to
> another election, we will not take part in it. We are in our own law. Now,
> I finish this small news. Can you reply to my letter at the address below?
> Gratefully yours,
>
>   Signed TOFOR
>   (Tofor 1977 [my translation from French])

In a comment to the letter, the French Resident High Commissioner admits that he didn't know quite what Tofor meant. It appears that both Tofor and the renowned Chief Bong of Pentecost were strongly opposed to the development of Vanuatu *politik*. They had been mastering the ways of the French and British colonial powers, and were bitter and resentful at the third 'thing' now on the scene: the Vanua'aku Party, which claimed to represent the heart and soul of New Hebridean *kastom*. The Vanua'aku Party was supported by the British, and collaborated with them in the process of violently smashing the Nagriamel movement, which fought for customary hierarchy (and which for a period had managed to involve Tofor and Tainmal in their ranks). Neither Tofor nor Tainmal had been opposed in a political sense to the Condominium government. On the contrary, they had been the consistent defenders and collaborators of *waetman*. The sudden emergence of the independent state took Tofor by surprise, since he and his father had always believed themselves to be heads of the indigenous nation, the *kastom* nation – a position they had been allowed to develop and maintain by the colonial government.

Conclusion

During this century of colonial encounters, the concept of *kastom* became the emblem around which the different changes in attitude towards the external world articulated themselves. At first, it seems that *kastom* was set up as a 'compartmental' concept, in Keesing's terms (1992), which wrapped up local power in order to hide its real contents from the new visitors. This was the protective reaction of Tainmal of Fanla and other high men towards the coercive apparatus of the colonialists. This defensive line, however, was modified in the 1950s and 1960s. Through the carving industry and tourist performances of status ceremonial, *kastom* was in fact opened up to new audiences, and moved from its hiding place in the interior of Ambrym social life to the intermediary space between island representatives and white official representatives and tourists. Then, by the end of the 1970s, *kastom* was democratized, and finally bestowed on the nation-state of Vanuatu upon its creation in 1980 (Rodman 1983). A national *kastom* was taking form, finally manifested in the policy of the National Council of Chiefs, wherein uniform principles of pig-exchanges, food-sharing and ceremonial prestations were outlined. It was only in this last process that *kastom* was really 'substantivized' (Thomas 1992) as in opposition to European ways. It now came to stand for the 'local style' in opposition to the ways of the 'white man'. Before that, *kastom* had been a fragmented concept, liable to stand in opposition to anything. The *kastom* of Tainmal of Fanla village could be in opposition to the *kastom* of Tintin of neighbouring Ranhor village, the *kastom* of Ambrym could be in opposition to the *kastom* of Tanna, in opposition to *skul* and Christianity – but as the biography of Fanla shows, it would not figure prominently in opposition to 'white man'. Paradoxically, *kastom* came to be in opposition to Western ways only when it was appropriated and used by the people who had themselves explicitly converted to Western ways.

The colonial state had to some degree implemented the ritual order in its own legislation and punitive system, through the high chiefs as ultimate authorities. In the process leading up to independence it had seemed for a moment to be feasible for the new nation to be structured on the ritual hierarchy of the Nagriamel movement and on chiefly authority. However, the nation of Vanuatu that dawned in 1980 first rushed against these movements with overt violence, and then firmly delegated a place for *kastom* at the outskirts of governance, designated to the realm of the National Museum and the National Council of Chiefs. In this domain, cultural heritage has been given its place as a property of the modern nation. As we outline in the introduction to this volume, and as seen in the contributions by Lindstrom, M. Scott, Bolton, and Regenvanu and Geismar, *kastom* can never be comfortable in that position and will continually try to explode those institutional limitations on its own forms of governmentality.

Notes

1. This article is based as much on archival material as my own research in North Ambrym. I want to give my gratitude to The Vanuatu National Archives for accommodating my requests regarding this archival material from North Ambrym in the colonial period. I want to thank the anonymous reviewer for comments and Edvard Hviding for reading earlier versions of this chapter.
2. *Nasara* is Bislama for 'ceremonial ground', the basis for island *kastom.* It turned out that importing the Ambrym *nasara* to the capital also imported the place of Ambrym itself in a significant way.
3. In the 1960s and 70s the political direction of the New Hebrides went in two different directions. The Nagriamel movement was established on Santo, as a nationwide ceremonial society with ideals of returning to *kastom*, taking back the land and, to a certain degree, upholding communalist values in terms of sharing community work and plantation surpluses. The Vanua'ku Party was initially a political movement in Port Vila. Under the name of National Party, it began as a protest movement for Anglophone and protestant elites who were unhappy with colonial subordination of land rights and civil rights. During the 1970s the tension between these very different types of movement became more pointed, a tension exacerbated by British support for the National Party. During the chaotic weeks of Independence in 1980, Nagriamel supporters were imprisoned, beaten up or excommunicated all over the new nation of Vanuatu, and Vanua'ku party members became the leaders and new political elites (see MacClancy 2002; Tabani 2008).

Bibliography

BDA 1961–9. Touring notes - Quarterly Report of the British District Agent, Central District no.2. Unmarked box, Vanuatu National Archives, Port Vila.

Bolton, L. 1998. 'Chief Willie Bongmatur Maldo and the role of chiefs in Vanuatu'. *Journal of Pacific History* 33(2):179–95.

Bonnemaison, J., C. Kaufman, K. Huffman and D. Tryon (eds) 1996. *Arts of Vanuatu.* Bathurst: Crawford House Publishing.

Campbell, I.C. 1997. 'Culture contact and Polynesian identity in the European age.' *Journal of World History* 8(1):29–55.

Deacon, B. 1934. *Malekula: A Vanishing People in the New Hebrides.* London: Routledge and Kegan.

Douglas, N. 1996. *They Came for Savages: 100 Years of Tourism in Melanesia.* Alstonville: Southern Cross University Press.

Eriksen, T.H. 2001. 'Between universalism and relativism: a critique of the UNESCO concept of culture.' In *Culture and Rights: Anthropological Perspectives* (eds) J.K. Cowan, M. Dembour and R.A. Wilson, 127–48. Cambridge: Cambridge University Press.

Foster, R. 1992. 'Commoditization and the emergence of kastam as a cultural category: a New Ireland case in comparative perspective,' in M. Jolly and N. Thomas (eds) *The Politics of Tradition in the South Pacific,* Special Issue of *Oceania* 62(4):284–94.

Frater, M. 1922. *Midst Volcanic Fires.* London: James Clarke & Co.

Geismar, H. 2005. 'Copyright in context: carvings, carvers and commodities in Vanuatu.' *American Ethnologist* 32 (3):437–59.

Goodenough, J.G. 1876. *Journal of Commodore Goodenough during his last command as senior officer on the Australian Station, 1873–1875.* London: Henry S. King.

Gosden, C. and C. Knowles 2001. *Collecting Colonialism: Material Culture and Colonial Change.* Oxford: Berg.

Guiart, J. 1949. 'Rapport sur la situation indigene dans le Nord-Ambrym.' Unpublished report to the Institut Francais d'Oceanie. In Archives Territoriales de Nouvelle Caledonie.

Guiart, J. 1951. 'Societe, rituels, et mythes du Nord Ambrym.' *Journal de la Societe des Oceanistes,* 7(7):5–103.

Harrison, S. 2006. *Fracturing Resemblances. Identity and Mimetic Conflict in Melanesia and the West.* Oxford: Berghahn Books.

Harrison, T.H. 1936. 'Living with the people of Malekula.' *The Geographical Journal* 88(2):97–124.

Keesing, R. 1992. *Custom and Confrontation: The Kwaio Struggle for Cultural Autonomy.* Berkeley: The University of Chicago Press.

Lamb, Robert 1905. *Saints and Savages: The Story of Five Years in the New Hebrides.* Sydney: William Blackwood and Sons.

Leach, M.J. 1967. Memorandum from the Information Officer and Co-Operative Societies Officer. 6 February 1967 F2/5. National Archives of Vanuatu, Port Vila.

Lindstrom, L. 1993. 'Cargo cult culture: towards a genealogy of Melanesian kastom'.
    Anthropological Forum 6(4):495–515.

Lindstrom, L. and White G. (eds) 1993. *Custom Today*. Special issue of
    Anthropological Forum 6(4):467–618.

Lini, W. (ed.) 1980. *Vanuatu: Twenti wan tingting long taem blong independens*. Suva:
    Institute of Pacific Studies, University of the South Pacific.

Lipuma, E. 1998. 'Modernity and forms of personhood in Melanesia'. In *Bodies and
    Persons*, (eds) A. Strathern and M. Lambek, 53–79. Cambridge: Cambridge
    University Press.

MacClancy, J. 2002. *To Kill a Bird with Two Stones*. Port Vila: Vanuatu Cultural
    Centre.

Patterson, M. 1981. 'Slings and arrows: rituals of status acquisitions in North
    Ambrym'. In *Vanuatu: Politics, Economics, and Ritual in Island Melanesia*
    (ed.) M. Allen, 189–237. Sydney: Academic Press Australia.

Philibert, J.M. 1983. 'Will success spoil a middleman? The case of Etapang, Central
    Vanuatu'. In *Middlemen and Brokers in Oceania* (eds) W. Rodmand and
    D.A. Counts, 187–207. Ann Arbor: University of Michigan Press.

Rio, K. 2002. The Third Man. Manifestations of Agency on Ambrym Island, Vanuatu.
    Ph.D. dissertation at the University of Bergen.

Rio, K. 2005. 'Discussions around a sand-drawing: creations of agency and society in
    Melanesia'. *Journal of the Royal Anthropological Institute* 11:401–23.

Rio, K. 2011. 'Policing the Holy Nation: The state and righteous violence in Vanuatu'.
    Oceania 81(1):51–72.

Rodman, W.L. 1983. 'Gaps, bridges and levels of law: middlemen as mediators in a
    Vanuatu society'. In *Middlemen and Brokers in Oceania* (eds) W. Rodman
    and D.A. Counts, 69–95. Ann Arbor: University of Michigan Press.

Rodman, W.L. 1985. '"A law unto themselves": legal innovation in Ambae, Vanuatu'.
    American Ethnologist 12(4):603–24.

Sahlins, M. 1991. 'The return of the event: again ...'. In *Clio in Oceania: Toward a
    Historical Anthropology* (ed.) A.Biersack, 37–101. Washington: Smithsonian
    Institution Press.

Speiser, F. 1923. *Ethnographische Materialen aus den Neuen Hebriden und den Banks-
    Inseln*. Berlin: C.W. Kreidel's Verlag.

Speiser, F. 1996. *Ethnology of Vanuatu: An Early Twentieth Century Study*. Bathhurst:
    Crawford House Press.

Strathern, M. 1992. 'Parts and wholes; refiguring relationships in a post-plural world'.
    In *Conceptualizing Society* (ed.) A. Kuper, 75–104. London: Routledge.

Strathern, M. and E. Hirsch. 2004. 'Introduction'. In *Transactions and Creations:
    Property Debates and the Stimulus of Melanesia* (eds) E. Hirsch and M.
    Strathern, 1–21. Oxford. Berghahn Books.

Tabani, M. 2008. 'A political history of Nagriamel on Santo, Vanuatu'. *Oceania* 78(3):332–57.

Thomas, N. 1992. 'Substantivization and anthropological discourse: the transformation of practices into institutions in neotraditional Pacific societies'. In *History and Tradition in Melanesian Anthropology* (ed.) J. Carrier, 64–85. Berkeley: University of California Press.

Thomas, N. 1993. 'Beggars can be choosers', *American Ethnologist* 20(4):868–76.

Thomas, N. 1997. *In Oceania: Visions, Artifacts, Histories*. Durham: Duke University Press.

Tofor 1977. Letter to the French High Commission. Unmarked Box, Vanuatu National Archives, Port Vila.

UNESCO 1996. *Our Creative Diversity. Report of the World Commission on Culture and Development*. Paris: UNESCO Publishing.

Wagner, R. 1986. *Asiwinarong: Ethos, Image and Social Power among the Usen Barok of New Ireland*. New York: Princeton University Press.

White, G. 1993. 'Three discourses of custom'. *Anthropological Forum* 6 (4):475–95.

Wilkins, Darral K. 1966. Touring notes - Quarterly Report of the British District Agent, Central District no. 2. Unmarked Box, Vanuatu National Archives, Port Vila.

Wilkins, Darral K. 1967. Letter, 16 March. F.297/3. National Archives of Vanuatu, Port Vila.

CHAPTER 10

Personhood, cargo and
Melanesian social unities

✳

LAMONT LINDSTROM

Introduction

London Missionary Society pioneer John Williams brought his ship, the *Camden*, into Tanna Island's Port Resolution on 18 November 1839. Two days later he was clubbed to death at Dillon's Bay, Erromango, along with his secretary James Harris. While on Tanna, as yet unaware of his fate, Williams attempted a Christian overture in the wake of earlier visits to the island by James Cook in 1774, Russian explorer Vasilii Mikhailovich Golovnin in 1809, and passing whalers and sandalwood cutters in the 1820s and 1830s. Williams attempted to make friends through things. George Baxter's commemorative 1841 oil-inked colour lithograph 'The reception of the Rev. J. Williams, at Tanna, in the South Seas, the day before he was massacred' (Figure 1), is the first illustration of European cargo come to Tanna. Williams' hand is empty and open in greeting, but, just behind him, his *Camden* shipmates flash mirrors, English cloth and a box full of beads and trinkets. Williams is pale-faced and sports top hat and boots. The Tannese on shore, who should be wearing penis-wrappers, are instead modestly draped in loincloth and feather headdress. A cultural intermediary, who stands barefooted on a gangplank spanning beach and boat, probably depicts one of Williams' Samoan or Cook Islander converts. The Tannese are not empty-handed. Yes, they bear aloft clubs and klaxon triton shell trumpets, but women in the background welcome Williams with armloads of coconuts. English beads meet Tanna

Figure 1 *'The Reception of the Rev J. Williams at Tanna' (George Baxter, 1841).*

coconuts, as one would expect they might given the importance of economic reciprocity and sociability on both sides of that beach. But these strangers bearing mirrors, beads and cloth also brought trouble. That gangplank led not just back onto Williams' boat, but outwards into an intensifying global system. New cargo opened up broader, if trickier, horizons.

Let me introduce three examples of more recent cargo flows into Tanna that occurred 140 years after Williams' brief visit and that also featured dangerous cargo. In 1979, the French colonial *délégué* on Tanna and his Resident Commissioner repeated Reverend Williams' gesture of friendship. Hands stretched out, these two Europeans offered gifts of cloth, tinned fish, rice, oil, cabin biscuits and tea to Tannese voters a month before the crucial elections of November 1979 that led to an independent Vanuatu. In this encounter, a Tannese man took the intermediary position of helping to transmit goods from European colonialists to islanders. During another exchange, this one with no Europeans in sight, the children and grandchildren of Sarei gathered up soap, tinned fish and money, which they ceremonially placed in front of the shawled old lady in appreciation of her venerable years – venerability, here, marked by imported goods. And one more, my young friend Marta much appreciated playing 'trade store' with cargo remnants she retrieved from trash I had thrown over the side of the hill on which her village is located. Island children nowadays, like their aged elders, play with store-bought things. Since Williams' visit, goods have continued to flow from hand to hand during these sorts of exchange events as in many others. Western cargo, as soon as it crosses the beach, trades from person to person on the island. Global flows have become local flows.

Cargoes of cloth, mirrors, beads, soap and an array of other goods have flowed into, and around, Tanna during the last two centuries of intensifying global connection. Such cargo flows have challenged people to rethink relations between islander and outlander, and also among themselves. New cargo has unsettled, notably, people's chronic, infrequently achieved social project of creating social unities. Tannese shifting attempts to incorporate new others, and to domesticate their new goods, are apparent in 150 years of social movements on the island. These began in the nineteenth century with the radical revision of a traditional moiety system into a new dualism, which united and opposed trading 'ship' people and 'men-of-war' (Bonnemaison 1994:168). They continued with the Christian conversion of the majority of islanders by the Presbyterian mission. Both these initial attempts at island social unity proved, in the end, ephemeral. Subsequently, the Tannese cooked up a celebrated series of 'cargo cults', including the exceptional John Frum movement (Lindstrom 1993a). Island efforts to jigger unity in the form of new moieties, new churches, new cults or new parties are ongoing, the most recent of which is currently led by the Prophet Fred (Tabani 2009). Although each of these ventures has promised a new unity, each in the end has crumbled, undermined by the island's fissiparous soil and by new global flows onto its beaches.

Melanesian dreams of social unity, and recurring efforts to achieve this, continue to be one of the cultural engines of political innovation throughout the region. Strange and exotic cargo has stoked and unsettled people's unificatory desires. Local attempts to achieve new and innovative social unities, whether pulled along by sweet dream or pushed by nightmare, also colour people's relations with the new Melanesian states and the broader sorts of national unity that these states both require and work to create. As Rio and Hviding (this volume) note, 'local cultural heritage has been a central element in political innovation in and beyond the local'. This 'beyond the local', in 1839 when Williams landed on Tanna, comprised an incipient and far-flung global system of trade and early Christian mission effort. In subsequent years, however, the global intensified and moved closer to the local, firstly in the form of the Franco-Britannic condominium of the New Hebrides/Nouvelles-Hébrides in which Tannese Islanders had become encapsulated (see Rio, this volume). Most recently, independent, post-colonial Melanesian states, like Vanuatu, comprise the larger political context within which local political innovation plays out. Such political innovation, with attendant revaluation of cultural heritage in the service of advancing local unity, frequently continues to 'call for responses of state legislation and regulation' insofar as it may threaten 'pre-assumed social orders such as those that the state attempts to hold together' (Rio and Hviding, this volume). Political innovation at the local level, responding to island worries about personhood and cargo, reflects back onto national and transnational structures of state and region.

Utopian unities

Anthropologists have repeatedly noted Melanesian dreams of unity and attendant fears of social disintegration. Islanders hope and work for community and for consensus, but expect the worst. There is unavoidable conflict between social harmony, on the one hand, and competitive status games, on the other. People's ongoing pursuit of status and power subverts the very sociability they hope to achieve. And careful accountings and balancings of everyday exchange relations on which island sensibilities rest are inevitably undermined by historic happenstance. Thomas Maschio, for example, describes 'pessimistic' ideals of person and conduct on New Britain that 'allow either for the continual recreation of or the undermining of community' (1994:103). Inevitably, unforeseen death, disease, accident, craziness, calamity, famine and misfortune dog the best-made plans for social equivalence. It does not help, in Melanesia, that untoward events often spark strong suspicions of sorcery, as much as they do fatalistic acceptance of coincidence, bad luck, nature or God's mysterious plans. Sorcery is inversely proportional, and intrinsically connected, to social unity or the lack thereof, as Nancy Munn has noted of Gawa consensus-building:

> ... speakers must attempt to create a new transformational level of
> spatiotemporal order consisting of a community consensus, a unity of
> wills unmarred by the hidden refusal of one or more individuals who put
> themselves above all others ... Group or community consensus constitutes
> an intersubjective spacetime that is the reverse of the witch's destructive
> bodily incorporation of the other. Rather than forming the radical
> superordination and domination of one actor over another, it creates a
> likeness of intention, or in Durkheim's terms, a 'mechanical unity'.
>
> (Munn 1986:264–5)

Failures of consensus evoke the witch, and the witch makes mechanical unity impossible. Sorcery is both cause and effect of disorder.

As cultural tragic flaws go, this one has generated interesting theory – in particular about Melanesian fondness for culting and social movements of various sorts (see Jebens 2004). Faced with heartbreaking, losing battles to establish enduring harmony and unity, Melanesians retreat into more tightly organized cults within whose narrower bounds they can construct a purer social world. These include the various men's cults and clubs into which guys across the region used to retire for a little pretend unity. Gilbert Herdt summarizes common functionalist accounts of the men's house: unstable social relationships, anxiety, mistrust, disruptions across generations, warfare, violence, chaos and calamity all impel men into 'the use of secret ritual initiation practices and the founding of an institutional complex called the men's house as the cultural and psychological solution to an otherwise intolerable and perhaps ultimately unsuccessful sociality' (2003:34).

Utopian cultic unities also characterized cargo as well as men's cults. Peter Worsley, famously, argued that cargo cults functioned to 'weld previously hostile and separate groups together into a new unity' (1957:228; Lindstrom 1993a:55–6); and that 'by projecting his message on to the supernatural plane', a cargo-cult leader demonstrates that his authority 'transcends the narrow province of local gods and spirits associated with particular clans, tribes or villages' (1957:237). Back on Tanna, 'John Frum provided the means to transcend Tanna's splintered society; the primary purpose of the John Frum approach was just as much to reunite society as it was to develop a religious belief system' (Bonnemaison 1994:254; see Guiart 1956:168). Ron Brunton similarly explained the unifying functions of the John Frum movement: new cultic organization overcame creeping social collapse – a twentieth century withering of traditional marital alliance in particular. According to Brunton: 'the movement was a rather sophisticated, and generally successful, attempt by pagans to halt and reverse a process of progressive social disintegration which came about because Tannese Christians refused to participate in traditional marriage exchanges' (1981:357–8; see also Brunton 1989:177).

We might turn, for a little more theoretical illumination on utopian unity, to Marilyn Strathern and her celebrated depiction of the Melanesian dividual in *The Gender of the Gift* (1988). Although Strathern's dividual has been criticized by some who find it too simplifying (e.g. Strathern and Stewart 1998; Lambek and Strathern 1998), or who stubbornly want to locate at least some measure of individuality in Melanesia or some dividuality in the West, her approach to personhood does capture the world of socially embedded personhood in Melanesia (and probably anywhere where kinship shapes and constrains personal agency). Taking Strathern seriously, dividual identity is always already conjoined with others – sociality colonizes the person:

> Far from being regarded as unique entities, Melanesian persons are as
> dividually as they are individually conceived. They contain a generalized
> sociality within. Indeed, persons are frequently constructed as the plural and
> composite site of the relationships that produced them. The singular person
> can be imagined as a social microcosm.
>
> (1988:34)

Following Strathern's decapitation of the individual to find the dividual therein, so we might also linguistically chip 'society' down to 'soc'. These labels grasp the person as society and also the society as person – as do American high-school students who decry the 'soc' as social zombies whose individuality is no longer distinguishable from the networks in which they are embedded. Here's one definition of the 'soc' from an online dictionary of youth slang:

> SOC. A pop-culture junkie so obsessed with following society's norms that
> they lose all sense of their own personal identity and become just another
> zombie of society. Soc's [*sic*] are typically between the ages of 16 and 39 and
> exhibit any or all of the following characteristics: wears makeup (women),
> owns a cell phone, owns a laptop computer, weights less than 150 lbs, drives
> an SUV, visits Starbucks frequently, and watches 'Friends'. *Hey dude, I'm
> bored ... let's go uptown and go beat up some soc's* [*sic*].
>
> (www.urbandictionary.com)

A young person's overpowering social networks – so we fear – colonize and transform him, or her, into the hapless 'soc' – society as macrocosmic person. Here appears not the witch but the zombie: An over-socialized American zombie arouses the same obloquy as the over-individualized Melanesian witch. The individualized Melanesian can be as repugnant, and creepy, as the dividualized Western person.

Strathern complicates the picture by distinguishing two sorts of dividualizing social relationships in Melanesia: dualistic husband/wife, clan/ clan or cognate/affine sorts of relations that are characterized by mediated exchanges of substances and goods (see also Brown 1988); and direct, composite parent/child kinds of relations characterized by unmediated flows. Both types, however, produce people whose personhood embraces parts of others. Failures of social cohesion obviously challenge individuals, but they also bedevil dividuals. Breakdowns of consensus and harmony in Melanesia (which must be fairly constant in the ordinary bustle of everyday life) threaten not just social order, as we in the West would expect, but also the fundamental constitution of persons themselves. Dangerous disconnects or breaches in sociality threaten to shatter the partible person. Melanesians, thus, have a doubled reason to yearn for unity insofar as this is the necessary foundation and origin of *both* society and person, which, as Strathern notes, are actually pretty much the same thing: 'Only under the condition of unity can the person or group then appear as a composite microcosm of social relations' (1988:275). The partible dividual, whose parts inhere within other related dividuals, coheres only insofar as everyone remains socially conjoined. Disunity dissolves the self. When social unity crumbles, this threatens not just social life, but life itself – and such failures of unity spark suspicions of deadly sorcery and witchcraft, as Munn (1986) and many others have observed (see Keen 2006).

Melanesians also have a doubled reason to worry about goods and substances insofar as flows and exchanges of these constitute the self. Strathern writes: 'since products are seen as constructed from multiple sources, sustained as multiple, the products themselves remain multiply authored' (1988:159); or this is so, at least, of 'local' projects. Flows of goods and substances from one person to another conjoin both into a shared personhood: 'Persons simply do not have alienable items, that is, property, at their disposal; they can only dispose of items by enchaining themselves in relations with others' (1988:161; see also Mosko's elaboration of Strathern's partible persons and partible things, e.g. 'for much of Melanesia there is thus no rigid distinction between persons and things' (2002:93)). Since 'objects act as persons in relation to one another' (1988:176), Melanesians may well keep a worried eye on strange goods whose flows appear wild or unmanageable. Such goods have included

Western wares – we are back to cargo here – that have sailed into the region over the past two centuries: *nari itonga*, as the Tannese say – strange cloth, beads and mirrors. Both outside goods, and outsiders themselves, present challenges to people whose sociality and whose personhood are defined by the bodily incorporation of the substances and labour of others. If Strathern is right, it is no surprise then that Melanesians have hopped into culting in the attempt to manage, and hopefully thereby incorporate, unruly outsiders with strange goods who appeared on their beaches. Wild people, and global goods, disconnected from known local flows of things into people and people into things, constantly endanger sociality and personhood (which, again, according to Strathern are much the same thing), and these must somehow be absorbed. Strathern suggests that traditional men's cults served to incubate the social/ personal unities that Melanesians crave, and one might expect the same of more recent social movements, cargoistic and otherwise:

> When men build fences around cult areas they create a unity both between
> themselves and in relation to the spirits with whom they are joined ... In
> so far as men's activity is thereby seen as the deliberate binding together
> of persons whose social orientations are otherwise diffuse and variously
> directed, the unifying nature of the collective action is inherently energizing
> in making the participants other than what they were.
>
> (1988:296)

Within cult fences, everyone and everything could possibly be unified, at least for a time.

Unitarianism/totalitarianism

Melanesian culting hopes to bind together and create new unities among, as Strathern put it, 'diffuse and variously directed people'. We might guess that culting, in historic times, was particularly stimulated by the appearance of strange anti-social (anti-personal) Europeans and their goods. These were scouts and forerunners of what, nowadays, has become a full-blown global system (or at least appreciated as such). Melanesians retreated behind cult fences within which they could better attempt to domesticate these global flows. Intractable alien threats to sociality and personhood appeared possibly controllable if only new unities, claiming to absorb new cargo and people, might be founded. Cults both nativized by working to contain global flows of people and cargo, and revitalized by performing triage on cultural heritage to preserve or revive those customs that made the best, most encompassing fences (see Harkin 2004). Globalization compels a retreat to fundamentals – or at least to some fundamentals. Revaluation and revitalization of *kastom* involves the nativization of old and new flows. Moreover, anxious to domesticate what crossed the beach, many Melanesian social movements were desperately and ambitiously totalitarian. Everything and everyone must be incorporated within the fence.

I have noted totalitarian dreams in one of the earliest published accounts of a twentieth-century Melanesian movement: Australian colonial administrator and anthropologist E.W.P. Chinnery's description of the 'Kekesi rites' (Lindstrom 1993b). This movement spread along the north-eastern coast of Papua between 1914 and 1928 (Worsley 1957:59–74). In 1917, Chinnery published the testimony of Bia from Binandere. Chinnery claimed that 'Bia himself gave me an account of the origin of the movement, and I reproduce here his own words' (1917:452). Bia's words reveal that he hoped to totalize a new social unity:

> I was visited by the Spirit of a man named Boinumbai ... I was told by this
> Spirit that a very powerful Spirit named Kekesi watched over all the people
> ... and controlled their food supply. Kekesi was a friend of Jesu Kerisu
> (Jesus Christ), and was able to see all that happened. Kekesi was going to
> make some laws for the people, and if they obeyed them, he would look
> after their interests, but if they disobeyed them, he would injure their food
> supply. A few nights later Boinumbai's Spirit again visited me ... and with it
> came the Spirit that Boinumbai introduced as Kekesi, the big chief of food
> and a strong Spirit, 'all the same as Jesu Kerisu and Government,' whom
> he told me to listen carefully to and to take notice of. Kekesi sat down and
> commenced making a gurgling sound in his throat, all the while bouncing
> violently and rapidly up and down, but keeping his sitting attitude. I was
> very frightened until Kekesi stopped doing this. But Boinumbai told me
> not to be frightened, as Kekesi was reciting the laws which he wished to be
> introduced by me to the people on his behalf. When Kekesi had finished,
> Boinumbai gave me this interpretation of Kekesi's speech: 'You, Bia, are
> to tell the people I am their chief, and they must obey me in all things ...
> Disobedience will mean the loss of his food supply to the defaulter. The
> people are to hear and obey the Government. The people are to observe
> the moral code of the tribe... And the songs I am giving you must be sung
> regularly by the people, otherwise trouble will come to you... When going
> to and from the gardens the people are not to straggle along, but to fall in,
> similar to the police working for the Government. The following commands
> may be given to the people whilst working in the garden or coming to and
> from the same: *A kush! A sha! A shun man! A shun be! A hon de shen! A
> som!*

(1917:452–3)

Here is a dream of law and order – a vision of obedience, regularity and totality. Everyone observes the moral code. Everyone obeys in all things. No one straggles. Utopian unity, moreover, is ritually demonstrated in collective drilling and marching. Many subsequent Melanesian movements pursued Bia's dreams of syncopated 'falling in, like the police'. *A kush! A sha! A sun man!* – the people parade off together to the gardens.

Cultic emphasis on undivided unity has resulted in a curious fondness for acronyms. These constructions, also devised from chippings of regional or subgroup names, make manifest within a cult's name itself the dream of new social and geographic unities. The Pitenamu Society, active near Lae in Papua New Guinea, for example, named itself with 'the first two letters of the four areas from which support was initially obtained: Pindiu, Tewai, Nawae and Mumeng' (Adams 1982:63). The Napidakoe Navitu of Bougainville 'derived its name from an anagram of the initials of the different ethnic groups in the vicinity of Kieta' (Griffin 1982:114). Balopa, on Manus, unites Baluan, Lou and Pam (Dalsgaard and Otto, this volume). Similarly, John Frum efforts to secede from independent Vanuatu in 1980 sparked the invention of the TAFEA Federation – an acronym composed of the initial letters of the five southern islands Tanna, Aneityum, Futuna, Erromango and Aniwa. The national government ultimately borrowed this construction, using it to rename the country's old Southern District. Other movements, such as New Hanover's Tutukuval Isukal ('Stand up together to plant' (Billings 2002)), that did not play with acronymy to name themselves, instead spoke unity directly into their names. The Prophet Fred's assistants on Tanna, along these lines, call themselves 'doctors of unity', and they name their organization itself the 'Movement of Unity' (Tabani 2009).

Within such amalgamations of villages and regions into new unities, cult leaders devised various divisions of labour. Unity does not necessarily mean uniformity. Yes, everyone marches off together, but they go to do different jobs. Tanna's Prophet Fred seems to be an expert elaborator along these lines. Whereas the orthodox John Frum movement merely divided folks into people of the red cross and people of the black cross (although it did boast its celebrated '26 teams'), Fred's supporters have split themselves up into a rainbow of colour: the red company functions as movement police; the black oversee *kastom* law; the green manage John Frum heritage and issues; the white seek out and destroy sorcery stones and other miscellaneous evils; and the yellow specialize in curing the sick (Tabani 2008). Now, back to 'soc', Strathern has argued that,

> The unity of a number of persons conceptualized as a group or set is
> achieved through eliminating what differentiates them, and this is exactly

what happens when a person is also individualized. The causes of internal
differentiation are suppressed or discarded. Indeed, the one holistic
condition may elicit the other. Thus a group of men or a group of women
will conceive of their individual members as replicating in singular form
('one man', 'one woman') what they have created in collective form ('one
men's house', 'one matrilineage'). In other words, a plurality of individuals as
individuals ('many') is equal to their unity ('one').

                                                                (1988:14)

And also that, within cults, the 'image' of unity 'is created out of internal
homogeneity, a process of de-pluralization' (1988:13). Munn, as already
mentioned above, has similarly suggested that consensus, in Melanesia,
presumes a 'likeness of intention, or in Durkheim's terms, a "mechanical unity"'
(1986:265). But this is a mechanical solidarity that dreams of being organic. If
a cult pursues unity by de-pluralizing and suppressing differentiation behind
its fences, it also unites by fabricating fantastic divisions of ritual labour
that promise an imaginary organic solidarity. People stick together not only
because of their homogeneous dividuality, but also because of heterogeneous
ritualized specializations that depend one upon the other.

Fred and other Melanesian prophets envision organic solidarities, and they
also propose that these new unities encompass everyone and everything (see
Rio 2005:418). These dreamed unities are totalitarian. Loose ends, rebels and
dissidents are dangerous. An obvious failure to totalize (if only to fence out)
the known world of things and people demoralizes the movement. Stubborn
evasion of the new collectivity undermines both sociality and personhood.
The drilling and marching that were characteristic of numerous movements
constituted a ritual mutualization of behaviour in the service of unity (see,
e.g., Worsley 1957:23 and 187; Adams 1982:69). People lined themselves up in
rows and paraded about the neighbourhood. Burridge (1969:127) called such
totality 'rigorism', noting that 'every millenarist believes he has grasped the
secret and is driven to enforce it on others' (1969:135; see also Guiart 1970:133).
Cults exacted uniformity at two levels: the ideological and the political. They
asserted one true *kastom*. Of note, here, are attempts that Melanesians have
made to codify their traditions – to put down on paper and standardize proper
kastom and do away with troublesome and disputed variants (see Keesing
1989:28). Second, everyone must believe and take part. Those who do not
are punished. Kekesi, after all, warned: 'Disobedience will mean the loss of
his food supply to the defaulter' (Chinnery 1917:452). After the fact, cultists
typically attribute the *failure* of their world to transform, or cargo to arrive, to
cracks in totalized unity and to the baneful influence of dissidents and covert
sorcery.

Cultists have called their particular constructions of unity the 'Law' (or *lo* in Pidgin English; see also Hviding, this volume). Thus, on Tanna, people talk about *lo blong John*. They combine in this usage two of law's English meanings: law that states the true ordering and relating of known things; and law that regulates personal behaviour (Lindstrom 1990:165–73). The Law aims to regulate people's bodily experiences, new orderings of space, time and things, and cooperative social relationships. It regularizes both the true and the permitted. Burridge concluded that 'the phraseology of millennial aspirations always envisages a new set of rules, new kinds of obligation' (1969:165). Cult luminaries typically instituted an arsenal of regularizing, and sometimes repressive, mechanisms to protect the Law's totality. The *kastom* school was one common ritual procedure that organized people's access to the new truth. Bia was not the first to organize a school for his Kekesi rite followers (Territory of Papua 1920/1921:62). Movement leaders also often commissioned guards and police to enforce their new unities, laws and truths (Guiart 1956:173). And they established courts to try and punish sinners and defaulters, to protect new totalities. The orthodox John Frum movement and Fred's Movement of Unity have both called forth their vigilant police. But Melanesian totalities that presume to encompass everyone and everything, and to fence away what they cannot, always at some point collapse – how could they not with the unremitting flows of strange people, knowledge and cargo that creeping globalization has dumped on island beaches?

Cult(ural) heritage

John Frum supporters on Tanna frequently claim that they saved island *kastom* (Bonnemaison 1994:251; Brunton 1981:374; Tabani 2009). We might translate *kastom* as 'cultural heritage', although the term has a complex genealogy and an increasing number of strategic uses (see Lindstrom 1993b:498–500, and many others). John Frum appeared just in the nick of time. A few years later, the Tannese might have forgotten how to dance, lost their stories, abandoned their kava plantations. What people mean, actually, is that John Frum saved at least some *kastom*. Islanders have cast off many of their notable, once common traditions and never comfortably or comprehensively revived these, John Frum or no John Frum: cannibalism, polygamy, lunar calendars, quinary numeration, sorcery stones, occasional widow sacrifice, traditional 'prostitutes', penis wrappers (not counting some men who live in several tourist-pleasing villages of south-west Tanna), and more.

Cult leaders and prophets, behind their fences, have specialized in telling people how they are living incorrectly and what they must do differently. They are especially concerned to eradicate practices they perceive to frustrate the harmonious life. Movements are only selectively nativistic. They weigh *kastom* against its effects on unity. Some practices pass muster ('the people are to obey the moral code of the tribe') but others do not. Sex and sorcery are particular worries given their essential function in originating flows that create or obliterate persons. Prophets aim to regulate sex and sorcery in order to dampen down possible disunities within their movements. Bia, for example, concluded his testimony to Chinnery with a string of nonsense words that he then interpreted for the anthropologist's notebook:

> Kekesi's speech was not in the Binandere language [but] I understood it, and
> it means that one boy had stolen his brother's wife, and that Kekesi was very
> angry with him and desired to tell him so.
>
> (1917:453)

Melanesian spirits and prophets frequently meddle in people's sex lives in this way (see Burridge 1969:167). Imbalanced sex and sorcery flows must be detoured.

Cultists who fix their attention on traditional customs of sex and marriage try to improve on them in various ways. Sometimes sex is liberalized. Concluding that sexual restriction is the cause of disunity, people in a number of movements established brothels or practices of ritualized sexuality in which they ignored customary restrictions of exogamy and incest (see, e.g., Worsley 1957:251; Kolig 1987:189). During Espiritu Santo's Naked Cult, for example, 'the sexual act was to take place in public, since there was no shame in it; even irregular liaisons should be open affairs. Husbands should show no jealousy, for this would disturb the state of harmony which the cult was trying to establish.' (Worsley 1957:151). In other places, cultists conclude that the best way to deal with possible sexual conflict is not to have any sex at all. And along with sex itself, cultists often attempt the reconstruction of marital custom. Those Naked Cultists also figured on abolishing *kastoms* of bridewealth and exogamy (Worsley 1957:151) to create a more perfect union.

People also typically turn their attention to disruptive problems caused by sorcery, or suspicion thereof. They often specialize in healing, as do Fred's unity doctors. If Strathern is right that the Melanesian person and society are tightly fused, then strange people, strange cargo and other loose ends may manifest themselves in personal illnesses; and sickness, furthermore, signals failures of unity. Cult attempts to reform sociability demand that prophets police disease and the wayward sorcerers responsible for it. For years, John Frum leaders have arrested and sentenced to a sort of internal exile a number of suspect sorcerers. In so doing, they reproduced the anti-sorcery practices of earlier Christian groups on Tanna.

Figure 2 *'Sacred men' killing Paton with sorcery (*nahak).

Missionaries and their island compradors likewise realized very early on that any hope of creating new heavens on Tannese earth demanded that they briskly attack sorcery. George Turner and Henry Nisbet, of the London Missionary Society, who held out for several months on Tanna in 1842, desperately preached against sorcery (*nahak* – which also means 'scrap' or 'mote' – some object a person has touched on which contagious sorcery techniques can be applied). They also condemned sorcery stones (*nukwei nahak*) and the men who knew how to use these – monstrous and disruptive sorcerers that they called 'disease makers' or, more politely, 'sacred men' (Adams 1984:67). (The Tannese, with some justification, in turn blamed the missionaries for causing a wave of epidemics that killed some thousands of people in the 1840s.) Presbyterian missionary John Paton, who followed Turner and Nisbet to Tanna between late 1858 and 1862, similarly lamented:

> ... the Tannese had hosts of stone idols, charms, and sacred objects, which they abjectly feared, and in which they devoutly believed;
>
> (1890:118)

and that,

> sacred men and women, wizards and witches, received presents regularly to
> influence the gods, and to remove sickness, or to cause it by the *Nahak, i.e.,*
> incantation over remains of food, or the skin of fruit, such as banana, which
> the person has eaten, on whom they wish to operate.
>
> (1890:118–19)

Paton featured his own confrontation with *nahak* in an autobiography,
written 30 years later. He took a few bites out of *nɨkori* fruit ('dragon plum',
Dracontomelon vitiense, Bislama: *nakatambol*; Paton called this 'quonquore')
and passed along his leftovers to three 'sacred men', challenging them to do
their worst (1890:226–31 and figure 2). Things turned out well, for Paton at
least. The week during which Paton was supposed to expire came and went
and he acquired new material for subsequent sermons on men's wickedness
and folly:

> This whole incident did, doubtless, shake the prejudices of many as to
> Sorcery; but few even of converted Natives ever get entirely clear of the
> dread of Nahak.
>
> (1890:231)

Christian missionaries on Tanna were suspicious of all power stones
insofar as these were central components in island magical practice and
avatars of spiritual presence. These included stone markers of spiritually
infused places, such as the origin points of the old moiety system, Kaviameta
and Numrukwen in East Tanna, and also those stones (*nukwei nari*), whose
powers ensure the fertility and abundance of kava, yams, taro and other island
crops. It was sorcery stones, however, which continued to provoke the gravest
mission concern. Just before Paton and his fellow missionary John Mathieson
fled Tanna in 1862, he boasted that 'the young chief Kapuku came and handed
to Mr. Mathieson his own and his father's war-gods and household idols.
They consisted chiefly of a basket of small and peculiar stones, much worn
and shining with use.' (1890:344). It was not until the successful coalescence
of new Christian unities at the turn of the twentieth century, however, that
church leaders convinced many islanders to part with their *nukwei nahak* by
casting these into the sea, cementing them into the foundations of recently
built churches and chapels, or giving them to passing tourists and museum
collectors.

In recent years, thanks partly to the success of John Frum action, islanders
have uncovered or otherwise retrieved many once lost stones – mostly those

that control the weather, eruptions of Iasur volcano, the fertility of cultigens and so forth. Few men, however, are willing to reassert rights to *nukwei nahak*. Sorcery still threatens dreams of unity, and people of all political persuasions guard against their retrieval. The orthodox John Frum and Fred's Movement of Unity have both deployed police to nab possible sorcerers whose un-dividualizing flows threaten disorder and disunity. Scores of anti-sorcery campaigns and movements have flared up across Melanesia in the last several decades. In Vanuatu, people on Paama and Ambrym islands, for example, have paid sorcery detectives (known locally as *kleva*, 'clevers') thousands of vatu to sweep their villages free of hidden sorcery paraphernalia (see Tonkinson 1982:54).

Beyond sex and sorcery, those dreaming of unity have also rejected other aspects of cultural heritage that might threaten totalitarian consensus. Intense cult frenzies in which people killed and ate as many pigs as they could catch may have been strategic responses to misgivings about the impact of exchange imbalances on prophesied social harmony (Guiart 1956:217; Golub 2006:275). No pigs, no imbalances. Anticipated movement unities might also be disrupted by strange cargo, and cult leaders have also tried to eliminate alien and dangerous goods from behind the fences they worked to build. They attempted to purge some global products to dodge their dangers. Money is the most risky of such strange goods. John Frum messages, early on, urged islanders to rid themselves of money either by hurriedly spending it all or dumping it at sea (Guiart 1956:155; Worsley 1957:154–5). A money-free world, like one emptied of pigs, would do much to narrow the odds of achieving total social unity (Golub 2006:286–7).

Initial John Frum messages, on the other hand, urged islanders to salvage island *kastom* that earlier church leaders had worked to prohibit or to replace with more Christian practice, such as dancing and kava drinking. This sort of revived cultural heritage might be employed strategically to beef up new unities. Kava continues to unite male drinkers (and female gardeners) each evening, as men gather to prepare and drink coconut shells of Vanuatu's 'national plant'. Dance, too – like ritual drilling and marching – conjoins people's bodies in shared cooperative and collective movement. Even simple woven baskets might symbolize and strengthen the warp and woof of local and, nowadays, national unities (Keller 1988). The revival of these communal practices of cultural heritage in the 1940s would have served John Frum strategies for achieving a new dream of island unity.

Osama bin cargo-Laden?

The initial waves of globalization that washed up on Tanna in the nineteenth and twentieth centuries triggered a certain sort of fundamentalism: people sorted through their cultural heritage – reviving this, discarding that – seeking ways better to digest (or fence off) strangers and their alien cargo. In so doing, they nativized ('glocalized' is the contemporary buzzword) much of what washed ashore. Islanders successfully nativized Christianity so that everyone lives happily with this, even if politically they stand in the John Frum or *kastom* camps. John Frum messages also remarkably managed to incorporate Pacific War events, people and cargo into a second new totality. Tannese stories digested American military personnel as lost island brothers and domesticated military equipment and symbols (such as red crosses, dog tags, airplanes) into familiar, local things. Alien flows of people and things were at least partly thereby reclaimed and put in the service of unity; island sociality and personhood were protected and renewed.

Political innovation in Vanuatu, as elsewhere in Melanesia, continues to reflect enduring worries about the constitution of personhood and, within this, the local consequences of imported goods and other foreign cargo. Insofar as young Melanesian states concern themselves with cultivating national identities they, too, are in the business of massaging personhood, partly by managing alien cargo flows, both material and informational. Local innovation can support, or subvert, efforts underway by state leaders to nurture broader sentiments of national identity and to assert control over national economies. Scott (this volume) reports on Arosi efforts to re-imagine their relations with the Solomon Islands through talk of a hidden, underground spirit army that parades vibrant *kastom* in support of island autonomy 'either as a federal state or an independent nation'. Such new autonomy, moreover, will motivate cargo flows: 'abundant resources and wealth will come out from and flow to the island and provide the foundation for Makiran development and regional ascendancy' (Scott, this volume). As on Tanna, Makiran political innovation aims at locating a 'true personhood' that should bring forth island autonomy and prosperity.

Hviding (this volume), likewise, traces the history of the Christian Fellowship Church (CFC) in Solomon Islands' Western Province (or, as some locals have proclaimed, the State of Western Solomons). Here, too, island political innovators, partly by controlling flows of money and other alien cargo, have achieved notable local autonomy, particularly within a Solomon Islands state weakened by interisland conflict. The CFC has established among its followers a degree of social unity only occasionally and irregularly achieved by John Frum people on Tanna – that sort of Melanesian unity that successfully conjoins dividuated persons and averts the divisive apparition of the sorcerer or witch. It has done so by looking beyond the state to transnational corporations willing to pay to harvest island hardwood forests. As Hviding notes, the CFC explains itself locally as a 'fellowship' that springs from its cultivation of 'peace, love, unity', so that everything once dividuated, including persons and things, recombine into a single companionship. Dalsgaard and Otto (this volume) explore parallel, although less successful, efforts by a Manus island leader to create, and lead, new island unities around exotic notions of public *kalsa* (culture) that transcend a traditional cultural copyright system still embedded within dividuated exchange relationships. This attempt to imagine a novel sort of public cultural domain upon which Westernized possessive individuals might freely draw in order to evoke broader sorts of social unity fell short, partly because adequate flows of cargo (money and other outside resources) failed to materialize. Unity of persons remained anchored to more traditional ideals of sociality.

The Tannese, too, continue to rummage through their cultural heritage to make sense of new personalities, and new cargo, that globalization is bringing onto their island. The several John Frum organizations have had both warm and cool relations with the new Vanuatu state, depending, largely, on which political parties have formed its government. But ever more serious threats to the person, and opportunities for local unity, now approach from far beyond the nation-state itself. Elsewhere in Melanesia, for instance, Papua New Guineans sometimes sport t-shirts featuring Osama bin Laden and George W. Bush. Anthropologist Daniele Moretti (who reproduces a West Papuan photograph of Osama t-shirts decorated with flying planes), reports that his Anga friends closely follow Bush's war on terrorism (2006:14). They circulated a story that local sorcerers, unlike Bush, easily located Osama to deliver to him this warning:

> You can hide from America; you can fight against that country and kill
> many of its soldiers. If you want, you can come to PNG and kill many of its
> people. But if you ever come to our villages, we will stop your weapons from
> working and your soldiers will die in the hundreds!
>
> (2006:15)

Osama is also now ashore on Tanna. One John Frum leader explains that he gave Osama some of the island's stones (*nukwei nari*) to resist the evil spirits that have taken over America, Tanna's erstwhile mythic ally: 'Only Tannese stones could give such a power to a man fighting alone against the world's greatest power.' (Tabani 2009). Tannese stones make Osama invisible to American power. Here, one totalistic fundamentalism refracts through the global system to stimulate reaction in a second: John Frum responds to and works to nativize Osama (if not, at least not yet, vice versa).

In addition to power stones, islanders continue to invoke the best, unificatory aspects of their *kastom* – their cultural heritage – to pull strange people and strange cargo flows into local circuits. Fred's followers, for example, recently have added trancing to the traditional Tannese toolkit of healing practices. Healing unifies. Faced with intractable secrets of health and wealth – secrets that globalization relentlessly makes more mysterious – islanders work to absorb the world into themselves. Tannese unity doctors continue to perform triage on Osama bin Laden and other global flows, and also on island cultural heritage, to find a way in the world.

BIBLIOGRAPHY

Adams, R. 1982. 'The Pitenamu Society'. In *Micronationalist Movements in Papua New Guinea* (ed.) R.J. May, 63–112. Canberra: Dept. of Political and Social Change, Research School of Pacific Studies, ANU.

Adams, R. 1984. *In the Land of Strangers: A Century of European Contact with Tanna, 1774–1874.* Pacific Research Monograph No. 9. Canberra: Australian National University.

Billings, D.K. 2002. *Cargo Cult as Theater: Political Performance in the Pacific.* Lanham, MD: Lexington Books.

Bonnemaison, J. 1994. *The Tree and the Canoe: History and Ethnogeography of Tanna.* Honolulu: University of Hawai'i Press.

Brown, D.J.J. 1988. 'Unity in opposition in the New Guinea Highlands'. *Social Analysis* 23:89–105.

Brunton, R. 1981. 'The origins of the John Frum movement: a sociological explanation'. In *Vanuatu: Politics, Economics and Ritual in Island Melanesia* (ed.) M. Allen, 357–77. New York: Academic Press.

Brunton, R. 1989. *The Abandoned Narcotic: Kava and Cultural Instability in Melanesia.* Cambridge: Cambridge University Press.

Burridge, K. 1969. *New Heaven, New Earth: A Study of Millenarian Activities.* New York: Schocken Books.

Chinnery, E.W.P. 1917. 'Five new religious cults in British New Guinea'. *Hibbert Journal* 25:448–63.

Golub, A. 2006. 'Who is the "original affluent society"? Ipili "predatory expansion" and the Porgera Gold Mine, Papua New Guinea'. *The Contemporary Pacific* 18:265–92.

Griffin, J. 1982. 'Napidakoe Navitu'. In *Micronationalist Movements in Papua New Guinea* (ed.) R.J. May,113–38. Canberra: Dept. of Political and Social Change, Research School of Pacific Studies, ANU.

Guiart, J. 1956. *Un siècle et demi de contacts culturels à Tanna*, Nouvelles-Hébrides. Paris: Musée de l'Homme.

Guiart, J. 1970 'The millenarian aspects of conversion to Christianity in the South Pacific'. In *Millennial Dreams in Action* (ed.) S. Thrupp, 122–38. New York: Schocken Books.

Harkin, M.E. (ed.) 2004. *Reassessing Revitalization Movements: Perspectives from North America and the Pacific Islands*. Lincoln: University of Nebraska Press.

Herdt, G. 2003. *Secrecy and Cultural Reality: Utopian Ideologies of the New Guinea Men's House*. Ann Arbor: University of Michigan Press.

Jebens, H. (ed.) 2004. *Cargo, Cult and Culture Critique*. Honolulu: University of Hawai'i Press.

Keen, I. 2006. 'Ancestors, magic, and exchange in Yolngu doctrines: extensions of the person in time and space'. *Journal of the Royal Anthropological Institute* 12:515–30.

Keller, J.D. 1988. 'Woven world: neotraditional symbols of unity in Vanuatu'. *Mankind* 18:1–13.

Kolig, E. 1987. 'Kastom, cargo and the construction of utopia on Santo, Vanuatu: the Nagriamel Movement'. *Journal de la Société des Océanistes* 85:181–99.

Lambek, M. and A. Strathern 1998. *Bodies and Persons: Comparative Perspectives from Africa and Melanesia*. Cambridge: Cambridge University Press.

Lindstrom, L. 1990. *Knowledge and Power in a South Pacific Society*. Washington, DC: Smithsonian Institution Press.

Lindstrom, L. 1993a. *Cargo Cult: Strange Stories of Desire from Melanesia and Beyond*. Honolulu: University of Hawai'i Press.

Lindstrom, L. 1993b. 'Cargo cult culture: toward a genealogy of Melanesian kastom'. *Anthropological Forum* 6:495–513.

Maschio, T. 1994. *To Remember the Faces of the Dead: The Plenitude of Memory in Southwestern New Britain*. Madison: University of Wisconsin Press.

Moretti, D. 2006. 'Osama Bin Laden and the man-eating sorcerers: encountering the "war on terror" in Papua New Guinea'. *Anthropology Today* 22(3):13–17.

Mosko, M.S. 2002. 'Totem and transaction: the objectification of 'tradition' among North Mekeo'. *Oceania* 73(2):89–109.

Munn, N. 1986. *The Fame of Gawa: A Symbolic Study of Value Transformation in a Massim (Papua New Guinea) Society*. Cambridge: Cambridge University Press.

Paton, J.G. 1890. *John G. Paton, Missionary to the New Hebrides. An Autobiography*. London: Hodder and Stoughton.

Rio, K. 2005. 'Discussions around a sand-drawing: creations of agency and society in Melanesia'. *Journal of the Royal Anthropological Institute* 11:401–23.

Strathern, A. and P.J. Stewart. 1998. 'Seeking personhood: anthropological accounts and local concepts in Mount Hagen, Papua New Guinea'. *Oceania* 68:170–88.

Strathern, M. 1988. *The Gender of the Gift: Problems with Women and Problems with Society in Melanesia.* Berkeley: University of California Press.

Tabani, M. 2008. *Une Piroque pour le Paradis: le culte de John Frum à Tanna.* Paris: Editions de la Maison des Sciences de l'Homme.

Tabani, M. 2009 'Dreams of unity, traditions of division: John Frum, *kastom* and inter-manipulation strategies on Tanna (Vanuatu)'. *Paideuma* 55:27–47.

Territory of Papua. 1920/21. *Annual Report.* Port Moresby: Government Printer.

Tonkinson, R. 1982. 'Vanuatu values: a changing symbiosis'. *Pacific Studies* 5:32–63.

Worsley, P. 1957. *The Trumpet Shall Sound: A Study of "Cargo" Cults in Melanesia.* London: Macgibbon & Kee.

CHAPTER 11

Solomon Islands cultural policy?

A brief history of practice

✳

LAWRENCE FOANA'OTA AND GEOFFREY WHITE

Introduction

'Culture' is a powerful idiom, frequently at play in defining national identities. In this chapter we focus on 'cultural policy' in order to call attention to the kinds of talk about culture that have emerged in national institutions in the Solomon Islands from the time of independence to the present. We are interested specifically in the role of the state in domains of culture/*kastom*/ tradition – even though locating the state can be as elusive as pinning down the meanings of 'culture'.

By placing a question mark in the title of this chapter we are calling attention to the fact that, at the national level, there has never been any kind of formal cultural policy in Solomon Islands or even a clear sense of what that would be. What is it? Who is it for? What could it do? As the national museum has on occasion been asked to draft such a policy, these questions are meant to provoke discussion that might inform this process. Our aims are as much practical as conceptual, seeking to examine this history critically in the context of this volume's comparative assessment of the politics of cultural heritage within Pacific states and social movements.

We begin by raising the question of why no viable national cultural policy has emerged in more than three decades since independence. To address this puzzle, we give a brief history of discussions of 'culture', '*kastom*' and 'tradition' in the context of the national museum and its local counterparts. Much of this history has already been outlined by Foana'ota in previous publications describing the role of museums and cultural centres in Solomon Islands national development (1994 and 2006).

Whereas our historical review focuses on the national museum, relations between the national centre and provincial locales are critical to questions of cultural policy. The importance of local *kastom* projects and their ability to tap into linguistic and cultural communities is evident in a number of contributions to the volume *Culture, Kastom, Tradition* (Lindstrom and White 1994; see Akin 1994; Bolton 1994; Burt 1994; Cole and Roga 1994). These same issues are taken up in many of the chapters in the present volume. Thus, whether it is the visionary movements described by M. Scott and Hviding for Makira and New Georgia, respectively, or the *kastom* ideologies discussed by Lindstrom and Rio for Vanuatu, the persistent and mutually defining relations between Melanesian localities and (new) nation-states remain of overriding importance. We see this chapter as an important opportunity for exploring questions about the articulation of local and national culture projects in the Solomon Islands.

Kastom and the new nation

Taking advantage of Foana'ota's experience as national museum director since the early years of independence, and White's perspective as an occasional visitor moving between Isabel Province and Honiara since 1975, we structure this chapter around a historical narrative of key events and projects that mark visible moments in the life of 'tradition' for national publics. Without attempting any kind of final definition of cultural policy, we have been attempting to track the language of 'culture' (or *kastom*) in the public sphere of the post-colonial Solomons. In many instances, the goals of such talk are purely rhetorical, a dimension of speech concerned with imagined identities and visions. In other instances, culture talk is more closely tied to the economics and politics of nation-building. In the historical overview that follows, we point to the interaction between formations of 'culture' and political-economic institutions at particular moments in postcolonial history:

1. During the colonial period, we see the operation of (European) concerns with the preservation and promotion of traditions and customs considered to be disappearing in the face of missionization and modernization.

2. Then, with independence from Britain on 7 July 1978, as indigenous voices emerge more strongly, 'culture' and 'custom' are deployed in the interest of defining a new national identity (Keesing and Tonkinson 1982).

3. In the 1980s and 90s, as large-scale resource projects take off and efforts are made to expand tourism (Hviding and Bayliss-Smith 2000), national 'culture' becomes a resource to be marketed in the context of national development.

4. Finally, as the 'ethnic tension' in the years around the 2000 coups caused economic and political ruin, followed by the Australia-led multinational intervention in 2003,[1] 'custom' became a means of gauging and regulating conflicts between local constituencies, especially in land disputes between populations around the national capital Honiara.

Despite its obvious simplifications, we suggest this historical overview as a means of identifying certain correspondences between talk of 'culture' and shifting political and economic circumstances. Despite these correspondences, however, another theme in our analysis is the relatively weak connection between prevailing rhetorics of culture and practical initiatives associated with economic development. Even though the preamble of the Constitution of the Sovereign Democratic State of Solomon Islands (1978) states that,

We the people of Solomon Islands, proud of the wisdom and the worthy customs of our ancestors, mindful of our common and diverse heritage ... shall cherish and promote the different cultural traditions within Solomon Islands.

There have been few government initiatives on matters of cultural heritage since independence. Having said this, those familiar with cultural activities in Solomon Islands may want to object to this gloomy view by pointing to the many events and projects that exemplify the constitution's concern with cultural traditions. What about Solomon Islands participation in regional arts festivals, for example? And what about the many conferences and research projects concerned with various cultural practices? Despite these bright spots, in surveying this landscape of cultural activity we see few sustained initiatives at the national level, but rather a continuing disconnect between rhetoric and socioeconomic reality.

Despite many significant accomplishments of individual projects, most cultural events and activities have depended on international interests and support for their origins and sustainability. Even though most cultural projects have long recognized the need to meet local and national interests, including training of Solomon Islanders, few have survived once foreign funding and participation are withdrawn. Whereas these problems might easily be laid at the feet of foreign donors, partners, researchers etc., our purpose is rather to focus on the absence of meaningful institutionalization of cultural practices in national (and local) institutions. We see little utility in analyzing these issues in terms of the inequities of colonialism, but rather would like to look more carefully at the interface of colonial (now national) institutions and indigenous practices.

Creating a national museum: conserving tradition – becoming modern

In reviewing the history of national cultural activities in and around the Solomons capital, Honiara, we find that that discourses of 'culture' and 'tradition' often say something interesting about social relations, political developments and formations of national identity. Of course these meanings are never monolithic, and talk of culture may well emerge from multiple visions or ideologies of culture colliding in the spaces of public culture. For example, the semantically dense Solomons Pijin term *kastom* carries a variety of connotations that only partially overlap with the English-language concept of 'custom' or 'traditional culture' (White 1993). Understanding the significance of talk of *kastom* in a multi-ethnic and multi-national space such as Honiara involves the recognition that key words and symbols, especially those used to represent a critical historical moment like independence, are at play in a field of diverse meanings.

What, then, are some of the ideologies associated with visions of culture/*kastom*/tradition in the national sphere? What is it? What is its value? How and why might indigenous practices be a more valued object of interest in education and development? In asking these questions, we begin by placing them in historical perspective, taking the establishment of the Solomon Islands National Museum as a case in point, a critical focus for converging interests in traditional culture in the years leading up to independence. As one of the most visible national institutions, the museum represents certain strands in colonial thinking about the place of indigenous culture in relation to larger trajectories of modernization and development. Although space does not permit adequate treatment of the history of the museum and the many individuals who contributed to its formation, we briefly consider the valuations of 'culture' that motivated the creation of a national museum in the years prior to independence, some of which continue to be relevant in the present. In doing so, we have benefited from comments on an earlier version of this chapter provided by several individuals who were intimately involved, including James Tedder, an administrator with long experience in the Solomons of the 1950s and 60s (Tedder 2008); Lindsay Wall, Honorary (volunteer) Curator of the Museum 1970–2, and Anna Craven, the first full-time paid Curator ('Curator Training') from 1973 to 1979.[2]

As Foana'ota has written in previous essays, the Solomon Islands National Museum had its origins in the collections of colonial officers serving in the British Solomon Islands Protectorate administration (Foana'ota 1994:96). These collections were the result of gift-giving associated with the touring of government officers as well as scientific collecting.[3] As noted in a brief history of the museum collection in the then new *Journal of the Cultural Association of the Solomon Islands*, 'Prior to 1952 various Resident Commissioners, District Commissioners and touring Officers of the Government had accumulated a considerable number of artefacts originating as gifts from prominent Solomon Islanders in various parts of the Protectorate.' (Dakei 1972:5). On the recommendation of the Resident Commissioner, these artefacts were brought together for public display under the care of an Honorary Curator, Mr Geoff Dennis, thus obtaining the status of something like a national collection in need of storage, curation and preservation. The collection, first placed in a room in the library, was then moved to the Lands and Surveys Department and then, finally, in August 1959, to the Assembly Hall of the Teacher Training College (Dakei 1972:6).

Thus, from the beginning, material artefacts, as the physical manifestation of traditional culture, provided a visible and public focus for more general concerns with cultural preservation in the context of rapid social and political change. The growing collection focused interest among expatriates and educated Solomon Islanders who 'regretted that facilitates were not available for the preservation of the old and fast disappearing handicrafts and artifacts' (Dakei 1972:7). In this context, especially in the culture of European and native elites in the national capital, awareness of the predicament of traditional artefacts and the knowledge associated with them inevitably turned towards construction of a museum. Concerned residents lobbied for construction of a museum, and formed the Solomon Islands Museum Association in 1969. James Tedder, as District Commissioner and Chair of the Honiara Town Council in the late 60s, was in a position to advance the cause of a national museum. He writes of the museum's origins as follows,

> the collection ... was stored at the teachers training college, where it
> collected dust and hardly a glance from the busy students and their
> lecturers. In 1951 the British Solomon Islands Society for the Advancement
> of Science and Industry had been formed and they formed the nucleus of
> the committee for the museum. Government was too poor and too busy
> to think about museums but in 1966 I asked the support of the Honiara
> Town Council, where I was then Chair, whether it would help to support
> the museum. I also asked all the larger Local Government Councils if they
> would be prepared to help. The replies were most encouraging and even the
> smaller Councils who were not approached offered help.
>
> (Tedder 2008:227)

With support from the Honiara Town Council and a grant of $12,500 from the Gulbenkian Foundation, a building was constructed and the Solomon Islands Museum opened its new gallery on 6 June 1969. The Association operated a craft shop that generated support for the museum, supplementing funds provided annually by the Honiara Town Council (paying, among other things, for a cleaner who would open and close the doors in the mornings and evenings). Expatriates involved in the creation of the museum recall that the effort received virtually no funding from government and depended on the interest and commitment of those who volunteered time and resources. One of these was Lindsay Wall, appointed to the post of Honorary Curator by the Museum Association in October 1970 and continuing through 1972. She worked at the museum from 10 a.m. till 12 noon each day and spent time advancing the work of the museum in Honiara. In addition, she 'researched the provenance and cultural background of the collection', which involved travelling to other islands and even overseas (Wall 2007 and 2009).[4]

Consistent with the need to curate the growing stock of traditional artefacts, the museum concentrated 'primarily on building up its ethnographic section'. Even though the original building had no storage space, artefact donations flowed in at an even faster pace. Lindsay Wall wrote in the first issue of the museum journal, 'More people are bringing custom items to the Museum. During 1970 and 1971 the Museum bought or was given about 180 items each year but already this year acquisitions number 175 items'. (1972:1). The museum's concern with the preservation of traditional cultural artefacts included stopping the flow of antiquities out of the country – a problem that has continued, uninterrupted, to the present. These concerns also extended to efforts to repatriate material culture that had already been taken out of the country to be lodged in museum collections elsewhere.

> In mission times there was a huge movement of artifacts out of the country. I went to several museums in New Zealand to see what they had and to try and negotiate return or loan of artifacts.... I came back with empty hands. While I was curator we made sure that legislation and information at customs tried to prevent the export of any old artifacts but people will collect and much was going out in private baggage. Instead, we tried to encourage the sale of the beautiful new carving and shell-inlay work as souvenirs.
>
> (L. Wall email to G. White, 5 March 2007)

In January 1972 the museum was placed under control of the central government and renamed the Solomon Islands National Museum and Cultural Centre. From that time onward, its mandate has been to 'collect, disseminate information, educate, entertain, and research' (Dakei 1972:6). When the Museum became, formally, the national museum, the Museum Association continued to assist with running the gift shop and publishing, notably the museum journal and occasional collections of custom stories. With these activities, it can be seen that the museum, in addition to its concern with the preservation and display of material culture, was already involved with a variety of educational outreach activities, some of which laid the groundwork for involvement in tourism (even if the latter has never developed as expected).

From the outset, the museum was more than a building. It was also a symbol of the interest in the preservation and promotion of traditional culture shared by the urban elite in and around Honiara. The institutionalization of these functions from the first moments of the museum's origins provided a clear focus for financial support of 'culture', however meagre, from the central government or international sources. With independence, however, the educational role of the museum in advancing a certain sort of cultural citizenship became more pronounced. Indeed, Solomon Dakei, one of the first Solomon Islander members of the Museum Association, wrote in the association's new journal: 'Apart from the ethnological and natural history subjects this handsome house now performs a most important function in educating the public by way of displays and illustrations in the cultural background of these Islands.' (1972:7).[5]

Indicative perhaps of its distance from the ongoing cultural life of local communities, the Museum Association encouraged 'interest in the culture and study of the Solomons by lectures and an annual journal' (Anon.1973:79). The audience for these activities was largely the elite, English-speaking population of Honiara and beyond. The first issue of the journal refers to sponsored talks by the 'Harvard Medical Team, Professors Monberg and Elbert and Dr. Kuschel, Dr. Roger Green.' (*The Journal of the Solomon Islands Museum Association* 1972:v). It was a logical step, then, to create a journal that would record this burgeoning scientific and cultural exchange. However, the editor of the journal, R.A. Keevil, lamented the absence of Solomon Islander voices right from the beginning, when he wrote in his preface to the first issue ' what we sadly lack is the word written by the Solomon Islanders, of our country's spent history. We need today the educated to sit with their elders, recording past history, before the old people die and it is lost forever.'(1972:v).

In the decades after the Second World War, the impulse to conserve readily expanded to include the stories and relics of war. The war years were, after all, a period in which the Solomon Islands was at the centre of world history. Once the museum was established, Honiara residents and international visitors came to see it as a locus for Second World War collecting and documenting. This sense of purpose, reinforced by the Europeans, Americans and Japanese who see the war as their history as well, intersects with local interests evident in oral histories and the material remains of war found throughout rural areas.

Indeed, local entrepreneurs have often created their own Second World War museum projects, most notably the outdoor Vilu War Museum created by Fred Kona on the outskirts of Honiara, with a collection of planes and relics on display (White 1996).[6] The National Museum, which stores donated objects but never developed its own approach to collecting or displaying Second World War artefacts, has tended to defer to such initiatives. As Jim Tedder described the situation in the early days of the museum,

> The war relics were beyond the finance of the museum and Fred Kona was
> doing a fine job which we did everything we could to encourage. I spent
> private time doing research as to places of war time interest around Honiara
> and the Town Council paid for a number of signs.
>
> (email to authors, 10 August 2009)

Anna Craven, the Museum's first Curator, reinforces this point by noting that the museum lacked the capacity to curate Second World War objects:

> Although we bought a few WW2 guns brought into the museum, we did
> not have the facilities to conserve metal objects; as it was I suddenly realized
> we had live bullets in the ethnographic store and had to find someone who
> knew how to de-fuse them!
>
> (email to authors, 9 August 2009)

From its early days onward, the museum has been almost continuously involved in various projects concerned to collect, conserve and display Second World War artefacts and histories, usually initiated by outside interests. In 1987, for example, the museum cosponsored a conference with the East-West Center in Hawaiʻi that brought together scholars and islanders who experienced the war to explore its significance from indigenous perspectives (Laracy and White 1988; White 1989). It has also engaged in discussions with external agents interested in documenting, collecting and even exporting crashed warplanes – the holy grail of foreign war collectors. One such effort, involving an Australian collector, focused on well-preserved planes in the Shortland Islands, and even involved a proposal to build a second museum gallery focusing on Second World War in exchange for permission to export one or more warplanes to overseas museums. The most recent example, publicized by posters in the Visitors Bureau office and Honiara hotels, is a private 'World War II Museum' in the form of a warehouse full of war relics in the Ranadi industrial area of Honiara.

As the above activities suggest, much of the rationale for the National Museum's involvement with Second World War history is related to its function in protecting and preserving cultural artefacts. In a draft of this chapter presented at a British Museum conference, we speculated that the museum's emphasis on preservation, symbolized most clearly by conventional interests in collecting and displaying traditional artefacts, was one reason for the apparent estrangement of many ordinary Solomon Islanders from the museum and its activities. In reaction to this characterization, several individuals involved in establishing the museum (Anna Craven, James Tedder and Lindsay Wall) observed that Europeans and native Solomon Islanders alike had all worked on a number of fronts, including support for art education, music, dance, oral history, customary storytelling, festivals and so forth. In other words, the focus on artefacts was only one aspect of a broader agenda concerned with preservation and protection of the indigenous. In these areas, the museum as a national institution functioned in the Solomons as it did in many Pacific states emerging in the 1970s – as a signifier of a modern nation concerned to protect native traditions in the context of accelerating social and economic change (Kaeppler 1994). For Solomon Islanders still living their traditions (however transformed by Christianity and Melanesian modernity), the museum has often been seen as a puzzling, even forbidding, form of self-objectification.

The history of the origins of the museum in the colonial context of pre-independence Solomon Islands repeats a story that has been often noted for museums throughout the newly independent nations of the Pacific, that is, of new nations inheriting institutions created on the basis of twentieth-century European models. Anna Craven, Curator Training in the mid 1970s noted this gap based on her previous work in Africa:

> museums in the first place – so obviously an alien introduction, which was obvious to me when I first started working with museums in Africa, [could be] a resource for education, but a place of wonderment and curiosity for local people, if they were brave enough to venture inside! They are a vehicle for the introduction and perpetuation of yet more external concepts...
>
> (Anna Craven, email to G. White, 19 March 2007)

As noted, everywhere that museums have been constructed as repositories of the traditional in modernizing or globalizing societies, the museum itself becomes a symbol of modernity, an institution that by its very existence signifies the objectification of traditional objects and practices as 'contained', bracketed off from a developing society embracing the 'new' with uncertain consequences for the 'old'. In this regard, the museum constitutes a kind of 'contact zone' in which multiple perceptions and subjectivities collide (Clifford 1997). Whereas Europeans involved in the museum opening tell a kind of frontier story about the success of a small group of committed individuals working against odds to instil respect for tradition and support cultural and creative activities,[7] at least some Solomon Islanders recall a different story, one that sees involvement of the educated elite, but confusion and even fear among many ordinary Solomon Islanders. Foana'ota recalls Solomon Islanders who did not feel free to enter the museum building due to fear of the powers of ancestor spirits that they knew were associated with the kinds of materials on display in the museum. Some would ask permission to enter, assuming the museum constituted a kind of tabu space. These attitudes have remained among local residents to the present time. For whatever reason, the postcolonial period saw a dramatic drop-off in the visitation rate, to the point where the gallery was simply left locked during the years of political instability.

Whereas ideologies of tradition as old ways of life threatened by modernity produced a view of museums as centres for preserving threatened traditions, some Solomon Islanders wondered about the purpose of an institution needed to store *kastom* objects that had either been cast off in recent decades or, in many cases, remained integral to daily life. Consistent with European hopes for the museum, some Solomon Islanders saw it as a kind of new 'custom house', or a place to keep heirlooms. Others, however, saw it as a foreign imposition in need of reform to make it relevant for the Solomons context. Thus began a long process of rethinking and reinventing the museum in ways that might be more relevant for a new nation of dispersed, rural, indigenous communities.

In tracing discourses of tradition in and around the museum, we note the strategic importance of transnational relations for national culture in the postcolonial era. Just as colonial actors were influential in advancing ideas of tradition and preservation that created the museum, so actors and institutions outside the Solomons played increasingly important roles in initiating cultural projects after independence. The forces that converged to create the museum at the end of the colonial period are joined by a complex array of global influences shaping cultural production in the new nation. Whereas concerns with collecting, recording, documenting and preserving cultural artefacts and knowledge remained, the needs of an independent Solomon Islands to use culture more actively in unifying and building a new nation placed a strong emphasis on educational projects and programmes. In some instances, preservation, education and entertainment all converged, as in the radio programmes of the 1960s and 1970s that broadcast custom stories and songs. The museum also produced custom-story booklets in a series published by the Cultural Association (cf. Bolton 1999).[8]

Local/national/transnational: cultural production in the new nation

In 1976, with the Solomon Islands now a self-governing state anticipating independence in 1978, and with a full-time expatriate curator in place, the Museum and Cultural Association became more active in education and publication. The Museum Association became the Cultural Association of the Solomon Islands, publishing a small journal and occasional lists of research being undertaken in the country. An example of the many projects and events that followed would be the 'festival of traditional music and dance' that the Association hosted in 1975. That experience led to construction of a wooden seating area adjacent to the Museum in 1976, as well as plans for an 'earth-bank open-air theatre'. Funding from the Australian government's South Pacific Cultures fund (see below) launched a number of visible national culture projects during the 1970s, including construction of a canoe house (across the street from the museum, next to the Mendana Hotel), an open air theatre next to that, and a historic photos project – developed by Lynne Auld (Anna Craven, email to authors, 9 August 2009).[9]

In 1976 the Museum then hosted a UNESCO workshop titled 'The Techniques of Recording Oral Traditional Culture', which in fact addressed interests in music, dance and material culture as well as oral traditions. At the same time, the museum began to address the need for outreach to schools in rural areas. An 'Oral Traditions Project' was initiated to involve students who would work in their home areas. Some years later, in the 1980s, the idea of 'School Mobile Kits' grew out of these efforts (see below).

As noted in our account of the creation of the National Museum, the original funding from the Honiara Town Council (chaired by James Tedder) had managed to secure commitments of financial support from the four administrative districts for local government, namely Central, Eastern, Malaita and Western, including the Honiara Town Council. As government began to centralize these functions prior to independence, the assistance from these four districts, including the Honiara Town Council, ceased. Although museum finances were centralized after independence, other initiatives kept the rural areas strongly in view. Whenever Solomon Mamaloni was in power, he ensured that the National Museum, National Archives and the National Library were part of a government ministry or department responsible for 'cultural affairs'. In order to ensure that these institutions actually reached people at the provincial level, Mamaloni introduced a policy to promote the development of provincial libraries and village-based museums and cultural centres throughout the country.

The emphasis on educational outreach at the museum was supported by the appointment of an Education Officer.[10] Educational activities included the development of a programme that sent 'mobile learning kits' to high schools around the country in an effort to extend the cultural curriculum (Rogers 1985). Due to lack of financial support, however, this project had to be stopped. Despite its termination, some of those who encountered the cultural materials contained in the kits as students have become teachers in the schools around Honiara, and now encourage their students to visit the museum.

The National Library was the only institution under the Cultural Affairs portfolio that attempted to implement this policy. In the mid 1980s, when one of Solomon Mamaloni's governments was in power, a branch of the National Library was established in Auki, in the provincial capital of Malaita. The plan called for creating space in the building for a small exhibition of artefacts from the National Museum. Unfortunately, this programme was abandoned when the government changed and, without the support for localization promoted by Mamaloni governments, never had the chance to expand to other provinces.

During this period in the 1980s a strong interest in building or restoring custom houses as cultural centres emerged in various parts of the country.[11] The Australian South Pacific Cultures Fund encouraged these projects by inviting interested communities to apply for support for their projects. Similar to cultural-centre projects, canoes and canoe houses also proved to be active areas of interest at this time. For example, in Natagera village on Santa Ana Island, the Australian fund supported the reconstruction of custom canoe and initiation houses that represented the different clans on the island. A canoe-building project on Gela was also initiated with support from the Australian fund and the University of the South Pacific Centre in Honiara, producing an attractive pictorial account (see Pule 1983). The Australian High Commissioner during this time, Trevor Sofield, was a person with a background in anthropology who strongly supported these investments in cultural projects. When he left the country support for these types of programme declined.

In addition to Australia, other international donors such as Canada, Great Britain, Japan and New Zealand contributed significantly to cultural activities and programmes following independence. A variety of forms of assistance supported the policy of expanding cultural services to provincial and community levels in different parts of the country. For example, at the National Museum, Canadian VSO or Volunteer Services Overseas provided a volunteer to help set up the Archaeology Section. In East Kwaio, Malaita, at the urging of anthropologist Roger Keesing, the US Peace Corps provided two volunteers to establish a cultural centre – an initiative that has evolved through several phases of development with assistance from anthropologist David Akin, one of the original volunteers (Akin 1994). This project inspired similar applications in East Kwara'ae. Even though their proposals were not funded, the process of applying focused efforts there to initiate several publication projects directed by Ben Burt and Michael Kwai'oloa (Burt 1994:182; Kwai'oloa and Burt 1997). In Western Province, Canadian volunteers were deployed to assist with the set up and management of a Cultural Affairs Division within the provincial government (Cole and Roga 1994). On Guadalcanal a VSO was assigned to assist the provincial government with their cultural centre.

Also in the early 1990s, the Japanese Overseas Corporation Volunteers provided assistance to the National Museum, as well as other government ministries and departments, in the form of volunteers and equipment. The single greatest contribution of Japan during this period was the MABO project, in which Japanese funding initiated a cooperative project involving the museum, archives and broadcasting services working with Osaka University. The Japanese government suspended its contributions of volunteers and equipment during the 'tension' conflicts, restarting them in 2006.

Most of these different forms of assistance from overseas governments, regional organizations and private donor agencies provided volunteers, who helped to train national counterparts and seek funding from their sponsors or other organizations. Such additional funding could be used to purchase equipment or set up administrative structures for provincial cultural offices. For the National Museum, the South Pacific Cultures Fund provided money for numerous projects, including the establishment of the School Mobile Kit, the Oral Traditions Project and the extension of the administration building to provide extra space for storing the archaeological collections, staff offices, a photographic darkroom, a workroom and an equipment-storage room.

Once the volunteers left, however, and the Australian government decided to end the South Pacific Cultures Fund, the activities and programmes that had been supported went into decline.[12] None exist today, with the exception of the Custom Training School in East Kwaio, which has been sustained in some measure through the efforts of David Akin and his Kwaio colleagues. At the National Museum, the archaeology section also survives, despite such basic problems as the failure of air conditioners in the main storage room. Museum archaeologists continue to plan joint work with provincial authorities, such as a recent archaeological survey of Santa Isabel island undertaken in cooperation with provincial authorities.

The obvious pattern in these examples is that organizations outside Solomon Islands have played a catalytic role in forming and developing cultural projects throughout colonial and postcolonial history. Despite wide recognition of the need to connect these projects with local interests and sponsors, however, few have proven capable of surviving the departure of outside support. Even though nationals were trained to continue with the programmes left by their overseas counterparts, they failed to find the financial, moral and political support necessary to maintain them. As a result, these programmes have either declined or collapsed, a consequence of the failure to institutionalize them in either local communities or national or local government. Nick Stanley, writing about the growth of cultural centres in Melanesia, noted that 'There is a distinct difference in emphasis between provincial centres and the national museum complex which is exacerbated by the prominence of overseas volunteers in the origins and direction of provincial centres.' (Stanley 1998:91). Whereas we agree that the prominent role of volunteers has been a factor in sustainability, we would argue that the same problems exist at the national level.

On the surface, this could be read as another chapter in the unfortunate story of dependency relations in the Pacific and elsewhere. Development theory has long recognized that it is easy for governments to accept financial assistance and gifts of equipment and new buildings funded by outside aid donors without any assurance that they have a life beyond the period of assistance. In the cultural domain, we see a repeated disconnection between rhetorics of culture and the development of capacity beyond the immediate goals of individual projects.

The same story of unsustainability evident in the experience of provincial cultural centres and custom houses may also be seen in the situation of the National Museum in Honiara. During the period leading up to independence in 1978, some individuals in the new generation of leaders that had returned from overseas studies and become prominent in national politics, started to acquire interest in the museum and its association. They included Francis Bugotu of Guadalcanal, Mostyn Habu of Santa Isabel, Geoffrey Beti and Milton Sibisopere from the West, Solomon Mamaloni from Makira, John Tuhaika and Leonard Kaitu'u of Rennell and Bellona and Francis Saemala and Wilson Ifuanao from Malaita, just to mention a few.[13] These leaders, active during the formative moments of indigenous scholarship, made important contributions. However, judging from the declining activity of the Cultural Association, the promise of those early years has not been sustained, at least not with a continued interest in development of the museum and its association.

There have been successive efforts to organize educational and cultural associations to support the work of Solomon Islands scholars, writers and artists.[14] A recent example is the formation of the Institute of Solomon Islands Studies, launched in 2003 as a locally initiated non-governmental organization with a board of advisors drawn from the College of Higher Education, the Ministry of Education and other cultural institutions. Yet these initiatives depend mainly on the vision of a few individuals, who persist despite the lack of institutional or programmatic support.

Whether at the national or provincial level, the attitude of policymakers toward cultural institutions such as the National Museum has long been ambivalent and weakly grounded in larger visions for the nation. Among the many contributing factors to the low valuation of cultural activities is the isolation of the concept of 'culture' (and, specifically, 'traditional culture') from the wider spectrum of social concerns. It is certainly the case for the National Museum, with its mission for preserving and promoting cultural heritage, that the more 'culture' is associated with the preservation of artefacts, the less it is regarded as relevant to contemporary society. The low level of support for the museum follows from the lack of understanding of its potential to contribute to a broad spectrum of national interests. Two areas where that potential has gained a degree of recognition from the state are education and tourism.

Kastom and the state: tourism and education

The location of 'culture' within the apparatus of the state has shifted many times during the various formations and reformations of government following independence. Most often, however, it has been coupled with either 'tourism' or 'education'. A clear example is the National Museum, which has been moved more than thirty times between the Ministry of Education, the Ministry of Home Affairs and the Ministry of Culture, Tourism and Aviation. As of writing, it is part of the Ministry of Culture and Tourism. The uncertainty of the location of the museum and of 'culture' in general in the setup of national ministries reflects uncertainties about the significance of culture and the role of the state in supporting it.

One of the more significant moments of attention to the state's cultural agencies occurred with the appointment of John Naitoro, an individual with graduate training in anthropology, to the position of Permanent Secretary in the Ministry of Culture, Tourism and Aviation in 1990. Seeing the need for coordination, he established a Culture Division within the ministry, and a position of Chief Cultural Officer with responsibility for policy development and coordination of cultural activities.[15] This position is today titled Director of Culture within the Ministry of Culture and Tourism. In practice, much of the attention in this office was devoted to organizing Solomon Islands' contributions to overseas arts festivals. Certainly a high point of national sponsorship for traditional performing arts came with hosting the first Melanesian Arts and Culture Festival, which included participation of provincial performing groups and delegations from all the Melanesian countries, as well as New Zealand and Taiwan (Kupiainen 2007).

Tourism in Solomon Islands has a long history, including even the war years, when troops moving through the Solomons were the catalyst for rapid growth in the production and sale of cultural artefacts (Douglas 1996). The state's role in the development of tourism in Solomon Islands begins with the establishment of the Solomon Islands Tourist Authority (SITA), established as a statutory body by an Act of the National Parliament. Its operating costs were covered by funds received from hotel and tourism-operator taxes as well as an annual subvention from the national government. Given the revenue-generating potential of the tourism industry, the government established an agency to deal with policy matters relating to its development early on (Tourism Council of the South Pacific 1990). It was hoped that such a division would attract funding from outside donors. So, in the early 1990s, the Solomon Islands Tourist Authority was changed to the Solomon Islands Visitors Bureau. The General Manager and staff of the Bureau are directed and monitored by a Board whose Chairman is either the Minister of Culture and Tourism or a government backbencher.

At present there is a division of responsibilities between the Director of the Tourism Division and the General Manager of the Visitors Bureau. The former concentrates on securing funds for the support of local initiatives attempting to develop small tourist facilities, such as eco-lodges and rest houses, while encouraging the improvement of various attractions throughout the country; the latter focuses on marketing and promoting tourism outside the country. While the Tourism Division developed a national tourism policy, the Visitors Bureau expanded and diversified its marketing strategy aimed at increasing the number of visitors into the country annually. No doubt driven by the hope of returns on its investment, the government puts more funding and emphasis on tourism development than other areas of cultural development, despite public support for cultural preservation and education.

The most visible national cultural initiative instigated by regional models for tourism development was the construction during the early 1990s of a 'cultural village' adjacent to the National Museum. In August 1990, the Honiara Municipal Authority allowed the building of a cultural centre or 'cultural complex' consisting of eight 'huts exhibiting the cultures of the provinces' on land adjacent to the museum (Tourism Council of the South Pacific 1990). The project was funded with about $300,000 from the EEC through the Fiji-based Tourism Council of the South Pacific. A year later, a new quarterly tourism newsletter would report:

> The country's main cultural centre is nearing its final stages of
> completion.... is expected to become one of the country's main tourist
> attractions.... Individually constructed, traditional houses depict the

diversity of the many cultures of Solomon Islands, and will enable visitors to get an insight of the country's history and cultural background.

> (*Tourism News: The Quarterly Newsletter*
> *of the Solomon Islands Tourist Authority* 2:1)

Despite the optimistic vision, the initial tourism-focused business plan for development of the cultural village proved unrealistic (Schouten 1992), and the space created by the ring of traditional structures now mainly hosts various local activities, including ceremonial functions of the museum.

Whether at the National Museum or in the provincial centres, the development of these cultural programmes is often seen by the general public and decision makers as tourism focused. From the beginning, one of the driving forces behind the construction of cultural centres or custom houses was to provide sites of interest to tourists who might visit and provide a source of income for the communities involved. The value of developing these places so that traditional knowledge, skills and architectural designs would be propagated in local communities, especially among younger people, was often regarded as less important than the economic incentives. As a result, when a weak business plan results in no tourists turning up, interest in the projects diminishes and the custom houses are left to rot. Anthropologists Pierre Maranda and Jean Michaud and their colleagues worked with local leaders in the Lau area of Malaita in the 1990s to create a tourism project (the Lau Cultural Preservation and Tourism Project) that would bring small numbers of 'adventure tourists' to support economic and cultural goals of the rural community (Michaud *et al.* 1994). Despite the involvement of anthropologists, filmmakers and North American tourism agencies, less than ten tourists ever visited the area under the auspices of the project.

One way to counter complacent attitudes towards cultural knowledge is to include it in school curricula, so that young people might realize its importance. During the 1970s, during the period around independence, educational institutions often introduced more material relevant to Solomon Islands cultural identities. At King George VI Secondary School, when it was the only government secondary school in the country, art classes included work with traditional designs and motifs (Tickle 1970). Students were encouraged to paint murals on the walls of school buildings, as well as a number of prominent buildings in Honiara town, depicting cultural objects or legends. Schools often organized cultural festivals during which students performed their own regional dances. These festivals were organized for the schools to come together at the end of the year to participate collectively.

Education, which receives most funding from international donors such as the EU and the New Zealand government, is an obvious focus for the development of policies that connect cultural knowledge with contemporary priorities. It is also one of the primary means by which governmental support may be directed towards (re)learning cultural and historical heritage. In the present National Education Plan Policy, the teaching of cultural values and skills is being considered for inclusion in the national curriculum. It is people who are concerned about losing their culture and language who are implementing cultural approaches. Everywhere in the rural Solomons, people see the importance of developing and promoting their own cultural heritage – as part of educating younger generations to appreciate, maintain and enjoy their own way of life. One area where Solomon Islanders in rural areas have long expressed an interest in cultural preservation, is in support for vernacular languages through the production of dictionaries and texts. Such efforts have been supported by many of the expatriate researchers who work in Solomon Islands, as well as by the efforts of bible-translation teams working with the Summer Institute of Linguistics.[16] In many other cases, village committees continue to seek support for dictionary and literacy projects.

In several locales people have established schools in their own communities in which they teach young people practical skills and methods of farming, building houses, making handicrafts and fishing, along with writing and reading. So far three such schools have been established: in Munda, Western Province and in Kwaio and Bita'ama in Malaita Province. The Ministry of Education recognizes these schools, and has provided limited financial assistance to one of them, Bita'ama. In 2007 the school at Bita'ama submitted an unsuccessful application for assistance to UNESCO through the Solomon Islands National Commission for UNESCO Secretariat. When the Kwaio Cultural School has been able to operate, it does so with very limited funding generated through the sale of handicrafts or from the Kwaio Fadanga funds.[17]

Finally, we offer a brief comment on some of the practical effects of cultural research and study, usually carried out by foreign scholars. Not surprisingly, projects and programmes associated with the work of individual scholars working in Solomon Islands have focused on the local communities that host them. Although many projects and activities have emerged from such collaborations, they have for the most part remained disconnected from national and provincial institutions. While the local focus of these efforts is in line with the priority given to the communities that host research, it has resulted in little learning across locales that share common concerns, as well as little support at the national level. Writing nearly two decades ago, Roger Keesing described the difficulties he encountered in his efforts at cultural development among the Kwaio of Malaita, from training local students to returning cultural materials. His statement remains as true today as it was then:

Many of us who have worked for years in Melanesian countries have hoped that we could help train advanced students, ideally from the communities where we have worked, so that indigenous scholarship can be fostered and cultural heritage materials entrusted to us put back where they best belong. That goal has been slow in realization, because the young countries of the region had higher priority needs for professional skills.

[Furthermore] the return of such materials is unsystematic and sporadic, and when it does take place, there may be inadequate means available to store and preserve them. The more serious problem is that, for the Solomons at least, there is no effective system for making such materials available to students of their own cultures.

(Keesing 1994:193)

On a more optimistic note, the advent of new electronic media and the increasing accessibility of the internet offer new possibilities for making cultural projects and programmes more widely available in the future.

Looking ahead: cultural policy in the making

In light of this brief (and partial) history of national cultural practices from the colonial period to the present, it should be clear that most of the projects and activities discussed have taken place in an isolated, fragmented environment with few connections to governmental institutions that might sustain them. Hence the urgent need for some form of cultural policy. If one examines critically the period from independence in 1978 to the early 1980s, it is clear that national cultural activities during the years immediately following independence were more visible and better organized despite limited funding. In some ways, this advantage was also undercut by the continuing influence of European visions of culture as pre-modern 'tradition' signified by objects and activities to be collected and preserved.

In recognition of the fact that support for cultural practices has actually declined over the years, a number of individuals working in the country's cultural institutions have taken on the task of writing a new national cultural policy. Although the need for such a policy has long been recognized, including at the 1992 conference 'Developing Cultural Policy in Melanesia', it has now been put on the national agenda, with recognition that cultural functions would be well served by a National Cultural Council analogous to the National Sports Council, which works to assure effective international representation and participation in sports activities. As conceived, the anticipated national cultural policy would provide guidelines for decision-makers engaged in national planning to encourage the integration of cultural considerations from the start. Connections between cultural institutions and educational, economic and political development should provide a stronger rationale for funding and implementation. This is particularly urgent as Solomon Islands takes responsibility for regional activities such as the 2012 South Pacific Festival of the Arts.

Currently the national government has a policy on culture that places its main emphasis on tourism development. As a result, 'culture' in the eyes of the state obtains value insofar as it can be commodified. One of the objectives of a new cultural policy is to provide a broader vision of culture that has practical significance for Solomon Islanders beyond the tourist gaze. While the potential monetary gain of tourism is certainly one of the benefits of cultural policy, the deeper significance of cultural development is in its contribution to people's own lives and histories. It is these connections that should be appreciated. With a strong grounding in local visions, a new cultural policy should also address the need for reviving the involvement of volunteers from organizations such as the US Peace Corps, Australian Youth Volunteer Ambassadors, Canadian Universal Services Overseas and the Japanese Overseas Corporation Volunteers without creating the dependencies evident in past initiatives. Rather, they would help the governments and communities rebuild their interest in their cultural practices and provide the support needed with their services.

A national cultural policy would have the benefit of providing continuity through changes in government. It would also guide the government in understanding the importance of programmes for cultural and artistic heritage, especially regarding the role of state institutions such as the National Museum, National Archives and the National Art Gallery. At the moment, major changes are often driven by extraneous political developments, such as the controversial sale in 2006 of the Old Government House that housed the National Art Gallery. The sale of the property to a hotel developer from Papua New Guinea forced relocation of the gallery to the grounds of the National Museum with a loss of exhibit space.[18]

Because of this sale, the government took steps to bring together the National Museum and Art Gallery under one administrative head. Although the catalyst for this move may be regrettable, it affords an opportunity to break down essentialized concepts of 'traditional' and 'contemporary' culture – a reflection of assumptions that 'traditional culture' derives from the pre-European past.[19] In fact, a number of recent activities sponsored by the museum already work to break down these boundaries. For example, the Peace and Unity Sculpture Project funded by a grant from the Solomon Islands Tobacco Company supported young artists to produce a series of carved posts, using innovative designs that were installed with the traditional houses in the museum's cultural centre. Another example is an Australian-funded

2007 workshop for young artists who produced several murals that now adorn the front gate area of the museum entrance.

Equally important, such a policy could set out more clearly the importance of cooperation between national institutions and their counterparts in provincial areas. The experience of the Vanuatu Cultural Centre in developing a fieldworker programme over many years, as discussed by Bolton in this volume, provides a set of possibilities for developing new models of cooperation between local and national spheres of cultural development. This stronger articulation of local/national relations would also minimize the disruption that follows when national cultural institutions move from one ministry or department to another. At the time of writing, the Ministry of Culture and Tourism had appointed a task force to evaluate options for creating a National Cultural Council to oversee a National Cultural Policy and related legislation. In addition to the obvious benefits of generating a national dialogue on culture, the hope is that a policy framework will help put programmes in place capable of fostering the development of Solomon Islands arts and culture as well as cultural awareness among younger generations. It will also be a useful reminder of values set out in the preamble of the National Constitution cited at the outset of this chapter, to the effect that 'the people of Solomon Islands are proud of the wisdom and the worthy customs of their ancestors; mindful of the common and diverse heritage; and agree and pledge that they shall cherish and promote the different cultural traditions within Solomon Islands' (Constitution of the Sovereign Democratic State of Solomon Islands 1978:1).

Acknowledgements

We want to thank Lissant Bolton, Ben Burt, Liz Bonshek, Edvard Hviding and other organizers of the British Museum Melanesia Project for the invitation to first present this chapter at the conference on 'Art and History in Solomon Islands: Collections, Owners and Narratives', 4–5 October 2006. Participants in the British Museum conference provided useful comments and discussion. We are especially grateful to Anna Craven, first Curator Training of the Solomon Islands Museum, for comments and contacts to numerous individuals who were active in the formative years of the Museum's history. James Tedder, Lindsay Wall, and Les Tickle all deserve special mention for offering detailed comments and criticism. We also thank David Akin, Jari Kupiainen and Knut Rio for comments on an earlier draft of this chapter.

NOTES

1. RAMSI ,or the Regional Assistance Mission to Solomon Islands, is the Australian-led multinational intervention in the political life of Solomon Islands. Invited by the Solomon Islands government after some years of violence around the capital, Honiara, a force of some 2,000 soldiers, police and administrators landed in the Solomons in July 2003 to restore peace and security and assist in rebuilding government institutions.

2. In response to the first draft of this chapter prepared for presentation at the British Museum conference in October 2006, Anna Craven and James Tedder raised concerns that it gave a distorted picture of the colonial context and diminished the role of the Europeans who worked to found the museum. Although our concern here is primarily with postcolonial cultural policy, we thank them for their acute comments. Their response helped correct a somewhat superficial characterization of 'the colonial'. At the same time, differences between their perceptions of the colonial situation and those of the first author remind us of the distinctly different lenses through which different actors might view the process of nation-building. Exploration of these differences is beyond the scope of this chapter.

3. The history of cultural documentation and collection has a natural science parallel. On the scientific side, post-war colonial administrators interested to document the natural and cultural worlds encompassed by British Empire, formed the 'British Solomon Islands Society for the Advancement of Science and Industry'. The Society was active from 1950–5, during which time it produced several small publications (Russell 1972:iii). In addition to cultural artefacts, they took an interest in collecting all sorts of faunal specimens, including seashells, butterflies and moths, and reptiles, as well as skeletal remains.

4. Lindsay Wall describes her curatorial work as follows, 'I worked flexible hours as I had three children, one under school age … I advertised that the curator would be available on site from 10–12am each day and at other times by appointment. This enabled me to spend time conferring with other offices and departments, meeting researchers, not to mention typing museum business and display labels at the Printing Office as there was not even enough money for a typewriter. I might add that it never seemed less than a full-time job!' (Wall 2007).

5. Solomon Dakei, from Western Province, was one of two prominent Solomon Islander members of the Museum Association at that time. The other was Silas Sitai from San Cristobal (Makira).

6. It was only the death of Fred Kona and the extreme disruptions of the 'tension' that finally closed the Vilu War Museum, which had become a well-known destination for military veterans from both the Allied and Japanese armed forces. While we could point to a list of economic and political difficulties that has made it difficult

for such local initiatives to survive, the absence of any national cultural policy relevant to the Second World War has compounded those problems.

7. By one account, the new museum was 'open most days of the week' with 'a constant flow of visitors'. (Anon. 1973:79). James Tedder in his memoir recalls that the museum (for which he helped obtain funding) 'was an immediate success with some 1,200 visitors a month – mostly Solomon Islanders – and valuable donations being made by villagers as well as previous residents of the Solomons who returned to their own countries.' (2008:227).

8. In comments on our earlier conference paper responding to our characterization of the colonial era, Tedder, who at one time was Director of Information and Broadcasting, underlined the role of the radio station in recording and broadcasting *kastom* storytelling and music 'in widening the cultural horizon of the villagers ... Luke Susuta for years was telling stories from the villages once a week in his splendid pidgin and it was one of the most popular sessions on the radio. Unfortunately broadcasting customary music was not so popular if it did not come from the area of the listeners or to some of the more sophisticates of Honiara. In 1974 in training exercises for new journalists we collected hundreds of tapes of old songs. These were properly documented but I believe most of these tapes have either been lost or deteriorated. However there was developing a new music based certainly on Western type but nevertheless distinctly "solomoni". For example one song so popular for many years was "Walk About Along Chinatown". Arising from such music new dancing based partly upon Fiji became the rage. It was loosely referred to as "tralala" and it became not only popular in Honiara but many feasts in villages ended with tralalas. Surely these activities showed that there were developing cultural activities during the "evil colonial days"' (Tedder 2008:2).

9. The Open Air Theatre was later converted for use as a boxing arena, with a ring constructed inside. 'It had been designed as a multiple use theatre, where films could also be shown, but the boxing ring meant that space no longer existed for dance performances.' (Anna Craven, email to authors, 9 August 2009).

10. Individuals who worked at Education Officer include William Talasasa, who was succeeded by Lia Ivupitu and then Shedrach Sesese. The latter, in particular, devoted considerable time to the Mobile Learning Kits.

11. For a fascinating visual account of a custom house/tourism project presented in a documentary film, see *The Lau of Malaita* (1987). This film, produced by Grenada Television for a 'Disappearing Worlds' series, depicts a project inspired by visions of local tourism in which villagers attempt to move various custom and sacred objects into a display house in their village. Anthropologist Pierre Maranda was an advisor for the film, which presents conflicts over the project among villagers with differing religious and cultural commitments.

12. With the centres that got involved in the collection or display of cultural objects, the question arises as to what happened to the collections when they ceased to operate. There may be information in the communities concerned, but the museum has no records. Guadalcanal is an unfortunate exception, because of the destruction of the provincial headquarters during the period of the 'tension'. This is an area that could be further explored, so that the situation regarding these institutions and the work they have done in the past can be better documented.

13 Like various other associations established by expatriates during the colonial period, membership frequently included relatively few Solomon Islander members. Of those who were involved in the early years, the list of members of the advisory committees of the Museum Association/Cultural Association reads like a Who's Who of leaders in Honiara society during the years leading to independence (list courtesy of Anna Craven):

> 1975 SIMA committee included: Henry Manuhea, Francis Saemala, Rosie Sibisopere, Mostyn Habu, Levy Laka, James Saliga, Milton Sibisopere, Kevin Misi, Simon Papage, Tebaka Kaitu.
>
> 1976 CASI committee included: John Sau (now Tuhaika), Jenny Sau (now Tuhaika), Geoffrey Beti, Dennis Lulei (Isabel Council), Henry Manuhea, Matthew Natei (Eastern Islands Council), Dominic Otuana (Western Council), A. Po'oia (Malaita Council), Joseph Puia, Tina Wawane (SI Christian Association), Lawrence Foana'ota, Peter Waleilia.
>
> 1977 CASI committee: Geoffrey Siapu, Jenny Sau (Tuhaika), Frank Kabui, Dennis Lulei (Isabel Council), Matthew Natei (Eastern Islands Council), Moira Piko, A. Po'oia (Malaita Council), Joseph Puia, Moffat Rukasi (Makira and Ulawa Council), John Sau (now Tuhaika), Tina Wawane (SI Christian Assoc.)

Despite the impressive presence of elite citizens at that time, the general view of the public was that these organizations belonged to the government or the mostly British community that established them. That kind of attitude made it likely that these institutions would be seen as foreign or irrelevant as the expatriates and volunteers left the country, and as the first generation of prominent Solomon Islanders involved in these associations passed away.

14. The University of the South Pacific Centre in Solomon Islands has also taken an active role in supporting cultural education and training, at various points in its history, particularly with its once active publishing programme that included support for the *'O'o Journal of Solomon Islands Studies* and publication of historical and literary works through the Institute of Pacific Studies at USP in Suva.

15. The position of Chief Cultural Officer was created by shifting the Cultural Education Officer from the museum's staffing.

16. One of the goals of the Museum Association/Cultural Association was to promote vernacular literacy by producing vernacular texts with English translation. In

the 1960s a member of the British colonial service in the Lands and Surveys Department, Brian Hackman, contributed to efforts to produce a national standard for spelling and pronunciation through publication of an exhaustive guide to place names (1968).

17. Although the Kwaio project has seen the emergence of a third generation of artists descended from those who learned in the early 1980s, the 'Kwaio Arts' organization has not survived due to the collapse of a market for its artefacts (David Akin, email to G. White, 29 September 2006).

18. In response to a motion by Mr Joses Tuhanuku, Member of Parliament for Rennell and Bellona, the Speaker of the National Parliament, Sir Peter Kenilorea, appointed a Special Select Committee to review the controversial sale. Unfortunately, parliament was dissolved before the report could be discussed.

    Interestingly, the loss of this important public land in the centre of the Honiara urban area was the second time that private interests had trumped public culture and resulted in the loss of national cultural property. In the 1980s the government of Prime Minister Mamaloni sold the land adjacent to the Mendana Hotel to an Asian hotel developer, requiring destruction of the Museum's Canoe House. The canoes were removed and subsequently destroyed during the years of the 'tension'.

19. The apparent dichotomy of 'traditional culture' and 'art' is widespread beyond the Solomons, evident, for example, in the separation of cultural (ethnology) museums from art museums or galleries.

BIBLIOGRAPHY

Anonymous. 1973. *Lukim Solomone: Introducing the Solomon Islands*. Honiara: Information and Broadcasting.

Akin, D. 1994. 'Cultural education at the Kwaio Cultural Centre'. In *Culture, Kastom, Tradition: Developing Cultural Policy in Melanesia* (eds) L. Lindstrom and G. White, 161–72. Suva: Institute of Pacific Studies.

Bolton, L. 1994. 'Bifo yumi ting se samting nating: the women's culture project at the Vanuatu Cultural Centre'. In *Culture, Kastom, Tradition: Developing Cultural Policy in Melanesia* (eds) L. Lindstrom and G. White, 147–60. Suva: Institute of Pacific Studies.

Bolton, L. 1999. 'Radio and the redefinition of kastom in Vanuatu'. *The Contemporary Pacific* 11(2):335–60.

Burt, B. 1994. 'Cultural development and anthropology in Kwara'ae'. In *Culture, Kastom, Tradition: Developing Cultural Policy in Melanesia* (eds) L. Lindstrom and G. White, 173–86. Suva: Institute of Pacific Studies.

Clifford, J. 1997. 'Museums as contact zones'. In *Routes: Travel and Translation in the Late Twentieth Century*. Cambridge, MA: Harvard University Press.

Cole, C.C. and K. Roga 1994. 'The relationship between cultural policy and programming in Western Province, Solomon Islands'. In *Culture, Kastom, Tradition: Developing Cultural Policy in Melanesia* (eds) L. Lindstrom and G. White, 105–13. Suva: Institute of Pacific Studies.

Constitution of the Sovereign Democratic State of Solomon Islands. 1978. Microfiche S40482. Law Library Microform Consortium. Hamilton Library, University of Hawai'i.

Dakei, S. K. 1972. 'A glance back … a look forward'. *The Journal of the Cultural Association of the Solomon Islands*. 1:5–8.

Douglas, N. 1996. *They Came for Savages: A Hundred Years of Tourism in Melanesia*. Lismore, Australia: Southern Cross University Press.

Foana'ota, L. 1994. 'Solomon Islands National Museum and Cultural Centre policy'. In *Culture, Kastom, Tradition: Developing Cultural Policy in Melanesia* (eds) L. Lindstrom and G. White, 95–102. Suva: Institute of Pacific Studies.

Foana'ota, L. 2006. 'Activity report from Solomon Islands National Museum after the problems of April 18–19 in the capital, Honiara'. *PIMA NEWS* (April–July edition):3–6. Port Vila: Pacific Islands Museums Association.

Hackman, B.D. 1968. 'A guide to the spelling and pronunciation of place names in the British Solomon Islands Protectorate'. Honiara: British Solomon Islands Protectorate.

Hviding, E. and T. Bayliss-Smith 2000. *Islands of Rainforest: Agroforestry, Logging, and Eco-tourism in Solomon Islands*. Aldershot: Ashgate.

Kaeppler, A. 1994. 'Paradise regained: the role of Pacific museums in forging national identity'. In *Museums and the Making of Ourselves: The Role of Objects in National Identity* (ed.) F. Kaplan, 19–44. London: Leicester University Press.

Keesing, R. 1994. 'Responsibilities of long-term research'. In *Culture, Kastom, Tradition: Developing Cultural Policy in Melanesia* (eds) L. Lindstrom and G. White, 187–97. Suva: Institute of Pacific Studies.

Keesing, R. and R. Tonkinson (eds). 1982. 'Reinventing Traditional Culture: The Politics of Kastom in Island Melanesia'. *Mankind* (Special Issue) 13.

Keevil, R.A. 1972. Preface. *The Journal of the Solomon Islands Museum Association* 1:v–vi.

Kupiainen, J. 2007. 'Kastom sur scéne n'est pas coutume mise en scéne. Reflexions sur le premier Festival des Arts et de la Culture mélanésienes'. In *Le Défi Indigene. Aux Lieux d'étre* (eds) B. Glowczewski and R. Henry, 235–255:. Paris.

Kwa'ioloa, M. and B. Burt. 1997. *Living Tradition: A Changing Life in Solomon Islands as told by Michael Kwa'ioloa to Ben Burt*. Honolulu: University of Hawai'i Press.

Laracy, H. and G. White (eds) 1988. *Taem Blong Faet: World War II in Melanesia.* Special Issue of *'O'o: A Journal of Solomon Islands Studies* 4. Honiara: University of the South Pacific Centre.

Lindstrom, L. and G. M. White (eds) 1994. *Culture, Custom, Tradition: Cultural Policy in Melanesia.* Suva: Institute of Pacific Studies.

Michaud, J., Maranda, P., Lafrenière, L. and Coté, G. 1994. 'Ethnological tourism in the Solomon Islands: an experience in applied anthropology'. *Anthropologica* 36:35–56.

Pule, R.T. 1983. *Binabina: The Making of a Gela War Canoe.* Suva: University of South Pacific.

Rogers, M.J. 1985. Establishing a School Loans Programme for the Solomon Islands National Museum: A Cross-Cultural Experiment. M.A. Thesis, James Cook University of North Queensland.

Russell, T. 1972. 'Foreword'. *The Journal of the Solomon Islands Museum Association* 1:iii–iv.

Schouten, F. 1992. *Solomon Islands Cultural Centre: Management and Operation Plan.* Suva: Tourism Council of the South Pacific.

Stanley, N. 1998. 'The revolt of the represented: the growth of cultural centres in the Pacific'. In *Being Ourselves for You: The Global Display of Cultures*, 85–114. London: Middlesex University Press.

Tedder, J.L.O. 2008. *Solomon Island Years: A District Administrator in the Islands 1952–1974.* Stuarts Point, NSW: Tautu Studies.

Tickle, L. 1970. 'Search for culture'. *The Art Teachers Journal* (Spring):4–13.

Tourism Council of the South Pacific 1990. *Solomon Islands Tourism Development Plan, 1991–2000* (vols. 1 and 2). Honiara: Tourism Council of the South Pacific for the Ministry of Tourism & Aviation, Government of Solomon Islands.

Wall, L. 1972. 'Curator's notes'. *The Journal of the Cultural Association of the Solomon Islands* 1:1–2.

Wall, L. 2009. Email communication to G. White. 7 August 2009.

White, G.M. 1989. 'The politics of remembering: notes on a Pacific conference'. *Cultural Anthropology* 4(2):194–203.

White, G.M. 1993. 'Three discourses of kastom'. *Anthropological Forum* 6(4):475–94.

White, G.M. 1996. 'War remains: the culture of preservation in the southwest Pacific'. *Cultural Resource Management Special Issue* 19(3):52–6.

CHAPTER 12

Describing knowledge and practice in Vanuatu

✳

LISSANT BOLTON

Introduction

This book addresses the intersection between political innovation and cultural heritage in Oceania, acknowledging the way Pacific Islanders draw on their own knowledge and practice to construct political and social forms which intersect with the new realities of the nation-state. In some cases, as in Edvard Hviding's discussion of the Christian Fellowship Church in the Western Solomons (this volume), such innovations are locally inspired and are aimed at a self-reliance that could potentially replace the state. The innovations that arise from the Vanuatu Cultural Centre (Vanuatu Kaljoral Senta or VKS) operate somewhat differently. They bring indigenous knowledge and practice together with the introduced concept of anthropological or ethnographic documentation, but in so doing, they subvert the conventional objectives of such documentation. Instead of documenting indigenous knowledge and practice as a first step to analysis and description, the Cultural Centre documents knowledge and practice with the objective of local cultural preservation, transformation and innovation. This happens through the Cultural Centre fieldworker project.

Vanuatu Cultural Centre fieldworkers set out to describe ni-Vanuatu indigenous knowledge and practice using some of the techniques of anthropological description, but aiming their project at a ni-Vanuatu, non-academic audience. In producing their descriptions, fieldworkers make use of the Bislama term *kastom*.[1] *Kastom* is a term of discrimination: it categorizes knowledge and practice of the place – from Vanuatu – in contrast to all that is not of the place – from outside. The fieldworkers' project is an appropriation and subversion of the techniques of anthropological and linguistic field research: as the programme has developed over the last thirty years, they have transformed those objectives into something that is very much their own. Whereas, as Marilyn Strathern argues, the objective of anthropology is description, for the fieldworkers, description is a precursor to action.

Marilyn Strathern reflects on ethnographic description in writing about the relationship between ethnography and anthropology. She discusses the ethnographic immersion of fieldwork, the imaginative re-creation that constitutes anthropological writing, and 'a continuing struggle with the language of description' (1999:xi). She argues for the distinctive character of anthropological description. Starting from Runciman, she suggests both that 'the distinctive problems of social science are ... those of description, not explanation', and that 'good descriptions in turn have to be grounded in theory' (1988:10). From this she argues that 'the concepts in which descriptions are grounded are unlikely to be those used by the agents whose behaviour is being described' (Runciman 1983:228 in Strathern 1988:10). Indeed, Strathern clearly distinguishes what she is doing in writing about Melanesians from what Melanesians themselves do. Much of the material of her book, she comments, rests on symbolic exegesis; Melanesian exegesis, by contrast, 'takes the form of transformation or symbolic innovation'. She argues that 'Anthropological exegesis must be taken for what it is: an effort to create a world parallel to the perceived world in an expressive medium (writing) that sets down its own conditions of intelligibility' (1988:17). In this chapter I look at the Pacific alternative that the VKS fieldworker project has developed: an alternative model of description, in which research leads to action. My description of their project is itself, of course, much more akin to anthropological exegesis in Strathern's sense.

The intersection between anthropology and the fieldworker project is also a function of the use of the term *kastom*. In this term introduced ideas about 'culture' have fused with ni-Vanuatu concepts to create its contemporary meaning. This convergence and divergence between *kastom* and introduced concepts of culture is all the more significant because *kastom* has a salience in Vanuatu that cognate terms do not have in the rest of Melanesia. The Cultural Centre and the fieldworker program have significantly determined both the meaning and the influence of this term in Vanuatu, and have drawn on academic understandings of culture in doing so.

In this chapter I discuss the fieldworker project of documentation and revival with reference to a specific instance, the revival of *nevsem* or yam towers on the southern Vanuatu island of Erromango. The chapter tracks between these two contexts – the fieldworker programme and Erromango – attempting to describe the one as it plays out in the other. I begin with an ethnographic description of the yam towers, and then discuss the fieldworker project. I then consider the ways in which Erromangans have been attempting to describe their own practice, and the transformations they intend those descriptions to effect. Specifically, this chapter sets out to consider some of the concepts in which the Cultural Centre fieldworkers ground their descriptions of their own practice.

Erromango and *nevsem*

To begin with an image: overleaf is a drawing of a yam tower at Pongil Bay on the west coast of Erromango, in southern Vanuatu. This drawing was made in 1850 by P.D. Vigors, a botanist on the voyage of HMS *Havannah* led by Captain Erskine. The drawing is the only European image of an Erromangan yam tower of which I am aware. Vigors described this tower in his diary:

> We came on a large quantity of yams stored in the open air in a way unlike anything we had seen before. The plan adopted seemed to secure the two important points of preserving them from vermin (Rats etc) and allowed a free circulation of air to pass at all times through them, they were however exposed to rain – whether this supply was the 'general store' or only that belonging to the chief I could not discover. A tree had been robbed of its branches, two smaller ones placed alongside of it fastened together at the top – on these 3 poles a number of cross sticks were placed from a few feet above the ground to the very top, and on these transverse pieces were the yams as shewn in the sketch ... they were placed regularly the largest at the bottom and getting gradually smaller as they went higher – I think they were probably all selected as being the best – many of them were of a very large size. Poles about 10 ft high laced round the base, on one of them was tied a 'wisp' of straw to shew that they wer '*taboo'd*' (sacred) or not to be touched. The whole framework was above 40 feet high, placed in front of one of their houses, this belonged to the chief and was curiously and nicely constructed.
>
> (Vigors 1850, cited in Weightman 1989:82)

Vigors assumed that the tower was a storage facility, a way of keeping yams in good condition until they were eaten. However the other expatriate eyewitness account of Erromango yam towers gives a different perspective. The missionary H.A. Robertson, who lived on Erromango from 1872–1912, and who wrote a book which includes two chapters about Erromangan practice, also briefly describes yam towers, which he reports are called *nevsem*. He reports that *nevsem* were central to a major feast, or *nisekar*. He says

Figure 1   'Yams stored at Bunkil bay'. *Philip Vigors Papers, Alexander Turnbull Library, Wellington, N.Z.*

For many months before, yams and other root crops had been gathered and tied on to an enormous scaffolding, about a hundred feet high. As the time of the *nisekar* drew near, pigs were placed within the scaffold enclosure, and fed till they were just rolling in fat; fresh yams and fowls were also added.

(Robertson 1902:391)

Erromango suffered grievously from the European incursion, far more than any other island in Vanuatu. It was exploited from 1840 by sandalwood traders, a trade that resulted in great bloodshed (Robertson 1902:35). By 1932, following the sandalwood trade, the labour trade and a number of epidemics, the population of Erromango had fallen from a mid nineteenth-century high, estimated at about 7,000, to a mere 381. No yam towers have been built since the early twentieth century. Some sites where they were built are still known, and in at least one such place (as it happens, near Pongil Bay) the hardwood poles that created the tower's frame still lie where they fell, in what is now bush. Five to six languages were spoken on Erromango at contact, of these only two survive, and one of those is almost extinct. Substantial amounts of knowledge and practice were lost during this period: many Erromangans today say with finality that they have lost their *kastom*.

What I know about Erromango, and about *nevsem* and the *nisekar* feasts for which they were built, I have learnt from scanty descriptions and references in the published literature, in photographs and in museum collections, and from the fieldworkers themselves. There are also evident analogies between knowledge and practice on Erromango and that of the adjacent island of Tanna, so that anthropological accounts of Tanna illuminate the fragments of Erromangan historic ethnography.[2] Like Tanna, Erromango was divided into districts. C.B. Humphreys, a student of W.H.R. Rivers who spent a few months on Erromango in 1920, reports that there were 'several districts, each with its high chief, *Fanlo*, who had jurisdiction over all the villages in his territory, while each village had its own *Fanlo* as well, who had local authority' (1926:132).[3] Like Tanna, the districts were interconnected by trade, warfare and, in particular, by *nisekar. Nisekar* seem to have been a major social focus for the whole of Erromango in the mid-nineteenth century. They were held to mark and effect certain events, and in particular to effect a number of transformations, such as funerals, and the installation and elevation of chiefs. Humphreys describes these as 'return feasts' (1926:181) while Robertson refers to the 'feasting season' (1902).

The Tannese food exchanges known as *niel* did not involve feasting per se, but rather the presentation and exchange of garden produce between allies; nevertheless, their material form echoes *nisekar. Niel* often focused on a specific food – so that a yam *niel* might be exchanged for a taro *niel*, a banana *niel* for a sugarcane or fish *niel*. Bonnemaison comments

> The aesthetic side prevails. When a group invites its ally to its own dancing
> grounds, it decorates them completely with the gifts it is about to give. Yams
> (or another item) make up huge piles at the centre of the ground, while
> all surrounding banyan trees drip with long braids of entangled yams that
> tumble down from the highest foliage.
>
> (Bonnemaison 1994:142)

There were at least three kinds of *nevsem*, corresponding to different feasting occasions. According to the southern Erromango fieldworker Jerry Taki, one *nevsem* type had three posts and was used in an exchange of food between two tribes or families. Vigors' drawing would appear to be of this kind of three-legged tower. In another type, the tower's platforms were connected by ladders. Painted barkcloths were displayed on one type of tower – possibly incorporating ladders – built for chiefly alliance rituals (Huffman 1996:136). The fieldworker Sempet Naritantop learned from an elderly woman that 'Sometimes dozens or hundreds of decorated barkcloths would be hung from long bamboo or wooden poles, radiating, like the rays of the sun, from the base of the ... *nevsem* towers'. The elderly woman 'broke into tears when reminiscing on the beauty of the spectacle' (Huffman 1996:136). Thus both *nevsem* and *niel* incorporated a strongly aesthetic dimension.

The *nevsem* system was closely linked to the chiefs, not only as the proximal cause for many *nevsem*, which was the creation or elevation of individual chiefs, but also because *nevsem* formally linked the different districts of the island. Jerry Taki reports that *nevsem* towers were controlled along 'roads'. There were sixteen nodal places on Erromango which had, in the person of the chief, the right to control the building of the towers. There were five such places in north Erromango, six in the central districts and five in the south. These places were linked by metaphorical roads, *helnivi* and *nival*, which Taki considers similar to the moiety-linked roads of *koyometa* and *numurkuen* on Tanna. Bonnemaison, Brunton and Lindstrom all describe 'knowledge roads' on Tanna, a series of formal links between places along which both ritual practice and knowledge can pass (Brunton 1979; Lindstrom 1990; Bonnemaison 1994). These roads might or might not follow the same course as physical paths linking places. Lindstrom (1990:124) describes knowledge roads as 'a system of major, named information highways' which connect 'nodal kava-drinking ground to kava-drinking ground from one end of the island to the other' (a kava-drinking ground is a ritual and residential centre). On Tanna, individual men inherit the right to control and transmit information along a certain section of these roads. It seems that the *nevsem* system linked all the districts of Erromango through one unifying system of exchange feasting.

The fieldworkers

Erromango and Tanna are islands in an archipelago distinctive for its cultural and linguistic diversity; they are two among 83 islands that lie north–south over 1,000 kilometres of ocean. Approximately 113 languages are spoken on the islands by a population, in 2009, of 234,000 people. Although Europeans settled in the islands from about 1840, the archipelago entered the colonial era very late: the subject of a joint naval agreement between Britain and France from 1887, it escaped colonial government until 1906. Independence was achieved in 1980. After independence the Vanuatu Cultural Centre (Kaljoral Senta or VKS) became one of the most effective institutions in the republic, implementing many programmes directed at the preservation and promotion of the diversity of knowledge and practice through the region (Regenvanu 2005). Crucial to this is the fieldworker programme.

The fieldworker programme was founded in about 1980 by Kirk Huffman, then a Cambridge anthropology postgraduate student working as curator in the fledgling Cultural Centre museum. The project arose out of an oral traditions recording project funded by the South Pacific Commission, and also out of a concern to document Vanuatu's many unrecorded languages. Huffman recruited Darrell Tryon, a linguist based at the Australian National University, to chair annual two-week training workshops for volunteers from across the archipelago. Initially, the context for the fieldworker programme was the fight for, and achievement of independence. Independence politicians made considerable mileage with the idea of the distinctive character of indigenous knowledge and practice in Vanuatu – *kastom* – as the foundation for national identity and national unity. The fieldworker programme was energized by this rhetoric (Bolton 2003).

The fieldworkers are recruited by the Cultural Centre to work voluntarily in their own villages and districts, documenting and reviving the distinctive *kastom* of their places. Each fieldworker represents his own region or district, and works independently there: a key concept for the programme is that each fieldworker is dealing with his or her own distinctive *kastom*. Thus the Erromango fieldworkers – James Nobuat Atnelo, Sempet Naritantop, Malon Lobo, Jerry Taki and Sophie Nempan – all support themselves through subsistence agriculture, and are involved in documenting and reviving Erromangan *kastom* in their own time. Fieldworkers may be paid to work on particular projects, in particular to assist academic researchers. In 1984, James Nobuat Atnelo was sponsored to do some research into Erromangan barkcloth by Kirk Huffman for a VKS exhibition (Huffman 1985 and 1996:139); Jerry Taki has often been employed to assist in archaeological surveys and excavations on Erromango itself.

From 1980 until 1994 the fieldworkers were all men. In 1989 I was recruited by Huffman and the VKS Board of Management to help found a women's fieldworkers group with a Cultural Centre colleague, Jean Tarisesei. The women fieldworkers began meeting in 1994, and every year since then I have chaired their annual two-week research and training workshop, as Tryon continues to chair the men's workshops. Although not everyone recruited as a fieldworker continues in the role, an appointment as fieldworker is often a lifelong commitment. There are many fieldworkers who devote significant amounts of thought and energy to their work through the year. Indeed, as was once observed to me, the fieldworker programme gives people somewhere to put their energy (Kate Holmes, pers. comm.). This comment was made in relation to women – opportunities for action are especially limited for ni-Vanuatu women – but it applies equally to men: the programme provides an arena for locally and/or nationally sanctioned action.

The format of the annual workshops is always the same. The fieldworkers each give two reports, one on their previous year's work (promoting and reviving *kastom*) and one on the topic of the workshop (documentation). For the last twelve years or so, the topic has always been nominated a year ahead, to give fieldworkers time to research it in advance. The idea of 'research topics' developed out of Tryon's early work with the men fieldworkers on language documentation. Early men's workshops used topics as a focus for the recording of language terms, recording words by semantic domain (Tryon 1999:11). These domains were decided at the beginning of the workshop, or announced a few months in advance over the radio. In 1991, for example, the workshop focused on birds, the VKS having a good collection of mounted bird specimens from the Vanuatu archipelago. Fieldworkers worked from these specimens to record names and other language terms. Inevitably, however, this process produced not just words but also stories and knowledge – reports of the significance of hearing a certain bird call on one's right-hand side, for example. When we started the women's workshops, we focused not on language terms, but on the stories, the knowledge, around a particular subject. These topics always relate to *kastom*, not to contemporary issues per se, although most workshops devote a session to issues such as marine environment preservation, logging or HIV/AIDS.

The fieldworker project is explicitly established as a project for Vanuatu: both for future generations and the present generation. The audience for fieldworker reports is other fieldworkers. Visitors may sit in on the workshops, but few visitors have the stamina to sit all day listening to the reports and discussion. The workshops are audio-taped with the intention that the reports be transcribed and subsequently published by the Cultural Centre in limited editions for the fieldworkers. Fieldworkers translate the knowledge they have, or which they have learnt, into Bislama, and into a form which can be presented to each other. The point of these reports is not a further audience, but each other and their own communities. They are working from and to the metaphoric and symbolic systems of knowledge and practice in their own places, while at the same time working from and to the knowledge and practice of the contemporary nation-state as it exists in the Cultural Centre.

From 1985 until 1994, the Vanuatu government imposed a moratorium on social-science research by expatriates. Anthropologists and linguists were banned from doing fieldwork, and archaeologists were banned from excavating. In this context, the fieldworker group was established as a distinctively indigenous project. When the ban was lifted, the new research policy imposed new research conditions of collaboration with local communities and contribution to local objectives. The objective of the policy is that 'ni-Vanuatu can perceive research as an exercise over which they have some control, in which they can meaningfully participate, and from which they can benefit' (Regenvanu 1999:99).

The early 1990s were also significant for the breakdown of the Vanua'aku Party (the political party which had dominated the independence movement and managed the transition into national independence), the splintering of political parties and the rise of self-interested government. This era saw the post-independence state-sponsored discourse of an indigenous or Melanesian form of development for Vanuatu replaced by a more orthodox and globally sanctioned approach to national development (Regenvanu 1999:98). More and more the Cultural Centre has become the locus for national-level negotiations in relation to *kastom*.

The national importance of the Cultural Centre is in no small measure due to its director from 1995 to 2006, Ralph Regenvanu. He has a deep personal commitment to the notion of Vanuatu's independence, not only at a political level, but also in other senses. Writing in 1999 about the lifting of the research moratorium, he made clear his attitude to the academic project: 'the body of knowledge currently being generated (by academic researchers) will augment the academic discourse about Vanuatu which has always been conducted and constructed outside it in the metropolitan countries' (1999:99). He commented further that while this discourse may only ever affect the lives of the subjects of research 'to a limited extent (if at all)', the Vanuatu research policy is designed to ensure that people in Vanuatu can take part in and benefit from research locally. Thus, like Marilyn Strathern, Regenvanu characterizes anthropological description as something apart from the concerns of Melanesians themselves.

Technologies of description in the workshops

The precursor to the fieldworker programme was an oral traditions training workshop held in 1976. It was taught by an ethnomusicologist, Peter Crowe, who focused on training the four participants to make good audio recordings. Using reel-to-reel tape recorders they recorded stories and songs and then put them together as a radio programme that was subsequently broadcast on the national shortwave station. Two of these trainees went on to become the core of the fieldworker group. From the beginning, then, fieldworkers were taught to interview and record other members of their own communities. In the early years of the project, all fieldworkers were given tape recorders and did make extensive recordings, now held in the National Film and Sound archive. These recordings were mediated, in the sense that the fieldworkers and their interlocutors selected what was to be recorded, but they were not re-presented or analysed. When the workshops began to have a specific topic, fieldworkers began to make recordings on those themes, which they sometimes played as part of their workshop reports. As the number of fieldworkers has grown (standing in 2008 at about 110 men and women), the provision of tape recorders and the emphasis on tape recording has diminished.

The workshops adopt the idea of enquiry as the key source of information. The expectation is that fieldworkers will ask other members of their communities for knowledge about *kastom* which they will then reproduce in reports for the workshop, and which they will also, if they can, return to the community translated into action. Especially in the early years of the workshops, this process of questioning was fraught with problems. The fieldworker project was not so widely understood, and individuals were seen to be seeking knowledge not properly theirs to know, from which they could be assumed to make money. One of the enduring roles for VKS staff – for example for Jean Tarisesei, as she has visited women fieldworkers in different parts of the country – is to explain that fieldworkers are not paid, and do not gain financially from their participation in the programme.

Writing has increased in importance as a fieldworker technique. Darrell Tryon first introduced the use of file-cards to record language terms, and subsequently suggested that fieldworkers should record the information they have researched in hardback exercise books. After each workshop, he suggested the fieldworkers 'write up their presentation as an essay' in their books, thus gradually building up 'an ethnography for their own group, section by section' (Tryon 1999:12). Some fieldworkers, notably Philip Tephahae from Aneityum, followed this suggestion faithfully; others have preferred not to write their accumulating knowledge down. In the last decade, more and more women fieldworkers have begun to write their reports in advance of the workshops, and either read those reports verbatim, or use them as an aide-memoire in presenting to the workshops. Recently, a fieldworker suggested to me that he would like to see his reports published as a book. In other words, over time, what fieldworkers do, has, in its material form at least, begun to look more and more like academic fieldwork – transforming knowledge and practice into text.

From the beginning Huffman introduced a central objective of revival to the project – it was not enough for the fieldworkers to record the knowledge and practices of their places, their objective was to make it alive again, or, in Huffman's metaphor, to wake it up again. Thus the work of the fieldworkers has never been just to research and report, but also to draw attention to knowledge and practice at the local level and to re-introduce it into contemporary life. At minimum, this involves making sure that knowledge is passed down the generations. Ralph Regenvanu argues that the process of documentation is in and of itself a technique for revival. Just asking the questions often results in several other people hearing the answers. The rationale for revival has to do with the evaluation of indigenous knowledge and practice, and the rhetoric that surrounds it has to do with identity: a positive affirmation that indigenous knowledge and practice is valuable and important and that ni-Vanuatu can be proud of who they are. A secondary object for revival is the creation of craft industries as a source of income (the making and selling of baskets). Huffman, Tryon, Regenvanu and myself, along with other VKS staff, have all urged fieldworkers to make objects again (textiles, for example), to revive ceremonies, to teach children songs and dances, to re-introduce indigenous land and sea-management techniques, and so on. There is also a sense that revival is itself a form of description: not the theorized anthropological description in Strathern's sense, but nevertheless an enacted description of practice that embodies a series of ideas about the nature of indigenous knowledge and practice.

Key concepts grounding fieldworker description

The concept of explicit analysis is alien to the fieldworker project. Fieldworkers do not set out to describe *kastom* by explaining it. They take the rationale, the significance, of any individual *kastom* for granted. I don't think I have ever heard a fieldworker question another about why a certain *kastom* takes the form it does, unless in incredulity that other people might – for example – make such a poor show of their marriage ceremonies. Rather, the questions they ask are about details, seeking to expand an account with further information. The concepts which underpin and inform the project are unexamined. I address several of these concepts here: addressing those relating to gender, the content of *kastom*, knowledge transmission and place.

The division of the fieldworkers into men's and women's groups is treated as self-evident in Vanuatu – as needing no comment. In fact, it has a complex history. As I have argued elsewhere, from earliest encounters, expatriates commonly read gender distinctions in ni-Vanuatu practice as a fixed discrimination between women and men in favour of the latter (Bolton 2003). In fact, it was the colonial system which introduced categorical distinctions between men and women through education, church and state systems. Commonly, only men were appointed to positions of authority in these systems, and in laying the groundwork for the independent state, the colonial government established that too as a domain for men. Huffman, trained in anthropology in the early 1970s, both perceived and privileged male domains in his understanding of ni-Vanuatu practice. Thus when he and Crowe founded the fieldworker group, the men-only focus was consistent both with colonially instituted arrangements of the new nation-state, and with a perception that the important domains in indigenous practice belonged only to men. The institution of the women's fieldworker groups resulted partly from pressure from feminist-influenced ni-Vanuatu women's groups that developed after independence. The move was supported by the men fieldworkers, however, who recognized the inadequacy of a men-only system.

For the women fieldworkers the turning point was in 1997, when the topic for the women's workshop was women and rank. At this workshop, as woman after woman made her research report, the fieldworkers realized the extent of women's status-alteration rituals through the country. These rituals, which dominate two-thirds of the country (from Epi to Torres), had been popularly (and anthropologically) regarded as a male-only system. But it transpired that in every place that men were involved in a status-alteration system, so were women; indeed, in some places a man was dependant on his wife's progress through the status rituals in order to progress himself. The kind of sophisticated conceptions of gendered practice which anthropologists (following Strathern) now use in descriptions don't have much importance for fieldworkers, but my contribution to the definition of *kastom* in Vanuatu has probably been to emphasize the equal contribution of women to all aspects of indigenous knowledge and practice. The women fieldworkers group certainly acts as a venue for the consideration and working out of ideas about the importance of women's contribution to *kastom*. It also offers another avenue for women who want to contribute to their home communities. As fieldworkers, they can and do act at community levels.

Ni-Vanuatu do not think of *kastom* as an all-encompassing system of belief and behaviour. Rather, they use the term to refer to those aspects of indigenous knowledge and practice which they identify as distinctive and important. The fieldworkers have a far more extensive definition of *kastom* than do many other ni-Vanuatu. In common parlance, the word is generally applied to a certain suite of practices: *kastom danis* (dances), *kastom singsing* (songs), *kastom stori* (stories, histories), *kastom dresing* (clothes), *kastom kaekae* (food, cooking), *kastom lif* (medicine) and, perhaps above all, *kastom seremoni*, often described simply as *kastom* (rituals, especially marriage). But the year-on-year accretion of the topics that the fieldworkers have addressed, and the discussions that the workshops develop, significantly extend the notion of what can be considered *kastom*. For the women's workshops, Jean Tarisesei and I have tended to alternate more strictly anthropological topics (marriage rituals, kinship terminologies) with environmental or practical ones (*kaekae blong disasta* – food preservation and disaster management; *kastom kalenda* – seasonal agricultural cycles). The topic I introduced which the fieldworkers found hardest to comprehend was water. That workshop elicited reports about water sources and uses, but people found it hard to think of this as *kastom*.

There are certain kinds of knowledge which the fieldworkers refuse to report in the workshops. Regenvanu's proposal that the women fieldworkers document women's knowledge about pregnancy and childbirth was met with a resounding refusal from the group. Women also refused to sing mourning songs, lest they elicit a death. When the men's workshop addressed traditional medicine, Tryon reported that the fieldworkers were very reluctant to reveal important (and valuable) knowledge, and it took him twenty years, he reports, to get the men fieldworkers to a point where they would report on principles of land-holding. In the sense that knowledge is a tradable resource in Vanuatu, some things are best not made public in workshops. Other kinds of knowledge are too powerful to be bandied about in such a context. Reporting on knowledge in a workshop is clearly not a traditional form of knowledge transmission. As the fieldworkers have developed a sense of their own project, and as education, business and development have made further and further inroads into rural life, the fieldworkers have in some ways become more willing to speak – have figured out how to speak and what not to say – and also, have less and less access to some kinds of knowledge as older people die.

In ni-Vanuatu practice a there are variety of ways in which knowledge can be properly transmitted and acquired. It can be taught by kin (formally or informally) and purchased with nominated payments, learned through participating in ceremony, acquired through conversation and observation, and, for men, through travel. Knowledge can also be acquired through dreams and other forms of engagement with non-human beings. Dreams not only act as the source of innovations (in song, in practice), but also as a source for important knowledge that has been lost. As Jack Taylor has demonstrated for north Pentecost, knowledge is also available in the landscape. He describes a place known as *abanoi*, a kind of 'invisible parallel dimension layered across or threaded within the lived world of human experience' (2003:114). This place is understood to contain the 'true and authentic knowledge of the ancestors' (2003:115). A person seeking wisdom should sit quietly so that 'sooner or later that which is sought will be made apparent to them' (2003:115).

I have also heard tell of living and awake people on the island of Efate who have had encounters with the past, via a momentary view of, or encounter with, people from the past apparently living in the landscape simultaneously with those living there now – as if seeing them through a gap in a screen (D. Luders, pers. comm.). Such sources have not been discussed in the workshops, but it is clearly one this kind that Huffman referenced when he talked about waking up *kastom*: *kastom* is in the landscape, it needs only to be retrieved from it. It may well be that such sources for knowledge are discussed outside the formal parameters of workshop sessions, perhaps especially by the men fieldworkers, whose conversations are often extended by nightly kava-drinking sessions.

Critical to the whole fieldworker project is a notion of *kastom* as varying across place, but not across time. The idea that *kastom* varies across place is, of course, the driver for the whole project – people from each place have both the capacity and the right to address the *kastom* of their particular place. What Huffman, Tryon and I have been less quick to observe, is the extent to which the fieldworkers do not think about *kastom* varying across time. Huffman, in writing about changing names for Erromangan barkcloth, has published a clear statement about change over time as a matter of changing fashions, and presumably discussed this with his fieldworker informants (1996:136). However, the notion of retrieving and reviving *kastom* implies a character to *kastom* which does not support the idea of change. This echoes the idea of the ethnographic present. The influence of expatriate ideas can be traced in many contemporary indigenous self-perceptions, it is possible that expatriate assumptions about the unchanging nature of indigenous practice may have influenced the idea of *kastom* on this point also. However, the idea that *kastom* belongs in a place liberates transformation, without marking that transformation as occurring over time.

In fact, *kastom* incorporates a specifically Melanesian idea of innovation as transformation. As Michael Allen long ago demonstrated in an article about innovation in the male-graded society in east Ambae, Vanuatu, people carefully negotiate the distance an innovation can take from established practice (1981). An innovation has to be a transformation which is still recognizably that which it transforms. Place literally grounds transformation, facilitating a greater degree of innovation. In recent years I have attempted to ask a number of people about the idea of *kastom* changing over time before the European incursion, and have often been met by genuine incomprehension. This is not to say that history and genealogy do not allow for event and transformation in that long era. People are well aware of stories of population movements, wars and the importation and adoption of rituals from other places. It is rather to say that the idea of *kastom* is of something which, because it is originates in place, has an integrity which cannot be conceived as subject to change. This is critical to the idea of revival.

Technologies of description on Erromango

Despite the ideology that *kastom* does not change, the key issue in relation to revival is that it is impossible to revive *kastom* without transformation. The motivations for ritual, the uses of objects, even specific relationships, no longer intersect with other aspects of people's lives in the way that they once did, because those aspects have also changed. Revival necessarily involves transformation and innovation. Erromango gives a particularly clear instance of this process, simply because the expatriate incursion was especially devastating there.

The massive population loss on Erromango from the 1840s was deeply dispiriting to those who remained. Partly as a response to violence inflicted by sandalwood traders, Erromangans murdered the first five missionaries who attempted to evangelize the island. This now hangs heavy on their collective conscience, and is often discussed as precipitating the loss of Erromangan *kastom* – a kind of punishment. Some of the first fieldworker research on Erromango encountered these ideas directly. James Nobuat Atnelo (who was born in Pongil Bay in 1935), was involved in researching barkcloth for a VKS exhibition curated by Kirk Huffman in 1984. Barkcloth manufacture had died out by the early twentieth century. Atnelo found three women who could teach him about barkcloth production and use. After he interviewed each woman, each, in turn, died. Atnelo travelled to the Cultural Centre to act as the exhibition guide. Just as he was about to set out to return to Erromango to revive barkcloth production, he was involved in a traffic accident and lost a leg. These events only served to reinforce opposition to the revival of *kastom* on Erromango.

Jerry Taki became a fieldworker in about 1985, after Atnelo's accident. Taki has a long history of participation in archaeological research, working before the research moratorium with Les Groube, during it with the VKS archaeological site survey, and since it with the Australian National University – VKS Archaeological Project. Both Taki and Sophie Nempan (the only woman fieldworker from Erromango) worked with Meredith Wilson when she surveyed Erromango's extensive rock art. Both Taki and Nempan have travelled outside Vanuatu as fieldworkers. Taki went to a World Archaeological Congress in Delhi in the early 1990s, while both Taki and Nempan have visited the important Erromango collections at the Australian Museum, Sydney. The determination of these fieldworkers, combined with changes in Vanuatu itself, has gradually brought Erromangans into a somewhat more open attitude to the revival of *kastom*.

Taki has taken *nevsem* as a long-term focus of his research. His objective is to build a tower again, but his awareness of gaps in his knowledge, and continuing opposition on Erromango, mean that this is a long-term goal. As a first step towards this, he learned enough to build a model of a *nevsem* tower, which now is now displayed, alongside a reproduction of Vigor's drawing, in the VKS museum. More significantly, in 2003 he and the other fieldworkers ran a *nevsem* workshop on Erromango, in his own village in the hills above Pongil Bay.

This workshop, planned for several years, was an innovative blend of Erromangan practice and introduced models of teaching and explaining. Taki sees *nevsem* as a key entry point into learning about Erromangan *kastom*. He said the importance of knowing about *nevsem* is that young people should understand the work of a chief, the responsibilities of leadership. He also reintroduced some of the kinship structures that underpinned the chiefly system – not only the inheritance of leadership itself, but also the inheritance of roles which provided support and assistance to the leader. To hold the workshop the Erromango fieldworkers activated the two *nevsem* roads, *helnivi* and *nival*, to draw people and contributions to the workshop, and subsequently sent kava and food back to the chiefs who remain at nodal points on those roads – four chiefs for *helnivi* and two for *nival*. Erromangan *kastom* dances, taught to young people for the workshop, were performed for the occasion. At the same time, those who attended the workshop sat in the meeting house and listened to Taki and others teach about the *nevsem* system. They used a large drawing of a four-legged tower to illustrate the talks and also built a small (2 metre high) tower in an enclosure, about which Taki spoke at some length. The workshop was audio- and video-recorded by VKS staff who came to Erromango for the purpose. They were the only non-Erromangans at the workshop.

Subsequently, Taki obtained permission from the chiefs to bring a group to participate in the Melanesian Arts Festival held in Port Vila in 2003. He took this group of young men out of the village to hide in the bush for a fortnight, so as to learn Erromangan dances, and then brought them to perform. He also built a small *nevsem* tower at the festival. This was not merely show; rather, he used it as an occasion to transact some business. He presented yams from two of the platforms in the model to the festival organizers; the yams from the third platform were given to representatives from the Loyalty Islands, New Caledonia, who attended the festival. In the past, the Loyalties had a trade connection to Erromango. The presentation opened that road of connection again.

Taki's research into *nevsem* has been built up through information gathered from various people on Erromango over a long period. This research is collaborative with the other Erromango fieldworkers – he has incorporated the results of their research into his own understanding. He has also benefited from discussions with the Tannese fieldworkers: for example, in his ability to compare the *nevsem* roads *helnivi* and *nival* with the Tannese *koyometa* and *numurkuen*. He has drawn on knowledge from his involvement in Meredith Wilson's rock-art research, and the information he has gained from museum collections, especially in Sydney. He has built up a dictionary of language terms for one of the Erromangan languages, which has presumably contributed further to his understanding. He has also learned from the men fieldworkers' workshops (and perhaps in other workshop contexts) how to present information in the form of a verbal report.

These workshops and models operate as descriptions at a number of levels. A model is in the most straightforward sense a description of something in three dimensions. The workshops involved verbal descriptions and images to explain the towers and the *nevsem* system. The young men were taught to dance the distinctive *kastom* dances that they had, until then, not known. At the same time, the workshop in Erromango started to enact the *nevsem* system, engaging with the *nevsem* roads around the island.

To this Taki has added his own understanding of the *nevsem* system as a form of agency, as a way to effect transformations. One of the enduring problems for the fieldworkers, which they often discuss, is how to carry knowledge and practice into the future; how these things can continue to effect sought-after transformations. In the past chiefs used *nevsem* to effect alliances and other kinds of transformations. Many of these transformations are no longer needed – not least because the population loss on Erromango has so drastically diminished those who might lead, and how they might relate to each other. In the *nevsem* workshop and at the Melanesian Arts Festival, Taki used *nevsem* to build relationships on and beyond Erromango and to effect changes in young Erromangans. The use of *nevsem* to reopen an alliance with the Loyalty Islands at the Melanesian Arts Festival is revival as innovation, creating a potential new role for *nevsem* in a wider context. Where the performance of *kastom* is merely just that, performance, and has no socially transformative effects that people value, it is hard to sustain: the key issue is to find a use for *nevsem* in contemporary Erromango. Taki has of course also used his research, as he freely admits, to change his own status: his knowledge and his achievements have given him different status and significance among his kin and elsewhere.

Taki and the other fieldworkers are drawing on anthropological research strategies to retrieve knowledge and to report it. At the same time, they are effecting something similar to Strathern's description of 'exegesis as transformation or symbolic innovation' (1988:17). They are explaining their own knowledge and practice to themselves in a way that transforms it, and they are making purposeful innovations with it, adapting it to new circumstances. They are effecting a transformation that enables them to take hold of their own practice and through it negotiate the new national contexts in which they find themselves.

NOTES

1. Bislama is Vanuatu's lingua franca, a neo-Melanesian pidgin spoken widely throughout the country.
2. The contemporary Erromangan population is mostly concentrated in the south of the island, and that is where the fieldworkers are based. The northern area of Erromango may have had stronger links to Efate. The information I discuss here probably relates principally to south Erromango.
3. Kirk Huffman, spelling *fanlo* as *fanlou*, reports that a high chief was called *fanlou nusian* (Huffman 1996:136).

BIBLIOGRAPHY

Allen, M.R. (ed.) 1981. *Vanuatu: Politics, Economics and Ritual in Island Melanesia.* Sydney: Academic Press.

Bolton, L. 2003. *Unfolding the Moon: Enacting Women's Kastom in Vanuatu.* Honolulu: University of Hawai'i Press.

Bonnemaison, J. 1994. *The Tree and the Canoe: History and Ethnogeography of Tanna.* Translated and adapted by J. Pénot-Demetry. Honolulu: University of Hawai'i Press.

Brunton, R. 1979 'Kava and the daily dissolution of society on Tanna, New Hebrides'. *Mankind* 12(2):93–103.

Huffman, K.W. 1985. 'An exhibition of Vanuatu Bark Cloth'. *COMA Bulletin* 16:49–50.

Huffman, K.W. 1996. 'The "decorated cloth" from the "island of good yams": barkcloth in Vanuatu, with special reference to Erromango'. In *Arts of Vanuatu* (eds) J. Bonnemaison *et al.*, 129–40. Bathurst: Crawford House Publishing.

Humphreys, C.B. 1926. *The Southern New Hebrides: An Anthropological Record.* Cambridge: Cambridge University Press.

Lindstrom, L. 1990. *Knowledge and Power in a South Pacific Society*. Washington: Smithsonian Institution Press.

Regenvanu, R. 1999. 'Afterword'. In *Fieldwork, Fieldworkers: Developments in Vanuatu Research* (ed.) L. Bolton. *Oceania* (Special Issue) 70(1):98–100.

Regenvanu R. 2005. 'The changing face of "custom" in Vanuatu'. *People and Culture in Oceania* 20:37–50.

Robertson, H.A. 1902. *Erromanga: the Martyr Isle*. London: Hodder & Stoughton.

Runciman, W.G. 1983. *A Treatise on Social Theory. Vol. 1: The Methodology of Social Theory*. Cambridge: Cambridge University Press.

Strathern, M. 1988. *The Gender of the Gift: Problems with Women and Problems with Society in Melanesia*. Berkeley: University of California Press.

Strathern, M. 1999. *Property, Substance, and Effect: Anthropological Essays on Persons and Things*. London; New Brunswick, N.J.: Athlone Press.

Taylor, J.P. 2003. Ways of the Place: History, Cosmology and Material Culture in North Pentecost, Vanuatu. Doctoral thesis, Canberra: The Australian National University.

Tryon, D. 1999. 'Ni-Vanuatu research and researchers'. In *Fieldwork, Fieldworkers: Developments in Vanuatu Research* (ed.) L. Bolton. *Oceania* (Special Issue) 70(1):1–8.

Vigors, P.D. 1850. Private Journal of a Four Months Cruise through some of the "South Sea Islands" and New Zealand in H.M.S. *"Havannah"*. Original ms, Alexander Turnbull Library, Wellington.

Weightman, B. 1989. *Agriculture in Vanuatu: A Historical Review. United* Kingdom: The British friends of Vanuatu.

Wilson, M. 1999. 'Bringing the art inside: a preliminary analysis of black linear rock-art from limestone caves in Erromango, Vanuatu'. In *Fieldwork, Fieldworkers: Developments in Vanuatu Research* (ed.) L. Bolton. *Oceania* (Special Issue) 70(1):87–97.

CHAPTER 13

Are the grassroots growing?

Intangible cultural-heritage

lawmaking in Fiji and Oceania

✳

GUIDO CARLO PIGLIASCO

Introduction

When this volume was still in its early stages, *Island Business* appeared on news-stands throughout the Pacific Islands with the attention-getting headline: 'The Pacific's stolen identity: how intellectual property rights have failed Pacific cultures' (Tabureguci 2008). Clearly, our intentions to articulate the complex relations between people and their tangible and intangible forms of cultural heritage in Oceania have been well timed to address issues of importance to Pacific Islanders today. In this chapter, I address some of the questions that emerged at one of the meetings[1] that guided our editors towards the conception of this volume; in particular, problems relating to the reproduction of tradition in contemporary Oceania, where issues of globalization, property rights and international policies intertwine with local practices around intangible cultural heritage. The emblematic example I employ throughout this chapter is Fiji, where the state's top-down cultural-heritage policies are meeting the bottom-up general adjudicative principles derived from customary law, and are based upon a regional, transnational consensus (see Rachlinski 2006).

Tangible piracy, intangible sanctions?

A question that increasingly preoccupies several communities in Oceania is whether they can in fact apply intellectual-property protection to performances and repositories of wisdom that identify their culture (Strathern and Hirsch 2004:3). The *Island Business* cover story argues that the IPR (Intellectual Property Rights) system is not well understood by Pacific Islanders. It is difficult for Pacific Islanders to understand that they could be restricted from using or commercially benefitting from what they have if someone else has filed a patent, copyright or trademark over it: 'A deficit that has left them exposed to outside forces who draw from local cultures to set up successful commercial or research ventures... Very often, when successes translate to profits, Pacific Islanders get nothing in return.' (Tabureguci 2008:16).

Lawrence Lessig (2004:64) explains that 'the physics of piracy of the intangible are different from the physics of the tangible'. However, the ideology that culture should be free and access open remains unclear to Pacific Islanders, who question why they get nothing in return from successful ventures that make use of their cultural property: gene prospecting by the Moorea Biocode Project; the band *Deep Forest* receiving a Grammy Award for "Sweet Lullaby", a song by the Baegu people of the Fataleka region in northern Malaita; kava 'from Vanuatu' sold elsewhere; 'Made in China' versions of Solomon Islands shell money; tattoo artists putting unique Pacific Island tattoo designs on foreigners' bodies; or more recently, directly related to my own work in Beqa, an island iconic in Fiji for its fire-walking practice, the cosmetic company Nu Skin selling a Firewalker® Relaxing Foot Cream with the extract of the *Cordyline terminalis* plant 'traditionally used by Polynesian firewalkers to absorb heat and to cool and soothe the skin'.

From the beginning, Pacific Islanders interested in protecting their traditional knowledge and expressions of culture (TKEC) debated whether to follow top-down Western legal models, or to establish a new grassroots system based on how traditional cultural custodians conceive ownership and protection.[2] In 'Recovering collectivity: group rights to intellectual property in indigenous communities', intellectual property lawyer Angela Riley (2000:205–6 and 224) observed a decade ago that any attempt to amend intellectual property laws to allow indigenous knowledge and cultural expressions to be copyrightable would face the most profound criticism. She argues that cultural property should be placed back into the hands of indigenous peoples. Unfortunately, indigenous declarations of cultural and human rights and intellectual property rights conventions (e.g. Rome Convention, 1961) are often unenforceable 'soft laws'. They neither establish the terms of protection nor provide any protection against unauthorized performance or fixation, reproduction, broadcasting or other communication to the public of traditional cultural forms. They often vaguely refer to unspecified 'works of folklore' (e.g. Art. 15(4) of the *Berne Convention*, 1967) while failing to protect the rights of their authors, thus contributing to commodification of cultural property (e.g. TRIPS, Art. 2.1; 14.1; 39. 3).[3]

A challenging task for the legal anthropologist in Oceania, but not only in Oceania, is to understand to what extent cases of misappropriation and misrepresentation spontaneously generate grassroots reactions, and how these reactions can highlight the imbalances and inequities orchestrated by traditional power structures and inspire national legislators and jurists to ensure that the cultural symbols and intangible cultural property of indigenous communities are respected. One example from Oceania: a legislative framework to extend protection to areas conventional IPR laws could not reach is under scrutiny, and aims to develop policies regarding recording and mapping cultural knowledge, and to uphold and eventually enforce the rights of indigenous people through tangible sanctions, while increasing community awareness of cultural-heritage management.

The Draft Model Law for the Protection of Traditional Knowledge and Expressions of Culture (hereafter Pacific Model Law) was initiated by the Secretariat of the Pacific Community (SPC) and the Pacific Island Forum Secretariat (PIFS), and developed under the aegis of UNESCO and WIPO. It is derived from the Regional Framework for the Protection of Traditional Knowledge and Expressions of Culture conceived in February 1999 in Noumea at the Symposium on the Protection of Traditional Knowledge and Expressions of Traditional and Popular Indigenous Cultures in the Pacific Islands, which brought together representatives from twenty-one states and territories of the South Pacific region.

The Pacific Model Law, an IP-based *sui generis* system which creates new IP-like rights for intangible cultural heritage, is designed to legislate traditional and moral rights over traditional knowledge and expressions of culture that might previously have been regarded as part of the public domain. Once a state classifies TKEC as a segment of its own public domain, it is able to control its usage. The Pacific Model Law represents a major advance in contributing to the international rights discussion without incurring a procedural uniformity that threatens cultural diversity (Pigliasco 2009a and b). The Pacific Model Law is not an 'indigenous declaration', however it provides a hybrid national and regional approach that includes enforceable sanctions.[4] It establishes a regional legislative framework, but leaves matters of implementation to policy-makers in accordance with their national laws and systems. The Pacific Model Law encourages the inclusion of customary law and traditional governance systems in national legislation over cultural property rights. It recognizes that the traditional custodians of TKEC should remain the primary decision-makers regarding the use of TKEC, following their customary forms of protection. It thus ensures that the creativity and innovation found in traditional cultures will continue to benefit local communities.

While the Pacific Model Law is currently under revision in Fiji, Vanuatu, Palau, Papua New Guinea and the Cook Islands, it will be interesting to see what kind of approach these countries' revisions will take: 'top down' or 'bottom up'. While libertarian professor of law Richard Epstein (1996:89) argues that, on the one hand, 'virtually every legal system contains a heavy bottom-up component', on the other, he admits that for every particular rule on the assignment and creation of property rights there exists a correlative imperfection. The task of legal systems is to minimize these. In this light, Fiji's pending legislation to Protect the Indigenous Intellectual Property Rights in Traditional Knowledge and Expressions of Culture (hereafter 'the legislation'), which has been drafted but not adopted yet by the government, shows an approach to law integrated with empirical research that listens to the indigenous communities' voice, minimizing assumptions that may not fit with actual traditional practices and knowledge.[5] While consultants are vetting the decree, its content remains confidential. However, in the nineteenth draft developed earlier, there is a clear indication of the struggle the legislation working group[6] faced in identifying the beneficiaries of such bill; a problem not new in post-racial, multicultural Fiji, and which might emerge in other Pacific Island nations as well.

> The usage and meaning of the term 'indigenous' varies across peoples in the world. For many, it is considered derogatory, and is associated with primitivism, poverty, and demeaning lifestyle. As such, many prefer to label their group as something different. The ideology is also prevalent in scenarios when the 'indigenous' or 'original' or 'aboriginal' people are considered minority and subservient to a larger ethnic group. In Fiji's case the use of the term 'indigenous' is acceptable because the original inhabitants are a majority and social and cultural consciousness of many non-indigenous people tends to consider or create an impression of their closeness to Fijians. The 19th Draft of the legislation is still tending to use 'indigenous Fijian', or *iTaukei* to emphasise that the particular group entrenched in the legislation are the indigenous people as per the requirements of the initial drafting of the legislation by the SPC [Secretariat of the Pacific Community], PIFS [Pacific Islands Forum Secretariat] and WIPO [World Intellectual Property Organization]. The two concepts are used simply to differentiate the latter from other ethnic groups in Fiji since the current connotation of the term 'Fijian' as used widely refers to every citizen of Fiji and not specifically the indigenous population. Although, some may argue that Fijian is defined in the Fijian Affairs Act as pertaining to indigenous people only as outlined in the *Vola Ni Kawa Bula* [Genealogical register of Fijians owners of the Native Land] but we must be realistic and should face the fact that as we proceed in this ever changing social, cultural and economic and political pursuits of our country, a separate term should be used to define the indigenous population. Although, *iTaukei* sounds nationalistic, it is the only identifiable indigenous term, just

as New Zealanders term their indigenous people as Māori or vice versa,
the indigenous people defined themselves as Māori to emphasize their
existence… *Kaiviti* is simply a translation of Fijian – thus have the same
connotation… There should be a national debate on the usage of the term
Fijian, because it is rather blatant when one is taught something else and
we hear conflicting commentaries, speeches, read contradictory reports,
journals, articles, books indicating that other races such as Indians in Fiji
regard themselves as 'Fijians'

(Rusiate Ratuyaqona [pseduonym], pers. comm.)

Fiji's prospected legislation clearly shows how cultural heritage is created
and recreated through a process of exhibition and control orchestrated
by the state (see Kirshenblatt-Gimblett 1995:369–70), and how the state
listens to cultural heritage claims. Sipiriano Nemani (Senior Policy Planning
Officer, Department of National Heritage, Culture & Arts), involved from the
beginning in the drafting process of the legislation, observes that it is designed
to bring awareness to the traditional custodians, and expects the *vanua* (the
people of the land) to take up the initiative.

The *vanua* considers land, water, customary practices, and human
environment as one and indivisible. Given this cultural context, the idea
of pursuing the promotion of traditional knowledge and expressions of
culture cannot consider only one element but the whole… No government
policy, no organized workshop, no financial assistance can help the
indigenous community in Fiji elevate its traditional values and identity.
All vests with the *vanua* and those at the helm of traditional leadership to
proactively pursue and reinforce to members of the *vanua* the importance
of maintaining key customs.

(Sipiriano Nemani, pers. comm.)

Intangible cultural-heritage protection: oxymoron or opportunity?

Another major difficulty faced by Pacific Island countries is that while
cultural heritage is interpreted locally accordingly to local epistemologies (see
Chief Willie Bongmatur quoted in Rio and Hviding, this volume; Rio, this
volume), at national and transnational levels a crossover rubric deriving from
diverse arenas – including the arts, humanities, human and cultural rights
movements, economic development and politics – is emerging. The result
is that the fault lines and common grounds of multi-disciplinary efforts have
yet to be articulated, and cultural heritage remains under-theorized. A central
argument of this volume is that 'throughout the Pacific, local cultural heritage
has been a central element in political innovation in and beyond the local'

(see Rio and Hviding this volume). Thus, in order to analyze issues related to safeguarding intangible cultural heritage in Oceania, it is important to examine the concepts involved, for the inevitable tension between customary and Western laws will requires continuous compromises and adaptations (as seen in Fiji's proposed legislation).

In Oceania concepts like heritage, ownership and property have different connotations than they do in Western interpretations. Strathern (2008) shows that while Western lawyers have fundamental ideas about property, in Melanesia there are multiple situations in which it is not appropriate to talk about property regimes, and how particular island 'inventions' appear to circumvent the implications of property thinking. In addition, Pacific Island legislators are now discovering that Western definitions of cultural heritage and cultural property are also highly varied and contested.

In Eurocentric discourse, cultural heritage suggests that cultural symbols and products rightfully belong to the cultural group with which they are identified; at the same time, these symbols and products by definition fall into the realm of public interest and are held for the public good (Shapiro 2005:4; Mason 1999). By contrast, cultural property is 'that specific form of property that enhances identity, understanding, and appreciation for the culture that produced that particular property' (Gerstenblith 1995:569). Note that if we turn culture into property, however, its uses will be defined and directed by law, and culture is going to become perforce the focus of litigation, legislation and other forms of bureaucratic control. As Arno observes, once expressions of culture are protected by copyright, patent or trademark laws,

> ... they could be bought and sold like material objects and contractual obligations, conceptualized as private property in the mode of classic capitalism. Presumably, cultural communities would have to be defined as legal persons, like corporations, who could own and dispose of intangible heritage property. Hypothetically, Viti (the Fijian word for Fiji), created as such a legal person, could cash out, go modern, and sell the rights to Fijian culture to Sony Corporation.
>
> (Arno 2005:59)

Strathern (2008) observes that indigenous communities in Oceania do not view their heritage in terms of property at all. 'That is, something which has an owner and is used for the purpose of extracting economic benefits... For indigenous peoples, heritage is a bundle of relationships, rather than a bundle of economic rights.' (Daes 1997:3). Indigenous scholar and advocate Tabureguci (2008), interviewed in the *Island Business* article, states that it is difficult to reconcile the concept of ownership in Pacific societies to that of the commercial world. In most cases, she points out 'we define wealth not in what we have but in what we give away' (Aroha Te Pareake Mead quoted in Tabureguci 2008:20).

All this becomes more problematic when the property in question is intangible. Brown (2003) points out that, unlike questions of monetary reparations or the return of indigenous lands, struggles over intangible resources lead to vexing questions concerning origins and boundaries. A fundamental question for both the Western jurist and the Pacific Island legislator is to what extent cultural heritage is a kind of property rather than a social, intellectual and spiritual inheritance (see Davison 2000; Aplin 2002). Hoebel (1966:424) argues that the essential nature of property is to be found in social relations rather than in any inherent attributes of the thing or object that we call property. Property, in other words, is not a thing, but a network of social relations that governs the conduct of people with respect to the use and disposition of things. Strathern (2005:104) shows that in Melanesia the right of ownership associated with property is 'a world through which people are indefinitely interconnected through the inclusions and exclusions of property relations'. On the other hand, property is not merely a relationship between persons and things. Property is a social practice that includes rights, privileges, powers and immunities, and that governs the legitimacy of socially recognized individuals to control tangible or intangible things (see Coombe and Herman 2004:561; Underkuffler 2003:30; Penner 1997:2).

In fact, property becomes meaningful only when relationships, conflicts or claims among people are at stake (Underkuffler 2003:12). However, while the term cultural property tends to embody a static view of culture by focusing on legal claims to tangibles owned by 'a culture', the term cultural heritage instead tends to emphasize group rights. It steers us away from ideas of control and possession towards a sense of belonging and shared enterprise, allowing us to recognize the value of intangible culture more easily than property. Employing the heritage concept therefore potentially empowers currently disempowered indigenous groups.

Cultural heritage is expressed through both tangible and intangible features – places, objects, rituals, myths, memory – and the social and contemporary significance they each have. While physical forms of cultural heritage are designed to survive after the death of those who produce or commission them, intangible cultural heritage is more closely related to its creators as it often depends on oral transmission.[7] This conceptualization was derived from earlier definitions of 'folklore' embedded in Western formulations of cultural property.

In the 1970s, the UNESCO Convention on the Protection of World Cultural and Natural Heritage began stimulating questions about intangible heritage. In the mid 1980s, WIPO[8] and UNESCO convened a Group of Experts on the Protection of Expressions of Folklore. Blakeney reports that representatives of Spanish-speaking countries took the position that the term "'folklore" was an archaism, with the pejorative connotation of being associated with creations of lower or superseded civilizations' (Blakeney 2005:3).[9] This terminological dilemma persisted until the conclusion of the World Forum on the Protection of Folklore, convened by WIPO and UNESCO in Phuket in April 1997,[10] where panellists suggested that the term 'folklore' had negative connotations as something dead that needs to be collected and preserved (Janke 1997). Western concepts of folklore tended to focus on artistic, literary and performing works, whereas among indigenous communities it encompassed all aspects of an evolving cultural heritage that is an integral part of people's lives (Janke 1997).

Such criticisms concerning the limitations of the term folklore made UNESCO ban its usage in the 1989 *Recommendation*.[11] Nevertheless, people persisted in using the term to refer solely to artistic creations, excluding belief systems and scientific traditions; folklore in this sense remained a 'sub-totality' of the cultural heritage of a nation (Lucas-Schloetter 2004:265). However, indigenous communities rarely differentiate between art and science, and abandoned the restrictive folklore concept in favour of 'traditional knowledge'. Two new terms therefore entered the arena: 'traditional knowledge' (TK) and 'traditional expressions of culture' (TCE), often conflated in the acronym TKEC.

Attempts to label indigenous heritage and knowledge have been presumed by indigenous peoples as the first step in imposing a uniform set of terms, rules and codes for managing TKEC. This has been reminiscent of the Pacific region's colonial past, and suggests that Western jurists and policy-makers have failed to recognize that the ultimate source of knowledge and creativity is the land itself (Strathern 2001 and 2005). From an indigenous perspective, clan rights to sacred knowledge cannot be separated from rights to land; clans' sacred stories and rituals are often focused on a specific part of their land and are seen as essential to its continued well-being. Thus, Brown (2003) argues that community rights in traditional cultural expressions must be approached as one element or reflection of a native title, a term that in the Australian context refers to Aboriginal land rights. Brown refers to the revolutionary 1992 decision of Australia's High Court in *Mabo and Others v. Queensland* (hereafter *Mabo*).[12]

With *Mabo* the burden of proof shifted to the Australian government, which was obligated to show that there were no prior occupants or that traditional owners had voluntarily abandoned their lands. The *Mabo* case, and four years later a decision known as *Wi* (which acknowledged Aboriginal claims to grazing districts), opened the eyes of the Australian Courts, and also of several High Courts in Oceania, to the role of customary law in the Australian legal system. A more recent example of indigenous legal epistemology deeply intertwined to their intangible cultural heritage comes in the controversial WAI 262 claim, recently ruled by the Waitangi Tribunal in New Zealand. This claim was founded upon the rights mentioned in Article 2 of the Treaty of Waitangi, which refers to both tangible and intangible heritage dimensions of Maori tribal groups' estates, including the use and development of knowledge, sacred sites, carvings, medicine, biodiversity, genetics, images, symbols and designs (Van Meijl 2009; see also Solomon 2001).

These cases indicate 'beyond any reasonable doubt' that Pacific Islanders' cultural expressions are more about 'custodianship' than ownership (Manek and Lettington 2001; Pigliasco 2007, 2009b and forthcoming). They share a sense of collective responsibility and identity regarding their traditional cultural expressions. Maybe the persistence of such collective responsibilities is the major reason why the formal intellectual property system produces inappropriate results (Dutfield 2003). Pacific Island communities own a communal right over their TKEC, which any of the custodian group's members may use under a directly fiduciary responsibility towards the group involving both moral and economic rights, which are inevitably intertwined.

Local custodians, global rights?

Albeit that exogenous elements such as modernity, Westernization, commodification and globalization have affected pre-existing patterns of sociality, ownership and kinship (Mosko 2002), property, in the case of the Pacific Island TKEC, should be still interpreted as a sociality, clearly operating outside the logic of 'possessive individualism' (Harrison 2000:676). In Pacific Island society the ownership of intangibles does not include the possibility of alienation, hence the notion of ownership should not be extended to the community's cultural heritage. The community's responsibility for its cultural heritage is embedded in a continuing relationship between the people, their land and other traditional and cultural resources. 'Custodianship' becomes a form of stewardship associated with an enduring sense of place and relationship to the village. Hence, the community shares collective responsibility toward their TKEC, just as their identity is philosophically vested in communalism and intertwined with their mythological and kin relationships. Custodianship in legal terms translates into fiduciary duty and responsibility. After all, Seneca in his *De Beneficiis* (1982:VII, 6) and modern philosophers like Kant (1923:79) and Fichte (1964:410) had already clearly outlined the difference between 'owning a thing' and 'owning the right to use it' (Pozzo 2005:9).

At the same time, the cultural heritages of indigenous communities may be critiqued by outsiders as closed domains, monopolized cultural expressions that no-one else is allowed to use. That is, attempts to protect cultural heritage are seen as violating principles of the public domain and open access to information. Attempts to protect cultural property may even undermine indigenous rights to limit usage of that property. For example, the *Bellagio Declaration*, a 1993 resolution aiming at reforming intellectual and property laws to protect works of cultural heritage, stresses the importance of maintaining and even extending the public domain, or the intellectual and cultural commons, as part of a utopian ideal of 'fair use' for 'those who have been excluded by the authorial biases of current law'. What the *Declaration* seems not recognize is that what is available in the public domain is often a misappropriation, misuse and misrepresentation of indigenous property.[13]

The tension between rights and culture is typically described as an opposition between universalism, in the form of a transnational but European-derived conception of rights, and relativism, in the form of respect for local cultural differences. Anthropologists Marie-Bénédicte Dembour (2007) and Sally Engle Merry (2007) observe that the two positions of universalism and relativism need not be considered mutually contradictory.

> Considering cultures as changing and interconnected and rights as
> historically created and transnationally redefined by national and local
> actors better describes the contemporary global situation. It also reveals
> the impossibility of drawing sharp distinctions between culture and
> rights or seeing relativism and universalism as diametrically opposed and
> incompatible positions. In drafting cultural rights legislation, we should
> therefore be able to draw upon two genres of law: the native protection of
> localized struggles, and the western protection of human rights based on
> historical, global experience.
>
> (Merry 2007:43)

The Pacific Model Law, and in particular Fiji's anticipated adaptation and revisions demonstrate that Western legal ideas can be translated into local realities as indigenous peoples pursue local struggles. In particular, it shows how the application of legal practices and concepts to traditional knowledge and cultural expressions has challenged modern law so as to recognize new forms of property. The issues of cultural property, cultural heritage and commodification have recently re-emerged at different local, regional and international levels. Undoubtedly, international heritage policies shape national ones (see Kirshenblatt-Gimblett 2004; 61), and UNESCO has sometimes been given a central role in this process as a chief villain, a tool for parochialism and relativism (Finkielkraut 1987). While heritage policy of the kind developed by UNESCO may recall top-down approaches, my research at UNESCO in Paris on traditional knowledge and model laws relating to *sui generis* expressions of culture suggests that three interconnected layers – transnational, regional and local – are actually dialogically engaged in establishing cultural property rights in Oceania (Pigliasco 2007).[14]

WIPO expert Anthony Taubman (2005:528) observes that an ideal foundational principle for *sui generis* traditional knowledge and traditional cultural expressions protection would be to defer to its customary normative context, giving effect more broadly to the rules or norms that already govern traditional knowledge and traditional cultural expressions in their customary context.[15] However, he also indicates that given the implicit transnational dimension of the national approaches to *sui generis* protection of traditional knowledge and expressions of culture, these measures should take the same trajectory, eventually allowing the traditional vectors of customary law to pass from the original jurisdiction to foreign jurisdictions and as well as in the reciprocal direction.[16]

Conclusion

However innovative and dynamic culture may be in practice, the concepts of heritage and property imply something more defined and static. Recent theoretical debates on the ontology of performance argue that intangible cultural-heritage interventions attempt to slow the rate of change. They conclude that performances cannot be saved, recorded, documented: once this is done, they become something other than performances. I would like to express some cautions regarding this perspective. If the 'performance's being … becomes itself through disappearance', as Kirshenblatt-Gimblett (2004:60) argues after Peggy Phelan (1993), than disappearance is the sine qua non of its existence, in other words, the performance's only life is in the present. However, this denies the diachronic, dialogic aspect intrinsic to any traditional cultural expression, ignoring 'the impacts of globalization in the present and historical transfer of cultural beliefs and practices in the past' (Merry 2007:43). Hence, time and change, which are central to the metacultural nature of culture, could not be accounted and studied.

On the one hand, the Pacific Model Law's endless consultations in Fiji and other Pacific Island nations reinforce the idea that culture is highly contextualized, always changing, and not always amenable to being managed or preserved through policy mandates (Handler 2002). On the other hand, model laws designed to safeguard cultural heritage should not be judged meta-ethically, by trying, perforce, to distinguish the good from the bad. This returns us to the tension between universalism and relativism discussed above, reminiscent of Moore's (1978:237) institutional and cognitive forces, and is partly the reason why it is so difficult to regulate in law, policy and practice, the protection, control and possession of cultural heritage (Bauer 2005).

Regardless of the complex political situation affecting the Republic of Fiji Military Forces at local, national and international levels, the discussions around its pending legislation to Protect the Indigenous Intellectual Property Rights in Traditional Knowledge and Expressions of Culture show that Fiji is distancing its laws from the Pacific Model Law pattern and is creating a template of its own for other Pacific Island countries' communities in the process of realigning IPR foci at grassroots level. Allowing exclusive and moral rights to traditional custodians would allow Pacific Island communities – like those mentioned in the *Island Business* article – to authorize, or prevent others from undertaking, certain acts in relation to their intangible cultural heritage. The appearance of *sui generis* tools and state institutions informed by local communities and their new struggles in the face of globalization signal an increased awareness of traditional transcultural rights in the Pacific milieu. These tools should encourage a novel concern for the effects of law in traditional custodians' everyday lives and experiences, allowing them to aspire for long-term group heritage interests, to reinforce communal custodianship, and to recreate communities.

NOTES

1. The European Society for Oceanists' seventh Conference, held in Verona, Italy, in July 2008.

2. For example, the Mataatua Declaration in New Zealand, the Julayinbul Statement on Indigenous Intellectual Property Rights in Australia and the Paoakalani Declaration in Hawai'i.

3. Trade-Related Aspects of Intellectual Property Rights Agreement (TRIPS) has been in force since 1995 and is to date the most comprehensive multilateral agreement on intellectual property.

4. See Part 5 of the Regional Framework for the Protection of Traditional Knowledge and Expressions of Culture, 'Enforcement' Division 1 – Offences: Art. 26 Offence in relation to traditional cultural rights; Art. 27 Offence in relation to moral rights; Art. 28 Offence in relation to sacred-secret material; Art. 29 Offences in relation to importation and exportation. In all these cases the person 'is guilty of an offence punishable on conviction by a fine not exceeding an amount equivalent to [Enacting country to determine] or a term of imprisonment not exceeding [Enacting country to determine] years, or both.'

5. The legislation goes hand in hand with a national Cultural Mapping Programme (Pigliasco 2007, 2009a and b) launched in 2004 by the iTaukei Institute of Language and Culture, which involves workshops with traditional custodians of knowledge and cultural expressions, so as to hear more about their own

understandings of their experience. Recently, the Institute of Fijian Language and Culture, has replaced its generic term Fijian with *iTaukei* [indigenous Fijians] to stress its concentration on indigenous Fijian matters.

6.   A working group was initially set up to spearhead the outlining of a 'policy' to serve as a guideline for the legislation, which will take the form of a decree; the group was composed of members from the iTaukei Institute of Language and Culture, the Department of National Heritage, Culture & Arts, the Attorney General's Office, and the Ministry of Fijian Affairs, assisted by Eliesa Tuiloma, former Principal Legal Officer and drafter of the legislation, and Gail Olsson, an independent consultant for the TradeCom Programme financed by the European Development Fund, which is currently financially supporting the drafting of the decree.

7.   The term intangible cultural heritage grew out of Japan's living-national-treasures programme (established in 1950) and the Japanese Law for the Protection of Cultural Properties.

8.   Although the origin of the World Intellectual Property Organization (WIPO) can be traced to the Paris and Berne Conventions adopted in 1883 and 1886, respectively, WIPO was formally established in 1967 as a special agency under the umbrella of the United Nations.

9.   The term folklore seems to have been used for the first time in 1846 by English archaeologist William J. Thoms, in his letter to *The Athenaeum*. The concept was adopted internationally to suggest the contents of the 'knowledge of the people' or 'culture of the people'.

10. The World Forum was convened in response to the recommendations in February 1996 of the WIPO Committee Experts on a possible Protocol to the Berne Convention and the Committee of Experts on a Possible Instrument for the Protection of the Rights of Performers and the Producers of Phonograms.

11. UNESCO's 1989 *Recommendation on the Safeguarding of Traditional Culture and Folklore* defined terms and strategies for the research, conservation and dissemination of intangible cultural heritage.

12. The decision recognized that the Aborigines had a pre-existing system of customary property law, reversing over a century of legal precedent which assumed that the lands were unoccupied and therefore under the power of the Crown except in cases where the native population could establish traditional ownership.

13. The Bellagio Declaration, sponsored by the Rockefeller Foundation in 1993, proposes to reduce the scope of intellectual property rights while creating new protection for traditional cultural expressions and knowledge.

14. Samoan lawyer Clark Peteru (pers. comm.) explains that the protection of traditional knowledge takes two forms in Oceania: 'one, in relation to cultural expressions and the other in relation to biodiversity'.

15. Antony Taubman is currently Acting Director and Head of the Global Intellectual Property Issues Division of WIPO, with responsibility for programmes on intellectual property and genetic resources, traditional knowledge and expressions of culture.

16. See Art. 39 of the Pacific Model Law: 'Recognition of other laws: In accordance with reciprocal arrangements, this legislation may provide the same protection to traditional knowledge and expressions of culture originating in other countries or territories as is provided to traditional knowledge and expressions of culture originating in the [Enacting country].'

BIBLIOGRAPHY

Aplin, G. 2002. *Heritage: Identification, Conservation, and Management.* Melbourne: Oxford University Press.

Arno, A. 2005. 'Cobo and Tabua in Fiji: two forms of cultural currency in an economy of sentiment'. *American Ethnologist* 32(1):46–62.

Bauer, A. 2005. '(Re)Introducing the International Journal of Cultural Property'. *International Journal of Cultural Property* 12(1):6–10.

Blakeney, M. 2005. International Developments in the Protection of Traditional Cultural Expressions. Arts and Humanities Research Board Network on New Directions in Copyright Law. Workshop on Theme 4: Protection of Traditional Knowledge and Culture, London, Queen Mary Intellectual Property Research Institute, 28 February, 2005.

Brown, M.F. 2003. *Who Owns Native Culture?* Cambridge, Mass.: Harvard University Press.

Coombe, R.J., and A. Herman 2004. 'Rhetorical virtues: property, speech, and the commons on the world-wide web'. *Anthropological Quarterly* 77(3):559–74.

Daes, E. 1997. *Protection of the Heritage of Indigenous People.* Geneva: United Nations, Office for the High Commissioner for Human Rights, No. E.97. XIV.3.

Davison, G. 2000. *The Use and Abuse of Australian History.* Sydney, AU: Allen and Unwin.

Dembour, M. 2007. 'Following the movement of a pendulum: between universalism and relativism'. In *Culture and Rights: Anthropological Perspectives* (eds) J. Cowan, M.B. Dembour, and R. Wilson, 56–79. Cambridge: Cambridge University Press.

Dutfield, G. 2003. *Protecting Traditional Knowledge and Folklore.* Geneva : International Centre for Trade and Sustainable Development (ICTSD), United Nations on Trade and Development (UNCTAD), Issue Paper No. 1.

Epstein, R. 1998. 'Intellectual property: top down and bottom up'. In *Capital For Our Time: The Economic, Legal, and Management Challenges of Intellectual Capital* (ed.) N. Imperato, 85–106. Stanford University, CA: Hoover Institution Press.

Eriksen, T.H. 2001. 'Between universalism and relativism: a critique of the UNESCO concepts of culture'. In *Culture and Rights: Anthropological Perspectives* (eds) J.K. Cowan, M.-B. Dembour, and R. Wilson, 127–48. Cambridge, UK: Cambridge University Press.

Fichte, J.G. 1964. *Gesamtausgabe I*. Stuttgart-Bad Canstatt: Frommann-Holzboog.

Finkielkraut, A. 1987. *La Defait de la Pensée*. Paris: Gallimard.

Gerstenblith, P. 1995. 'Identity and cultural property: the protection of cultural property in the United States'. *Boston Law Review* 75:559–672.

Handler, R. 2002. 'Comments on Nas, Peter "Masterpieces of oral and intangible culture: reflections on the UNESCO world heritage list"'. *Current Anthropology* 43(1):144–5.

Harrison, S. 2000. 'From prestige goods to legacies: property and the objectification of culture in Melanesia'. *Comparative Study of Society and History* 20:662–79.

Hoebel, E.A. 1966. *Anthropology: The Study of Man*. New York: McGraw-Hill.

Janke, T. 1997. 'UNESCO-WIPO World Forum on the Protection of Folklore: lessons for protecting indigenous Australian cultural and intellectual property'. *Copyright Reporter* 15(3):104–27.

Kant, I. 1923. *Kant's Gesammelte Schriften VIII*. Berlin: De Gruyter.

Kirshenblatt-Gimblett, B. 1995. 'Theorizing heritage'. *Ethnomusicology* 39:367–80.

Kirshenblatt-Gimblett, B. 2004. 'Intangible heritage as a metacultural production'. *Museum International* 56:45–65.

Lessig, L. 2004. *Free Culture: How Big Media Uses Technology and the Law to Lock Down Culture and Control Creativity*. New York: Penguin Press.

Lucas-Schloetter, A. 2004. 'Folklore'. In *Indigenous Heritage and Intellectual Property* (ed.) S. von Lewinski and M. von Hahn, 259–368. The Hague: Kluwer Law International.

Manek, M. and R. Lettington 2001. 'Indigenous knowledge rights: recognizing alternative worldviews'. *Cultural Survival Quarterly* 24(4):8–9.

Mason, R. 1999. 'Conference Reports: "Economics and Heritage Conservation: Concepts, Values, and Agendas for Research, Getty Conservation Institute, Los Angeles"'. *International Journal of Cultural Property* 8(2):550–62.

Merry, S.E. 2007. 'Changing rights, changing culture'. In *Culture and Rights: Anthropological Perspectives* (eds) J. Cowan, M.B. Dembour and R. Wilson, 31–55. Cambridge: Cambridge University Press.

Moore, S.F. 1978. *Law as Process: An Anthropological Approach*. London: Routledge & Kegan Paul.

Mosko, M.S. 2002. 'Totem and transaction: the objectification of "tradition" among north Mekeo'. *Oceania* 73(2):89–109.

Penner, J.E. 1997. *The Idea of Property in Law*. Oxford: Oxford University Press.

Phelan, P. 1993. 'The ontology of performance: representation without reproduction'. In *Unmarked: the Politics of Performance*, 146–66. London: Routledge.

Pigliasco, G.C. 2007. The Custodians of the Gift: Intangible Cultural Property and Commodification of the Fijian Firewalking Ceremony. Ph.D. dissertation, Anthropology, University of Hawai'i at Manoa.

Pigliasco, G.C. 2009a. 'Local Voices, transnational echoes: protecting intangible cultural heritage in Oceania'. In *Sharing Cultures 2009: International Conference on Intangible Heritage* (eds) S. Lira, R. Amoêda, C. Pinheiro, J. Pinheiro and F. Oliveira, 121–7. Barcelos, Portugal: Green Lines Institute.

Pigliasco, G.C. 2009b. 'Intangible cultural property, tangible databases, visible debates: the Sawau Project'. *International Journal of Cultural Property* 16(3):255–72.

Pigliasco, G.C. 2010. 'We branded ourselves long ago: intangible cultural property and commodification of Fijian firewalking', *Oceania* 80(2):161–81.

Pozzo, R. 2005. 'Introduzione'. In *Immanuel Kant, Johann Albert Heinrich Reimarus, Johann Gottlieb Fichte: L'Autore e i Suoi Diritti, Scritti Polemici sulla Proprietà Intellettuale*. 7–35. Milano: Biblioteca di Via Senato Edizioni.

Rachlinski, J. 2006. 'Bottom-up versus top-down lawmaking'. In *Heuristics and the Law* (eds) G. Gigerenzer and C. Engel, 159–73. Cambridge, MA: The MIT Press.

Riley, A.R. 2000. 'Recovering collectivity: group rights to intellectual property in indigenous communities'. *Cardozo Arts and Entertainment Law Journal* 18(1):175–225.

Seneca, L.A. 1982. *De Beneficiis*. Pisa: Giardini.

Shapiro, D. 2005. 'Cultural property and the international cultural property society'. *International Journal of Cultural Property* 12(1):1–5.

Solomon, M. 2001. 'Intellectual property rights and indigenous peoples: rights and obligations'. In *Motion Magazine* (http://www.inmotionmagazine.com/ra01/ms2.html).

Strathern, M. 2001. 'Introduction: rationales of ownership'. In *Rationales of Ownership: Ethnographic Studies of Transactions and Claims to Ownership in Contemporary Papua New Guinea* (eds) L.K. Kalinoe and J. Leach, 1–12. Wantage, UK: Sean Kingston Publishing.

Strathern, M. 2005. *Kinship, Law and the Unexpected: Relatives Are Always a Surprise*. Cambridge: Cambridge University Press.

Strathern, M. 2008. 'Sharing, stealing and borrowing simultaneously', paper presented at the Ownership and Appropriation, Joint Conference of the SA, ASAANZ and AAS. University of Auckland, New Zealand, 8–12 December

Strathern, M. and E. Hirsch 2004. 'Introduction', In *Transactions and Creations: Property Debates and the Stimulus of Melanesia*. (eds) E. Hirsch and M. Strathern, 1–18. New York: Berghahn.

Tabureguci, D. 2008. 'The Pacific stolen identity: how intellectual property rights have failed Pacific cultures'. *Island Business* (September):16–21.

Taubman, A. 2005. 'Saving the village: conserving jurisprudential diversity in the international protection of traditional knowledge'. In *International Public Goods and Transfer of Technology Under a Globalized Intellectual Property Regime*. (eds) K. Maskus and J. Reichman, 521–64. Cambridge: Cambridge University Press.

Underkuffler, L.S. 2003. *The Idea of Property: Its Meaning and Power*. Oxford: Oxford University Press.

Van Meijl, Toon 2009. 'Maori intellectual property rights and the formation of ethnic boundaries'. *International Journal of Cultural Property* 16(3):255–72.

Notes on the contributors

✳

Guillaume Alévêque is a Ph.D. candidate at the École des Hautes Études en Sciences Sociales and is affiliated to the Centre de Recherche et de Documentation sur l'Océanie (CREDO) in Marseilles, France. His research focuses on social and cultural change in French Polynesia, and involves both historical and anthropological approaches. After studying 'first contacts' and Christianization in the late eighteenth and early nineteenth centuries, Alévêque carried out fieldwork on the emergence of new rituals of identity and their political stakes in the present.

Lissant Bolton is Head of the Oceania Section at the British Museum. An anthropologist, she has worked for many years with the Vanuatu Cultural Centre advising the Women's Culture Project. Her monograph *Unfolding the Moon: Extending Kastom to Women* was published in 2003. Her more recent work focuses on exploring the diversity of Melanesian responses to museum collections and co-editing a major survey of this topic (*Melanesia: Art and Encounter*). She has also curated a number of exhibitions including 'Power and Taboo: Sacred Objects from the Pacific' (British Museum, September 2006 – January 2007) and 'Baskets and Belonging: Australian Indigenous Histories' (British Museum, May – September 2011).

Steffen Dalsgaard is Assistant Professor of Anthropology and Ethnography at Aarhus University, Denmark. Since 2002 he has worked in Manus Province, Papua New Guinea, specializing in cultural property and, more recently, on state formation and politics, with a particular focus on tradition, exchange and elections. In addition, he has recently worked as a consultant on a liquid natural-gas project in Papua New Guinea operated by Esso Highlands Ltd.

Lawrence Foana'ota recently retired after 38 years as Director of the Solomon Islands National Museum. He is an Adjunct Senior Research Fellow at James Cook University, Australia, and a former President of the Pacific Islands Museum Association. Trained in anthropology and archaeology, he has published on the cultural heritage of Solomon Islands and museum policy in the Pacific, and has in recent years documented intangible heritage for UNESCO. He is an Officer of the Order of the British Empire. Currently he carries out research on the contemporary use and abuse of customary compensation payments in Solomon Islands.

Haidy Geismar is Assistant Professor of anthropology and museum studies at New York University. Since 2000 she has been working in collaboration with the Vanuatu Kaljoral Senta, studying the circulation of traditional material culture, the formation of value in museum and marketplace, and the emergence of indigenous regimes of intellectual and cultural property. She has curated two exhibitions about Vanuatu: 'Vanuatu Stael – Kastom and Contemporary Art' and 'Port Vila Mi Lavem YU', a visual exploration of Vanuatu's urban centre. Her book, a collaborative visual anthropology entitled *Moving Images: John Layard, Fieldwork and Photography on Malakula since 1914* (with Anita Herle) came out in 2010 and a monograph *Treasured Possessions: Culture, Property and Indigeneity in the Pacific* is forthcoming from Duke University Press.

David Hanlon has returned to the University of Hawai'i at Manoa's Department of History after six years as Director of the Center for Pacific Islands Studies. A former editor of *The Contemporary Pacific*, he is the author of *Upon a Stone Altar: A History of the Island of Pohnpei to 1890* (1988), *Remaking Micronesia: Discourses Over Development in a Pacific Territory 1944–1982* (1998) and, with Geoff White, has co-edited *Voyaging Through the Contemporary Pacific* (2000). He is currently working on a biography of Tosiwo Nakayama, the first president of the Federated States of Micronesia. His research interests include culture contact, missionization, development, Micronesia, historic preservation and ethnographic approaches to the study of Pacific pasts.

Rosita Henry is Associate Professor and Head of Anthropology in the School of Arts and Social Sciences at James Cook University, Australia. Her research concerns relationships between people, places and the state in Australia and the Pacific as expressed through cultural heritage and the politics of festivals and other public performances. She is co-editor with Barbara Glowczewski of the book *Le Défi Indigène, Entre Spectacle et Politique* (2007), which has been revised and republished in English as *The Challenge of Indigenous Peoples: Spectacle or Politics?* (Oxford: The Bardwell Press, 2011).

Edvard Hviding is Professor and Head of Social Anthropology at the University of Bergen, Norway, and Director of the Bergen Pacific Studies research group. He is an Adjunct Professor of anthropology at James Cook University, Australia and an Honorary Fellow of the Cairns Institute. With many periods of fieldwork in Solomon Islands since 1986, his research record includes sea tenure, kinship, ecological anthropology of reef and rainforest environments, social movements and globalization, centred on the Marovo area of the Western Solomons. Among his publications are the monographs *Guardians of Marovo Lagoon* (1996), *Islands of Rainforest* (with T. Bayliss-Smith, 2000) and *Reef and Rainforest: An Environmental Encyclopedia of Marovo Lagoon* (2005), and several co-directed films including *Chea's Great Kuarao* (2000). In 2010 he was awarded the Solomon Islands Medal for his long-term development of vernacular education in the Marovo language.

Lamont Lindstrom is Kendall Professor of Anthropology at the University of Tulsa. He is the author of *Cargo Cult: Strange Stories of Desire from Melanesia and Beyond* and *Knowledge and Power in a South Pacific Society* and has also published on kava, chiefs and governance, Pacific War ethnohistory, and written a dictionary and grammar of Kwamera language (Tanna, Vanuatu). In addition he has co-edited *Chiefs Today: Traditional Pacific Leadership and the Postcolonial State* (with G. White, 1997) and *Culture-Kastom-Tradition: Developing Cultural Policy in Melanesia* (with G. White, 1994)

Ton Otto is Professor and Research Leader (people and societies of the tropics) at James Cook University, Australia, and Professor of Anthropology and Ethnography at Aarhus University, Denmark. He has conducted long-term fieldwork in Papua New Guinea since 1986. His research focuses on issues of social and cultural change, including religious movements, political and economic transformation, warfare, the politics of tradition and identity, the management of natural resources, and processes of design and intervention. He also writes about methodological and epistemological questions and engages with material and visual culture through exhibitions and films. His recent publications include the co-edited volume *Experiments in Holism: Theory and Practice in Contemporary Anthropology* (with Nils Bubandt, 2010) and he has co-directed and two prize-winning films *Ngat is Dead* (2009) and *Unity through Culture* (2011)

Guido Carlo Pigliasco is Lecturer in Anthropology at the University of Hawai'i. He has practised international law for twelve years. His long-term work in the Pacific has resulted in ten film documentaries on contemporary Oceania for Italian television (1992, 1993, 1994), the ethnographic novel *Paradisi Inquieti* (2000), the multimedia *A Ituvatuva Ni Vakadidike E Sawau* (The Sawau Project) (2005), and the monograph *Na Vilavilairevo* (2009). He currently researches and publishes on the theorization and application of intangible cultural-heritage policies in Fiji and Oceania, combining academic with applied work.

Ralph Regenvanu is a Member of the Vanuatu National Parliament for the constituency of Port Vila, Vanuatu's capital. A trained anthropologist, he was Director of the Vanuatu Cultural Centre and the National Museum of Vanuatu from 1995 to 2006, and until 2010 he was also Director of Vanuatu's National Cultural Council. He was a member of the drafting committee for the UNESCO Convention for the safeguarding of the intangible cultural heritage. During 2010–11 he held cabinet portfolios as Minister of Cooperatives & Ni-Vanuatu Business Development and Minister for Lands.

Knut M. Rio is Professor of Social Anthropology at the University of Bergen, Norway, and is responsible for the ethnographic collections at the Bergen University Museum. He has worked with Melanesian ethnography since 1995, with fieldwork in Vanuatu. His work on social ontology, production and ceremonial sacrifice on Ambrym Island has resulted in journal publications and the monograph *The Power of Perspective: Social Ontology and Agency on Ambrym Island, Vanuatu* (2007). He has also co-edited *Hierarchy: Persistence and Transformation in Social formations* (with Olaf Smedal, 2009).

Michael W. Scott is a Lecturer in Anthropology at the London School of Economics and Political Science. Since 1992 he has been conducting fieldwork among the Arosi of Makira/Ulawa Province, Solomon Islands, and has written on such themes as matrilineal land tenure, historical transformations of ontology and cosmology, and Arosi interpretations of Christianity. His publications include 'Hybridity, vacuity, and blockage: visions of chaos from anthropological theory, Island Melanesia, and Central Africa', *Comparative Studies in Society and History*, 2005, and the monograph *The Severed Snake: Matrilineages, Making Place, and a Melanesian Christianity in Southeast*

Solomon Islands (2007). He is currently writing a book about the Makiran underground army.

Rolf Scott is a Ph.D. candidate in social anthropology at the University of Bergen, Norway. His research interest is the phenomenology of the global, which he defines as the global grid of latitude and longitude, and the positioned individual as a centre of a logical coherent and measurable cosmos. He is also interested in the phenomenology of the photograph and film, which he sees as deriving from the same system. Scott's fieldwork has been focused on the Western practice of circumnavigating the world on yachts, on the revitalisation of Polynesian voyaging in Hawai'i, and on the making of documentary film.

Geoffrey White is Professor of Anthropology in the Department of Anthropology at the University of Hawai'i. His long-term work in the Pacific is based on fieldwork in Santa Isabel, Solomon Islands. His research on problems of historical memory and identity formation focuses on representations of Christian conversion and the Second World War as well as the politics of postcolonial nation-making. Among his publications are *Identity through History: Living Stories in a Solomon Islands Society* (1991) and many co-edited volumes including *Chiefs Today: Traditional Pacific Leadership and the Postcolonial State* (with L. Lindstrom, 1997) and *Culture-Kastom-Tradition: Developing Cultural Policy in Melanesia* (with L. Lindstrom, 1994).

Index